THE *Misfit* OF THE FAMILY

SERIES Q

Edited by Michèle Aina Barale,

Jonathan Goldberg, Michael Moon,

and Eve Kosofsky Sedgwick

THE *Misfit* OF THE FAMILY

Balzac and the Social Forms of Sexuality *Michael Lucey*

DUKE UNIVERSITY PRESS DURHAM & LONDON 2003

Printed in the United States
of America on acid-free paper ∞
Designed by Rebecca M. Giménez
Typeset in Carter and Cone Galliard
by Tseng Information Systems, Inc.
Library of Congress Cataloging-in-
Publication Data appear on the
last printed page of this book.

PARA *Lalo*

CONTENTS

ACKNOWLEDGMENTS

This book has been a long time in the writing. I first began working on it in 1990–1991, when I held a Junior Faculty Fellowship from the University of California at Berkeley's Doreen B. Townsend Center for the Humanities. The center's director at the time, Paul Alpers, and the other members of its fellowship group provided a supportive context in which to get the project off the ground. The project turned out to be a lot more demanding than I had imagined, and over the years I've benefitted from many sources of encouragement to keep me going. Undergraduates and graduate students in my classes in Berkeley's French and Comparative Literature Departments graciously put up with my ways of relentlessly including both obscure and well-known works by Balzac in my courses during those years. Many of those students contributed substantially to my efforts to find the right framework to say what I had to say about the works I examine in this volume. The Townsend Center provided further resources in 1995, allowing me the luxury of team teaching an interdisciplinary seminar with Carolyn Dinshaw. Together with a very smart group of graduate students we were able to pursue some of the theoretical reading and thinking that helped me find new ways of looking at much of this material.

Eve Kosofsky Sedgwick's kind invitation to contribute to the anthology she edited, *Novel Gazing: Queer Readings in Fiction* (Duke University Press, 1997) provided me with the occasion to bring an early version of chapter 3 to completion. An invitation from Yopie Prins to give a lecture at the University of Michigan helped me along to that end as well. Moreover, Eve, Yopie, and Ross Chambers all helped out with encouraging comments on different versions of the material for that chapter.

I'm grateful for the early interest in the project along with the encouragement that came from the editors of Series Q and from Ken Wissoker at Duke University Press, and from James Creech and the other, anonymous, readers of the manuscript. A fellowship from the National Endowment of the Humanities allowed me to spend 1997 rethinking what I was up to. Thanks to an invitation from Leyla Ezdinli, I was able to try out a version of chapter 1 on an audience at Smith College in March of that year. More recently, the readers on the editorial board of *Representations* helped me to make further refinements to that same material, some of which appeared as "Legal Melancholy: Balzac's *Eugénie Grandet* and the Napoleonic Code" in *Representations* 76 (fall 2001): 1–26.

Margaret Waller also provided a helpful reading of the *Eugénie Grandet* chapter, and then kindly recommended to Michal Peled Ginsberg that she invite me to contribute to a volume she was preparing on *Le Père Goriot.* An earlier version of part of my introduction thus appeared in the volume Michal edited: *Approaches to Teaching Balzac's Old Goriot* (Modern Language Association, 2000), and is reprinted by permission of the copyright owner, the Modern Language Association of America. A further invitation from Michal to participate in an institute on the Family, Sexuality, and the Law sponsored by Northwestern University's French Interdisciplinary Group in spring 2002 provided me with a wonderful forum in which to think through some final revisions to the manuscript in the company of Michal, a friendly group of students, and four other helpful interlocuters: Rachel Fuchs, Marcela Iacub, Remi Lenoir, and Patrice Maniglier.

Carla Frecerro's invitation to speak at the *Queer Encounters II* conference at the University of California, Santa Cruz, in spring 2000, provided a welcome occasion to try out the first half of the introduction. I was able to try out the whole of the introduction at the seminar "Sociologie des homosexualités" run by Didier Eribon and Françoise Gaspard at the École des Hautes Études en Sciences Sociales in January 2001.

Trips to France have been crucial to my work on this book. Financial support obtained from Berkeley's Committee on Research, from its Freshman Seminar Program, and from the Department of Comparative Literature by way of its chair, Tony Cascardi, made a few of those essential trips possible. On the Parisian side of things, it's a great pleasure to thank Didier Eribon, Claude Servan-Schreiber, Françoise Gaspard, and Marie Ymonet and her family for some of the finest examples of hospitality I have experienced.

My encounter with Pierre Bourdieu and his work was crucial in shaping this book. At his invitation, some of the material in chapter 3 appeared in French as "Drôles de cousins" (translated by Christian Marouby) in *Actes de la recherche en sciences sociales* no. 125 (December 1998), but more important was the intellectual example and the inspiration that he and his work provided.

Closer to home, my conversations with Doug Beaton have been another crucial form of encouragement over the years. David Copenhafer's research assistance helped speed along my work. Carla Hesse gave me some crucial bibliographical advice early on. Many colleagues in the French and Comparative Literature Departments have been immensely supportive over the years. Let me mention gratefully here Ann Smock, David Hult, Suzanne Guerlac, and Eric Naiman. Leonard Johnson kindly left a book on the Marquis de Custine in my box one day. Ted Rex's inimitable form of friendly and attentive interest has been endlessly cheering. Numerous other colleagues have kindly read and commented on versions of these pages, including Susan Maslan, Debarati Sanyal, Robin Einhorn, Lydia Liu, Nancy Ruttenburg, Karl Britto, Linda Williams, Noah Guynn, Katherine Bergeron, and Elisabeth Ladenson. As for Tim Hampton, Leslie Kurke, Celeste Langan, and Sharon Marcus, I believe they have helped me with nearly every page. Having such a group of close readers to help say better what is trying to be said is surely as wonderful a gift as any intellectual could hope for. I'd like to mention my colleague Bill Nestrick as well. He was a great friend from my earliest days in Berkeley and he eagerly supported this project at its outset. I wish he were still with us to read the finished product.

A friend of Gerry Gomez's gave him a copy of *Cousin Pons* to read one day when he was in Guadalajara, making him a Balzacian before we had ever met—a happy coincidence that delights me. As for Gerry, he brings me joy every day.

PREFACE

There is nothing particularly original in the observation that for Honoré de Balzac the novel was an instrument for historical and sociological analysis. Georg Lukács's well-known praise of Balzac for his skillful creation of "types" in his characters is one critical acknowledgment of Balzac's successful efforts in this direction. For Lukács, Balzac's achievement is to be found in large measure in his way of linking individual characters to social history: "In his writings the unfolding of material problems is always indissolubly bound up with the consequences arising from the personal passions of his characters. This method of composition—although it seems to take the individual alone for its starting-point—contains a deeper understanding of social interconnections and implications, a more correct evaluation of the trends of social development than does the pedantic, 'scientific' method of the later realists."[1] I share Lukács's high estimation of Balzac's sociological acuity, although I will in this book choose to locate Balzac's sociological insight differently than did Lukács. As I will demonstrate shortly Lukács's notion of "types" does not permit much critical purchase on Balzac's interest in sexuality—in particular in the institutions that organize sexual interaction. In this preface I intend to offer a way of perceiving the forms of Balzac's sociological curiosity, a way that allows us to appreciate his achievement in analyzing sexuality.

That Balzac and a certain part of his public read novels as programmatic historical or sociological writing is evident in the paragraphs in

Illusions perdues (*Lost Illusions*) where Daniel D'Arthez advises Lucien de Rubempré on how to make his mark as a novelist:

> If you don't want to ape Walter Scott you must invent a different manner for yourself, whereas you have imitated him. . . . Dealing with France, you will be able to oppose to the dour figures of Calvinism the attractive peccadillos and brilliant manners of Catholicism against the background of the most impassioned period of our history. Every authentic reign from Charlemagne onwards will require at least one work, and sometimes four or five, as in the case of Louis the Fourteenth, Henry the Fourth and Francis the First. In this way you will write a pictorial history of France in which you will describe costume, furniture, the outside and inside of buildings and private life, whilst conveying the spirit of the times instead of laboriously narrating a sequence of known facts. You will find scope for originality in correcting the popular errors which give a distorted view of most of our kings.[2]

(These overly earnest remarks are, of course, presented with a certain amount of irony, further evident in the fact that Balzac had abandoned a project a bit like this for what would become *La Comédie humaine*.)[3] It should be equally clear, in thinking of some of the later novelists most deeply marked by Balzac's novelistic practice (among others, Marcel Proust, Henry James, Willa Cather, and William Faulkner) that much of what they learned from Balzac had to do with the possibility and the methods of a novel devoted to careful sociological analysis—analysis not only of economic relations but of sexuality and gender as well.[4]

The Marxist tradition of Balzac criticism has demonstrated the importance of the sociology of class relations in Balzac's writing.[5] It has been argued that Balzac had a special relation with some of his women readers, who found in his novels both a representation and an analysis of their gendered situations that they considered significant,[6] and there have been numerous feminist accounts of his work.[7] It has often been noted that Balzac presents us with many characters who are not heterosexual.[8] Yet I believe that it remains to imagine how the representation of gender and the sexual division of labor, in conjunction with the representation of characters who express a diversity of sexualities, fits into the large sociological demonstrations that make up *La Comédie humaine:* this is my task in the following chapters.

When I began working on this book in 1991 I thought of it as an investigation into the question of why there had been so many psychoanalytically inclined critical readings of Balzac in the United States in the 1970s and 1980s. This volume has not turned out precisely to be an account of that investigation, but some of the questions crucial to that early formulation of my project remain central here. What had psychoanalytic criticism enabled us to see in Balzac and, at the same time, what had it masked? It did strike me that in that critical literature there were no satisfactory accounts of the nonheterosexual characters (throughout this book I often choose to refer to them as *queer*) who so frequently appear in the novels, and who were clearly so popular with Balzac's readers[9] (see the epilogue on the latter topic). Over the course of my investigations of the ways in which Balzac's novels construct a relation between individuals and family forms and systems of law, of inheritance, and of sexuality, it has come to seem to me that psychoanalytic criticism has helped to reveal only a certain side of these kinds of relations and has perhaps obscured other aspects. Moreover, if psychoanalytic criticism seemed during a certain period so "appropriate" to a reading of Balzac, perhaps the fit between the novels and the theory should be understood as a historical phenomenon in its own right. That is, if a psychoanalytic reading of Balzac has at times seemed so convincing, perhaps in part it is because Balzac's novels reflect and reflect on the creation of a kind of society that finds comfort in psychoanalysis, and in part because one current in the novels helps produce an understanding of that society that runs along psychoanalytic lines. But perhaps the novels also do more than this. My goal in the following pages is never really to show that psychoanalytic readings of Balzac are, in general, *wrong*—although certainly I do find a number of them to be, in their particulars, wrong-headed. Rather, I would claim that certain psychoanalytic readings are burdened, not to say handicapped, by historically overdetermined interests in particular ways of understanding both family and its relation to larger social constructs.[10]

In *The Logic of Practice,* Pierre Bourdieu observes that "the 'unconscious' . . . is never anything other than the forgetting of history," by which he means that by the time some historically produced social mechanism has been widely and efficaciously instituted in a large number of individual psyches, its historical production is likely to have been forgotten.[11] I find this a useful insight when it comes to thinking about Balzac, who through his novelist practice might help us *remember* a history that certain kinds of psychoanalytic reading might rather tend to reify into ahistorical psychic mechanisms. Indeed, such an insight has been present from the earliest days of French sociology. Consider these remarks from near the end of Durkheim's *The Division of Labor in Society:*

> Social facts are not the mere development of psychological facts, which are for the most part only the prolongation of social facts within the individual consciousness. This proposition is very important, for to uphold the opposite viewpoint exposes the sociologist at every moment to risk taking the cause for the effect, and vice versa. For example, if, as has often happened, we see in the organisation of the family the necessarily logical expression of human sentiments inherent in every consciousness, we reverse the real order of facts. Quite the opposite is true: it is the social organisation of kinship relationships that has determined respectively the sentiments between parents and children. These sentiments would have been completely different if the social structure had been different. . . . Most of our states of consciousness would not have occurred among men isolated from one another and would have occurred completely differently among people grouped together in a different way.[12]

When in chapter 1 on *Eugénie Grandet* I suggest that we might profitably take a moment to consider melancholy in that novel to be an aspect of a historically located *habitus* rather than a general, ahistorical form of neurosis, I am drawing much of my inspiration from sociological insights such as those found in the citations above by Bourdieu and Durkheim.

Some fifty years before Durkheim, Balzac seems to have constructed his novels to demonstrate what it would mean, as Durkheim famously says in *The Rules of Sociological Method,* to treat social facts as if they were things. Durkheim notes that what he calls social facts are phenomena that "reside in the society itself that produces them," and that are "different from those which occur in consciousnesses in isolation." *"They have a different substratum,"* he says, but "this does not mean that they are not in some sense psychical, since they all consist of ways of thinking and acting."[13] It is often noted that Balzac is not much given to psychological description. This might in some ways amount to saying that he is a sociological novelist in the Durkheimian sense, that his primary interest is not in the substratum of *psychic* facts but in that of *social* ones. "Collective ways of acting and thinking," Durkheim writes, "possess a reality existing outside individuals, who, at every moment, conform to them." He continues: "They are things which have their own existence. The individual encounters them when they are already completely fashioned and he cannot cause them to cease to exist or be different from what they are. . . . In order for a social fact to exist, several individuals at the very least must have interacted together and the resulting combination must have given rise to some new production" (45). I understand Balzac's method in his novels, his experiments in narrative form, as part of an effort to envision the substratum of social facts, the complicated locus of social forms.[14]

Part of my project in this book is to call attention to Balzac's analysis of the relations that exist between large social changes and changes in the specific social forms that enable sexual interaction, including, in particular, same-sex interactions. Such forms are, to use Durkheim's term, *institutions,* and they evolve, just as do institutions.[15] As part of his sociological analysis, Balzac inquires into the ways a set of shared practices might come to constitute a sexuality or a sexual identity; he inquires into the historical and social processes in which and through which such sets of practices, such social forms, become fixed or unfixed, come to seem consequential or inconsequential, come to seem open to revision or written in stone, and so on. In the remaining pages of this preface I offer, by way of a reading of some passages from Henry James's essays on Balzac, some observations by Pierre Bourdieu in his *Pascalian Meditations,* and some passages from Balzac's *César Birotteau,* a fuller account of what it means to think about the Balzacian novel's active relation to a sociological knowledge of sexuality.

In 1880 Henry James, in a quite unfavorable review of Zola's *Nana,* insisted that in order to be rightly understood the novel in general needed to be thought of "as a composition that treats of life at large and helps us to *know.*" Zola's particular novel, he asserted, makes no "contribution to our knowledge of ourselves."[16] Like Balzac, then, James thought of the novel as an instrument of knowledge, and in his writing he takes care in reflecting on the ways in which Balzac used that instrument to serve particular kinds of knowledge. In his *Pascalian Meditations,* Pierre Bourdieu offers a caveat regarding novels and narrative, rooted in what he refers to as "ordinary language and its grammatical constructions ready-made for teleological description." That "teleological description" corresponds to a particular "philosophy of mind . . . which cannot conceive of spontaneity and creativity without the intervention of a creative intention, or finality without a conscious aiming at ends, regularity without observance of rules, signification in the absence of signifying intention." As for the nineteenth-century novel, it is riddled with such a philosophy of mind and philosophy of the subject, Bourdieu suggests, citing Michel Butor in support of his claim, that "the novel . . . in the eighteenth and nineteenth centuries was, as [Butor] points out, almost entirely identified with the narration of the adventures of an individual and almost always takes the form of strings of 'decisive individual actions, preceded by a voluntary deliberation, which determine one another.' "[17] Such a novel, it seems, could not be an instrument of sociological knowledge because, to go back to the basic lessons one might learn from Durkheim, it has not taken the necessary first step of setting aside what Durkheim refers to as *notiones vulgares* or *praenotiones.*[18] As Durkheim warns us, when we do not first construct a scientific understanding of the object that we intend to investigate, we are likely to remain closer to the ideas offered about the world through "common sense" than we are to the world itself:

> Man cannot live among things without forming ideas about them according to which he regulates his behaviour. But, because these notions are closer to us and more within our mental grasp than the realities to which they correspond, we naturally tend to substitute them for the realities, concentrating our speculations upon them.

> Instead of observing, describing and comparing things, we are content to reflect upon our ideas, analysing and combining them. Instead of a science which deals with realities, we carry out no more than an ideological analysis. (60)

This might suggest that the more a novel can be experienced as "realist" in its portrayal of the world and of the people in it, the more it is simply supplying a confirmation of commonsense "prenotions" about the world rather than opening a way to a critical understanding of that world. Yet I think that within certain traditions of novel writing, techniques of structuration or narration (in short, methods) are developed that can serve to push beyond commonsense approaches to a life, or to "vulgar" ideas about subjective agency, intentionality, and expressivity. (James's critique of Zola—that he doesn't help us to *know* anything—amounts, on one level, to saying that Zola's thought never leaves the level of ideology, of vulgar prenotions, and that he never approaches his subject matter with any kind of rigorous sociological insight.)

There are, I think, even among the "realist" novels of nineteenth-century Europe, plenty of works that do not correspond to the stereotypical pattern evoked by Butor and Bourdieu, or to the critique James makes of Zola. It will be part of my argument in this book that at least a few of Balzac's works are among them. It may seem odd to invoke a novelist so apparently aesthetic and psychological as James in the service of an attempt to renew our understanding of the novel's sociological potential. The oddity of James's devotion to Balzac was, of course, apparent to James as well. He freely admits that Balzac is his major influence as far as the novelistic enterprise goes, but he also often expresses bafflement as to how someone like Balzac, who apparently went about writing novels in what was for James an entirely incorrect way, managed to have any success at all:

> All painters of manners and fashions, if we will, are historians, even when they least don the uniform: Fielding, Dickens, Thackeray, George Eliot, Hawthorne among ourselves. But the great difference between the great Frenchman [Balzac] and the eminent others is that, with an imagination of the highest power, an unequalled intensity of vision, he saw his subject in the light of science as well, in the light of the bearing of all its parts on each other, and under

pressure of a passion for exactitude, an appetite, the appetite of an ogre, for *all* the kinds of facts. We find I think in the union here suggested something like the truth about his genius, the nearest approach to a final account of him. Of imagination on one side all compact, he was on the other an insatiable reporter of the immediate, the material, the current combination, and perpetually moved by the historian's impulse to fix, preserve and explain them. One asks one's self as one reads him what concern the poet has with so much arithmetic and so much criticism, so many statistics and documents, what concerns the critic and the economist have with so many passions, characters and adventures. The contradiction is always before us; it springs from the inordinate scale of the author's two faces; it explains more than anything else his eccentricities and difficulties.[19]

Given James's system of aesthetic value, the favored terms here are "intensity of vision," "passions," and "imagination." The "historian's impulse to fix" or "arithmetic" or "criticism" are all apparently threats to the novel, which, for James, only works well when it works as an appeal made from one richly receptive imagination to another, an appeal that is best conveyed in a private, personal, and intensely affective experience of reading that has little to do with "arithmetic." Yet, as James points out, the lesson to be learned from Balzac is that, in the right hands, the novel can produce knowledge about the relationship between "passion" and "arithmetic."

Zola is, for James, an example of a novelist for whom only the arithmetic, statistics, and documents seem to have importance. Zola is thus mostly mechanical; Balzac, on the other hand, James understands as more often than not inspired:

> It is exactly here that we get the difference between such a solid, square, symmetrical structure as "Les Rougon-Macquart," vitiated, in a high degree, by its mechanical side, and the monument left by Balzac—without the example of which, I surmise, Zola's work would not have existed. The mystic process of the crucible, the transformation of the material under aesthetic heat, is, in the "Comédie Humaine," thanks to an intenser and more submissive fusion, completer, and also finer. . . . It is hard to say where Zola is fine; whereas it is often, for pages together, hard to say where

> Balzac is, even under the weight of his too ponderous personality, not. (130)

James is implying, I think correctly, that when Zola took on a sociological project that resembled Balzac's, but pursued it in a series of novels that are formally more predictable than Balzac's, some of the richness of Balzac's analytical project was lost, as was some of the acuity of his sociological perception. Indeed, one might well imagine that Zola could not borrow more extensively from Balzac in formal terms precisely because Zola's sociological vision was so much more limited. Yet James is also straining a great deal in order to force Balzac into his own highly aestheticized discourse of refined form and discourse, of intense experience, of the mystical transformation of the brute material of life within the heated crucible of aesthetic activity. (Indeed, it is practically miraculous that a project as rigorously sociological as Balzac's is able to survive the process of relentless aesthetic refinement to which James subjects it in developing his own novelistic practice—although this is altogether another story.) How astonishing—given this aestheticizing bias—to discover what a precise sense James has of Balzac's sociological project. At one point he writes: "Nothing appealed to him more than to show *how* we all are, and how we are placed and built-in for being so. What befalls us is but another name for the way our circumstances press upon us—so that an account of what befalls us is an account of our circumstances" (135). And elsewhere he comments: "The novel, the tale, however brief, the passage, the sentence by itself, the situation, the person, the place, the motive exposed, the speech reported—these things were in his view history, with the absoluteness and the dignity of history. This is the source both of his weight and of his wealth. What is the historic sense after all but animated, but impassioned knowledge seeking to enlarge itself? . . . His imagination achieved the miracle of absolutely resolving itself into multifarious knowledge" (110). James seems to be redeeming Balzac's historical and sociological tendencies by portraying Balzac's imagination—the novelistic faculty par excellence for James—as in itself sociological and historical. For James, Balzac, by acting aesthetically, performs sociology. There is something in the *imaginative form* of Balzac's novels that *is sociological.* For James, in Balzac's hands, sociology becomes for a moment an aesthetic (a novelistic) practice.

I find this to be an interesting claim for the relation between Balzac and sociology, in part because it includes an aspect missing from most accounts of that relation, accounts that have usually not found a way to take novelistic form and practice into consideration. The usual accounts of Balzac's relation to sociology start from a consideration of Balzac's relation to other sociological thinkers of his moment. A typical version of the history of French sociology in the early decades of the nineteenth century divides the nascent field into two camps with two different impulses.[20] The first is based on an effort to establish rigorous protocols for the use of statistics to study social phenomena, and is associated with those like Adolphe Quetelet who in 1835 published a text discussing the concept of the "average man" (*l'homme moyen*). As Michelle Perrot puts it: "The 'average man' sketches out a norm, and the distance from the mean provides the measure of a deviance that can be estimated through calculations of probability. Thus Quetelet 'treats social facts as things,' and by doing so opens the way for Durkheim, who will coin the phrase. A science of society becomes imaginable: a sociology whose instruments will be statistics, tables, and calculations."[21] The second sociological impulse of Balzac's historical moment is that which led to the development of the *enquête,* the survey or inquiry or site study, which Perrot associates mainly with the efforts of public health officials in the production of documents like the 1834 *Report on the Spread and Effects of Cholera in Paris and the Rural Areas of the Seine District;* and with investigations of working-class communities, such as the work of Louis-René Villermé published in 1840, *An Account of the Physical and Moral State of Silk, Cotton, and Wool Workers.* In *The Taming of Chance,* Ian Hacking associates the *enquête* with the figure of Fréderic Le Play, and sees a close parallel between Le Play's enterprise and Balzac's:

> A man no less ambitious than Balzac, [Le Play's] vision of his life's work was formed exactly when Balzac's was. He dated it 1829. Like Balzac's *Comédie humaine* it started with the idea of classifying the various types of humanity, sorted first according to their conjugal situation, their families, and then according to their location, their work, and above all their domestic budget. It was directed not at the prospering classes of France but at the labourers of Europe. It was cast not in the form of novella but as quantitative studies of

> individual household expenses. It was numerical but, like Balzac's masterpiece, antistatistical. It did not study Quetelet's averages but used representative individuals to display the chief features of their type, as a rock or plant might serve the natural historian as a paradigm.[22]

Hacking is particularly interested in the contrast between Quetelet's *l'homme moyen* and Le Play's representative individuals. Le Play's aim was in fact to produce monographs on representative *families,* not individuals. He describes his goal as being to "ground the study of populations on the study of a few judiciously chosen working-class families."[23] Still, one can assume that some notion of "typicality" is important to him. Le Play insists that in any given locale, one should—for typicality's sake—always choose a family originally from the area, as well as one representing some kind of norm ("qui réunisse à peu près des conditions moyennes" [15]). This means that certain households are best excluded from consideration: those without children, for instance, or households of unmarried people.

From Lukács onward, many have praised Balzac for his ability to produce *typical* characters. As Lukács puts it, "The central category and criterion of realist literature is the type, a peculiar synthesis which organically binds together the general and the particular both in characters and situations. What makes a type a type is not its average quality, not its mere individual being, however profoundly conceived; what makes it a type is that in it all the humanly and socially essential determinants are present on their highest level of development"[24] Lukács's typicality is thus different from Le Play's, for Lukács often insists that it has nothing to do with the "reproduction of 'average' reality" (60). Yet both forms of typicality have their limitations. Le Play's "typical" exclusion of unmarried people and of households with no children means that his sociology will have nothing to do with a thorough investigation of the social forms of sexuality. Lukács's typicality may have little to do with "averages," yet his concept of typicality is nonetheless normalizing (in a way Balzac rigorously fails to be). Because of Lukács's insistence on types in relation to his particular version of the social, there will be, for him as for Le Play, no place for a nonjudgmental investigation of sexuality in his sociology. "Individual destinies," he says, "are always a radiation of the socially typical, of the socially universal, which can be separated from the individual only by an analysis *a posteriori*. In the novels themselves the individual and the general are inseparably united, like a fire with the heat it radiates" (55). Lukács's normalizing impulse lies within his version of what he here chooses to name the "universal" and the "general." In his essay "Healthy or Sick Art?" he speaks out more specifically against what he sees as the "substitution of pure psychologism for the representation of the real and complete, that is, social, human being." The social, and therefore typical, person will certainly not be "a shapeless bundle or uncontrolled torrent of free, undisciplined associations." When artists turn to a depiction of such a state, "love becomes mere eroticism; the erotic declines into mere sexuality; finally sexuality is reduced to mere phallicism."[25] Of all the things that might be said about the point of view behind such commentary, it will suffice here to note that when it grapples with the imbrication of social processes and sexual forms, it does so in terms that are not sufficiently capacious to capture the full range of sexual forms that any society will evince. Nor will it come as a surprise to discover that Lukács is thus not well positioned to appreciate either the richness or the extent of Balzac's sociological approach to sexuality.

Henry James is much more helpful when it comes to apprehending the kind of sociological interests that Balzac's novels demonstrate. His comment that for Balzac "nothing appealed . . . more than to show *how* we all are, and how we are placed and built-in for being so" nicely calls attention to Balzac's open-mindedly curious interest in sociologically structuring processes (in how we come to be built-in). Lukács's "typicality" assumes the shape of a "complete human personality" to be already known, to be normatively given. Balzac knows social forms to have histories too complicated to accord with that point of view. It is via Balzac's interest in the *production* of social agents (rather than in the "typicality" of any given agent) and his interest in the particular kinds of existence possessed by the social forms taken on by those agents that we will gain access to his insights on sexuality.

Thus I want to suggest, *pace* Lukács, that what is important sociologically about Balzac has little to do with the typicality of his characters, a quality that might be disputable in many cases. How is it that Balzac's practice of novel writing, his formal choices, allow him analytic purchase on the particular substratum of social facts and forms?

How is it that he focuses attention on what it means to be "built-in," or that he elaborates on the meanings of the verb "to press" in James's other phrase, "how our circumstances press upon us"? Elisheva Rosen is one critic who has helpfully directed attention to this capacity in the Balzacian novel. She speaks of "the importance that [Balzac] gives in the definition of a field to the social actors that constitute it, to their concrete aptitudes, to their particular personalities." She continues: "The situations that Balzac imagines always have something unique about them. They are tied to a particular conjuncture that can be quite complex, to a precise moment in History. This is why the presentation of a social actor by Balzac is always oriented toward a particular moment in that actor's trajectory, a moment that cannot be fully deduced from its antecedents, yet whose antecedents must be known in order to comprehend the strategies for action that the actor will adopt."[26] Rosen valuably directs our attention to Balzac's interest in the way particular moments of crisis reveal something about a social actor, who is then required to produce strategies of action that reveal how he or she has been "built-in" or "pressed upon" by past experience. In another article, Rosen names what she is describing here as the "interactional competence" of a Balzacian character, a particular sociological capacity that, as she puts it, is not "equally distributed" among his characters. Understanding that capacity and the mechanisms of its distribution is at the heart of Balzac's sociological project. "There are certainly, in Balzac's universe, interactional prowesses that are more remarkable than others, and social mobility is often the prize related to the finest strategies. But talent in this area does not guarantee success."[27] Rosen and James help us to understand that Balzac's methodical efforts to apprehend, on the one hand, successful and unsuccessful forms of social action and, on the other, the productive nature of the relation between a given individual and equally given social facts and forms, make up the primary areas of his sociological inquiry.

Balzac sometimes gives theoretical summaries of the principles that govern his sociological insight. Consider the description in *César Birotteau* of why Césarine Birotteau chooses to marry Anselme Popinot, a skinny, befreckled, red-headed shop assistant who limps:

> There are moralists who hold that love is the most involuntary, the most disinterested and least calculating of all passions, a mother's

> love always excepted, a doctrine which contains a gross error. . . . Any sympathy, physical or mental, is none the less based upon calculations made by brain or heart or animal instincts. Love is essentially an egoistical affection, and egoism implies profound calculation [Qui dit égoïsme, dit profond calcul]. For the order of mind which is only impressed by outward and visible results, it may seem an improbable or unusual thing that a poor, lame, red-haired lad should find favor in the eyes of a beautiful girl like Césarine; and yet it was only what might be expected from the arithmetic found in bourgeois matters of feeling [Néanmoins, ce phénomène est en harmonie avec l'arithmétique des sentiments bourgeois]. (6:132, 113–14)[28]

Balzac's direct mention here of what he designates profound *calculation* or the *arithmetic* of bourgeois feeling is a helpful reminder of one of the central sociological phenomena he is interested in grappling with. Only rarely does he, in constructing his novels, turn to situations in which the calculus or the arithmetic, or, to use Bourdieu's term for this capacity, the *habitus* with which they are endowed, serves his characters well.[29] Within *César Birotteau,* even if the marriage between Césarine and Anselme does end up being a happy one, it is only recounted within the bounds of a novel mainly devoted to a short period in the life of Césarine's father, César, during which he unsuccessfully attempts to move a step up the social ladder. He enters into some financial speculations, renovates his house, and gives an extravagant ball to celebrate his being named to the Legion of Honor, only to find that once he has made all these changes he is no longer able to perform the day-to-day calculations necessary to guarantee his economic survival:

> A week after the ball, that final flare of the straw-fire of a prosperity which had lasted for eighteen years, and now was about to die out in darkness, César stood watching the passers-by through his shop window. He was thinking of the wide extent of his business affairs, and found them almost more than he could manage. Hitherto his life had been quite simple. . . . But now . . . the poor man had so many things to think of that he felt as if he had more skeins to wind than he could hold. . . . Birotteau was very careful to hide his thoughts from his wife and daughter, and from his assistant; but

> within himself he felt as a Seine boatman might feel if by some freak of fortune a Minister should give him the command of a frigate. (6:181, 171)

The contrast between César and his daughter is instructive. Through her marriage to Anselme she and her husband will, over the course of a few decades, rise to the highest circles of social distinction, gaining success after success, title after title. Further, unlike many in the Balzacian bourgeoisie, Césarine will reveal an internal nobility that will correspond in a satisfying way to the aristocratic titles she will assume. This very success may well be why we will only see her in the margins of future Balzac novels; indeed, even in *César Birotteau,* the novel in which she plays a major role, it is clear that for Balzac the analysis of the sudden failure of her father's ability to act successfully in his social world is more interesting than his daughter's potential successes. Balzac's interest in the fluctuations in the ways different social agents are enabled or disabled from acting successfully—his particular interest in social action—corresponds to a Bourdieusian insight expressed in many places, including *Pascalian Meditations,* where Bourdieu writes that "habitus is not necessarily adapted to its situation nor necessarily coherent. It has degrees of integration. . . . As a result, it can happen that, in what might be called the Don Quixote effect, dispositions are out of line with the field and with the 'collective expectations' which are constitutive of its normality. This is the case, in particular, when a field undergoes a major crisis and its regularities (even its rules) are profoundly changed."[30] Balzac's novels indeed do portray a variety of "Don Quixote" effects, and one could do worse than to imagine that an analysis of that effect is the centerpiece of his novelistic enterprise. That Bourdieu should have recourse to a character from a novel to label this phenomenon is perhaps a sign that within the history of the novel there is a practical knowledge of the phenomenon in question, a knowledge that Balzac was able to actualize as fully as perhaps any novelist could be expected to do.

We might say, then, that Balzac is sociological novelistically in the sense that he is able to use the novel to encapsulate a knowledge of social practice, of the ways a habitus functions, especially in moments of social crisis when that habitus no longer necessarily serves its agent well. And, more specifically for my purposes in the chapters ahead,

Balzac is sociological in his ability to understand the shifting social forms of sexuality (especially sexuality in some kind of social crisis) in relation to the habitus of individual agents who both *work within* and *do work on* the social forms through which their sexuality comes to expression.[31]

Balzac's interest in sexuality as a social institution causes him often to turn to the relation of sexuality to other social institutions—to the family, of course, but also, for instance, to the state. I will wind up this preface by offering three reflections regarding sexuality as it appears in Balzac's novels, regarding its institutional status, and regarding the imbrication Balzac sees and allows us to see between state, sexuality, and habitus.

First, Balzac demonstrates that some sexualities serve to bring agents into reasonably satisfying conformity with the position that they occupy in a given social field; other sexualities create dissonances that can give rise to critical awareness of one's social positioning; and sometimes both of these will be the case for the same person in different circumstances. Here again Bourdieu can be quite helpful, as when he writes in *Pascalian Meditations:*

> The relationship between dispositions and positions does not always take the form of the quasi-miraculous and therefore mostly unremarked adjustment that is seen when habitus are the product of stable structures, the very ones in which they are actualized. . . . In particular because of the structural transformations which abolish or modify certain positions, and also because of their inter- or intragenerational mobility, the homology between the space of positions and the space of dispositions is never perfect and there are always some agents "out on a limb", displaced, out of place and ill at ease. The discordance . . . may be the source of a disposition towards lucidity and critique which leads them to refuse to accept as self-evident the expectations and demands of the post, and, for example, to modify the post to the demands of the habitus rather than the habitus to the demands of the post.[32]

For Balzac, this sexual out-on-a-limbness sometimes results only in intense social vulnerability (Cousin Pons and his friend Schmucke, for instance), whereas it sometimes also makes possible a lucidity that allows for room to maneuver socially (Vautrin, but not in every moment; Eugénie Grandet).

Second, in order to grasp Balzac's understanding of sexuality it will not help to consider homosexuality as a sexual-identity category that is in opposition to heterosexuality (those terms themselves being anything but sociologically self-evident). Such a categorical division (itself a product of a certain history) is not sufficiently supple nor sufficiently universal to allow one to grasp the relation between sexuality and habitus in all times and all places, certainly not in the times and places about which Balzac was writing. Suppose we understand (as Balzac does) sexual commerce or behavior or desire or interaction to be a "profound calculation." There is no reason to assume that the division of sexual actions, exchanges, decisions, calculations, desires, or strategies into categories based on an opposition between same-sex and opposite-sex forms will succeed in capturing the whole set of processes in question—even though, as Balzac shows us, during the mid-nineteenth century such a categorical division becomes an increasingly important factor in the minds of social agents themselves.

Finally, if we want to understand Balzac's sociological vision of sexuality, we might do well to understand sexual acts, exchanges, and desires as being part of a logic of practice rather than as expressive of some subjective set of intentions. A final quotation by Bourdieu from *Pascalian Meditations* can be our guide here:

> The world is comprehensible, immediately endowed with meaning, because the body, which, thanks to its senses and its brain, has the capacity to be present to what is outside itself, in the world, and to be impressed and durably modified by it, has been protractedly (from the beginning) exposed to its regularities. Having acquired from this exposure a system of dispositions attuned to these regularities, it is inclined and able to anticipate them practically in behaviours which engage a *corporeal knowledge* that provides a practical comprehension of the world quite different from the intentional act of conscious decoding that is normally designated by the idea of comprehension. (135)

What would it mean to think of sexuality as a form of practical corporeal knowledge through which one comprehends the world as best one can, and not always well? What would it mean to understand sexuality as a set of social forms, of institutions, differentially distributed across a social field, subject to modification both by external social forces and by the cumulative effect of individual actions? What do people express as they move through these social forms? These are the questions Balzac can help us to pursue.

INTRODUCTION

Balzac and Alternative Families

In chapters 1 and 2 of this book, I will focus on forms of misfit—the "out-on-a-limbness" evoked in the preface—that manifest themselves as failures of reproduction, both biological and social. In chapters 3 and 4, I turn to forms of misfit that involve specifically same-sex relations of various kinds. In the interlude between chapters 2 and 3 I hope to make clear that for Balzac in particular, and for his world more generally, certain social forms existed that enabled something like what we today think of as socio-sexual identities based on sexual preference. Yet despite what this division into chapters might suggest, it is also the case that there was not in place in Balzac's world or in his mind any widely accepted and durable distinction between homosexual and heterosexual identities such as is taken for granted by many today.

Perhaps, for Balzac, when studying the range of alternative sexualities he saw in the world, categorization for its own sake was not quite so interesting as it was to become later. Balzac seems to have been more interested in the process by which sexual forms in general prove responsive to circumstance or prove adaptable when it comes to providing a means of expression. Eugénie Grandet (discussed in chapter 1) and the various people who do not marry in *Pierrette* (chapter 2) exist within the same spectrum of affective and erotic possibilities as do Cousin Pons or Cousin Bette (chapter 3) or Lucien de Rubempré (chapter 4). Their stories respond to similar historical and sociological conditions. Their sexualities, for Balzac, arise out of and work within and on the same set of expressive possibilities.

I would like in this introduction to begin to establish the common social context for the analyses that make up the two halves of this book. I take up the issues of chapters 1 and 2 here by way of a discussion of Balzac's *Ursule Mirouët* and the issues of chapters 3 and 4 by way of a discussion of *Le Père Goriot.* I introduce my analysis of each of these two novels with a discussion of a different moment in the history of France's Civil Code (Le Code civil), the body of law that regulates the institution of the family. To frame the discussion of *Ursule Mirouët* I focus on the concerns about the institution of *adoption* that can be found in the debates among the first architects of the Code, concerns that Balzac scrutinized in his novel. To frame the discussion of *Le Père Goriot,* I turn to the debates in the 1990s concerning the project to revise the Code to take account of same-sex domestic partners. I contrast the analytical radicalism of Balzac's novel with the conservatively structured imagination of many of the opponents of the legislative efforts of the 1990s. That conservative imagination, I claim, is the historical product of the mid-nineteenth-century moment about which and in which Balzac was writing.

FAMILY FEELING / PROPERTY RIGHTS

Les liens du sang qui unissent et qui constituent les familles sont formés par les sentimens d'affection que la nature a mis dans le cœur des parens les uns pour les autres. L'énergie de ces sentimens augmente en raison de la proximité de parenté, et elle est portée au plus haute degré entre les pères et les mères et leurs enfans.

Il n'est aucun législateur sage qui n'ait considéré ces différens degrés d'affection comme lui présentant le meilleur ordre pour la transmission des biens.

[The blood ties that unite and constitute families are formed by the sentiments of affection that nature has placed in the hearts of relatives for each other. The energy of these sentiments increases with the closeness of the kin relation, and finds its highest point between fathers and mothers and their children.

There is no wise legislator who has failed to consider that these different degrees of affection provide him with the best order for the transmission of property.]—M. Bigot-Préameneu, presenting the articles of the proposed Civil Code regarding wills to the corps législatif in 1804

La science de l'homme fait partie de la science du gouvernement. . . . Que les philosophes pénetrent donc de plus en plus dans l'abyme du cœur humain: qu'ils y cherchent tous les principes de son mouvement, et que le Ministre profitant de leurs découvertes, en fasse selon les tems, les lieux et les circonstances, une heureuse application.

[The science of man is part of the science of government. . . . Let philosophers then probe ever more deeply into the human heart: let them seek out its workings, and then let the Ministers profit from these discoveries, let them apply them wisely to a given time, place, and set of circumstances.]—Claude-Adrien Helvétius, *De l'homme* (1773)

Here is what Jean-Étienne-Marie Portalis, one of the architects of the French Civil Code, had to say about the right to the property of a deceased person: "Property rights cease with the life of the proprietor." This being the theory, there are some basic practical questions that Portalis then poses: "Will the possibility of leaving your estate to someone be allowed or forbidden, or will it suffice to place limits on that possibility?" A state itself exists, Portalis suggests, so as to have an agency to answer that question. And the particular answer in this case is that the French state will choose to limit in dramatic ways a citizen's freedom to dispose of her or his property after death: "State intervention is essential in all these matters, because it is necessary both to grant and to guarantee to people the right to inherit, and it is necessary to establish a mode for dividing up the inheritance. For goods rendered ownerless through death, the only real claim on them one sees initially is the State's claim. Let there be no mistake, the State's claim is not to inherit, but to order and to administer the inheritance."[1] Portalis's qualifications in the final clause of this citation notwithstanding, the level of state intervention incorporated into the French Civil Code was to be substantial. Starting from the premise that "no member of a deceased person's family has a rigorous title to property over the deceased's goods," it was the state that would answer in great detail all of the following questions: "How will the estate be divided between children, or, when there are no children, between close relatives? Is one sex to be favored over the other? Is primogeniture a relevant consideration? Are illegitimate children to be treated equally with legitimate ones? If there are no children, will any collateral relative suffice, no matter how distant?"[2]

The Civil Code, in answering these questions, fixed deeply within French culture a particular social category, that of the *héritier,* the heir. All persons of property with legal family necessarily, by law, accumulate heirs around them.[3] Whether you can or cannot be someone's heir in France depends on the law and on your familial relation to that person as defined by the law. Thus it is that the concept of *héritier* lies at the center of a complex legal, historical, cultural, and psychological web that could be thought of as the French epistemology of the family. This epistemological web is *felt* as well as *known.* How it is felt and known in the 1820s, 1830s, and 1840s, both by those woven into it and by those woven out of it, was one of the primary theoretical concerns of Honoré de Balzac.

In the *avant-propos* to *La Comédie humaine,* Balzac lays claim to a certain conservative social position regarding the family. He writes, "I also consider the Family and not the Individual as the true social unit. In this regard, taking the risk of being considered a backwards thinker, I place myself alongside de Bossuet and de Bonald, instead of following modern innovators" (1:13). Yet Balzac is not telling the whole truth here. For there is nothing necessarily backwards about focusing on the family, especially if one realizes, as Balzac does, that the term itself designates no fixed, transcendental object—that, as is the case of early nineteenth-century France, numerous conflicting family forms exist in uneasy proximity to one another. Different social groups, different classes, different regions are all likely to think differently about what a family is, or, one might better say, they are likely to enact the concept of the family in different ways. Some family forms will seem backwards to some, some will seem innovative to others. Within and between different social groups, attitudes toward the evolution of family forms will be different and often in conflict.

Balzac's analytical gaze on the family will thus not confirm the conservative polemic he voices in the *avant-propos.* His novels attest to a rambunctiously radical curiosity about all of the different ways in which "family" might be understood or enacted. Those novels portray a world in which all family forms seem to be in crisis; in which there is no clear, fixed, hegemonic form to the family but in which there are clear ambitions to assert or establish the hegemony of this or that form. For Balzac two of the forces most clearly overdetermining the contested space of the family are, first, the reorganizations of civil society undertaken by Revolutionary and post-Revolutionary governments and, second, the accelerated economic changes concomitant with the onset of modern industrial capitalism. Balzacian novels portray any given family as a space in which competing historical and economic interests find their material instantiations. Thus generational tensions, marital strategies, reproductive intents and accidents, sexuality, gender, as well as emotions and affects all can be seen as in part the overdetermined products of large social forces at work in and on any given practice of family.

One of Napoleon's major achievements in the first decade of the nineteenth century was to renovate the legal codes that governed France. The Napoleonic regime produced five legislative codes: the Civil Code, the Code of Civil Procedures, the Code of Criminal Procedures, the Penal Code, and the Commercial Code—new laws for the new empire. Napoleon himself was intimately involved with the writing of the Civil Code, which is often referred to as the Le Code Napoléon. This body of law, which—with modifications—remains in effect today, was of great interest to Balzac. It regulates civic identity and sets out family law, marriage law, forms of inheritance, and forms of property. For Balzac, it was a source for plot devices. But it also prompted more theoretical forms of questioning: What are the relations between law and custom? What effects will law have on custom, on family forms, on forms of sexuality, and on individual psychologies?

In the "Discours préliminaire" given by Jean-Étienne-Marie Portalis in 1800 (*le 24 thermidor, an VIII,* in the republican calendar) that opens the discussion of the project of a new civil code, Portalis asserts that "good civil laws are the greatest good men can give and receive; they are the source of custom and morals."[4] Certain Revolutionary and Enlightenment thinkers had understood legal reform as a direct way of modernizing the psyches of their citizens. There is, in the rhetoric of the architects of the Civil Code, an explicit hostility to this Revolutionary discourse. "Nature" is to be the basis (at least rhetorically speaking) for the Civil Code. About marriage, for instance, Portalis would say: "Doubtless, the general desire drawing one sex to the other belongs uniquely to the physical order of nature. . . . The mutual regard, the reciprocal duties and obligations that are born of their union once formed, that grow up between reasoning and feeling beings, all that belongs to natural law" (1:483–84).

It is nonetheless perfectly clear that the architects of the Civil Code understood themselves to be crafting a political document that advanced a particular program, and that they intended to favor certain interests and not others—in particular, they wanted to favor a certain practice of the family. In the eyes of its architects, according to one historian of the Code, "spontaneously, affections within the family are scarcely more than inclinations; the dispositions of patrimonial law correlative to them are meant to perpetuate them artificially, to turn them into 'synthetic' feelings, thereby lacking any natural freshness, but no longer marked by the inconvenience of their evanescence."[5]

Alongside this vision of a civil code that uses inheritance laws as a form of subtle psychological manipulation ("a game of implicit patrimonial blackmail, mechanically creating good social habits," as that same legal historian says at another moment [10]), we could add a vision of a code that has more direct political agendas, of which I will give two examples. The first has to do with the well-known fact that post-Revolutionary law did away with the *droit d'aînesse* (primogeniture) as a way of breaking the power of the aristocracy.[6] The Civil Code formalized this in its article 745, which states that neither sex nor primogeniture makes any difference; all legitimate heirs inherit equally.[7] As emperor, however, Napoleon decided that he would in fact prefer to have certain families of great power and wealth, where the wealth would remain entailed to the name and not be subject to division among heirs. To enable this, in 1806 he reinstituted *majorats* (a form of entailment) in France. With imperial approval, it would again be possible to attach a fortune to a title, so that the fortune could pass directly from titleholder to titleholder. In a letter to his brother Joseph, king of Naples, Napoleon had this to say:

> My brother, I want, in Paris, one hundred large fortunes, all of which will have grown up with my throne, and which will be the only large fortunes . . . the others, by the effects of the Civil Code, will have been split up. . . .You must set up the Civil Code where you are. It consolidates your power because, by its means anything that is unentailed falls, the only large fortunes that remain are the ones you set up as your fiefdoms. This is why I advocated for the Civil Code and what convinced me to establish it.[8]

Napoleon's realpolitik was not directed merely at the rich and famous. It could be found even in the attitude toward adoption taken by the Code. Some of the limitations the Code placed on adoptions in articles 343–346 are as follows: The person adopting must be at least fifty years old, have no legitimate descendants, and be at least fifteen years older that the person being adopted. The person adopting must have provided six uninterrupted years of support to the person being adopted while that person was a minor. (An exception was made for cases where the person being adopted had in a war, a fire, or a case of near drowning saved the life of the person adopting.) The person being adopted must have reached the age of majority.[9] Napoleon himself provided the rationale for these kinds of severe restrictions:

> Why would one marry, if it were possible to have children without all the costs of marriage? We are told these are chimerical fears. But we must be farsighted. Who could have warned Spain that the discovery of the new world would destroy its population? Things of this kind don't happen overnight; they take effect over centuries. It's the drop of water that cuts through granite. [Adoption] would not be a cause that acts immediately on marriage and population; but its long term effects might be felt. Marriage, we are told, is in vogue. This is true, but measures must be taken so that it remains so. If we want adoption among our customs, it can only be as a rare supplement to the effects of marriage, not as a way of avoiding marriage.[10]

In the debates concerning adoption, one sees how much these legislators feared irregularities in the inheritance system they were seeking to establish. One legislator worried: "Direct your attention to the old bachelor who sees his wealth on the point of being disbursed in numerous parts. He will choose to adopt, and how? He will choose his favorite among his relatives, and cheat all the others."[11] We see here traces of the obsession with rooting out all tendencies toward primogeniture. For Napoleon himself, this argument does not seem crucial. It would appear that the provision that one had to be at least fifty years old in order to adopt was sufficient to calm his fears about depopulation. He was therefore willing to be generous to older folks who had no descendants and for whom adoption "is a way of preparing for one's old age surer support and consolations that could be expected from collateral heirs."[12] In these differing positions on adoption and in the general sense they give of the *productive functionality* of the Civil Code as a vehicle for state interests, we can find the subject of Balzac's novel of 1841, *Ursule Mirouët,* where the possibility of an adoption taking place weighs heavily on the minds of a certain pack of *collatéraux* (collateral relatives).[13]

URSULE MIROUËT

Balzac most often writes in specific opposition to the set of interests he sees being furthered by the Civil Code. He views the legal form not as something to be valorized but something to be combated. He places himself in conservative opposition to it, considering it to be a vehicle through which the bourgeois class dehumanizes personal relations in order to advance itself as a class. We will see that Balzac also has an analytic interest in the formative and deformative relations between legislated and unofficial practices. His plots are, we will find, sometimes vehicles for analysis, sometimes vehicles for polemic. They can be, when they are polemically inclined, melodramatically normative, but there is no guarantee that the norm being valorized will coincide with the norm the legal code valorizes.[14]

Within the novel *Ursule Mirouët,* one of the main villains, Minoret-Levrault, is a denizen of the town of Nemours where the novel unfolds. Here is how Balzac gives his readers an indication of his character's villainy: "A son of the revolution, an observer of the Empire, Minoret-Levrault had never involved himself in politics; as for his religious beliefs, he had only once set foot in church, to be married; as for the principles of conduct of his private life, they could be found in the Civil Code: anything that the law did not forbid, or did not touch upon, he believed to be allowed" (3:771–72, 27).[15] Minoret-Levrault forms himself to the Code—which is not to say that the Code produces quite the effects that its architects intended. Balzac suggests that his character shapes himself both to the Code's dictates *and* to its outside: that which the law leaves unaddressed.[16] Minoret-Levrault and his wife have pretensions to accumulating a fortune and founding a bourgeois dynasty. Thus it seems hardly accidental that they have only one child, a son named Désiré. The narrator of the novel suggests by way of a few physiological details that perhaps Minoret-Levrault is not particularly fertile: "Especially upon hearing his high, squeaky voice, which made for a ridiculous contrast with the thickness of his neck, a physiologist would easily have understood why this big, tall, thick farmer adored his only son, and also perhaps why the son had been so long in appearing, as the name Désiré made clear" (3:773, 28–29).[17] Yet such matters are clearly subject to many overdeterminations. To respect the Civil Code (which demands the equal distribution of an estate among children) and simultaneously establish an economically powerful dynasty, one had best limit oneself to a single child, and marry off that child well.[18] The name Désiré, too, may have many overdeterminations, the product of a desire constrained by the terms of the Code, or the product of a desire slowly being formed by the Code—even though the architects of the Code clearly did not intend it to encourage such stringent family planning.

Minoret-Levrault is the nephew of a certain Doctor Minoret, who had left Nemours early in life and made a name and a fortune for himself practicing medicine. In 1815 he retires, childless and a widower, to Nemours, where it turns out he has three collateral heirs: his nephew; a niece, Mme. Crémière; and a distant cousin/niece on his mother's side of the family, Mme. Massin, who seems to be five degrees away from him on the family tree.[19] The careful construction of the opening of the novel shows Balzac willfully forcing his reader to read and reread carefully, to backtrack, to take notes, all in order to do the cognitive work of establishing the family tree in question so that the plot can be followed. There is an opening scene in which the collateral heirs are introduced *before* details about family structure are provided, in which people are insufficiently identified in terms of filiation, surname, and spousal affiliation for the reader to be able to establish clearly their exact relation to each other or to the doctor. As further information is provided in the pages that follow, the novel becomes a bit like a logical puzzle that the reader has to solve: a woman who refers to Minoret-Levrault as "cousin" and Minoret as "uncle" is named Mme. Massin; then there is a woman named Mme. Crémière, who also calls Minoret "uncle"; Mme. Crémière and Minoret-Levrault have the same grandfather, and so on. It only becomes possible to build the exact family tree after piecing together bits of information provided slowly during roughly the first twenty pages of the novel. Even more crucial than constructing the family tree is to understand that these three people from that tree enter into a new relation thanks to the arrival of the doctor in town. He accumulates heirs around him. On his first visit to the town, as he thinks about moving back, he asks his nephew: "Ai-je d'autres héritiers? [Do I have other heirs besides you?]" (3:786, 43).[20] The novel is clear: their identity as heirs comes from the fact of his existence (and his apparent wealth)—of which, prior to the novel's opening, they had been unaware.

If *Ursule Mirouët* opens with the sociological creation of three heirs, its plot is set in motion when the heirs discover that the doctor will not be retiring to Nemours on his own:

> From the indiscreet remark of a young man sent down to set out the library, Madam Minoret-Levrault . . . discovered that the doctor was responsible for an orphan named Ursule. This news caused strange havoc amongst the people of Nemours. Eventually, however, the old man arrived at his new home towards the middle of January 1815, and settled down there on the sly with a baby girl of ten months and her nurse.
>
> "Ursule can't be his daughter. He's seventy-one!" the heirs cried in alarm. (3:789–90, 47)

The entire plot of the novel has to do with the question of what the relation is between the doctor and Ursule—in law and in fact—and how the form of that relationship will reflect on the distribution of the doctor's estate. The novel reveals the actual relationship of Ursule and the doctor to be the following: she is the daughter of the doctor's dead wife's illegitimate brother. She might thus be recognized as practically part of his family, but is without any blood relation to him and thus without legal claim on his wealth. She belongs on the *étranger* (nonkin) side of the divide between *étranger* and *héritier.* The doctor serves as Ursule's godfather, but that is not a legal relationship. Sometimes third parties refer to Ursule as his *pupille,* his ward. This is a legal relation, but not one that makes Ursule an heir. When she turns twenty, in February 1835, a few days before the doctor dies, he makes a legal accounting to her of the wealth he has administered as her guardian, and he turns that wealth over to her.[21] There is, after this point, no legal relation between them.

Yet they make up a family.[22] In the roughly twenty years the doctor lives in Nemours between his retirement and his death, he has as little contact as possible with his heirs, whom he finds not to his liking. Instead, he builds around himself and Ursule a circle of close friends, all elderly men: a retired soldier, the curate of the town, and a justice of the peace. Of this circle, the novel says: "Thus, seven or eight months after the doctor's arrival in Nemours, the four old men playing whist and backgammon formed a compact, exclusive group: a group which each felt to be a sort of autumnal brotherhood, and whose delights were all the more to be appreciated because they were unexpected. This family of like minds found in Ursule an adopted child—adopted by each according to their inclinations [Cette famille d'esprits choisis eut dans Ursule une enfant adoptée par chacun d'eux selon ses goûts]: the curate thought of her soul; the justice of the peace became her trustee; the soldier was intending to become her tutor; as for Minoret, he was father, mother, and doctor all in one" (3:798, 57). If we recall the debate about adoption at the moment of the construction of the Civil Code, we can see the two positions evoked there being exemplified here. Adoption was allowable when it added comfort to an old age, Napoleon suggested. Adoption was a danger when it threatened to provide a way of short-circuiting the appropriate division of an inheritance. The heirs in *Ursule Mirouët* fear precisely that. Ursule is "the heirs' *bête noire,* their sword of Damocles" (3:801, 60). And the narrator apparently has some sympathy for their "family feelings": "Let's admit it! The fears of the heirs arose from what are some of the strongest and most legitimate of social sentiments—family interests" (3:802, 61).[23]

But the heirs are also a bunch of ruthless vultures, who do their best the moment the doctor dies to kick Ursule out of the house in order to make sure that she doesn't steal anything. Worse than that, Minoret-Levrault himself actually steals both the doctor's will and his instructions to Ursule revealing how she has been provided for, and then burns them to ensure that he and his fellow heirs inherit everything. The doctor has to come back from the grave as a ghost to reassert his intentions. It would be possible to go into greater detail here, into all the twists of the novel, to discuss the fears of the heirs that the doctor will outwit them by either adopting or marrying Ursule, the plans they lay to forestall these eventualities, the reasons why the doctor considers both legal avenues—marriage and adoption—and rejects them both,[24] but I will limit myself to observing that the doctor's intention was (and thanks to his ghostly reappearance he pretty much gets his way in the end) to provide appropriately *both* for Ursule *and* for his heirs. He respects both claims, as does Ursule. She has a deep respect for legal and/or blood families and their rights; and, having no liking for the heirs, she is quite pleased to be able to acknowledge in one of the closing scenes that she has no blood connection to them: "We are barely kin, and friends even less than that . . . I wouldn't know how to feel any affection for you" (3:966–67, 244). Balzac makes it quite clear then that there has been a chiasmic exchange of terms. The alternate family of Ursule and the doctor, or, to use the terms current in French sociology today, their *famille recomposée,* incarnates the sentiments that are supposed to adhere in "natural" families, whereas the natural family is heartless yet rigorous in its pursuit of respect for the legal norms by which it stands to profit. Pierre Bourdieu describes precisely the situation represented in Balzac's novel in his article "Des familles sans nom" ("Families Without a Name"), which discusses the difficulties members of *familles recomposées* have knowing how to address each other:

> It is not that objective structures, backed by the law and by the social order generally, provide the ground for sentiments. It is on sentiments, with their instabilities and their intermittence that a certain unit [the recomposed family] rests, a unit ceaselessly called into question as to its boundaries, its hierarchies, its common interests. It is constantly obliged to reaffirm its continuity in the face of a social order that, far from supporting it, as it would an ordinary family, contributes—by refusing it the banality and the securities that go with a simple name and a simple destiny—to its being confined to the category of "family at risk."[25]

In the chiasmic exchange that Balzac narrates in his novel and that Bourdieu describes in terms of our own historical moment, we see the misfit of the family, the painful experience of which reminds us of the distance between, on the one hand, institutionalized forms that would be normative and, on the other, practices crafted out of the day-to-day experience of life.

In 1904 a group of feminists got together to mark the hundredth anniversary of the promulgation of the Code by burning a symbolic copy.[26] They had a clear sense that the law embodied a particular set of interests that were not theirs. This lesson of the particularity of the law's interest, one that both the feminists and Balzac strove to disseminate, at different times and in various ways, turns out to be difficult to hold on to. The debates that preceded the establishment in fall 1999 of national domestic partnership legislation in France provide clear evidence of this lesson, echoing in various ways both Balzac and the Napoleonic legislators and suggesting, among other things, that we still have much to learn from a careful reading of Balzac.

The 1999 legislation establishing the new Pacte Civil de Solidarité (PACS) created a new section in the Civil Code and modified certain other codes, principally the tax code. The debates around the PACS legislation constitute a recent episode in the ongoing struggle in France to legislate the relation between family structures, sexuality, and reproduction. It is worth noting that the category of *héritier* was in no way changed by the PACS legislation. It might also be worth noting that in the original 1804 version of the Code, spouses themselves could only inherit in extreme circumstances. In 1804, article 767 of the Code read: "When the deceased leaves behind neither *relatives of a heritable degree* nor illegitimate children, the goods in the estate belong to the surviving nondivorced spouse."[27] Relatives were considered potential heirs even with *twelve* degrees of separation, which means that one's great-great-great-grandfather's brother's great-great-great-grandson would inherit before one's spouse. Spouses are better off today, and the degree of successibility has also been reduced. Article 755 now reads, in part: "Collateral relatives beyond six degrees do not inherit, with the exception of descendants of brothers and sisters of the deceased."[28] In today's France, spouses are no longer *étranger* to the estate of their partner. But people united by a PACS are in no way assimilated to the category of spouse in terms of inheritance law. Juridically speaking, they do remain *étranger* to their partner, just as if they were an unmarried heterosexual couple. According to French law, as we have seen, everyone has for inheritance purposes a *portion disponible* of their possessions, of which they are free to dispose as they please.

The size of that share is carefully regulated, varying from one-quarter to three-quarters of the total value, depending on the structure of the family tree. Thus only if the family tree is empty up to six degrees of separation can a person freely leave all of his or her possessions to someone who does not legally qualify as an heir or a spouse.[29]

Although it would be possible to go into further detail, what is evident is that in its symbolic dimensions the PACS legislation was constructed as a grudging concession and care was taken so that the rights of what is imagined to be the "real" family are not impinged on. The rights of this putatively real family were, during the legislative debate leading up to the adoption of the PACS, sometimes invoked in Napoleonic terms. For instance, in one stunning moment in 1995 the then minister of justice declared, "There is no question of creating domestic partnership legislation; to the contrary, it is a question of encouraging marriage and births so that France will be stronger!"[30]

The distinction between *héritier* and *étranger* within the structure of the family was one of the unspoken stakes in the PACS debate. Thus also present in the discussion of the PACS legislation—just as in the debates around the establishment of the Civil Code—was a conflict over whose interests are represented by a legal code, and an effort by different people to control the *perception* of whose interests are embodied in a given code. One position in the PACS debates was voiced by Didier Eribon, who insisted that it be recognized that a legal code represents and advocates for a specific set of interests within a society, not the general interest, and that demands for legal change constitute an effort to alter the set of interests furthered by the law: "It is, I believe, through reflection on the possibility of defining new modes of sociability . . . but also through new demands made on the law by these new modes of relation, that we may find new doors opening before us. . . . What might the law be, once we have said—and it must be said over and over again—that the law is not fixed and frozen, but is one of the stakes in a political struggle?"[31] Given France's legal history, given how the legal codes governing France have been the product of historically specific political agendas and how they have been written with the intention to favor certain social practices and to hinder or eliminate others, it might seem surprising that the interested nature of the law is so easily forgotten. Much ink was spilled during the debates around the PACS in an effort to control the public perception of whose interests were represented by the law, with many ideologues endeavoring to convince their readers that the law in its current state represents a general, not a particular, set of interests.

Among the people in the PACS debate working in a non-Balzacian way to obfuscate the relation between the law and a particular set of interests—to make the law seem like a general set of interests—was Françoise Héritier, an anthropologist at the Collège de France. She is one of the signatories of an article that was published in *Le Monde* on January 27, 1999, titled "Let's Not Leave the Critique of the PACS to the Right." The article states: "Must we act as if it goes without saying that the right to choose alternative sexual life styles should be granted institutional recognition? Must we find it normal that any form of difference be claimed as a discrimination and that those who chose to live or assume the life of a certain difference should demand at the same time that that difference be neutralized for the sake of equality?"[32] Héritier's position, evident here, and in numerous passages from her 1996 book *Masculin/Féminin,* would seem to be that the law represents the interests of anthropology, and that those living in anthropologically transgressive ways should be content to live outside the law. To question the current state of the law would thus be to question not a given particular historical order but *social order* in general. Héritier consistently confuses the idea that there is some kind of juridical convention being enforced in any given society with the idea that there is *one singular* "juridical convention that grounds the social."[33] In an article on new reproductive technologies involving sperm and egg donations, for instance, Héritier writes: "Regarding the protection of secrecy and the anonymity of donors, the examination of what goes on in other societies shows that it is perfectly possible, *in a situation where a social consensus has been established and where filiation is defined by law,* to live in harmony with yourself and others while dissociating completely the functions of genitor and Pater, of genetrix and Mater" (274; my emphasis). What seems problematic here is the conception of the social world as a space of consensus, and the implication that the law embodies that consensus. Indeed, it would be difficult to imagine how anthropological work could succeed if it takes as a point of departure the notion that a legal code somehow represents the actual, the dominant, the preferred, or even the most frequently attested set of practices within a culture.[34]

Héritier frequently uses a tone of common sense, similar to that of the Napoleonic architects of the Civil Code, to insist that law and nature walk easily hand in hand: "The rules that govern filiation, that unavoidable place where we also find the law and on which depends the ability to recognize a child's place in the family and in society—those rules are anchored in that most irreducible part of the human body, and thus of human nature: the difference of the sexes."[35] Yet what is clear here, as was clear in the case of the Napoleonic legislators, is that such talk about nature and sexual difference—riddled with the most unexamined ideological preconceptions—is in fact little more than an alibi for discussion and for legislation that is much more centrally about property rights and inheritance practices, as well as about sexual oppression.

As an alternative to Héritier's practice, one might consider the observations of John Borneman in his "Until Death Do Us Part: Marriage/Death in Anthropological Discourse." There he writes: "Marriage, gender, and the symbolics of blood, then, enter into social relations not as prior to sexuality but as part of a matrix of power relations."[36] Speaking of his work on forms of marriage in East and West Berlin, he comments:

> I identified marriage more as a radial pattern than as a central referent for measurement of all variant forms. . . . I tried to account for the various official forms as strategic devices for exclusion—for the regulation of the nation internally and for the demarcation of the nation from outsiders. And I accounted for the various unofficial forms, often merely practiced and unnamed, as marital tactics for inclusion that grew out of individual pragmatics that were historically contingent. I concluded that no single model of marriage, no universal equivalent, is able to account for all of the types that go by the name; they do not order themselves into normal and deviant forms except in the legal model, nor does any form exactly reproduce itself uncontested over time. (229–30)

Borneman's observations can help us appreciate both the theoretical and the practical weaknesses of Héritier's anthropological work: an inadequate conceptualization of the relations between the "official forms" of a given culture and the range of actual practices within that culture. Crucial to Balzac's analytic brilliance is his subtlety in perceiving and revealing the myriad effects of encounters and misencounters between official forms and actual practices. *Le Père Goriot* is a stunning case in point.

KINSHIP, ECONOMICS, AND SEXUALITY IN *LE PÈRE GORIOT*

L'enfant conçu pendant le mariage a pour père le mari [A child conceived during the marriage has the husband for father].—French Civil Code (1804), article 312

In the example of an alternative family provided by *Ursule Mirouët* we have seen only slight hints that for Balzac the heterosexuality (not, of course, a word he had at his disposal) of the normative family could also be called into question. Bourdieu observes that the efforts of families that are not heterosexually organized to achieve recognition by the law pose the same questions to the social order as do the struggles of "recomposed" families:

> If "recomposed" families and, *a fortiori,* homosexual families are somehow disturbing or even menacing for the social order and for the moral order on which it is founded—especially so, paradoxically, when they make an effort somehow to come to terms with the common norm, to "bring themselves into line"—this is because such attempts at normalization or regularization by entities that seem essentially outside the norm, that seem fundamentally to break the rules, can only be perceived by those who remain rooted in the age-old doxa of the family and the home as ambiguous acts of homage offered up to orthodoxy by the heretical.[37]

The construction of a belief in orthodoxy, the construction of a menacing heretical threat, a struggle for recognition that calls into question the status of that which would be normative—Balzac understood all of these factors to be part of the family history of the first half of the nineteenth century as well. He seems implicitly to understand that what we now know as the norm of the heterosexual family is under construction as he writes, and therefore that the form of family heresy we might today recognize as a homosexual household is slowly developing its modern aspect in counterpoint to the ideological construction of the heterosexual family.

In *Ursule Mirouët,* Doctor Minoret sets out to respect both his obligations to his heirs and his attachment to Ursule, both the normative and the alternative. As Ursule could not easily be made into one of his heirs, he sets aside some savings from his yearly income and invests those savings carefully, placing them in bonds *au porteur,* that is, in bonds that would belong not to any named individual but to the person who had them in hand. He also sets aside in a hiding place a certain amount of cash intended for Ursule, and in his will he leaves his *portion disponible* to the man he knows Ursule intends to marry.

How does one leave money to someone who is not an heir? By way of the *portion disponible,* by slipping them cash, or by using a modern financial instrument such as a bond.[38] The Civil Code was originally more concerned, it seems, with regulating the transmission of landed property than with the transmission of liquid property.[39] The twists and turns possible thanks to new financial instruments, and the relations between those forms of liquid property and landed property, attract a great deal of attention in Balzac's novels, precisely because they allow for economic relations as well as those of affection that escape the provisions of the Code.[40] As Armine Kotin Mortimer puts it, in discussing the *inscriptions de rente au porteur* (bonds payable to the person who has them in hand) in *Ursule Mirouët,* "the money that has been converted to these inscriptions no longer has any connection to the succession or the doctor's estate, any more than Ursule has to Minoret, legally speaking. Rather, these written papers have value only for the hands that hold them."[41] Kinship relations, for Balzac, are established and maintained in part by way of economic practices. The Code dictates and enforces certain kinship relations. Different kinds of financial instruments and economic practices allow a variety of people to resist some of the forms of kinship dictated by the Code, and that resistance can be, as the case of *Le Père Goriot* well illustrates, in the service of a nostalgic allegiance to older forms of family politics than those favored by the Code. Alternatively, that resistance can be in the service of various practices of kinship that have never been officially recognized as providing the basis for a family.

One version of family crisis frequently proffered by Balzacian narratives evinces a nostalgia for a pre-Revolutionary family, a putative locus of natural human sentiment. In *Le Père Goriot* this nostalgic position is represented at certain moments by Eugène de Rastignac, in particular through his relationship with his mother and sisters, who were left behind in the provinces when Rastignac went to Paris to get rich quick. In this particular version of family history—for which Balzacian narrators often piously advocate—true human, family-based sentiment is rapidly being corroded and denatured in the modern economic world: "His thoughts carried him back to his home and his family. He remembered the pure happiness of his uneventful life there: he recalled the days spent among beings who loved him dearly. Those dear creatures conformed to the natural laws of the domestic hearth, and in so doing found a full and constant happiness there, unmarred by such torments as his" (3:262, 271).[42] This narrative of the corrosion and denaturalizing of family sentiment is in fact often mimicked in a certain kind of psychoanalytic account of Balzac's novels, one that focuses on the perversions of modern sexuality, which are assumed to devolve from a disruption of traditional family structures. Such readings need to be understood as uncritical in their failure to grasp that the narratives they mimic are themselves ideologically interested, contestatory, and polemical in their original social and historical context, and often contested in the novels themselves.[43]

To state it another way, any reading of a Balzac novel that casts the social world portrayed in the novel as existing in an unstable moment that is to be read in contrast to an earlier stability—that is, any reading that accepts a version of reality in which the unbridled, perverse, overweening, inappropriate desires and interests of the Balzacian moment are held in contrast to some more grounded, natural moment of properly regulated desire and interest (even if that moment exists only in some utopian or purely theoretical space)—is a reading whose ideology conforms to only one of the ideological positions available in the Balzacian world, and obviously to a naive and conservative position at that. From such a vantage point it will not be easy to see some of the more challenging thinking about sexuality and family relationships that occurs in and around these novels.

In the specific case of *Le Père Goriot,* the numerous ways of conceiving of the interests embedded in family structures might be taken as making finally untenable a reading of *any* family structure as presocial, natural, human, disinterested. It is common and sensible to read the novel's protagonist, Eugène de Rastignac, as positioned at the charged crossing of many visions of family structure and interest and as having difficulty choosing among them. There is no denying his nostalgia for his mother, his sisters, and his family's country estate. At least two other discourses of kinship emerge out of the two possible paths to wealth that Rastignac considers in the course of the novel. Vautrin (Balzac's well-known charismatic criminal genius), seeing that the young Victorine Taillefer is in love with Rastignac, offers one path, asking Rastignac to become an accomplice in a murder that will make Victorine a rich heiress. This whole scheme is overlaid by a complicated discourse of homoerotic friendship, and indeed kinship, between Vautrin and Rastignac, a discourse I examine in more detail below. The other remaking of kinship would enable Rastignac's insertion into the Goriot family by way of both an adulterous relationship with one of Goriot's married daughters and his sentimental devotion to an old man who would be a father-not-quite-in-law. It would be possible to view Rastignac's implied kinship with Vautrin and his links to the Goriot clan as perversions or failures of certain normative models resulting both in and from a moment of general crisis in family structure. Here is one formulation of such a position:

> Despite a certain amount of jealousy, Goriot gives his daughter to Rastignac, indeed entreats him to take her. And Vautrin, as self-appointed guardian of Victorine's hand, bestows it upon the prospective suitor. Here we begin to confront the gaping chaos that the novel desperately seeks to order. For both prospective fathers—Goriot and Vautrin—ultimately abdicate their position, relinquish their authority to say no; whence an unregulated circulation of women, an uncontrolled flow of money, a mad proliferation of familial and social relations. As we begin to look at the perturbed relationships which arise in a frenzied attempt to supplement the missing core, we enter into a truly Yeatsian turmoil.[44]

We see here a tendency toward a discourse of panic regarding a perceived challenge to a particular conception of what is sometimes called the "paternal function." Yet this panic (based on a somewhat exaggerated diagnosis of an unregulated, uncontrolled, mad, perturbed, frenzied turmoil) might indicate a susceptibility to, rather than a critical distance from, the conservative polemics of the novel, a polemics that would convince us that panic is an appropriate response to the fearful perversions the novel menacingly reveals to us.[45]

We can read *Le Père Goriot* differently by keeping firmly in mind that all discourses (even nostalgically normative ones) of family relationships are polemical, and that the novel itself both stages polemics and acts polemically. We would thereby be taking seriously the polemical nature of the novelistic project Balzac sets out in his *avant-propos* while also noticing that his novels do more than merely give voice to that project. The analytical richness of *Le Père Goriot* arises from the way in which the juxtaposition of competing discourses on family can be taken to clarify the competing interests of any and all of these discourses.

Consider the situation of Victorine Taillefer, the unrecognized daughter of a rich banker. Vautrin concocts a scheme to use her familial situation to enrich both Rastignac and himself. How the relations between "illegitimate" children, "natural" affection, and inheritance were to be understood was a subject of great dispute for both Revolutionary legislators and the men who drew up the Civil Code in the first years of the nineteenth century; the novel is clearly referencing this dispute with regard to both Victorine and the children of Goriot's daughter, Madame de Restaud. Vautrin renders Victorine's situation ruthlessly: "If it were the will of Heaven to take his son from him Taillefer would acknowledge his daughter. He would want to have someone or other to leave his money to, it's a weakness of human nature, and he's not likely to have any more children, I know. Victorine is gentle and sweet, she will soon twist her father round her little finger, and make him spin like a humming-top with the whip of sentiment!" (3:144, 134). The fungible "nature" of family sentiment, the quickness with which family sentiment can be abusively attributed, the different economic interests at stake in the determination of who gains sentimental and legal inclusion in the family are all well understood by Vautrin, as they were by the Revolutionary and Napoleonic legislators who argued over how to fix inheritance rights for male and female heirs, as well as for legitimate and illegitimate offspring. Victorine's situation is unusual: "Her father believed he had sufficient reason for not recognizing her, refused to have her near him, allowed her only six hundred francs a year, and he had realized his property in order to disinherit her and leave his whole fortune to his son." This translation actually removes some legal complexity from the text; in French it reads: "Son père croyait avoir des raisons pour ne pas la reconnaître, refusait de la garder près de lui, ne lui accordait que six cents francs par an, et avait dénaturé sa fortune, afin de pouvoir la transmettre en entier à son fils" (3:59, 38). Legally, her father cannot *not* recognize her: "L'enfant conçu pendant le mariage a pour père le mari," as the Civil Code has it: "A child conceived during the marriage has the husband for father." The law is a frank acknowledgment that allowing parents easily to disown children born of adultery would be too disruptive of the order of property in France. Articles 312–318 of the Code put into place an elaborate set of rules making it clear that as long as a husband and wife were in rough proximity to each other during the estimated period when the child would have been conceived, the child is to be considered legitimate. It is also not easy for a father to disinherit a child, male or female, by realizing his property (that is, exchanging land for capital) as long as the property remains recognizably his. In an effort to put a definitive end to primogeniture, as we have seen, the Code left parents little control over the share of their estate that went to each child. Thus, as the French text suggests: "[il] avait *dénaturé* sa fortune" (my emphasis). Taillefer is performing some kind of financial sleight of hand (more far-reaching and ambitious than that practiced by Minoret in Ursule's favor) in order to cheat Victorine out of a share of his estate.

The direct relation between law and "natural family sentiments" proposed by the brave legislator M. Bigot-Préameneu (cited in the epigraph near the beginning of this chapter) is transparently absent from the actual Civil Code he is discussing, as it is from the world of Balzac's novel. Indeed, Balzac's image of the humming-top spun by the whip of sentiment seems much more appropriate. Sentiment and a variety of economic interests chase one another's tails. Sometimes sentiment comes in handy after the fact. With the death of her brother, Victorine will be able to put a new spin on her father's previously misogynistic, or stubbornly primogenitural, or genetically suspicious sentiments; she will perhaps "renaturalize" his relation to his estate and thereby bring him into conformity with the law, which paradoxically has no intention of preserving anything but the appearance of a direct relation between blood ties and the transmission of wealth across generations.

Instead of imagining Vautrin, for whatever reason, as somehow exterior to a system linking in various ways reproduction, kinship, and the transmission of wealth across generations, we should imagine him as trying to shift the parameters of that same system to suit his own ends, financial and sentimental as well as reproductive. Vautrin's discourse of homoerotic friendship, combined with his striking patriarchal slave-plantation fantasy, imply his promotion of willed kinship relations whose artificiality hardly differs from the more legally willed "natural" kinship between Taillefer and Victorine, or, as we shall see shortly, between Restaud, one of Goriot's sons-in-law, and Restaud's wife's children.[46] In one conversation with Rastignac, Vautrin observes: "I possess at this moment fifty thousand francs, which would give me scarcely forty negroes. I need two hundred thousand francs, for I want two hundred of them to carry out my idea of the patriarchal life properly. Negroes, you see, are children ready-made that you can do what you like with, without a nosy Public Prosecutor coming to ask you questions about them" (3:141, 131). In a later conversation, he continues: "I mean to leave this country in a few months for America, to go and plant my tobacco [aller planter mon tabac]. I will send you the cigars of friendship. If I make money, I will help you. If I have no children (which is likely to be the case: I am not anxious to plant scions of my own stock here [je ne suis pas curieux de me replanter ici par bouture]), I will leave you my fortune. . . . Is that acting like a friend?" (3:186, 182). Vautrin is denaturalizing his fortune, assigning and recognizing sentiment where he will, dissociating "ready-made" children from the function of "heir" usually assigned to children, designating his heirs "freely." Rastignac, as the designated heir, appreciates this, at least on one level, in a silent acknowledgment of kinship made at the moment Vautrin is arrested: "Rastignac lowered his eyes, acknowledging, in expiation of his secret evil thoughts, the kinship [ce cousinage criminel] with him that the criminal claimed" (3:219, 221).

But when, a moment or two thereafter, this denaturalized kinship system is rendered consciously affective and erotic (and also public), Rastignac violently demurs. The treacherous elderly spinster, Mademoiselle Michonneau, spins his top for him:

> "This gentleman sides with Collin [one of Vautrin's other names]," she said, scrutinizing the student, with an expression of venomous inquiry on her face. "It's not difficult to understand why."
>
> Eugène sprang forward as if to throw himself upon the old maid

and strangle her. The treacherous intention of her look was obvious, and it had let a flood of hideous light into his mind. (3:222, 224)

What the queer Michonneau does is to suggest publicly Eugène's queerness; in a moment of perfectly modern homophobia she explicitly sexualizes the kinship relation Eugène had tentatively been experiencing between himself and Vautrin.[47] As these two queer denizens of the Vauquer boardinghouse struggle briefly to establish which one of them can be more homophobic than the other, we might notice the family discourse of the novel working to cash in on their struggle by using it to demonize Vautrin and queer kinship, and by creating an affective inclination not to notice that "queer" and "natural" kinship systems are not as distinct as one would like to believe.[48]

Rastignac's sentimental top will be spun at least one more time, as the novel once again manages to reveal what its surface polemics might seem to deny. The scene in question again specifically links Vautrin to another of the plot's currents, this time to the woes of Goriot's daughter, Anastasie de Restaud, who has sold the family diamonds to pay the debts of her lover. Her husband has caught her in her shenanigans, and has forced her to reveal which of his children are "really" his ("Answer me this: have I one child which is my own?" [3:247, 253]). Her husband has extorted as well a promise from her to divest herself of her personal fortune in his favor when he asks her to, thereby disempowering her from transmitting her premarital family fortune along her (not his) bloodline, to the children he is legally obligated to recognize as his own.

To make matters worse, her lover still has debts, and since her child by her lover is now likely to require some "extrafamilial" financial assistance at some point, she turns to her father for help in keeping her lover out of debtor's prison, to the tune of twelve thousand francs. Her father has just spent that amount furnishing an apartment for Rastignac and Delphine, Goriot's other daughter, where Goriot expects to reside as well, as the odd trio begin to build their own version of an alternative family. Goriot therefore has nothing left with which to help Anastasie, and the two daughters begin a nasty verbal tussle that drives their father to distraction, until Rastignac, listening in the next room, chooses to intervene:

> Eugène, horror-stricken, took the bill he had signed for Vautrin, the stamp on which was sufficient for a larger sum; he changed the figures and made it into a proper bill for twelve thousand francs payable to Goriot's order; then he went into the room next door.
>
> "Here is the whole amount, Madame," he said, handing her the piece of paper. "I was sleeping, your conversation wakened me, and so I was able to learn what I owed Monsieur Goriot. This bill clears my debt, and you can convert it into cash. I will pay it off punctually on the proper date." (3:251, 258–59)

Earlier in the novel, Rastignac, owing debts of honor to several aristocratic dandies, was tempted into borrowing some money from Vautrin, signing a note rather than taking on a debt of honor to such a dubious character (3:185, 180–81). That note (Vautrin is safely imprisoned and therefore Rastignac's debt to him apparently forgettable) is somehow conveniently at hand at this crucial moment. Symbolically, this transaction is thus extremely rich, as the note exists at the outset as a token of Rastignac's "kinship" with Vautrin, and yet here is sentimentally overwritten, as if to forget that relationship. Rastignac provides Goriot with the filial devotion he finds nowhere else; devotion that overcompensates both for Rastignac's now reneged queer openness to Vautrin and for Rastignac's guilt at participating in a world where adulterous couples and their children mix and match in open secrecy with legally regularized families.

Le Père Goriot reiterates that families are, in the social world under scrutiny in the novel, only confusedly related to blood; appropriate family sentiment is another structure perfectly capable of being exploited to numerous complex ends, and the relation of sentiment to blood is itself insistently rhetorical. Goriot, attempting to convince his daughter to accept Rastignac's help, exclaims, "But he's my son, our dear child, your brother, your saviour! . . . Oh! my child! [he is now speaking to Rastignac] I will be more than a father to you, I want to be an entire family" (3:252, 259). This family delirium of Goriot's makes explicit the possibility that all family structures represent social (and not natural) interests that overdetermine and help reproduce certain forms of sentimental and economic dependence, as well as certain forms of sexuality. Such a reading necessarily understands that sentiment and sexuality themselves in part enact complex interests coming from elsewhere.

Vautrin's and Goriot's versions (not necessarily perversions) of kinship structures need not be seen, through some process of degradation, because of some implied excess, or through the structures' homosexual or incestuous possibilities, as revealing in negative a prior stability that, while now elusive, represents some utopian familial normativeness. Instead, by pluralizing and revealing the competition between the versions or visions of kinship and appropriate sentiment available at a given moment, Vautrin's and Goriot's versions could facilitate the development of critical distance on the currents of interest (economic, institutional, reproductive, erotic) that inhere in any of the novel's extant versions of kinship and family. For instance, one could choose to read the cruel patriarchy of Vautrin's slave-plantation fantasy as offering an implicit critique of the economic exploitation embedded in many heterosexually reproductive structures. One could choose to read in Goriot's affective volatility a critique of the contradictions internal to a family form in which the affective and economic components of paternal interest in daughters dwell in such uneasy proximity.

Analogously, we could learn something from the juxtaposition of these competing family forms about the rhetorical construction of a certain homophobia and about how homophobia draws on certain forms of family sentiment to sustain itself. When Mademoiselle Michonneau observes homophobically that we all know the true nature of Rastignac's relation to Vautrin, Rastignac's homosexual panic is, as much for a polemical reason as for any other, given ample room to express itself in counterbalance to his previous avowal of kinship to Vautrin. This suggests that even the ersatz version of family relationships Rastignac espouses in joining Goriot's "family" makes use of a hostility to queer sexuality, perhaps in order to hide the dubiousness of its own relation to some putative naturalness. To understand fully that in Balzac's critical understanding of the world all family structures are queer would mean understanding that *both* the homophobic hostility enacted by Michonneau and Rastignac *and* the expression or representation of homosexuality the novel nonetheless provides are contributions to a polemical struggle regarding the normalization of a new heterosexual family form. Rastignac's panic, should we allow the novel to encourage us to mimic it, might well blind us to the critical insights the novel offers even as it participates in this polemical struggle.

IN CHAPTERS 1 AND 2 I will investigate further the concerns highlighted in my reading of *Ursule Mirouët;* that is, Balzac's vision of the relations between law, economics, family practices, and the structure of individual psyches. Chapter 1, through a reading of *Eugénie Grandet,* pursues in particular Balzac's understanding of the social construction of femininity in certain parts of French society in the first three decades of the nineteenth century. Chapter 2 focuses again on ways in which Balzac's polemical bent is often belied by the social analysis he undertakes within his novels—in this case an analysis of people who either choose not to marry or simply end up not marrying.

In the second half of the book I return to the concerns of my reading of *Le Père Goriot:* an investigation of the place of queerness in Balzac, in particular of the place and function of same-sex intimacies in his works. The interlude between chapters 2 and 3 discusses some relevant historical and biographical material before turning to some theoretical reflections and a reading of *La Fille aux yeux d'or* (*The Girl with Golden Eyes*) that attempts to present in more detail the sociological and historical content of Balzac's interest in queer sexuality. Chapter 3 then opens with a return to some methodological reflections on the project of this book and on what I mean by calling Balzac a sociologist. The remainder of chapter 3 offers a reading of Balzac's last two novels, *Le Cousin Pons* and *La Cousine Bette,* investigating further his understanding of the imbrication of economic history, histories of family practices, and histories of sexuality, this time focusing on the queer figures at the center of those two novels. Chapter 4 turns finally to *Illusions perdues* (*Lost Illusions*) and *Splendeurs et misères des courtisanes* (the inexactly titled English translation is *A Harlot High and Low*), among the most complex and most brilliant of Balzac's novels. My goal there is to understand, with the help of the insights gained in previous chapters, why it is that male same-sex relations are so central to the historical and sociological arguments of those late novels. In my epilogue I take a brief look at how those novels and, in particular, the character of Vautrin became the foundation of a tradition of writing about male same-sex relations that extends well into the twentieth century.

One final observation here: I have learned that it is crucial in reading Balzac to hold in mind that the works in question are not ideologically consistent or coherent, but rather are arenas in which ideological conflicts are being played out. The voice of the narrator, for instance, is never ideologically trustworthy—it cannot be said that the narrator speaks for anyone or anything other than the narrator. Other aspects of the work may not share the narrator's ideological predispositions. Consider, along with the reading of *Le Père Goriot* given above, the two *Cousin* novels I explore in detail in chapter 3. The narrators of Balzac's two final novels both let it be understood that their protagonists (Cousin Pons in one case, Cousin Bette in the other) are of ambiguous sexuality. Bette is a spinster and Pons an elderly bachelor, and both have developed close friendships with persons of the same sex: Valérie Marneffe for Bette and Wilhelm Schmucke for Pons. The normalizing curiosity the narrators show for these queer cousins is part and parcel of their effort to naturalize not only a certain family structure but even heterosexuality itself. Yet the analytic clarity with which the novels themselves regard family structure *denaturalizes* that structure, revealing the historical, social, economic, and personal interest it contains. In *Le Cousin Pons* and *La Cousine Bette* we find simultaneously an investigation into certain characters' sexuality and an analysis of the interests that would produce such an investigation.[49]

In his two late novels, as in Balzac generally, I argue, sexuality is understood as an integral part of a social order, an economic system, a system of inheritance, and a psychological (affective) system that subtends the others. To remain with the example of the last two novels, we might observe that Pons's entire story—to whom should he leave his art collection?—reveals the entanglement of these systems. Imagining that he might be useful to his "cousin" Cécile (who is looking for a husband) by settling his valuable collection on her, he thereby imagines a perfect correspondence between his aesthetic identity (a sublimated form, the novel suggests, of his sexuality), his desire to belong to a family, and his own economic best interests. Once this project fails, Pons will try to leave his collection to his friend, Schmucke, and a detailed analysis of the plot surrounding this project (also doomed to failure) reveals the complex imbrication suggested by the novel between friendship, sexuality, family strategies, inheritance, affect, and social interests.

The novel *La Cousine Bette* has a hard time finding a name for the social relation between Bette and Valérie. Sister, friend, lover, daughter—the proliferation of available categories suggests that this relation cannot be reduced to any given modality. Similarly, Bette cannot quite manage to name what she feels for Wenceslas, whom she loves at one and the same time as if she were his mother and his lover. We notice in Bette's case a certain slack in the cord that links sentiment or affect or sexuality to family structure. If we were to consider merely the novel's plot, we would notice that it ruthlessly eliminates everyone who plays with this slack. Nonetheless, *La Cousine Bette* entertains an interest in different possible manifestations of sexuality outside the family system. What would sexuality be if it were no longer linked to inheritance? This question is the more radical one the novel poses, however hesitantly. But to get at that question—indeed, to grasp the full complexity with which sexuality is understood in Balzac—it is always necessary to ask about its relation to history, to economics, to law, and to all the various structures—especially that structure we call family—that provide the wherewithal, the medium, in which a sexuality takes on its forms.

CHAPTER ONE

Legal Melancholy: Balzac's *Eugénie Grandet* and the Napoleonic Code

The individual himself regards sexuality as one of his own ends; while from another point of view he is only an appendage to his germ-plasm, to which he lends his energies, taking in return his toll of pleasure—the mortal vehicle of a (possibly) immortal substance—like the inheritor of an entailed property who is only the temporary holder of an estate which survives him.—Sigmund Freud, "On Narcissism"

"A quoi servent donc les enfants!" [What, then, is the use of children?]—Monsieur Grandet, in *Eugénie Grandet*

FAMILY JOYS

My point of departure for this chapter is a moment toward the beginning of Balzac's novella, *Le Contrat de mariage* (*The Marriage Contract*). The twenty-something aristocrat Paul de Manerville is living in Bordeaux and has fallen in love with and decided to propose marriage to the nineteen-year-old Natalie Évangélista. Once Natalie and her mother have accepted unofficially, the time comes to negotiate the marriage contract. This is a moment Mme. Évangélista dreads, for it necessarily involves revealing her rather precarious, indeed irregular, financial situation. She is a widow. When her husband died, their daughter Natalie should have inherited one-third of his estate. Mme.

Évangélista never paid her daughter this money—her dowry, in point of fact. Indeed, the mother has been slowly consuming the estate of her late husband by continuing to lead, with her daughter, the rich life to which they are accustomed. Female observers throughout Bordeaux's high society have already imagined that Natalie will have difficulty finding a husband: "Whenever, upon Natalie's arrival at a ball, they would hear an eligible bachelor say with ecstatic admiration, 'What a beauty!', the mothers present would reply: 'But an expensive one'" (3:539).[1]

Not only would Natalie be expensive to keep, she may well, by getting married, cost her mother everything she has. For to give her the fortune to which she is entitled from her father's estate would now cost Mme. Évangélista more than she possesses: "The widow owed her daughter a third of the fortune M. Évangélista had left, twelve hundred thousand francs. She found herself unable to pay the debt, even were she to sell everything she owned" (3:554). Also, if Paul, finding out the truth of Natalie's financial situation, withdraws from the marriage, the entire town will hear of it, and Natalie may well truly become unmarriageable. As Mme. Évangélista ruminates on the impending conversation about her daughter's marriage contract, on this turning point in her life after which she will no longer be able to say to herself that she has always acted honestly, the narrator describes what goes on in her mind, as follows:

> There rose up in her soul, in regards to Paul, a slight movement that couldn't yet be called hatred or aversion, or even anything bad. Yet was he not her opponent in the trial she was secretly undergoing? Was he not unwittingly becoming an innocent enemy who must be vanquished? Who has ever been able to love the person they are required to deceive? Obliged by the circumstances to be cunning, the Spanish noblewoman resolved, as would any woman, to deploy all her superiority in this battle, whose shamefulness could only be obliterated by an absolute victory. (3:554)

One sees here a common characteristic of Balzac's novels: an acute perception and portrayal of the causes and conditions of women's economic disadvantage, and simultaneously a misogyny that expresses itself through a discourse on the nature of "all women." Yet what I would like to call particular attention to in this description is its interest in linking the birth of affect to a moment of economic crisis, where that crisis is intimately related to the legal structures that fix relations between men and women. That the affect could initially be unnamed, unfixed—a movement that has yet to take on an identity as hate or aversion, and yet seems about to do so—reveals the interest Balzac has in the productive relation between legal and financial orders and affective patterns. Affective patterns would seem to be constantly available for renewal and revision, and the outcomes of those renewals and revisions will necessarily be linked to economic, legal, and social forces and histories.

The very vocabulary of this passage suggests that the emotional relationships between men and women are heavily determined by their legal standings: Paul is the opposing party in some kind of legal ordeal. The reader has been prepared earlier in the novella for the understanding that law contributes to the shape of affect. Paul's close friend, Henri de Marsay, advises him against marriage, in the following terms:

> So you want to be married and will soon do so. Have you ever pondered the Civil Code? Myself, I have never sullied myself in that overly loquacious slum known as a Law School, and certainly I've never opened the Code, but I have observed its application in the real world. I am a legal thinker the way a clinician is a doctor. Sicknesses are not found in books, but in sick people. The Code, my dear friend, made women into wards, it considered them as minors, as children. Now how are children best governed? By fear. Here, Paul, is where you find the beast's bridle. Take your own measure. Do you think that someone as gentle, as sweet, as friendly, as confiding as you are can carry off the role of a tyrant? (3:536)

Henri de Marsay proves clear-sighted here regarding Paul's fate; Paul, on the other hand, will never grasp this way of looking at things, and so he will suffer miserably at the hands of his wife and his mother-in-law. He gives voice to a different understanding of what marriage should be: "The life of the large group of people to which I belong in perfectly bourgeois fashion is made up of emotions for which I now feel a need. . . . I want to live in close enough intimacy with a dear creature so that our affection will not be dependent on minor things. . . .

I feel that I am well suited to family joys, and want to place myself in the circumstances society requires in order to gain a wife and children" (3:534).

Paul understands himself to belong to an affective universe that is different from the one in which Henri lives. Paul wishes to understand affection as independent of the social order. Granted, one has to fulfill certain social conditions in order to get married and have children, but, those conditions filled, the world of family intimacy is to be imagined as separate from the larger world of legal and economic forces. Paul would willingly label himself bourgeois for espousing this way of looking at the world. We know from elsewhere in Balzac (*Ursule Mirouët,* for instance) that not every member of the bourgeoisie is as dewy-eyed as Paul. Yet *Le Contrat de mariage* is clearly suggesting that Paul, in all his sentimentality, is as ideologically structured and as marked by class in his affective leanings as is anyone else. Indeed, he may well incarnate a perfect instance of bourgeois sentimentality. That same sentimentality might well mark him, in the eyes of both Henri and the narrator, as too feminine in his affective structure for his own *personal* interests—thus making him unsuitable for clearheaded negotiations of a marriage contract, and unlikely to be able to conduct himself appropriately in relation to the wife he has chosen. Still, the sentimentality he embodies—even if it brings him only disaster—may well represent a set of class interests that would function appropriately elsewhere. In a certain way, it is unfortunate for him that he never met Eugénie Grandet.

EUGÉNIE'S MELANCHOLY

In his essay "On the Family as a Realized Category," Pierre Bourdieu observes: "The family is the product of a labour of *institutionalization,* both ritual and technical, aimed at durably instituting in each member of the instituted unit feelings that will tend to ensure the *integration* that is the condition of the existence and persistence of the unit." He goes on to speak of the "constant maintenance work on the feelings," of the "countless acts of reaffirmation and reinforcement that aim to produce, in a kind of continuous creation, the *obliged affection* and *affective obligations* of family feeling (conjugal love, paternal and maternal love, filial love, brotherly and sisterly love, etc.)."[2] This "labour of institutionalization"—the social production of family affect and the material supports and instances of that affect—is a major preoccupation of Balzac's novels, novels that reflect in complicated ways on the historical and material contingencies that overdetermine family feeling, gender, and sexuality. In what follows, I investigate this preoccupation in the case of *Eugénie Grandet* (1833), pursuing in the case of this novel what it means to talk about the production—indeed, the materialization—of family feeling.

More than that, I am interested in the hints Balzac gives (for example in the discussion between Henri de Marsay and Paul de Manerville in *Le Contrat de mariage*) that one can almost become conscious of the social production of affect and thereby almost actively intervene in shaping one's own psyche. Any such intervention probably remains a bit of an "almost" in *Eugénie Grandet,* whose protagonist is nonetheless said by the end to be "gifted with the delicate intuition that a solitary person comes to possess through perpetual meditation and by way of the acute vision with which such a person perceives the things that come within his orbit" (3:1197, 191).[3] Eugénie is also said to be "accustomed by sorrow and her recent education to figuring most things out" (3:1197, 191). In fact, there is, I will try to show, a reasonable amount of evidence that Eugénie has by the end of the novel critically understood—and attempted to intervene in—the socially and historically constructed nature of what Bourdieu would call her *habitus* and her bodily *hexis.*[4]

I begin with an example from *Eugénie Grandet* of the famous socially conservative Balzacian narrative voice,[5] preaching social stability to the post-Revolutionary, post-Empire, post-Restoration world of France's July Monarchy (which began in 1830), a world of intense social flux: "Misers do not believe in a life to come. The present is everything for them. This thought casts a terrible light on the present day, when, more than ever before, money dominates the law, politics, and social behaviour. Institutions, books, men, and doctrines, all conspire to undermine the belief in a future life, which has been the foundation of the social fabric of eighteen hundred years" (3:1101, 84). Ostensibly a plea for a return to religious values, the passage also has an analytic side, as part both of the extended Balzacian reflection on the institutional support necessary for the reproduction of any social order, and of the particularized effort to comprehend the effects of post-Revolutionary secularization on the patterns and possibilities of social reproduction.

Institutionalized religion, as it is understood in novels such as *Eugénie Grandet,* exercises its socially reproductive force partly through its role in the production of affective systems that discourage change. Consider, for instance, the first few sentences of the opening paragraph of *Eugénie Grandet:*

> In certain provincial towns there are houses whose appearance arouses a melancholy as great as that of the gloomiest cloisters, the most desolate moorland, or the saddest ruins. There is perhaps, in these houses, a combination of the silence of the cloister, the desolation of moorlands and the sepulchral gloom of ruins. In them life is so still and uneventful that a stranger would think them uninhabited, if his eye did not suddenly meet the pale, cold look of a motionless figure whose almost monk-like face appears above the window-ledge at the sound of an unknown step. These melancholy characteristics are to be found in the appearance of a house in Saumur, at the end of the steep street which leads to the château through the upper part of town. (3:102, 3)

Among the many things to notice in this bravura opening is the ambivalence in the rendering of the social status or function of melancholy. I'd like to avoid specifying too quickly how precisely one might understand the concept of melancholy in Balzac until I've discussed how the word is used and what work it does. Melancholy might seem, first of all, profoundly antinovelistic.[6] It thrives in a somber and religious silence that would seem to eschew storytelling; it evinces a passivity and a slowness so exaggerated one might think that life itself would be inhibited.

To the extent that the novel's opening passage also foreshadows the novel that is about to unfold—the figure at the window being an avatar of Eugénie and the unknown footstep in the street that of her Parisian cousin Charles, whose arrival startles her into some (novelistic) movement—we might also understand melancholy, as well as being ill-suited to an eventful story, as an antimodern or anachronistic affect. As the narrator states a few pages later: "The melancholy dwelling where the events of this story took place was, in fact, one of those houses. They are the venerable remnants of a century when men and things had that quality of simplicity which the French way of life is losing daily" (3:1030, 6). If the house is melancholic, it is apparently so because it comes from another time when time itself was experienced differently. It is melancholic for being forced to remain standing and inhabited in a time where life moves at a pace no longer conducive to the stillness of "the silence of the cloister, the desolation of moorlands and the sepulchral gloom of ruins."

If Eugénie, one of the house's key inhabitants, is the melancholic face at the window of the melancholic house, perhaps it is because she—like her habitation—is emotionally structured in such a way as not to be able to cope with the novelties likely to be walking down her street. This novel of melancholy could then be a novel about the ways institutional structures and institutionalized structures of affect lag behind in times of rapid change. And the novel should be understood to structure itself in both an allegorical and an ironic relation to the form of melancholy it adduces. Allegorically, it mimes (especially in certain ideological exhortations of its narrator) the point of view of the sad buildings forced to contain social relations that seem inappropriate to the structure of feeling implied in the buildings' construction. Ironically, it refuses to sustain a full allegiance to that melancholy, whose stillness and claim to ahistoricity would contradict the novel's own analytic position—that affect is an effect.

Alas, melancholy is not used consistently enough in Balzac always to give it the same specific diagnostic force. Alongside what we might call the "architectural melancholy" described in the opening paragraphs of *Eugénie Grandet,* for instance, there is also a peculiar variety we might call the melancholy of unmarried young women. Balzac lays out this syndrome clearly toward the beginning of *César Birotteau,* in his description of the young Césarine: "If her happiness deprived her figure of that certain poetry painters insist on supplying their compositions by rendering them a little too pensive, nonetheless that vague physical melancholy that afflicts young girls who have always been under their mother's wing imprinted her features with something ideal" (6:103, 79). Eugénie shares Césarine's "physical" predisposition:

> In the innocent, monotonous life of a young girl there comes a day of delight when the sun's rays flood into her heart, when a flower seems to express her thoughts, and when her heartbeats convey

their fertile warmth to her brain, so that all her ideas dissolve into a vague longing; it is a day of innocent melancholy and tranquil happiness. When babies begin to see, they smile; when a girl first becomes aware of the feelings of nature, she smiles as she smiled when a baby. . . . The moment of seeing the things of this world clearly had arrived for Eugénie. (3:1073, 54)

This melancholy might seem quite distinct from the architectural one. And the two kinds in fact suggest different avenues for reading the novel. Architecturally speaking, we could read *Eugénie Grandet* as a novel about social structures left over from a past social dispensation, straining to encompass the new reality that tries to inhabit them. But Césarine's and Eugénie's girlish melancholy might encourage us to see their novels as representing transhistorical crises common to "the family": the moment a girl is ready to leave the paternal household and become a wife and mother; the natural script that is inevitably played out when that moment arrives.

Such encouragement is probably best refused. But there's no reason not to think about the social content this pseudobiological discourse represents. If *César Birotteau* and *Eugénie Grandet* both have families consisting of a mother, a father, and a melancholy young woman of marriageable age, perhaps it is because that constellation was so well chosen for investigating the particular historical pressures on systems of family affect. The "legal melancholy" of my title is an ad hoc and somewhat awkward category of my invention, an attempt to pin together the girlish melancholy and the architectural melancholy described above. For it is hardly surprising that, given the upheavals in the French social order, there should be profound shifts in the functioning of gender and affect within families. My analysis of *Eugénie Grandet* focuses on this conjuncture.

I am particularly interested in the way *Eugénie Grandet* constructs relations between, on the one hand, individuals, family forms, and what we might call the practice of family; and, on the other, systems of law, inheritance, and sexuality. *Eugénie Grandet* foregrounds Balzac's use of the details of the Napoleonic Code to structure his plots. Eugénie and her father, Felix, find themselves in a situation of possible conflict at the moment of her mother's impending death, because with the death of her mother Eugénie would, by the terms of the

Code, inherit her mother's share of the family's wealth, and her father would be accountable to her for it. Grandet's notary tries to convince Grandet that it is in his best legal interest to be on friendly terms with his daughter at this crucial moment, whereas Grandet cannot believe the law would ever put him in a losing position vis-à-vis his daughter. The ways children can inherit separately from their mothers—even though those mothers, as married women, have no control over their own finances—means that the death of the mother is one of the most tumultuous and narratively productive events in the life of a Balzacian family.

At a certain point in *Eugénie Grandet,* Felix Grandet has confined his twenty-three-year-old daughter Eugénie to her room because she refuses to tell him how she has disposed of a rather large sum of money she has been accumulating through his annual birthday presents to her. The Code in fact grants fathers certain rights regarding the imprisonment of their disobedient minor children. Eugénie is no longer a minor, but she submits to the imprisonment anyway. Her father's notary, feeling a bit more compunction than does Grandet, and also recognizing the legal significance of the impending death of Grandet's wife, tries to convince Grandet that it is not in his best legal interest to treat his daughter (and his wife, deeply affected by Eugénie's treatment) harshly. Should her mother die, Eugénie would be in a position to demand that her father liquidate the estate he has accumulated using the combined wealth of the marriage in order to pay Eugénie her mother's inheritance. Here is Grandet's exclamation of disbelief at his legal situation: "Montrez-moi le Code, je veux voir le Code! [Show me the Code; I want to see the Code!]" (3:1165, 155). While the text of the Code doesn't make an actual appearance in the novel, it becomes clear how much the Code's provisions exert pressure on Balzac's characters and their development. "I will be picked over, betrayed, killed, devoured by my daughter," Grandet exclaims. The notary is firm: "She inherits from her mother." "What, then, is the use of children?" Grandet wonders (3:1165–66, 155).

The Napoleonic Code was not intended to empower women; in fact, it clearly dispossesses them in most circumstances. But Eugénie is no longer a minor and is as yet unmarried. Her mother is on her deathbed, and even though her mother gave up all control over her own goods by marrying, the nuptial contract can still insist that her children inherit what she brought into the marriage. If Eugénie were still a minor there would be no problem, because her father would in that case still control her finances. But he has inadvertently left her a window of opportunity by not marrying her off before she reached her majority. At her mother's death she can therefore demand an accounting of her inheritance, which means her father will have to liquify all his assets in order to share them out with her in the proper proportion.

What a mother brought to a marriage, how the marriage contract was written, the number of children born within the marriage, the sex of those children, and their age and marital status at the moment of their mother's death thus become important facts in understanding any given Balzacian family structure. Balzac's analyses of the various permutations of inheritance, and especially inheritance through the mother, show an acute awareness of the material causes of gendered family structures, including affective ones.

The Napoleonic Code is one of the material conditions that provides Balzac with his plots. The matrix of narrative potentiality it establishes makes family financial dramas a satisfying plot strategy. Thus in *Eugénie Grandet,* for instance, we have a family of father, mother, and daughter, in which the daughter is of age but unmarried at the time of the mother's death. In *La Recherche de l'absolu* (*The Quest of the Absolute*) (to choose another text often cited in discussions of the Napoleonic Code in Balzac's novels) one reads of four minor children at the moment of the mother's death, one of whom could use marriage as a way of making her father account to her for her mother's inheritance.[7] In focusing on *Eugénie Grandet* in what follows, I'd like to pursue not only the well-demonstrated fact that Balzac uses the terms of the Code as plot devices but also the ways that his novels show the imbrication of law and psychology.

MELANCHOLIA

I have yet to mention the rather well-known Freudian account of melancholy. In part this is to allow the term to resonate within the Balzacian context, and in part it is also because too swift a turn to the Freudian reading of melancholy seems to me to run the risk of leaving behind too quickly the social and historical components of affects.

Freud, in elaborating his ideas on melancholy, relies on a distinction between "sexual instincts" and "ego-instincts." That distinction is made, for instance, in this passage from "On Narcissism":

> The individual does actually carry on a double existence: one designed to serve his own purposes and another as a link in a chain, in which he serves against, or at any rate without, any volition of his own. The individual himself regards sexuality as one of his own ends; while from another point of view he is only an appendage to his germ-plasm, to which he lends his energies, taking in return his toll of pleasure—the mortal vehicle of a (possibly) immortal substance—like the inheritor of an entailed property who is only the temporary holder of an estate which survives him. The differentiation of the sexual instincts from the ego-instinct would simply reflect this double function of the individual.[8]

For Freud, the appropriate differentiation of sexual instincts from ego-instincts is required for heterosexuality. What he calls "narcissistic object-choice" results from a failure to sustain the appropriate differentiation of the two instincts:

> The sexual instincts are at the outset supported upon the ego-instincts; only later do they become independent of these, and even then we have an indication of that original dependence in the fact that those persons who have to do with the feeding, care, and protection of the child become his earliest sexual objects: that is to say, in the first instance the mother or her substitute. . . . We have found, especially in persons whose libidinal development has suffered some disturbance, as in perverts and homosexuals, that in the choice of their love-object they have taken as their model not the mother but their own selves. They are plainly seeking themselves as a love-object and their type of object-choice may be termed *narcissistic*. (68–69)

The "disturbance" in the libidinal development to which Freud refers is thus one that could conceivably cause a failure of entailment, the alienation of germ-plasm rights through an overweening individualism. Balzac himself wrote a trio of stories and novels he grouped together under the title *Les Célibataires* (*Unmarried People*), whose purpose, he said provocatively, was to "stigmatize" such people—"any unproductive being . . . old spinsters and old bachelors" (4:24, 4:21). In a letter written slightly before the first appearance of *Eugénie Grandet,* he compared *Eugénie Grandet* to one of the stories collected in *Les Célibataires* (see 3:1644), perhaps an indication that he saw in this novel another aspect of his investigation of certain failures of reproduction within French society. Yet Balzac's project is as much sociopolitical as psychological. There may therefore be more to be gained for a reading of Balzac by considering melancholy to be a historically specific aspect of *habitus* rather than a general and ahistorical neurosis.

This same distinction Freud makes in "On Narcissism" between ego-instincts and sexual instincts is important to the oft-read 1917 essay "Mourning and Melancholia," in which "narcissism," an undesirable relation between the two forms of instinct, is once more a key analytic term. Mourning, according to this second essay, is a process in which libido is slowly withdrawn from a lost object and given to a new one. Melancholia arises when such a transfer of libido is not successfully undertaken or completed:

> The result [in a loss of an object leading to melancholia] was not the normal one of withdrawal of the libido from this object and transference of it to a new one, but something different for which various conditions seem to be necessary. The object-cathexis proved to have little power of resistance, and was abandoned; but the free libido was withdrawn into the ego and not directed to another object. It did not find application there, however, in any one of several possible ways, but served simply to establish an *identification* of the ego with the abandoned object.[9]

Freud then theorizes that one of the conditions that makes this melancholy identification between ego and lost object more likely would be that the original object choice of the melancholic patient was a narcissistic one:

> Certain things may be directly inferred with regard to the necessary conditions and effects of such a process. On the one hand, a strong fixation to the love-object must have been present; on the other hand, in contradiction to this, the object-cathexis can have had little power of resistance. As Otto Rank has aptly remarked, this contradiction seems to imply that the object-choice had been effected on a narcissistic basis, so that when obstacles arise in the

way of the object-cathexis it can regress into narcissism. The narcissistic identification with the object then becomes a substitute for the erotic cathexis, the result of which is that in spite of the conflict with the loved person the love relation need not be given up. (170)

All this theoretical speculation, Freud suggests, needs some empirical confirmation. Such confirmation would be the successful clinical finding that those people whom Freud considers most given to narcissistic object-choice (homosexual men and beautiful women are Freud's examples—perhaps beautiful, young, protected, provincial women like Césarine and Eugénie) are also most given to melancholy. "The conclusion which our theory would require," Freud states, "namely, that the disposition to succumb to melancholia—or some part of it—lies in the narcissistic type of object-choice, unfortunately still lacks confirmation by investigation" (171).

Writing about *Eugénie Grandet* in her 1985 book *Breaking the Chain: Women, Theory, and French Realist Fiction,* Naomi Schor refers to precisely this moment in which Freud is worrying about empirical justification for his ideas about what kind of person would be most susceptible to melancholy. Schor writes: "*Eugénie Grandet* offers us, I would argue, precious literary confirmation of Freud's hypothetical conclusion, for, viewed in this optic, Eugénie's undying passion for [her cousin] Charles appears to be motivated by [an] insidious form of narcissism."[10] I would like here to dispute Schor's claim and her procedure. When Schor offers Balzac's novel as literary confirmation of Freud's hypothesis about narcissistic object-choice, she suggests a theoretical truth to the ways of marshaling the concepts of narcissism, melancholy, and gender identification offered by Freud, a truth that would also be revealed through some representational accuracy in Balzac's novels. What if we suppose instead that Balzac's and Freud's ways of marshaling notions such as narcissism, melancholy, and gender identification share a common interest? Rather than proposing that Freudian family romances and Freudian models of gender identification can illuminate the representational work of the Balzacian novel, what if we propose that the juxtaposition of Freudian family romances with Balzacian novels encourages one to notice (and perhaps by noticing to continue) only one kind—and a conservative kind—of cultural work those novels are doing? The juxtaposition might not then be illuminating. It might not illuminate so much as sustain a particular set of habits of thinking about gender that a certain current in the novel (its most conservative ideological voice) may be asserting or advocating, but that may be perfectly contestable, even within the novel itself, say by its set of analytical interests in the historical production of affect.[11] In particular, it might be worth watching the ways in which a Freudian deployment of words and phrases such as "homosexual object-choice" or "homosexual relation," "narcissism," and "melancholy" abets not so much the *analysis* of as it does the *production* and *reproduction* of—the very belief in—a heterosexual order. *Eugénie Grandet* may well be (on one level) out to abet that same process. (Heterosexuality is never a given in Balzac novels, although it is often trying to become one.) Yet by way of its thoroughgoing attention to family structure and gender, and to the ideological struggles and institutional transformations bearing on family and gender, it might also reveal a great deal about the roles and interests of specific institutions in producing and reproducing normative affects and identifications. It might also evince a curiosity for the failures of normativity.

The novel opens in 1819, on Eugénie's twenty-third birthday. The evening in question is an extraordinary one because it also brings a previously unknown cousin, the twenty-one-year-old Charles Grandet, to the house. A young Parisian dandy, he has been sent away from Paris by his father, who is on the verge of bankruptcy and planning to kill himself rather than face dishonor. The father sends with his son a letter to Eugénie's father, asking him to assist Charles in setting out to remake his family's fortune. Charles, on learning of his father's suicide, enters into a period of intense grief. Eugénie falls in love with Charles, and, when he finally sets out as a trader to make his fortune in the wide world, she gives him a hefty sum of money—the accumulation of twenty-three years of birthday presents. Charles, growing to believe himself in love with his cousin, gives her in exchange a dressing case or elaborate toilet kit worked in gold, a present from his mother, who has been dead for some time.

Schor's reading of Eugénie as a Freudian melancholic relies on two assertions: that Eugénie's bond with her mother is too strong and based in narcissism, and that her "pathological" (92) love for her cousin Charles is nothing other than a reenactment of her bond with her mother. According to Freud, it is the boy's object-choice of his mother (what Freud calls "anaclitic object-choice") that challenges his primary narcissism. A girl's object-choice of her mother, Freud asserts, cannot have the same effect. Boys who follow a normative path of libidinal development, one more given to anaclitic object-choice, take the mother as their love-object and in the slow separation of sexual instincts from ego-instincts keep the sexual instincts directed toward the mother and gradually transfer the ego-instincts to the ego-ideal. "Observation of normal adults," Freud notes, "shows that their former megalomania has been subdued and that the mental characteristics from which we inferred their infantile narcissism have vanished."[12]

A girl's primary narcissism, it would seem, rather than entering into conflict with the choice of the mother as object, threatens to become complicit with it, allowing sexual and ego-instincts to remain confused. Schor tells us that Eugénie "never transcends her homosexual bond with her mother."[13] This is part of her argument for Eugénie as a melancholic. Eugénie's bond with Charles, so this logic goes, must be a new version of her bond with her mother, which is a form of narcissistic object-choice, and thus likely to produce melancholy when the object is lost. Such an argument clearly depends on accepting Freud's assertion that for women the distinction between anaclitic object-choice and narcissistic object-choice cannot be the same as for men. As Freud says:

> Complete object-love of the anaclitic type is, properly speaking, characteristic of the man. . . . A different course is followed in the type most frequently met with in women, which is probably the purest and truest feminine type. With the development of puberty the maturing of the female sexual organs, which up till then have been in a condition of latency, seems to bring about an intensification of the original narcissism, and this is unfavorable to the development of a true object-love with its accompanying sexual over-estimation; there arises in the woman a certain self-sufficiency (especially when there is a ripening into beauty) which compensates for the social restrictions upon her object-choice. Strictly speaking, such women love only themselves with an intensity comparable to that of the man's love for them.[14]

Schor's reading of *Eugénie Grandet* chooses not to accept all of Freud's suggestions about female development. In discussing the passage from

Freud cited above, Schor comments: "However questionable not to say mystified Freud's remarks on female narcissism, there is one observation in that famous or infamous passage that bears rereading."[15] Schor is speaking about Freud's comment that a woman's narcissism may be some sort of compensation for the "social restrictions" she faces in choosing an object. Schor continues: "Seen in this light, it would appear that the female protagonist's melancholic retreat into narcissism may in fact be the only form of autonomy available to her in a society where woman's assigned function in the Symbolic is to guarantee the transmission of the phallus" (106). The relevance of such an insight to a reading of *Eugénie Grandet* is unquestionable. Eugénie's struggle for and against autonomy is, as I shall discuss shortly, crucial to the novel. But I wonder if the psychoanalytic framework Schor adumbrates is fully successful in capturing what the novel has to say about Eugénie's relation to autonomy.

For Schor, Eugénie's primary, unbroken narcissistic, "homosexual" relation to her mother includes a particular negative component: her identification with her mother includes identifying with her mother's servility and melancholy stoicism in the face of a woman's "necessary" suffering. Schor reads Eugénie's love for her cousin Charles as a protomelancholic narcissistic object-choice that replays the relation to her mother. To do so, she reads the primary axis of Eugénie's identification with Charles as an identification with *melancholy.* Of Charles's mourning of his father's death, the novel comments: "He was not simulating grief; he was really suffering, and the cloud spread over his features by sorrow gave him that interesting air that women find so attractive. Eugénie loved him even more for it" (3:1108, 93). When, after a nine-year absence, Charles returns from abroad, having made a fortune as a slave trader, and, not realizing that Eugénie is incredibly wealthy, rejects her hand in order to marry someone with an aristocratic name, Schor reads Eugénie's reaction as her development into a typical Freudian melancholic: "In a very real sense the narcissistic object Eugénie chooses to love . . . is melancholy itself. . . . Small wonder, given the nature and depth of her identification with both her mother and her cousin . . . that Eugénie responds to Charles' desertion by withdrawing from life and regressing into narcissism: she has always already been in mourning" (103). The form of what Schor calls

Eugénie's "melancholic retreat into narcissism" (106) after her rejection by Charles involves an agreement to marry a longtime suitor, the President de Bonfons, on the condition—of her stipulation—that the marriage never be consummated. "In short," Schor writes, "Eugénie submits to the laws of exchange but without relinquishing her most autistic fantasy; against all expectations grounded in masculine developmental models, she enters into the Symbolic, while remaining fixated in the Imaginary" (99). For Schor, it almost seems that autism is as close to autonomy as Eugénie Grandet can get. Eugénie's evasion of reproduction is here both a self-conscious relation to gender oppression *and* a sign of neurosis. Such a reading would seem to leave in place a stigmatization of Eugénie that recalls Balzac's own comments on *célibataires*.

Here we might recall Eugénie's father's frustrated outburst, quoted at the opening of this chapter, on hearing that Eugénie could take him to court if he doesn't give her an accounting of the estate of her recently deceased mother: "A quoi donc servent les enfants! [What is the use, what is the point, of children?]." This question can be heard in many ways, but let's choose to hear it, as Eugénie might, as a political question, as a question that could give rise to a critical and productive alternative practice of gender. Schor's characterization of Eugénie's predicament at the close of the novel is perspicacious, yet her way of stating the case allows Eugénie almost no room for action outside of psychological pathology; it leaves her no space for a political education about psychological forms, about affect. Might she not have learned something from watching her mother's death at her father's hand? Might she not have learned something from the way Charles values over her a woman with an aristocratic name? Might she not have learned something—about, perhaps, the political economy of modern heterosexuality, and her own affective participation in it—from the forms of attention her various suitors pay her, and the kinds of marriage contracts they would agree to? Might she not learn something, at the very end of the novel, from the choice of her faithful servant Nanon to marry only reasonably late in life?

I'd like to begin pursuing questions such as these by first examining Eugénie's father's way of understanding gender. This will serve as a prelude to my attempt to read the scene where Eugénie *fails* to use the

Napoleonic Code to her advantage and at her father's expense, as well as to understand what might be going on in the marriage agreement she finally arrives at with the President de Bonfons.

MONSIEUR GRANDET

Eugénie's father, M. Grandet, obsessed by the accumulation of wealth, might be thought of as a totally unsentimental character. His vision of the world is almost entirely governed by perceptions of how value can be realized as gold and then hoarded. The novel consistently claims to be shocked by or critical of this vision, which leaves almost no place for human feeling, although it may well be that the novel, at its most analytical level, shares more of Grandet's vision than it would care to admit. For Grandet, gender itself is primarily a system of signification within a social field, a system he can manipulate in order to extract value from the social field. One example of this would be his wise decision to hire as his household help "la grande Nanon":

> At the age of twenty-two, the poor girl's looks were so unattractive that she could not get a job anywhere. This feeling was, to be sure, unfair, for her face would have been much admired had it been on the shoulders of a Grenadier Guardsman. But, as they say, everything in its proper place. Having had to leave a burnt-down farm where she had looked after the cows, she came to Saumur to look for a job. . . . [Grandet] noticed this girl who was sent away from door to door. As a cooper he was a judge of her physical strength and he was aware of the use to be made of a female built like Hercules, planted as firmly on her feet as a sixty-year-old oak on its roots, with powerful hips, a broad back, a carter's hands, and a sturdy honesty as unassailable as her untarnished virtue. (3:1042, 19)

His keen sense of how to use everything in the world to realize value gives him an analytic vision of the way gender can be exploited. As a woman, Nanon will earn lower wages. As a strong woman, she can be employed for tasks that might otherwise require a man. As a virtuous woman lacking in traditional appeal, she is unlikely to find a lover or husband and so become pregnant and therefore less useful to Grandet. All this he calculates to his profit. I will discuss shortly his view of his wife, but first I will discuss how he views his daughter, because she would appear to be the one object not fully subsumed into his dominant way of looking. She is, according to the novel, "le seul être qui lui fût réellement de quelque chose, sa fille Eugénie, sa seule héritière [the only being that seemed to him really to be anything, his daughter Eugénie, his sole heiress]" (3:1036, 12). This is an interesting way of putting things. She is the only being who is of any substance to him, one might say; all other beings only signify potential for exploitation. She alone, as his heir, has substance. Consequently, he is willing, on her birthday, her saint's day, and other holidays, to make her presents of money: "It was, after all, merely a question of moving his money from one box into another and, in a manner of speaking, of fostering his heiress's avarice: he would occasionally ask her for an account of her/his treasure [son trésor], that had at one time been enlarged by the La Bertellières" (3:1045, 22). The syntax of the French leaves it ambiguous whose treasure it is.

Notice those last few words: "enlarged by the La Bertellières." The La Bertellières are Eugénie's maternal relations, all of whom (except for her mother) died in the course of a single year, thirteen years before the beginning of the novel, when Eugénie was ten years old. The novel glancingly yet quite specifically tells us that Grandet's gifts to his daughter started thirteen years previously: "In the morning, following his custom for the noteworthy days of Eugénie's birthday and saint's day, Monsieur Grandet had come to her room before she got up and had solemnly given his paternal present, which for thirteen years had been a rare gold coin" (3:1045, 22). Moreover, the casual way the La Bertellières are given brief mention in a subordinate clause, as vague deceased contributors to the Grandet fortune, might draw attention away from the telling coincidence the novel almost accidentally insists on: Grandet's presents to his daughter commenced thirteen years previously, precisely at the moment when her maternal relations ceased to exist. Grandet's paternal relation to his daughter is haunted by maternal wealth.[16]

I'll return shortly to the complexities of the maternal inheritance, but first I want to examine further Grandet's relation to his daughter, for it almost becomes sentimental, as if her uniqueness in his system as the recipient of his germ-plasm (to use Freud's term) and the future recipient of his (and his wife's) wealth would be sufficient grounds for some other level of relation. When, late in the novel, he learns that Eugénie has done something with "her" *trésor* without asking him, and when he finds that she is unwilling to tell him what she has done with it (recall that she has given it to her cousin/lover Charles), he puts her under house arrest—confining her to her room and placing her on a regime of bread and water. But he then finds himself obliged to sneak into the backyard to catch a glimpse of her through her window: "When the old man reached the big walnut tree, he would hide behind its trunk and stay for a few moments to look at his daughter's long tresses; he was no doubt wavering between the thoughts inspired by his temperamental obstinacy and the desire to embrace his child" (3:1163, 153). Is this longing to embrace his daughter the natural expression of his humanity, repressed too well by his monomaniacal avarice, or is it to be understood as in fact the product of the financially and socially structured relation to his daughter as his sole heir? Is wanting to embrace her of a different order from his compulsive need to count his gold? This may well be one of the more radical questions the novel is asking. Grandet's way of refusing all sentimentality, of speculating on—exploiting—the sentimentality of others, is often described by the narrative voice of the novel as an attitude that constitutes one of the scourges of the modern world. Yet it is hard to deny that in fact the novel shares Grandet's view of the economic and social predeterminants of family relations, and of family practices—of which gender is one. Eugénie, too, will come to share some of her father's and the novel's perspective, and this is what will make her decision to marry so complex.

Consider, for example, the fascinating description of Grandet's wife provided early in the novel:

> Quoique ridicule en apparence, cette femme qui, par sa dot et successions, avait apporté au père Grandet plus de trois cent mille francs, s'était toujours sentie si profondément humiliée d'une dépendance et d'un ilotisme contre lequel la douceur de son âme lui interdisait de se révolter, qu'elle n'avait jamais demandé un sou, ni fait une observation sur les actes que maître Cruchot lui présentait à signer. Cette fierté sotte et secrète, cette noblesse d'âme constamment méconnue et blessée par Grandet, dominaient la conduite de cette femme.

> [Although ridiculous in appearance, this woman, whose dowry and inheritance had brought Père Grandet more than three hundred thousand francs, had always felt so deeply humiliated by a dependence and slavery against which the gentleness of her heart forbade her to rebel that she had never asked for a penny nor made any comment on the documents for signature which Maître Cruchot set before her. This foolish, secret pride, this nobility of soul which Grandet never understood and constantly wounded, dominated her behaviour.] (3: 1046, 24)

There is something intensely Balzacian about this pair of sentences, whose seeming awkwardness, not to say semantic irregularity, carries a heavy, multilayered burden of meaning. Syntactically speaking, the apparent ridiculousness of this woman is never given the direct contradiction the *quoique* leads one to expect. Only by understanding her hidden noble soul as the implicit counterbalance to her ridiculous way of appearing and conducting herself can one justify the opening word of the first sentence. If the syntax becomes derailed, if it takes so long to get to the beautiful soul one should perceive under the ridiculous appearance, it is initially because of a financial detour that might seem to be quite off the subject. What is the relation between the size of Madame Grandet's dowry, the wealth of her dead relations, and the balance between her ridiculous appearance and her beautiful soul? The semantic range of the passage also suggests its ambivalent agenda. She is humiliated and has a marvelous sweetness of soul, yet her strange pride is *sotte* as well as *secrète*. What seems to be going on in this passage is a clear-sighted though rhetorically clouded explanation of why Grandet would have chosen to marry this woman—the size of her dowry, the wealth of the relatives from whom she would inherit, the timidity of her character—slightly papered over with a moralistic discourse that the novel consistently shows not only to work at the expense of women, but in fact to be part of their training in gender. The fact that she experiences her humiliation within the marriage in such a way that she never asks a question of the notary when he obtains her signature on the documents by which Grandet makes use of the wealth she brought to the marriage may well explain the somewhat incongruous use of the adjective *sotte,* hardly well chosen in an effort to praise the femininity of her soul. Nonetheless it sets the stage for an important later scene where a notary tries to give Eugénie some information about her signature, information she will refuse in what we might call a family practice of femininity.

The particular act she signs, "la déclaration par laquelle Eugénie accomplissait elle-même sa spoliation," by which she despoils herself in renouncing her mother's succession, comes as part of the series of events by which the Napoleonic Code enters the novel. When Eugénie secretly gives her cousin her little fortune, they swear eternal, sentimental love: "Ange de pureté!" Charles exclaims, "entre nous, n'est-ce pas? l'argent ne sera jamais rien. Le sentiment, qui en fait quelque chose, sera tout désormais [You are as pure as an angel. Between us, money will never matter, will it? Only feeling, which can give it some value, will be everything from now on]" (3:1131, 116). It is when Grandet discovers his daughter no longer possesses her money that he sentences her to house arrest, an act whose violence and whose repercussions ultimately send his wife, her mother, to her deathbed. "Où est votre or?" he asks her, "Where's your gold?"

> "Father, I love and respect you in spite of your anger, but I must very humbly point out to you that I'm twenty-two [*sic*] years old. You've told me often enough for me to know by now that I am of age. I have disposed of my money as I chose to. . . . Was I free, yes or no, to do what I liked with it? Was it mine?"
>
> "But you are a child."
>
> "I am of age." . . .
>
> . . . "Eugénie, you are in my house, in your father's house. If you are to stay here, you must obey my orders. The church commands you to obey me." Eugénie bowed her head. "You hurt me in what I hold most dear," he continued. "I don't want to see you until you do as I say. Go to your room. You will stay there until I allow you to leave it. Nanon will bring you bread and water. You heard me, go!" (3:1154–56, 143–45)

It would appear that Grandet has always imagined his authority to be civilly grounded. Religion has never been any particular object of attention to him, except that he began accumulating his wealth by using his money and his wife's dowry to buy an abbey, some vineyards, and a few dairy farms—all former church property, being sold off by the state after the Revolution. But because, civilly speaking, Eugénie was entitled to do whatever she pleased with her money (to be so entitled under the Napoleonic Code a woman would have to be both over twenty-one and unmarried or widowed), Grandet chooses here to ground his authority in religion, and Eugénie submits.

But Grandet has a few more things to learn about the Civil Code. Promulgated in 1804, it established for the first time in France a uniform set of laws concerning marriage and inheritance. Until the Revolution, marriage had been a church affair and mostly governed by canon law, and there was no uniform national code regarding inheritance. In 1867 one perhaps tendentious legal commentator, Paul Gide (father of André), had this to say about marriage:

> The civic equality of the two sexes is a fundamental principle of our modern law. It is true that this equality ceases in marital relations: by engaging herself in the ties of a marriage, a woman alienates a part of her rights and submits to a sort of temporary incapacity. But this incapacity—and I am not sure we should even call it that—is not inherent to the sex, its cause is not to be found in the physical or the moral constitution of woman, but in marital power itself, which is to say, in an exterior and accidental fact. Considered in and of herself . . . woman, in the eyes of civil law, is in almost every point man's equal.
>
> This principle, which today seems to us an uncontestable axiom of reason and justice, is nonetheless a recent conquest of social progress, and the honor of first proclaiming it belongs to the codes that came out of the French Revolution.[17]

The accidental fact of becoming a minor again should one marry after having reached the age of twenty-one might seem a more substantial civic inequality to some than Paul Gide claims here. Consider Eugénie. She is of age. She is the heir of her mother and her father. She is unmarried and will someday be wealthy. But her father controls all the family money. Her mother has no legal right to help Eugénie at this point, and Eugénie has given Charles all her ready cash.[18]

It is true, thanks to the Civil Code, that Eugénie is more or less (more less than more) the civic equal of her father. He has, according to the terms of the Code, no right to imprison her. When the lawyer Bonfons and the notary Cruchot hear from Eugénie's mother of her daughter's sequestration, the lawyer exclaims: "To put a girl of twenty-three on bread and water! . . . But that constitutes *excessive cruelty; she can take action against him, both in and on*" (3:1163, 152). Eugénie comes out of her bedroom at this point (her father apparently doesn't lock the door) to refuse her civil liberties in the name of religion: "My father is master in his own house. As long as I live in his house, I must obey him. His conduct should not be subject to the approval or disapproval of other people; he is answerable only to God" (3:1163, 152). The notary Cruchot nonetheless takes it on himself to have a conversation with Grandet, in which he points out that Grandet should get back on friendly terms with his daughter for two reasons. Grandet is killing his wife and alienating his daughter by the way he is treating her. Neither is a wise financial strategy:

> "After all, you don't want to kill your wife. She's too useful to you. Just think of the situation you'd be in with regard to your daughter if Madame Grandet were to die. You would have to give an account of your assets to Eugénie, since you and your wife are joint owners of your property. Your daughter would have the right to demand her share in your fortune, to sell Froidfond. In short, she will have the inheritance from her mother and you cannot have it."
>
> These words were like a thunderbolt to the old man, who was not as knowledgeable about the law as he might be on business matters. He had never thought that his jointly owned property might be sold by auction. . . .
>
> . . . "Cruchot," he continued solemnly, "you wouldn't deceive me, would you? Swear to me on your honour that what you're telling me is legally sound. Show me the Code. I want to see the Code."
>
> "My poor friend," replied the notary, "don't I know my job?"
>
> "So it's really true. I shall be despoiled, betrayed, murdered, pillaged by my own daughter."
>
> "She is her mother's heiress."
>
> "What, then, is the use of children? Oh, but I love my wife. Fortunately she's tough. She's a La Bertellière." (3:1164–66, 154–55)

What Grandet means by love for his wife is quite clear here. One of her advantages, coming from La Bertellière stock, is that she is supposed to be long-lived. This was a bother with the other members of her family, whom Grandet wanted to die so that his wife could inherit from them, but an advantage with her, since he controls her wealth as long as she lives: "'You're really a good woman and I don't want any harm to come to you because of your age, although, on the whole, the La Bertellières are a tough lot . . . Eh, isn't that so?' he called out after a pause. 'Still, we inherited their money, so I forgive them'" (3:1149, 138). Before the existence of the Civil Code, Grandet could perhaps have relied on custom to avoid having to give control of any money to Eugénie upon her mother's death, and he could have postponed marriage or written a marriage contract for her that would have allowed him all he desired. With her "modern" civil status, however, the law is on her side. As it is, at twenty-three she could, with a little difficulty, legally arrange to marry according to *her* choice, not her father's. With her mother's death she could force her father to give her her maternal inheritance and thereby be financially well equipped for whatever marriage she should desire. Yet, even knowing her father's hostility to her beloved Charles, Eugénie, at her father's behest, legally renounces her maternal inheritance and agrees to remain dependent on her father until his death. Here is part of the conversation that takes place between her, her father, and the notary, shortly after her mother's death:

> "But, Monsieur Cruchot, what do I have to do?," asked Eugénie, impatiently.
>
> "Well," said the notary, "you would have to sign this deed, by which you would renounce your inheritance from your mother and allow your father the use during his lifetime of all the property you hold in common and of which he guarantees you the full ownership."
>
> "I don't understand a word of what you are saying," replied Eugénie. "Give me the deed and show me the place where I have to sign.". . .
>
> "Little girl," [her father] said, "I would rather you didn't sign that deed, which would cost a lot to register, but instead purely and simply renounced your inheritance from your poor, dear, late mother and relied on me for the future. I would make you a good, substantial allowance of a hundred francs a month. Look, you could afford as many masses as you wanted to be said for anyone you choose. What about it? A hundred francs a month in livres!"
>
> "I'll do whatever you like, father."

"Mademoiselle," said the notary, "it is my duty to point out that you are divesting yourself . . ."

"My goodness," she said, "I don't care about that." (3:1172, 162–63)

The adjective *sotte* comes to mind, especially since Eugénie is reenacting here her mother's gesture—of signing without questioning—from the passage where the narrator used that same word. There is no narrative commentary on Eugénie's actions in this particular scene, where she gives up the chance to use one of the few situations the new Civil Code allows her—or any woman—to achieve some independence.[19] It is as if she and the events of the novel are in a battle: the novel keeps trying to make her a woman of independent means and she continues to find ways to refuse the opportunity.[20]

Much of the philosophical discussion around the establishment of the Civil Code during this period had to do with the relation of civil law to established customs, to *moeurs.* Jean-Louis Halpérin's *L'Impossible Code civil,* works to explain why it turned out not to be possible to establish such a code during the Revolutionary period in France: "It is easier to vote in a constitution than to revolutionize a civil law with deep roots in customs, regional habits, patterns of family conduct, even when a certain quarter of public opinion aspires to change and claims to express the *expectations* of the whole society."[21] What we see in *Eugénie Grandet* is precisely how "customs, regional habits, patterns of family conduct"—firmly grounded in individual psychologies, in religious discourse, and in sentimental discourse—resist the effects of the new Civil Code, which lawyers and notaries grant an authority that Eugénie flatly refuses even to see.[22] *Eugénie Grandet* is part of Balzac's effort in *La Comédie humaine* to think through the relation between law and customs, between law and psychology; indeed, between law, gender, and sexuality. Finely tuned to the situation of women, though no feminist, Balzac seems content in *Eugénie Grandet* to reveal a woman's predicament to her at the same time that he denies her the necessary discursive and psychological malleability to turn her predicament to her advantage. Yet if it seems, at the moment when Eugénie renounces her mother's estate and refuses to challenge her father in any way, that she has understood precisely nothing about her place in a changing world, the pages just prior to the end of the novel, leading up to her decision to marry, suggest that in fact she does learn something about the possibilities open to her, and that she gains some ability to act accordingly.

After Eugénie's father dies, she is, despite her best efforts, independent and wealthy, and seems to have nothing to do but wait around for the return of her beloved cousin in order to enter into a marriage where wealth will be subservient to sentiment. When Charles returns to France it is 1827 and the Restoration is in full swing (although its demise in the July Revolution of 1830 looms on the horizon). Charles —ignorant of Eugénie's wealth—would just as soon marry into an aristocratic family. He is very much of his moment in this regard, the combination through marriage of new bourgeois wealth with an old aristocratic name being a common strategy during the Restoration. Charles thus sends Eugénie a letter, kindly returning (with interest) the money she gave him on his departure and telling her quite frankly, "I shall confess to you, my dear cousin, that I don't care in the least for Mademoiselle d'Aubrion, but, by marrying her, I guarantee to my children a social situation whose advantages will, one day, be incalculable. . . . We owe ourselves to our children" (3:1187, 180). "A quoi servent donc les enfants!" The novel once again poses Grandet's question.

Charles's calculation is understood by the novel to be standard for its time, and it is one that Bonfons, Eugénie's soon-to-be husband, has in mind too. As we shall see shortly, Bonfons imagines outliving Eugénie and inheriting her wealth, after which he will use it to buy a second wife, an aristocratic one this time. In Balzac's novels dealing with the years just prior to the July Revolution, where titles were understood to be purchasable through marriage, the title's price tag was based both on its position in the aristocratic hierarchy and on the estimated beauty of the woman in question.[23] (Title and capital were fighting for predominance well before 1830, and were seen by Balzac as increasingly fungible long before that date.) Within *Eugénie Grandet* it is made perfectly clear that Charles, had he known in time of Eugénie's wealth, would have seen her as a preferable match to Mlle. d'Aubrion. Recently returned from Africa and the Caribbean, he has accumulated a tidy but not extravagant sum in the slave trade, a sum of 1,900,000 francs in gold (3:1182, 174). The novel shortly thereafter makes a point of giving Eugénie's fortune as precisely ten times that (3:1195, 188). A fortune of 1,900,000 francs appears to be enough to buy Charles the hand of a not particularly good-looking girl from a down-and-out aristocratic family: "Monsieur and Madame d'Aubrion . . . now reduced to an income of about twenty thousand livres a year, had a rather ugly daughter, whom the mother wanted to marry off without a dowry. . . . So Madame d'Aubrion herself, when she looked at her daughter, was almost in despair of encumbering anyone at all with her, even a man who was besotted with the idea of an aristocratic connection" (3:1182, 174). Yet there is a chance that even such a transparently calculated marriage as this might not work out. Monsieur d'Aubrion threatens to cancel the marriage when he hears that Charles's father died with substantial debts that have never been paid, leaving the family name besmirched. Could opportunity yet knock for Eugénie?

In the end it is Eugénie herself who, through a careful, consciously calculated set of actions, renders a marriage between herself and Charles impossible. This fact can, of course, easily go undetected in a novel so insistent on the melodrama of her victimization. Hearing that Charles's planned marriage is on the point of breaking down, Eugénie retires for an afternoon of reflection before descending that evening to a crowded salon of people curious to know how her sentimental attachment to Charles will cause her to act:

> She appeared in the evening in time for the arrival of the usual circle of visitors. The Grandet living-room had never been as full as it was that evening. The news of Charles's return and of his foolish [*sotte*] treachery had spread through the whole town. But although the visitors looked and listened with great attention, their curiosity was not satisfied. Eugénie, expecting them to be very inquisitive, did not allow any of the painful emotions that were ravaging her to appear on her calm face. She turned with a smile to those who wanted to show their sympathy by melancholic looks or words. (3:1192, 185)

She gives a crafty, antimelancholic performance. At the end of the evening, as the guests leave, she asks one of her suitors, Bonfons, to remain behind for a few minutes. In her conversation with him she arranges simultaneously to become engaged to him, to pay Charles's father's debts so that there is no impediment to his marriage to Mlle. d'Aubrion, and to be sure that he will be informed of her generosity and her wealth at the same time that he is informed of her engagement.

"So you're going to marry Eugénie," Charles says to Bonfons when Bonfons informs him of Eugénie's actions:

> "Well I'm pleased; she's a good girl. But," he continued, struck by a sudden enlightening thought, "she must be rich then!"
>
> "Four days ago, she had nearly nineteen million," replied the President [Bonfons] in a bantering tone, "but today she has only seventeen left."
>
> Charles, dumbfounded, stared at the President.
>
> "Seventeen . . . mill . . ."
>
> "Seventeen million, yes Monsieur." (3:1195, 188)

Along with the documents regarding the payments of his father's debts, Eugénie has also arranged to return the gold dressing case Charles had given to her. It is as if, in this small symbolic gesture, as well as in her larger, extravagantly spiteful display of her wealth, Eugénie reveals her clear sense of how her own sentiments have played her false, how they have participated in the construction of her own instrumentality.

Eugénie's marriage to Bonfons is to be a frank and disillusioned one,[24] involving a direct refusal of sentimentality:

> "Monsieur le Président," said Eugénie agitatedly, when they were alone, "I know what you find attractive about me. Swear to leave me free for the whole of my life, to claim none of the rights which marriage gives you over me, and my hand is yours. Oh," she continued, seeing him go down on his knees, "I haven't finished yet. I must not deceive you, Monsieur. I have an inextinguishable feeling in my heart [J'ai dans le coeur un sentiment inextinguible]. Friendship will be the only feeling I can offer my husband. I do not want to hurt him, nor to contradict the dictates of my own heart [contrevenir aux lois de mon coeur]." (3:1193, 186)

There is a magnificent ambiguity in the sentence "J'ai dans le coeur un sentiment inextinguible." Of course the novel suggests that that sentiment would be an ongoing masochistic attachment to Charles. Bonfons understands as much himself, hurrying to fulfill all his promises to Eugénie for fear of a possible reconciliation between her and Charles. But suppose instead that inextinguishable sentiment were something more complex, a mixture of shame and pride arising from a critical reflection on past sentiments, arising out of a political education as to the correspondence of her social positioning and her psychic construction. Such a critical distance from one's own *habitus* might well produce that clairvoyance that is said to characterize her at the end of the novel, that "acute vision" with which she sees all that falls within her purview.

The novel does halfheartedly suggest that Eugénie gives up her independence—or at least her wealth—to Bonfons because of some sense of religious duty. Having spoken to her priest about entering a convent, she is roundly upbraided:

> But you have great obligations to society to fulfil, Mademoiselle. Are you not the mother of the poor to whom you give clothing and wood in winter and work in summer? Your great wealth is a loan that you must repay, and you have always piously accepted it as such. To bury yourself in a convent would be selfish. As for remaining an old maid, you ought not to. First off, could you manage your enormous fortune by yourself? You might perhaps lose it. You would soon be engaged in countless lawsuits and you would be involved in interminable difficulties. Believe your pastor. A husband would be useful to you, for you have a duty to preserve what God has given you. (3:1190, 182–83)

We owe ourselves to our children, it might seem. Yet Eugénie sees clearly the conflicting ideological agendas motivating the priest's discourse: is she to marry in order that she may have children to whom to pass on her fortune, or so that a man will supervise the wealth? When he tells her that she has a duty to "preserve what God has given her," he is ostensibly suggesting that she has a duty to pass on her fortune to the next generation. Perhaps she hears another, oblique suggestion to follow in the priest's verb "preserve." A few paragraphs later, she has another question for him: "'Monsieur le Curé,' asked Eugénie with a dignified composure inspired by the thought she was about to express, 'would it be a sin to remain a virgin while being married?'" (3:1192, 185). The priest claims not to know the answer, and promises to consult his library and return with the answer the next day, but Eugénie proposes an unconsummated marriage of convenience to Bonfons before hearing the priest's answer. Perhaps it was in his inability to give an immediate answer that she found the response she needed. For he had just offered her two reasons to marry: so a man would manage her wealth for her and so that she would pass the wealth on to her children. If, a few short moments later, he was willing to entertain the possibility of a chaste marriage, it seems rather clear what would have been the primary reason for his encouragement to marriage.[25]

The discourse of economic utility never stops. Grandet's wife was useful to him just by staying alive. Does Eugénie herself succumb to the discourse of utility that her spiritual counselor offers her? Perhaps Bonfons could be useful to Eugénie. If she can arrange not to have to sleep with him, at least she won't have to think about her money anymore. But, in fact, the novel has another hard lesson to teach her. Her husband, too, as we have seen, thinks in terms of utility. It is 1827. He, too, could profit from an aristocratic marriage. Eugénie's desire not to have children means that were she to die before him, he would get all her money. Unlike the relation of her mother to her father (because of Eugénie, he could control their community property only while she was alive), Eugénie would be more useful to Bonfons dead, the novel suggests. Perhaps to make sure she doesn't have an affair and produce illegitimate children he might have to recognize, perhaps to be free to pursue an aristocratic wife, perhaps merely to realize the terms of the marriage contract he wrote so carefully ("in which the two future spouses gave each other, *in the event of their not having children, all their property, both landed and personal, without exception or reservation, in absolute ownership, dispensing even with the formality of an inventory*" [3:1197, 190]), Bonfons would prefer both a childless match and a quick demise for Eugénie. One might think that he has learned a thing or two from Grandet's miscalculations. Unfortunately for Bonfons, however, he has forgotten that Eugénie is a La Bertellière and he isn't. The novel thus happily and summarily kills him off about two years into his marriage to Eugénie, denying him his aristocratic yearnings. With a cruel sense of symmetry, the novel makes sure that Bonfons has been as useful to Eugénie as was her mother to her father. Bonfons had received two large inheritances during the short marriage, which then go to enrich the communal property that Eugénie possesses outright after his demise. She couldn't have made a better match:

> Eugénie had, thanks to her sorrow and her recent education, become accustomed to figuring most things out. So she knew that the

> President wished for her death in order to be the sole owner of their enormous fortune, which had been increased still further by the estates of his uncle the lawyer and his uncle the Abbé, whom God had seen fit to call to himself. The poor recluse pitied the President. Providence avenged her for the shocking, calculated indifference of a husband who respected the hopeless passion she fed on, as the strongest guarantee of his own interests. To give life to a child, that would surely put an end to the selfish hopes, the delightful ambitions, cherished by the First President. (3:1197, 191)

Providence has a strange way of avenging Eugénie: teaching her lesson after lesson about the fact that she is continually misplaced historically and psychologically, a family misfit formed to react sentimentally in ways that seldom correspond to anything that might be in her own interest and unable to escape from a regime of social utility in sufficient flux almost to have offered her a way out—a way out (take the money and run) that the novel seems to present to us without allowing her to see. "Such is the story of a woman who," the novel says in its cloying closing paragraph, "made to be a magnificent wife and mother, has neither husband nor children nor family" (3:1198–99, 192).

This concisely melodramatic attempt at closure cannot successfully tie up all the loose ends of a narrative so ruthlessly and analytically interested in the gendered consequences of the social, historical, legal, and psychological unrest of the decades immediately following the French Revolution. It might be worth giving a last mention to la grande Nanon in this regard. Nanon, from a different class position, does seem to find a marriage outside of the system of social utility that has frustrated Eugénie. And if Nanon does find such a marriage—at the age of fifty-nine—it is thanks to Eugénie's friendship. "You are the only one who loves me," Eugénie says to Nanon on the novel's closing page. To Nanon she has (immediately on her father's death) given a gift of money that apparently remains a successful sign of love:

> One of her first acts was to give an annuity of twelve hundred francs to Nanon, who, as she already had six hundred francs a year of her own, became a rich match. In less than a month she changed her state from spinster to married woman, under the protection of Antoine Cornoiller, who was appointed head keeper of Mademoiselle Grandet's land and property. Madame Cornoiller had an

> immense advantage over her contemporaries. Although she was fifty-nine years old, she did not look more than forty. Her coarse features had resisted the assaults of time, and, thanks to her monastic way of life, she could defy old age, with her ruddy complexion and iron constitution. Perhaps she had never looked better than she did on her wedding-day. Her plainness had its own advantages and she looked big, strong, and rounded, with an expression of happiness on her indestructible face which made some people envy Cornoiller's lot.
>
> "Her colour's fast," said the draper.
>
> "She could still have children," said the salt merchant. "She's been as well preserved as if she'd been kept in brine, if I may say so."
>
> "She's rich, and that fellow Cornoiller's done very well for himself," said another neighbour. (3:1176–77, 167–68)

The townsfolk, voices of custom, provide all the reasons of social utility that could contain this marriage, reasons that find themselves somehow inscribed in the legal codes that then serve to help reproduce the family structures that then produce the subjects that reason in this way. The narrator's analysis is slightly different. For him, she has bided her time well—avoided historical melancholy, one might say—to the point that (thanks to certain monastic features in her day-to-day life and thanks to the way other women have aged) she has the market advantage in looks. It is hard to know exactly what to do with this passage. Surely the narrator's snide analysis could be read as just as nugatory as those of the townsfolk he satirizes. After considering the many overdeterminations of this marriage, is there anything left over? Balzac is fascinated by the, for him, recent history of France precisely because the post-Revolutionary period is one where customs, *moeurs,* family practices (and therefore gender and sexuality), and legal inscription were all subject to revision. The conservatism of novels like *Eugénie Grandet* lies in the effort, legible in Balzac's particular use of sentimental and melodramatic plots, to naturalize a melancholic practice of femininity that takes no advantage of any Revolutionary revisions. But some of the radical social analysis of his novels can be found in the detailed reconstruction of the social and historical moments where revision actually presents itself as a possibility, even if it is never quite grasped, and where melancholy would not be naturalized but understood as historically produced and available for critical apprehension. I wonder if some trace of that critical apprehension remains in Eugénie's friendship with Nanon, the only person who loves her, and someone who marries, perhaps for pleasure, at age fifty-nine, thanks to the help of her friend.

CHAPTER TWO

On Not Getting Married in a Balzac Novel

Imagine a reader in 1833 who found in Eugénie Grandet's chosen celibacy a recognition of the need to struggle against the instrumentalization of women and children within a rigidly structured system of inheritance practices. That reader would have been surprised and disappointed upon reading the preface that Balzac wrote for his short novel *Pierrette* in 1840. At that moment, he chose to group *Pierrette* together with another short novel, *Le Curé de Tours* (1832), under the omnibus title *Les Célibataires* (*Unmarried People*). To that same grouping he would add, a few years later, the longer novel *La Rabouilleuse,* making the group into a trilogy.

"L'état du Célibataire est un état contraire à la société," Balzac wrote in the preface to *Pierrette*—"The condition of being unmarried is inimical to society." He continues: "At one point the Convention had the idea of fixing on unmarried people double the taxes of those on married people. That was one of its most equitable fiscal ideas, and one of the easiest to put into action. See how much the Treasury would have to gain from a small amendment such as this: *All forms of personal taxes will be doubled should the taxpayer in question not be or have been married*" (4:21).[1]

The exact degree of humor and irony that Balzac employs in his preface is a bit hard to ascertain. He is unmarried himself at the moment he composes this text, and he makes a disclaimer to this effect a few sentences after those cited above: "The publication of this idea, recalled from the Convention's files, is all the more courageous given that the person putting it forward is still an unmarried fellow; but in certain cases social interests must take precedence over particular interests. This is a principled stand, and the principle is the profound hatred the author feels for all unproductive beings, for all unmarried people, elderly spinsters and unmarried men, those drones in the hive!" (4:21).[2] The rhetoric Balzac employs seems to foreshadow specific forms of homophobic discourse that would become widespread in the twentieth century. This seems especially apparent when we hear the novelist proclaim, a few pages later: "Do not think of accusing the author of a prejudice that causes him to attack certain people as would a rabid dog: he is not celibatairophobic." Balzac suggests that his readers distinguish between "obsessive hatred" on the one hand, and, on the other, his position in the preface, which is to "brand" (*flétrir*) those he considers to be "adamantly unmarried [célibataires sérieusement célibataires], stealing from civilization while giving nothing in return" (4:24).

Whatever ambiguity, humor, and irony may be present in Balzac's preface, it is worth insisting on the symbolic violence it also contains—its effort to justify the exclusion of certain people from full participation in the social domain, to refuse them equal treatment before the law. It is also remarkable that Balzac elaborates his celibatairophobia in the context of a fiscal fantasy. The plan to stigmatize "unproductive" people by way of the fiscal code calls our attention to links between sexual forms and economic practices and traditions. The organization of sexuality and the organization of civil and economic life are understood to be inextricable.

Also worthy of note in Balzac's expressed celibatairophobia is his recourse to a legal idea from the Revolutionary period. What is this supposed monarchist doing having recourse to the proposals of Revolutionary legislators to justify his proposed social program? To what set of interests does the prejudice he is advocating here belong?

There is, of course, no reason to believe that a prejudice against unmarried people belongs to any one set of interests, and thus no reason to believe that the interests of the Revolutionary legislators in stigmatizing unmarried people would be exactly the same as those to which Balzac is lending his voice in 1840. Jean Borie opens his 1976 book, *Le Célibataire français,* by noting the apparent paradox of Revolutionary legislators celebrating the *individual* as the category to which rights are accorded at the same time as they treat with such suspicion *le célibataire,* who might have been viewed as a fine case of individualism. Borie notes at another point in his book the extent to which the Revolutionary legislators might have had specific symbolic targets in mind: priests and aristocratic libertines for example.[3] In his preface to *Pierrette,* Balzac recalls that last category specifically by describing his well-known character, the rake Maxime de Trailles, as "one of our most horrific *célibataires*" (4:22). Balzac informs us of his plans to marry off Maxime in a soon-to-appear work.[4] Balzac's attention in his trilogy (despite the implications of the title *Le Curé de Tours*) in fact seems more drawn to newly enriched bourgeois figures than it is to priests and other enemies of the Revolution. Bourgeois reticence to reproduce is attributed by Balzac to a pathological attachment to wealth. Two such unreproductive figures, the odd couple of a brother and a sister, lie at the heart of *Pierrette.* So while it may seem strange to find Balzac, often an ardent advocate for the family and the monarchy, vaunting the legal initiatives of the Revolutionary period, the paradox may in part be understood as arising from his hostility to certain aspects of a developing bourgeois social order, a hostility that would allow him to imagine many fleeting allegiances with those who held otherwise divergent political and ideological beliefs.[5]

One scholar of the legislative efforts of the Revolutionary period recalls for us the extent to which "happiness" within a family was, for Revolutionary legislators, only conceivable in a marriage that produced offspring: "A family was never simply two spouses, whatever the juridical status of their union: individual happiness came only by way of maternity and paternity. . . . Marriage itself can only be a source of happiness for the spouses when it is fecund. Thus for the Revolutionaries, the end of marriage remained, as under older law, as under canon law, procreation."[6] The Revolutionary legislators were not attached to particular formal procedures for marriage. In claiming an equal inheritance status for illegitimate and legitimate children, for instance, the legislators affirmed that official state recognition of a union was far from essential. It sufficed for parents to recognize their children for "happiness" to be achieved and for legal procedures of inheritance to pertain. Revolutionary law was also much less restrictive regarding adoption than would be the Napoleonic Code that followed it, so that "happiness" (and the transmission of wealth to an heir) would not be out of the reach of couples who were having problems producing children.

The Revolutionary legislators also knew that not *all* illegitimate children were likely to be born to *couples* who had specifically chosen not to have their marriage recognized by the state. They knew that many unofficial fathers would not be interested in recognizing their unofficial offspring. Their answer to this problem was not to lay any constraint on unofficial fathers. (Quite the contrary: just as would be the case in the Napoleonic Civil Code, the Revolutionary lawmakers opposed establishing any legal grounds for any *recherche de la paternité* [paternity claims].) Some legislators saw the state as therefore called upon to assist single mothers in the upbringing of their children, and saw a tax on obdurately unmarried people (*les célibataires endurcis*) as an appropriate way of financing that project. The only way unmarried people would be able to escape such a tax would be by marrying or by adopting.[7]

The Constitution of Year III of the Revolution actually excluded unmarried people from the upper chamber of the legislative body. As the scholar Xavier Martin puts it, the unmarried were severely targeted by Revolutionary legislators because they "deprive society of their reproductive faculty or exercise it only in an anarchic way. . . . Unmarried people form within the social body so many individual enclaves of the state of nature, and thus regrettably perpetuate the presumed egotism of that primitive state within the very heart of society."[8]

Balzac's preface thus has a long discursive tradition behind it. Scholars often hold that whereas Revolutionary legislators were willing to experiment with alternative family forms and to protect certain unofficial forms, the legislators of the Napoleonic Code were only interested in protecting the interests of a particular (bourgeois) kind of officially structured family, and considered the legal family mainly as a structure through which wealth could be transmitted between generations in a more or less orderly, regulated fashion. Balzac would often polemically accuse the Civil Code of fostering throughout the entire population the kind of egotism the Revolutionary legislators saw enacted in a concentrated fashion by people who did not marry. A typical example of this accusation can be found in the programmatic speech given by Doctor Benassis in *Le Médecin de campagne:* "These days, in order to prop up society, the only support we have is *egotism*. Individuals believe in themselves. But the future lies in the social man. . . . Nations, like individuals, draw energy from great feelings. A people's feelings are its beliefs. Instead of having beliefs, we only have interests" (9:430). *Pierrette,* surely one of Balzac's cruelest stories, sets itself up as the struggle of feelings (in particular, "family" feelings) against interests (in particular the interest in acquiring or holding on to personal wealth). The "feelings" are embodied in the young girl, Pierrette, and her childhood companion, Jacques Brigaut, who are compared at several points in the novel to Bernardin de Saint-Pierre's Paul and Virginie. The "interests" belong to just about everyone else in the novel, but especially to the brother and sister Jérôme-Denis and Sylvie Rogron, Pierrette's two "cousins" (they are the children of Pierrette's mother's half-sister), and to a group of shady characters interested in their money. Yet, as we shall see, this opposition between feelings and interest is not fully upheld by the novel, which also understands that feelings and interests exist in productive (and sometimes counterproductive) relation to each other: interests often produce feelings; feelings are often the embedded and psychologized forms of past interests; feelings often cause actions that represent or further an interest opposed to the one a person may have consciously calculated for her or himself.[9]

The sociological analysis performed by *Pierrette,* as is the case for many Balzac novels, does not in the end support many of the polemical assertions inserted elsewhere within the novel's own rhetoric. The most polemical and melodramatic accounts of social history in Balzac's novels often rely on a particular way of marking 1830 as a watershed in French history. The narrator of *Illusions perdues,* speaking of the forms of social dissatisfaction that led up to the Revolution of 1830, describes that dissatisfaction as composed of a group of "deep, underground hatreds which were to inspire a terrible unanimity in those who engineered the insurrection of 1830 and destroyed the elements of a durable social community in France" (5:152, 34). The symbolic importance of 1830 in the structure of many Balzacian novels has been remarked on by numerous critics.[10] Novels set in the decade before 1830 (for instance, *Eugénie Grandet, Illusions perdues, Splendeurs et misères des courtisanes,* as well as all three of the works making up *Les Célibataires*) often foreshadow in their plots the success and failures that will fall to the winners and losers of 1830.[11] The intense social and sexual anarchy of a novel such as *La Cousine Bette,* which opens in 1838, perhaps illustrates what the narrator of *Lost Illusions* might have meant by the destruction in 1830 of whatever factors might have produced "a durable social community in France." To understand how 1830 figures in *Pierrette,* it is necessary here to recount a bit of the story.

Pierrette has been orphaned before the story begins, and she has been living in Brittany with her maternal grandparents, who are kind-hearted but lacking in business acumen. Their business goes bankrupt and they are forced to move into a community home for senior citizens and the indigent, in which Pierrette is not entirely welcome. They know of the existence of some relatives of her mother's in the town of Provins, on the other side of France, and so write to them to inquire if they have the means and the willingness to take in their granddaughter. The letter eventually finds its way into the hands of Sylvie and Jérôme-Denis, both unmarried and in their forties, who are at that moment in fact shopkeepers in Paris, but contemplating retiring to their native Provins, where they will, with their savings, be able to fix up a house and live in style. Never having been loved or cared for by their parents (nor ever having been particularly lovable, it would seem), the only form of human relation known to them in any detail is the relation of a tyrannical shopkeeper to an oppressed employee.

It would seem that if the two siblings have remained unmarried into their forties, it is in part due to their asocial habits and unpleasant personalities, yet in part it is also due to certain strategical maneuvers. About the brother, the narrator tells us that: "His sister had always prevented him from marrying, perhaps fearing to lose her influence in the establishment, seeing in marriage to a woman necessarily younger and doubtless less ugly than she, a cause of expense and even ruin" (4:44). Both brother and sister had been more or less abandoned by a father whose philosophy about how to raise children was rather simple: raise them as cheaply as possible, give them a small stake to start with, and kick them out on their own. If there is any money left when you die, your lawyer can find them and let them know (4:41). They were both thus farmed out as young as possible to Parisian shopkeepers who had previously moved to Paris from their native Provins. At a certain point, they combined savings to set up a shop of their own, which they ran with the help of labor provided by their own connections back in Provins: “Old man Rogron sent to his children all of the unfortunate offspring of Provins whose parents destined them to commerce; he ran a trade in male and female apprentices for them. . . . Many sent the child who was an inconvenience in the household off to the establishment run by these two unmarried people” (4:45). The two siblings thus are childless, but intimately related to surplus children in their society. There is a way in which they perversely enact the scheme imagined by the Revolutionary legislators to tax the unmarried in order to allow the state to aid in the upbringing of children of single mothers and orphans. Sylvie and Jérôme-Denis provide for excess children (as cheaply as possible), precisely because, childless, they need young people to help tend the shop.[12]

The letter from Pierrette’s grandparents, asking for assistance, arrives at roughly the moment the two Rogron siblings are thinking of selling their business and returning to Provins to lead a life of leisure. Being only distant relatives of Pierrette’s and not having associated much with any relatives at all, it takes Sylvie and Jérôme-Denis roughly an hour’s conversation to establish their genealogical relation to the young orphan, and they are not particularly well-disposed toward her: “To take on the care of an orphan, a young girl, a cousin who, despite everything, would be their heir should neither of them marry—this was grounds for a serious discussion. . . . Suppose Rogron found a shoe that fit among the young heiresses of Provins, wouldn’t it be a better idea to save their money for his children?” (4:49). In any case, Pierrette is more or less forgotten among all the preparations for the move back to Provins, and she remains forgotten during the busy period when, having moved back, the brother and sister are renovating their house. At the same time as they are making the renovations, they try to establish themselves among the “high society” of Provins, but are found a bit too vulgar and uncultivated for the best society, which is grouped around “la belle Mme. Tiphaine.”

With the renovations completed, the predictable failure in joining the Provins society, and the lack of a business to tend, intense boredom sets in quickly. At this point, Sylvie suddenly remembers her young cousin, and invites her to come live with them—in part to stave off her boredom and to provide an object for her and her brother’s domineering impulses, but also in part to make herself interesting in the eyes of Mme. Tiphaine and her circle, to create a social identity for herself as the guardian of a "pretty young heiress" (4:67). Yet the clever high-society members quickly trick Sylvie into revealing that she and her brother have callously waited nearly a year and a half before responding to the urgent letter they received from Pierrette's grandmother. The revelation of this unfeeling behavior seals the exclusion of the Rogrons from Provins's finer circles and as a result gives rise to an alternate society: "From this day forth, the Rogrons no longer hid their hatred for the great bourgeois families of Provins and their followers. . . . The very day on which Denis Rogron and his sister Sylvie began publicly speaking ill of the clique was the day on which, without knowing it, they became persons of note and put themselves in the position of accumulating a society of their own: their salon would become the center of a set of interests that was seeking a theater in which to declare itself" (4:68–69). The Rogrons will agree to finance a new, liberal, journal in Provins, run by a down-and-out lawyer named Vinet and a Napoleonic soldier named Colonel Gouraud. Thus the Tiphaines, landowners of independent means who are loyal to the Restoration monarchy, create, via their exclusion of the Rogrons (small capitalists) an opposing party that will declare its allegiance to the opposition to the government in place. And the Rogrons, previously of no particular party, rapidly take on the political positions suggested to them by their status in the opposition.

Pierrette is thus, on the one hand, a case study of the way small-town politics worked just prior to the Revolution of 1830. Yet, on the other hand, it is a demonstration not so much of anything specific about 1830 as it is a picture of the ways in which social oppositions that come into being within a given limited context take a certain form thanks in part to the form already taken by the larger social oppositions governing the world around them. This implies further that the melodramatic account of child exploitation within the novel (the Rogrons drive Pierrette to her death by way of the demands they place on her) is itself perhaps not sufficiently understood as simply a critique of the psychological excesses found in the egotism that might characterize the French shopkeeping class around 1830. The novel studies in a more general way the forms of interpenetration between—the synergies and conflicts between—competing national interests, competing local interests, and competing practices of family and sexuality. The narrator in fact suggests as much toward the novel's end.

Near the conclusion of the novel, Pierrette's childhood friend, Brigaut, and her grandmother have realized the extent of the abuse she has suffered at the hands of the Rogrons, and have rescued her from the Rogron household—but too late. Pierrette's health is so damaged that she is unable to recover. While she is dying, a process that takes a few months, a legal procedure is undertaken to nullify the Rogrons's guardianship of Pierrette. The proceedings involve all the parties in the Rogron/Tiphaine conflict, in various roles such as lawyers, judges, and witnesses. The conflict is worsened by the political tensions and ambitions that are increasingly dividing all parts of French society in 1827–1828. The narrator comments, at the moment Pierrette has been rescued from the Rogrons's house:

> At this point in time, the war between the Vinet party and the Tiphaine party had reached its high point. . . . Everywhere in France, party spirit—excessively violent at this moment—was linking up with other interests that were threatened, or with personal slights and militant personalities. . . . So, for instance, the magistrate saw, in the proceedings between Pierrette and the Rogrons, a means to strike down, to shame, to dishonor, the leaders of the salon in which plans against the monarchy had been formed, in which the opposition journal had been born. (4:143)

In the final pages of the novel the narrator looks back from a moment well after 1830 to observe how many of the opposing parties in the drama of the novel have had successful political careers in the July Monarchy, how people from both sides of the struggle between Pierrette and the Rogrons have successfully curried favor with those newly arrived in power, and how, in the new social arena, old enemies have even become friends, Pierrette's former supporters being as willing to forget the wrongs done to her as are those who wronged her. The cruel irony and intense melodrama of the novel notwithstanding, then, there is a way in which it can be understood as most interested in an analysis of social conflict and social process in moments of crisis, and in an analysis of the uses and effects of discourses and ideologies of reproduction within such moments of crisis.

Of particular interest at the end of the novel is the fact that Jérôme-Denis Rogron is no longer *célibataire*. It is, in a certain way, his fortune that has been at stake throughout the novel. The person who has successfully laid hands on it is his wife, the reasonably young, elegant, and beautiful Bathilde de Chargeboeuf, a poor aristocrat without a dowry who has traded on her name and beauty to gain some financial leverage: "There was in Bathilde's desire to be married nothing vulgar. She was not marrying in order to become a mother, nor in order to have a husband. She was marrying to gain some freedom, to have an editor-in-chief, to be called Madame and be able to act in ways that men can act" (4:119). At the end of the novel, having successfully used Rogron in order to achieve a public position, she is now waiting for him to die so that she can marry the Marquis de Montriveau, who is already courting her. One can assume she is unlikely to have any children in her first marriage.

Had the law of which Balzac spoke in his preface existed, it would seem that Rogron would have substantially reduced his tax burden thanks to his marriage to Bathilde, yet quite likely was never to have had any children. Of course, all of the hostile rhetoric directed at *célibataires* has begged the question of the relation between marriage and children, and Balzac's plot clearly shows his awareness of the shaky ground on which the polemics of the preface exist. The demonstration that Balzac undertakes in *Pierrette* does not support the position taken so vociferously in his preface: that is, first of all, *Pierrette* demonstrates that marriage implies no intent to have children. Further, neither the motives of those who do plan to have families *nor* the motives of those who do not choose to do so correspond in any coherent way to a concern for the social good. (Think of the Rogrons's father.) Further still, the novel demonstrates the degree to which it is incorrect to imagine that people are fully aware of what they enact as they plan to have children, or plan not to. Balzac's vision of how people are formed to the social roles that they enact includes a perception that childbearing intentions are produced or inflected by social forces and forms of which it is difficult to be fully conscious.

Balzac consistently refuses to see sexuality as a phenomenon of a natural order. It is always tied to economics, to family structure, to material and psychological forms of inheritance, to large historical and political movements. In all three works that make up *Les Célibataires*, for instance, Balzac invents sexually troubled scenes that are simultaneously scenes of problematic inheritance—inheritance that often, in these tales, threatens to move collaterally because a given person has not produced offspring. In *Pierrette,* Balzac directly confronts the premenopausal spinster Sylvie Rogron, with her premenstrual "cousin" Pierrette, in order to call attention to the ways in which a woman's changing relation to reproduction at different periods of her life is woven into a complex web of social practices related to inheritance. Of the many intriguing scenes regarding sexuality within this story, noteworthy for my analysis is a discussion with a doctor about the dangers of pregnancy for a woman in her forties who has never given birth before. Equally important is the thematization of Pierrette's difficult arrival at menstruation.

Speaking of the "reproductive strategies" developed by the French bourgeoisie in the nineteenth century as they strove to achieve social dominance, Robert A. Nye writes:

> Taken in its largest sense, this reproductive strategy did far more than decide how many children should be born or how they should be spaced; it was inseparable from what Foucault has called a "technology of sex," a set of tactics for longevity, maximizing vitality, and ensuring fertility that became a "political ordering of life." As has always been so, these "tactics" circulated in the form of folk beliefs on health, and as traditional moral and religious injunctions, but in the course of the nineteenth century, they were further developed and systematized by scientific "disciplines" specializing in sex and reproduction—embryology, physiology, psychiatry, and medical hygiene.[13]

In presenting Pierrette's medical condition, the heart of the novel's melodrama, *Pierrette* enacts the tactics of the technology of sex of which Nye and Foucault speak, partly, as we shall see, in order to encourage in the reader the celibatairophobia of the novel's preface. On the other hand, in discussing the reproductive situation of Sylvie, the novel ironically displays others deploying those same cruel and manipulative tactics, and thereby renders them available for critique.

Pierrette, in perfect health when she arrived at her cousins' house, falls victim to chlorosis while she lives with them. Chlorosis was the name given to a condition related to what we now know as anemia, involving excessive paleness or even a slightly green complexion. It was associated mostly with girls arriving at the age when they would normally begin to menstruate, and usually involved a failure to begin menstruating or a suppression of menstruation if it had begun. It was associated with eating disorders and bizarre forms of craving (for raw green salads or grass, leaves, roots, and even printed paper [see 4:107 and 128]). It was thought to be brought on in part by harsh physical and emotional treatment and by excessive demands for physical labor, all of which characterize Pierrette's situation in her cousins' house. The medicine of the time conceptualized the condition as a disruption of the proper flow of blood within the young female body. Blood that was meant to flow through and out of the reproductive organs was thought to be displaced onto the digestive system, causing disorders of the appetite, and subsequently perhaps to be displaced further upward to the lungs, where it could cause pulmonary problems, perhaps even tuberculosis (4:109). Pierrette eventually succumbs to what seems to be a kind of tubercular abscess in her skull—the final displacement upward of her disordered reproductive potential.[14]

If the Rogrons felt a certain ambivalence about inviting Pierrette, who will be their "collateral" heir should neither of them marry and have children, to live with them, for Sylvie that ambivalence only intensifies as Pierrette approaches marriageable age. The marriageable age established in the Civil Code is fifteen for girls and eighteen for boys. "There is no need to explain the difference it has been felt necessary to establish in the age at which one reaches majority as a girl or as a male," declared Portalis, one of the architects of the Civil Code:

> All legislators have established this difference because all legislators have felt struck by the same reasons. Nature develops more rapidly in one sex than in the other. A girl who would have to languish painfully in too long a waiting period would lose some of the attractiveness that might favor a good situation for her, and often she will find herself exposed to dangers that could taint her virtue; for what a girl sees in her marriage is the conquest of her liberty. The same fears do not exist in the case of our own sex, which is only too disposed to remaining unmarried, and to whom one can unfortunately all too easily offer the reproach of fleeing from marriage as one would from slavery or poverty.[15]

It is not exactly clear why the lesser willingness of men to marry indicates that they should have to wait three years longer in order to be entitled to do so. But Portalis's words make clear how a legal dissymmetry (fifteen versus eighteen) is dubiously linked to a biological one (girls should be able to be married as soon as they can reproduce, which will be at a younger age than for boys) and immediately given a social face as well (a girl's attractiveness is crucial to her marriageability, and apparently is greater at age fifteen than at age eighteen). Portalis and his law both make clear the social expectation that there will often be a disproportion in ages between an older husband and his younger wife, and that marriage would lose meaning for an older woman in the way it does not for an older man.

The novel opens as Pierrette's childhood friend, Jacques Brigaut, ventures to Provins to see her again after their three-year separation caused by her move to her cousins' house. After the opening scene of their reunion, the novel retrospectively recounts the horror of the three-year separation, and then catches up with the opening scene and moves on to recount rapidly the tragic denouement that ends in Pierrette's death. During the opening scene, it is revealed that Pierrette is "just coming to the end of her fourteenth year" (4:35) whereas Jacques was "somewhere around sixteen years old" (4:29). Jacques has figured out which house Pierrette lives in, and he arrives at the break of day in the square in front of the house to sing a traditional Breton song that will reveal his presence to Pierrette and call her to her window. The song just happens to be one intended to be sung to a bride the morning after her wedding, beginning "We have come to wish you happiness in marriage" (4:31). It successfully wakens Pierrette, who is overjoyed to rediscover her childhood friend but sends him away quickly, for fear of what will happen if her evil cousins discover her in conversation with a young man. The serenade has, in fact, wakened Sylvie, who appears at her window in time to see a figure running away from the house: "No man would deprive himself of his matinal slumber for a troubadour, only a girl [*fille*] wakes up for a song of love. So it was a girl [*fille*], an old girl [*vieille fille;* French for spinster] in fact, [who was opening her window]. . . . Is there anything more horrible to see than the morning apparition of an ugly spinster at her window?" (4:32–33). The unflattering description of Sylvie (who is forty-one) continues for a good number of lines.

It is not hard to conceive how much social encouragement there is for the hostility of an unmarried and not particularly good-looking forty-one-year-old woman in the face of her beautiful, nearly fifteen-year-old cousin. Especially when, as the novel tells us, Sylvie "still cherished the idea of marriage" (4:97). This longing of hers is evidence within the story of how carelessly the two siblings think through the means to the realization of their desires. They invited Pierrette to come live with them because their existence was so boring, and because they needed some symbolic capital in their efforts to establish a social position in the town to which they had just returned. Yet a young, nearly marriageable heiress in the household is also likely to become an obstacle to whatever desire either of them may harbor to be married in the years ahead. For what makes one or the other of the pair marriageable is their fortune. If you can find your way to their fortune via a beautiful young girl, why find your way to it via them? This is, in fact, more of a problem for Sylvie than for Jérôme-Denis. Several women do appear on the scene with an interest in marrying the brother. If they would be willing to bear a child of his, that child would for inheritance take precedence over Pierrette. Bathilde de Chargeboeuf, who eventually marries Jérôme-Denis, feels a great deal of hostility toward Pierrette (4:96), clearly because her desire is to marry Rogron, to have no children, to outlive Rogron, and to marry again, keeping the money. Sylvie even finds a suitor in the fearless veteran, Gouraud, who would apparently be willing to brave a marriage with her that no one else could face in order to enhance the comfort of his later years. Yet Sylvie suddenly realizes he could achieve the same end by marrying Pierrette (and, of course, by maneuvering to prevent any marriage by her brother): "Sylvie, who still cherished the idea of marriage, finally came to see that Pierrette represented an obstacle: Pierrette was nearly fourteen [the story has jumped back in time from its opening scene, in which Pierrette is nearly fifteen], and the paleness caused by her illness—whose symptoms the ignorant spinster neither noticed nor did anything about—made her all the more beautiful" (4:97). Indeed, instead of paying heed to the child's worsening condition, Sylvie at this point vengefully insists that Pierrette take on the duties of the household servant in order to earn back the cost of her upkeep. Pierrette's worsening domestic situation in turn worsens her medical condition to the point that "irremediable damage was done to her developmental processes" (4:98).

The novel combines its attention to the cruel fate suffered by the innocent and noble Pierrette with a meticulous attention to the health of her reproductive organs, as if somehow her innocent character and her reproductive potential were linked. It also insists at great length on the cryptogamic Sylvie's ignorance in all matters relating to reproduction, causing her never to have an inkling as to Pierrette's chlorotic condition:

> At the sight of the symptoms of this illness, a mother . . . would have taken the child on her knees, questioned her, . . . would have figured out her illness and understood that the humors and the blood that were not flowing along the proper paths had now started attacking the lungs after having already troubled the digestive system. . . . But a spinster, in whom family sentiments had never been awakened, to whom the needs of childhood and the precautions required by adolescence were unknown, had no access to the indulgences and sympathetic feelings that would have been inspired by the many occurrences of life in a conjugal household. (4:109)

Here the narrator's way of putting things is interesting, for he suggests both that there is a failure of feeling on Sylvie's part and that that failure of feeling is caused by a failure in her education and experience. Without the knowledge or experience of the processes of biological reproduction that would have been gained by living in a "normal" household, it does not occur to her to be concerned with Pierrette's distress.

Sylvie's ignorance is not only a cause of further distress for Pierrette, it leaves Sylvie open to exploitation as well. One of the women interested in Sylvie's brother, and who will eventually lose out to Bathilde de Chargeboeuf, is the thirty-year-old Mlle. Habert, whose brother is a priest in the town. The Habert siblings are in some ways a mirror of Sylvie and her brother, and the two spinsters quickly become fast friends. But the Haberts have a scheme: the brother is going to inspire great religious fervor in Pierrette and then convince the Rogrons to send her to a convent—thus removing the inheritance obstacle she represents. The sister is then going to capture Jérôme-Denis's hand and produce offspring who are to inherit all the Rogrons's wealth. The possibility of Sylvie marrying the fearless Colonel Gouraud and somehow semimiraculously producing an offspring is another obstacle that Céleste Habert needs somehow to take precautions against. To do this she endeavors to convince Sylvie that Gouraud (forty-five years old) is the kind of fellow who is likely to want lots of children. She then takes Sylvie to a doctor to hear what a doctor would say of a woman in her early forties bearing a child. "A married woman of forty who has had other children has nothing to fear," the doctor replies. When Céleste specifies that the woman in question would not have had any previous children, the doctor qualifies his remarks: "In that case a happy delivery is a kind of miracle that God allows for, but rarely." The narrator goes on to provide further details: "The doctor responded further with a terrifying pathological description. He explained that the natural elasticity of muscles and bones present during one's youth no longer exists after a certain age, especially in women such as Mlle Rogron, whose profession had rendered them sedentary for many years" (4:102). Asked specifically whether what he is saying implies that a "virtuous" woman over forty should no longer marry, the doctor replies quite specifically: "Or else she should wait a few years . . . but in that case it is no longer really a marriage, but rather an association of interests" (4:102). The doctor's observation about marriage for a postmenopausal woman is rendered in sharper tones by the priest, Céleste Habert's brother, whom Sylvie also consults and who affirms that the church "sees in marriage only the propagation of humanity . . . and disapproves of passions that make no social contribution" (4:103).

If in the case of Pierrette's chlorosis and the novel's finally tuned attention to the state of her reproductive organs we see an example of a certain social ideology in action in the novel, quietly (or not so quietly) insisting that reproductivity is destiny and that only those who reproduce contribute to the social good, in the case of Céleste Habert and her brother's manipulation of Sylvie around questions of her own reproductivity we see the novel displaying critically the cynical deployment by a certain set of characters of that same reproductive ideology in the service of a particular set of interests. (Céleste's "concern" for the sentimental well-being of her "friend" Sylvie also makes for a sharp contrast with Eugénie Grandet's concern for Nanon, whom she helps to marry at age fifty-nine.)

Pierrette has thus been concerned with the social form of marriage and with the ways that form's links to biological reproduction are theorized, calculated, spoken of, experienced, controlled, manipulated, believed in, or disbelieved. This analytical interest is elaborated in the novel by way of the interrelations between the various members of its baroquely constructed set of characters. Many of these characters are in competitive pursuit of the same fortune while possessing various degrees of awareness of the ways in which their own desires for money, for marriage, for children, or their own aversions to marriage or children contribute to the strategic decisions they make. Clearly, this analytical interest in the way reproductive ideology functions exists in tension with the celibatairophobic discourse the novel lays out in its preface and then continues to emit at various moments. In its analytic project, the novel seems to objectify its own use of celibatairophobic discourse, and to begin to question the interests that such discourse furthers. It seems hardly surprising, then, that the same novelist who constructed *Pierrette* and wrote its preface would be intrigued by the social forms and meanings of nonreproductive sexual relations in the world around him, and in particular by same-sex relations. In the remainder of this book I move on from the analyses of Balzac's interest in evolving strategies of reproduction and inheritance, in strategies for limiting reproduction, and in strategies that result in failures of reproduction to an examination of his interest in the forms of same-sex relations he saw in the world around him and to his analyses of these forms in his novels.

INTERLUDE

Balzac and Same-Sex Relations in the 1830s

Balzac, on the whole, is a very dangerous writer.—G. H. Lewes, "H. de Balzac," *The Monthly Magazine,* May 1842

JUST FRIENDS

In 1832 or 1833, Eugène Sue sent the following letter to Honoré de Balzac:

> What a cruel fellow you are, here in Paris without letting me know, not the slightest sign—would you like to make some reparations for this ignominious behavior? Ask me to lunch, to dinner, to supper, to bed, to chat, to kill some time—anything you want—I'll be in town until Monday or Tuesday of next week.
>
> Mr. Vimont, *bookseller,* who will remember you with no problem—has a huge hard-on for you. If necessary, I would have wanked him to produce it, but as full of yourself as you are, you well know the erection produced merely by the mention of your name. Go see him. He's a good fellow. . . .
>
> But for God's sake, come see me, I have a million things to say to you.
>
> With admiration for your foreskin, I am yours truly,
>
> Eugène S.

[Vous êtes un grand misérable, vous à Paris de ne m'avoir pas dit un mot, un seul mot—voulez-vous réparer cette ignominie? Venez me demander à déjeuner, à dîner, à souper, à coucher, à causer, à bêtiser—tout ce que vous voudrez—je reste ici jusqu'à lundi ou mardi de la semaine prochaine.

Mr Vimont *libraire* qui vous remettra sans douleur—bande pour vous jusqu'au sang—s'il avait fallu le branler pour cela, je l'aurais fait, mais fat que vous êtes vous savez bien que l'érection vient à votre nom seul—voyez-le donc. C'est un excellent homme. . . .

Mais pour Dieu venez, venez, venez, j'ai un million de choses à vous dire.

J'admire votre prépuce et suis le vôtre.

Eugène S.][1]

The letter, or bits of it, is often cited in discussions having to do with Balzac's literary, and perhaps personal, interest in sexualized relations between men. Often cited as well is the sentence in a letter from Hyacinthe (known as Henri) de Latouche to Balzac from 1828: "You who have told me to go fuck myself, apparently because friendship is like a woman and you have a hold on me because of what I feel for you, why don't you come here and get fucked; as quickly as possible [Vous qui m'envoyez faire foutre, apparemment parce que l'amitié est femme et que vous me prenez moi-même par le sentiment que j'ai pour vous, venez donc vous faire foutre ici; et au plus vite]."[2] One of the lengthier treatments of such materials can be found in Pierre Citron's 1986 *Dans Balzac*.[3] Citron is fond of the term "ambisexuality," which, in Balzac's case, is linked for Citron to "the will to apprehend life in all its forms" (85). Thus Balzac is *not* to be thought of as being like "notable homosexuals such as Custine or H. Auger [homosexuels notoires comme Custine ou H. Auger]"[4] with whom he might have been friends. In his recent biography of Balzac, Graham Robb also helpfully covers much of this ground, and repeats a version of Citron's apparently disinculpating (and also dehistoricizing) gesture: "Balzac's tendencies might best be described not as homosexual, heterosexual or both, but simply as sexual."[5] After reviewing a whole set of cases of the close friendships with men that Balzac is known to have experienced,[6] Suzanne Jean Bérard offers a slightly different conclusion: "We are inclined to believe that Balzac, without ever having physically practiced homosexuality [*la pédérastie*], nonetheless had a repressed and sublimated attraction for young men. He gave—as is often the case—a noble name to this latent sodomy: he called it friendship, fidelity, protection . . . and he allowed it to play in his life a role that, while avoiding any offense to public morality, nonetheless inflicted deep, heartfelt emotions."[7]

All of these discussions of the evidence in question have at least the advantage of acknowledging the serious presence of the notion of a sexualized intimacy between men within Balzac's own personal life. In this regard, they serve us better than the astonishing assertions of the translator of the Penguin edition of Balzac's *Splendeurs et misères des courtisanes* (titled in translation *A Harlot High and Low*). In an introduction to the English version of that novel, the translator Raynor Heppenstall writes, in connection with the relations presented in the novel between Jacques Collin (aka Vautrin) and Lucien de Rubempré:

> How the homosexual thing came in, I don't know. To us, it is certainly there. How much it was there to Balzac is a different matter. He knew about the existence of male prostitutes, that is certain. He knew that prison life tended to foster homosexual practices. I am nevertheless far from certain that he conceived the relations between Lucien and his Mephistopheles to be anything like those we now regard as normal between men whom we describe as consenting adults. Not to put too fine a point upon it, if he did, the sum total of sexual services then required of Lucien would be such that we need hardly feel surprised that, on his free evenings, all he wanted to do was recline on a divan and smoke a hookah. The idea of Jacques Collin as homosexual Mephistopheles to a succession of young Fausts was, I suppose, first suggested by Proust. . . . I remain unconvinced that it is what Balzac had in mind.[8]

We could perhaps charitably ascribe Heppenstall's naïveté (if, indeed, that is what it is) to his apparent ignorance of the historical materials that attest to the rich and varied sexual culture that surrounded Balzac. Robb's and Citron's ways of presenting some of those materials reveal perhaps a different form of naïveté—the belief that a different (previous) sexual culture can adequately be thought about by way of the nonce categories present in one's own culture. The situation is, of course, rendered more problematic by the fact that the deployment of terms we find in Robb and Citron is haunted by an ideology we might call homophobic: an ideology evident in the effort to distinguish Balzac from clearly recognizable "homosexuals," the effort to name his sexual activities or proclivities or interests with some other, more palatable, word. Historically speaking, we should note that whatever Custine and Auger were notorious for, it could not exactly have been their "homosexuality"—whatever confused category that word can be said to designate and whatever assortment of people it brings together.[9] The word was obviously not yet around. This is why evaluations such as Robb's and Citron's risk being dehistoricizing: they apply words that had yet to be invented (and that, by way of their invention, allow certain acts of grouping to be performed) to social and historical contexts in which different sets of practices, different social forms, different institutions, words, categories, concepts, and habits of thought were in play. (Balzac himself, as we shall see in this interlude and in the following two chapters, fully understood that the social forms through which sexual relations come to be enacted are historically variable.)

As for which words *were* around, Balzac is well known for his use, in the final section of *Splendeurs et misères des courtisanes* (first published in 1847) of the word *tante* (fairy; or, more literally, auntie) and of the expression *le troisième sexe* (the third sex), one he added to the proofs, having previously written *le dernier sexe* (the final sex) (6:840, 6:1466). He could have picked up the expression *tante* from a number of contemporary sources, including the slang dictionary published by the convict-turned-chief-of-police, Eugène-François Vidocq, in his *Les Voleurs* of 1837. Vidocq gives the following definition for *tante:*

> [A] man who has the tastes of women, the woman of men's prisons. . . . It should not be believed that pederasty is always caused by a vicious constitution; phrenologists, who have found the bumps on our skulls corresponding to all the forms of love, have yet to find the bump of Socratic love. . . . Sometimes prison wardens and guards have even allowed *marriages* to be celebrated with a certain amount of pomp and circumstance.

> [Homme qui a les goûts des femmes, la femme des prisons d'hommes. . . . Il ne faut pas croire que la pédérastie soit toujours le résultat d'une organisation vicieuse; les phrénologistes, qui ont

trouvé sur notre crâne la bosse propre a chaque amour, n'y ont point trouvé celle de l'amour socratique. . . . Les directeurs et surveillants de maison centrale ont même quelquefois souffert que des *mariages* fussent célébrés avec une certaine pompe.][10]

Vidocq compares such marriages to a contract of marriage that King Henri III signed with Maugiron, "his favorite *mignon* [minion]," and goes so far as to cite a satiric pamphlet occasioned by that earlier episode. He also makes reference to the trial (1835) of the poet-murderer Pierre-François Lacenaire, one of whose bloody crimes included the murder of the Tante Chardon and his mother, the crime and the victims being discussed both in court and in accounts in the popular press.[11]

Balzac could also have learned about same-sex prison slang from the contribution of M. Moreau-Christophe, "Les Détenus" ("Detainees"), in the omnibus project to which Balzac also contributed, *Les Français peints par eux-mêmes: Encyclopédie morale du dix-neuvième siècle*. Moreau-Christophe writes:

> There exist in men's prisons, men whose degradation has caused them to descend to such a low level that they no longer belong to their own sex.
>
> As children, they are called *mômes,* or *gosselins* [little kids]; as adolescents, they are *cousines* [female cousins]; older, they are *tantes* [aunts].
>
> These individuals begin to act like women, imitate feminine ways of dressing, and feminine manners and voices. Some of them wear scarves, which they arrange as effeminate bonnets [*un bonnet à la folle*]. They all wear corkscrew curls in their hair.[12]

The other readily available bits of lexicon for referring to same-sex relations would include, of course, "vice," that omnibus category that grouped together same-sex couplings, drinking, gambling, drugs, prostitution, and a number of other things. One can also find references to "unnatural" passions ("cette passion outre nature"), usages of the adjectives *particulier* (particular or peculiar) and *équivoque* (dubious), as in "cette passion équivoque et plus qu'italienne" (this dubious and extremely Italian passion), as well as references to classical literature, as in the description of someone as "the personification of Anacreon's most beautiful ode or Theocritus's most handsome verse."[13]

Bérard's evaluation of the material on Balzac's possible same-sex inclinations shows a slightly different methodological problem than does Robb's or Citron's. She imagines that categories such as friendship, protection, fidelity, or devotion are sublimated forms of "homosexuality," thereby missing the occasion to inquire into the particular shape taken by social forms such as friendship within Balzac's time and within his circle. Further, by imagining that Balzac's "homosexuality" is only "latent" or "unconscious," she misses the occasion to notice *both* Balzac's sociological curiosity (quite conscious) about the social forms that help shape same-sex sexual behavior *and* his epistemological curiosity about the ways in which the available social categorizations of sexual behaviors affect the very conditions of their perception.

In this interlude, I would like to provide some background about some of the social forms of same-sex intimacy with which Balzac was familiar, and then turn to look at his investigation—in works such as *La Fille aux yeux d'or* or *Sarrasine*—of the way in which what one is or is not able to perceive about sexuality (and, in particular, same-sex sexuality) in one's world depends on epistemological categories already assimilated. It would further seem that Balzac understood there to be a variety of epistemologies in competition in his social universe, and that he understood the conflicts between those epistemologies to be related to other conflicts structuring the social field.

GENDER, SEXUALITY, STATUS, FRIENDSHIP

For all my reservations about the ways Robb, Citron, and Bérard handle their materials, it is also the case that their work has participated helpfully in the project of keeping the materials alive and available. Had their curiosity limited itself in ways similar to Heppenstall's, figures such as Auger and Custine might have been more completely relegated to the dustbin of forgotten memoirs held by increasingly fewer libraries as years go by.

Even the most straightforwardly homophobic treatment of some of this material in the past few decades has nonetheless helped disseminate it, thereby working for the benefit of readings that might approach it with a better-informed sense of the history of sexuality. In *Balzac et le mal du siècle,* Pierre Barbéris is most ardent in his efforts to ensure that Balzac's sexual reputation remain unbesmirched.[14] Balzac is, for Barbéris, a "woman's man," and Balzac's penchant for passionate male friendships is something altogether respectable:

> It is in no way an actual homosexuality. It is in no way an anomaly, a full-blown neurosis. It is merely—but this is a great deal—a form of human relation that, in order to have access to a certain truth, is obliged to exclude women and love. Did Balzac practice homosexuality? In the end the question is unimportant. . . . It does not seem that Balzacian homosexuality, doubtless the expression of deep psychological needs, was experienced by Balzac as a *destiny,* as a cross he had to bear. It did not exile him in any way, certainly not from normalcy in love. It did not turn him into a pariah. It did not prevent him from seeking out women, devoting himself to marriage, or from becoming the most important novelist, above all, of the intimate secrets of couples. . . . That which served to *separate* Proust helped Balzac—during a century of wide-spread separation—to affiliate.[15]

As the next chapter will make clear, Balzac—apparently unlike Barbéris—was quite capable of imagining couples that involved two members of the same sex. The heterosexism in evidence in Barbéris, one that foregrounds a certain discourse devoted to the pathologization of homosexuality, seems also to inhibit an adequate historical perception of Balzac's novels and their interests in same-sex couples. In spite of all this, Barbéris helpfully provides interesting material about what he calls Balzac's "liaison" ("aucun autre mot ne s'impose [no other word will do])" with Jules Sandeau in 1835, an early member of a series of young men who will make up what Barbéris calls Balzac's "harem of secretaries." As evidence of the nature of the relationship between Balzac and Sandeau, Barbéris provides two passages from the first edition of Sandeau's "autobiographical novel" of 1839, *Marianna.* Sandeau would apparently tone down one of them in later editions of the novel: "Georges was in his room, writing. Lying on a sofa near him, a slight, young, blond man with a soft and melancholy air about him gazed at him silently. In the candlelight, looking a bit extenuated, pale, with his forehead resting on his white, feminine hand, he would have seemed to a poet a beautiful lily whose stem was bending under its weight." A bit later, the older Georges says ("with a voice like a caress") to the younger Henry, "Je t'aime." "I love you. You have an ineffable charm about you, the scent of my native soil that awakens in me all the feelings of my youth. . . . And he pressed him gently to his chest. Seeing them together—the one in the flower of his graceful youth, an adolescent with a virginal brow, a limpid gaze, a slender and flexible waist, a happy child whose youth had so far only known smiles—the other worn by pain, his face already etched with wrinkles—it was like seeing a young beech tree near an oak cleft by lightning."[16] Pre-Raphaelite or symbolist before their time, Sandeau's descriptions exist in a realm of explicit sexual vagueness characteristic of a great deal of French writing in the 1830s. Whether Balzac practiced anything that might be called homosexuality may well be "unimportant" to Barbéris, but what the materials in fact show is that Parisian literary men of the time were quite strongly aware of the possibility of their friendships being sexualized, and they had little problem publicly expressing this awareness.[17]

In his "How to Do the History of Male Homosexuality" David Halperin writes of the ways in which the discourse of male friendship has managed at various times to discriminate between friendship and sexualized same-sex relations:

> Sexual love, at least as it is viewed within the cultural horizons of the male world, is all about penetration and therefore all about position, superiority and inferiority, rank and status, gender and difference. Friendship, by contrast, is all about sameness: sameness of rank and status, sameness of sentiment, sameness of identity. It is this very emphasis on identity, similarity, and mutuality that distances the friendship tradition, in its original social and discursive context, from the world of sexual love. So why include it here, in a genealogy of male homosexuality? Because the friendship tradition provided socially empowered men with an established discursive venue in which to express, without social reproach, sentiments of passionate and mutual love for one another, and such passionate, mutual love between persons of the same sex is an important component of what we now call homosexuality.[18]

Halperin in his article helpfully separates out different discursive traditions often tangled up in our present-day notion of homosexuality (effeminacy, sodomy, friendship, inversion, homosexuality). Yet to understand the French material from the 1830s we need to find a way of relating Halperin's static discursive grid to the kinds of dynamism in the French cultural context that cause the various threads to tangle, untangle, and retangle in particular ways as various social forms for same-sex interaction evolve. The Sandeau passages, for instance, are about friendship but not about sameness; they are about (and written by) literary men in pursuit of superior social position without necessarily having obtained it; and they are fully aware of the sexual implications in their imagery and tone.

Halperin's characterization of friendship draws on ancient models (Gilgamesh and Enkidu, David and Jonathan, Achilles and Patroclus, Orestes and Pylades) as well as on early modern ones (Montaigne and La Boétie). Balzac's contemporaries knew these models as well, and invoked them precisely in order to note discrepancies between the friendships of their moment and these earlier models. George Sand, for instance, in her *Histoire de ma vie,* just after describing her arrival in Paris in 1831, her garret lodgings, and her trips to the theater disguised as a man, turns to a long reflective passage on Montaigne and friendship:

> From my youth, indeed, from my earliest childhood, I had a dream of an ideal friendship and I was filled with enthusiasm for ancient examples, where I suspected nothing malicious. Later I would have to learn that such friendships were accompanied by that senseless or sickly deviance of which Cicero said: *Quis est enim iste amor amicitiae?* [What then is this "love of friendship" of which you speak?] This terrified me, as did anything that seemed wild or depraved. I had imagined such pure heroes, and now I had to imagine them as brutal and depraved! I was again seized with a saddening disgust when, old enough now to read whatever I wanted, I understood the whole story of Achilles and Patroclus, of Harmodius and Aristogiton. Indeed, it was Montaigne's chapter on friendship that brought me this disillusioning, and from that point on that very chapter, so chaste and ardent, that holy and masculine expression of a sentiment so elevated as to be virtuous, became a kind of sacred law that corresponded to one of my soul's aspirations.[19]

Of course Sand's *Histoire de ma vie* is a retrospective text, first published in the mid-1850s when French sexual culture had arguably undergone some changes from the 1830s, and also when Sand was at a very different point in her career and was taking care of her reputation in rather different ways than she did in her more daring early years.[20] She is using this digression on friendship in part to make the point that nonsexualized relationships with men were extremely important, both affectively and professionally, in her life. She refers specifically to her close friend François Rollinat, a lawyer, whom she sometimes called "mon Pylade," and to the difficulty contemporaries had in believing in the nonsexualized nature of such a relationship.[21] Yet Sand insists: "This friendship was on a par with the most beautiful novels of chivalry [cette amitié est restée digne des plus beaux romans de la chevalerie]."[22]

In that last remark of Sand's we find an indication of one of the contributing elements to the dynamism in this cultural system, a system in which male friendship and the possibility of sexualization exist in such close proximity to each other. In *Histoire de ma vie,* Sand *explicitly* discusses the way the *gendering* of the discourse of friendship makes it difficult for her to appropriate for her relationship with a man. *Implicitly,* by mentioning novels of chivalry, she indicates another appropriation going on here: the appropriation by literary bohemians of an aristocratic discourse. Sometimes bohemians and aristocrats could forge a successful coalition around antibourgeois sentiments, and around an opposition to certain bourgeois cultural practices (particularly as related to sexuality). Yet such coalitions, when successful, could not fully dissolve the class tensions between the two groups, and such tension often shows up in attempts to appropriate the aristocratic discourse and aristocratic social forms of friendship within a bohemian context.[23]

I would like to elaborate more fully on this tension, and to do so I will remain with Sand for a moment but also bring Astolphe, marquis de Custine (1790–1857) into the discussion. It was in Sand's garden at Ormesson that she says she read and meditated on Montaigne and friendship. It was also at Ormesson that a strange episode she mentions, but fails to recount fully, took place in the mid-1820s:

> My husband sometimes spent the nights in Paris, my manservant slept in a building a ways off. I was alone with my maid in my pavilion, itself isolated from any other inhabited building. My mind

> was clouded with fearful thoughts ever since the foggy night—one of those nights whose sonorities are so strangely lugubrious—on which I had heard the calls for help of a man who was being attacked, whose throat seemed to be being slit. Since then, I have learned the key to this mystery; but I neither can nor wish to reveal it.[24]

Sand's rhetorical coyness is a fairly clear signal that something sexually suspicious is involved. Georges Lubin, editor of the Pléiade edition of Sand's autobiographical writings, suggests that what Sand heard was Custine being beaten up by a group of guardsmen, with one of whom he had sought out a sexual rendezvous. This event took place on October 28, 1824. Sand's house was apparently situated on the road that newspaper accounts indicated Custine was following on his way to his rendezvous.[25] Sand is thus plausibly both recording and failing to record an attack on a man for seeking out sex with another man.

Anka Muhlstein, one of Custine's biographers, suggests two slightly different hypotheses about Custine's social fate after the newspaper coverage of his attack and the rumors surrounding it. Custine had been briefly married but his marriage ended shortly before the attack, when his young wife died of tuberculosis. Even before his wife's death, he had brought into his household the Englishman who would become his lifelong companion, Edward Saint-Barbe (who came to be known as Édouard de Sainte-Barbe). Custine and his wife had an infant son who died of meningitis slightly more than a year after the attack on his father, who was to live the rest of his life openly with his companion, Sainte-Barbe. Muhlstein suggests on the one hand that while some of Custine's aristocratic connections abandoned him after the scandal of 1824, many others of them (including Sainte-Barbe) were perfectly loyal: "Those near to him who knew of and had accepted his tastes would never have burdened him with reproaches simply because his singularity had become public."[26] On the other hand, Muhlstein also suggests that it was in part the hostile reaction to the scandal within the aristocratic circles in which he had moved that encouraged Custine to begin associating more with the literary bohemians of his time, to begin seriously to pursue literature himself, and to choose to become an important patron and host to the literary stars of his time: "There was another world he could turn to, more exciting, more amusing, more varied than the Faubourg Saint-Germain, a new society open to artists and writers. One only had to cross the river."[27]

Custine, because of his literary ambitions as well as the way his social trajectory was inflected by the scandal of 1824, finds himself drawn to bohemian circles. Sand, searching for new forms of social relations, tries to appropriate the model of aristocratic male friendship for her own bohemian friendships with certain men, yet has to recognize that that very aristocratic discourse may often have sheltered sexualized relationships among male aristocrats. The example in her own circle of Custine and Sainte-Barbe could only make these problematic aspects of the appropriation of the discourse more salient.[28]

As further evidence of the ways this particular tension was constantly being played with in the 1830s, both by bohemians and by an aristocrat such as Custine, consider Custine's contribution to an 1831 omnibus set of volumes in which different literary figures took turns describing various aspects of contemporary Parisian culture. Custine's contribution to *Paris; ou, Le Livre des cent-et-un* was called "Les Amitiés littéraires en 1831," which might well have seemed provocative to someone aware of Custine's reputation. Toward the end of his essay Custine declares: "In this century of increased publicity, indiscretion is permitted and even demanded. A secret would be a privilege: no more privileges! That is today's call to order . . . or to disorder! [Dans ce siècle de publicité, l'indiscrétion est permise et même commandée. Un secret serait un privilége [*sic*]: plus de priviléges! C'est le mot d'ordre . . . je veux dire de désordre!]"[29] Custine here seems explicitly to link himself and his fate (the loss of his secret) to his privileged aristocratic status, and hints at his opposition both to democratic political discourse and to the growing association of literature and journalism. In this first-person essay he describes himself trying to write a play, and being glad of the interruption provided by the arrival of two friends. Yet as they converse with him and advise him about what he should be writing, it becomes clear that rather than being devoted to literature they are devoted to literary politics and success by any means. Topics should be chosen strategically, they advise him, and should be topical. After their departure, Custine chastises them for not respecting the *sacerdoce,* the sacred calling, of literature.

Particularly interesting in this essay is the description Custine gives of the play he was beginning to write before his friends interrupted him:

> The play I had been sketching out, one I had begun during a trip [to Andalucia and Africa] suddenly presented itself to me in all its simplicity. I imagined a drama without a love story, motivated by nothing more than the painting of Moorish and Christian chivalry on the one hand, and by the struggles of maternal tenderness on the other. It seemed to hold potential for new and sublime forms of beauty. . . . I felt myself transformed into a creative spirit; a greater force took hold of my soul; a fountain of life sprang up in my heart: all my desires were new, all my impressions unknown! . . . To feel deeply is always a way of making new discoveries! . . . What delicious tears the love of duty and of one's country drew from me!!! . . . How I, along with my hero, suffered the pains of a noble and legitimate ambition!! . . . and a mother's love! . . . how many secrets it revealed to me! . . . I composed verses and sketched scenes with the rapidity of thought; in my poetic intoxication, it seemed to me impossible that I would not manage to share my emotions and enthusiasm with the whole world; I felt myself the master of hearts: I was happy![30]

Custine may well have had the aristocratic credentials to carry off this hyperromantic performance of enthusiasm for archaic forms of chivalry and mother-love without it falling into a camp satire. It seems clear, given what was known about Custine by his contemporaries, that there is, in this performance, a kind of flagrantly displayed aristocratic disregard for what was known about him. That public opinion could choose to chastise this kind of pretension, at least when it was not backed by serious aristocratic status such as Custine's, can be seen in an unsigned newspaper article from 1830, a review in *Le Figaro* (of which Latouche was the editor) of the young Sainte-Beuve's new collection of poetry, *Les Consolations,* which he dedicated to his friend and fellow poet, Victor Hugo. The review begins by noting that a "friend" is dedicating a book to another "friend," with Sainte-Beuve, the reviewer scoffs, finding ways to place Hugo's name almost on every page.

Les Consolations indeed begins with an effusive sixteen-page preface dedicated to Hugo and devoted to a discussion of friendship.[31] Sainte-

Beuve writes with the same tone of effusive excess that characterizes Custine's prose. Yet Sainte-Beuve's reviewer will call him to task for invoking a discourse of friendship to which he has no title. In a tone that, on reflection, is difficult to pin down, the reviewer declares:

> The friendship of two poets? Fie! Orestes and Pylades could be friends—all things have a time and place! But Sainte-Beuve and Hugo, let's not be ridiculous! Greek *comradery* is permissible; Parisian comradery is forbidden. . . . There can never be enough catcalls, enough epigrams, to punish two romantics who indulge in a commerce of friendship—licit only in Greece—in the rue de Notre-Dame-des-Champs in Paris!
>
> Orestes and Pylades, Nisus and Euryalus, that is fine; Victor Hugo and Sainte-Bueve is not. So, let's be quick about it, sharpen our pens and daggers, let's ridicule these men who are not being pursued by furies, who are not part of Aeneas's army, and yet who take it into their heads to be so devoted to each other, because they have the same tastes, the same ideas, the same poetic leanings, the same literary sympathies, the same love of work and glory.
>
> [L'amitié entre deux poétes, fi! Oreste et Pylade pouvaient être amis, à la bonne heure! mais Sainte-Beuve et Hugo, c'est du dernier ridicule! La *camaraderie* grecque est permise, celle de Paris est défendue. . . . Il n'est ni assez de sifflets, ni assez d'épigrammes pour punir deux romantiques qui ont, dans la rue de Notre-Dame-des-Champs, à Paris, un commerce d'amitié, licite seulement en Grèce!
>
> Oreste et Pylade, Nisus et Euryale, bien; Victor Hugo et Sainte-Beuve, non. Et vite, et vite, taillons nos plumes, affilons nos pointes, ridiculisons des hommes qui ne sont point poursuivies par les furies, qui ne font point partie de l'armée d'Énée, et qui s'avisent d'être dévoués l'un à l'autre, parce qu'ils ont les mêmes goûts, les mêmes idées, le même penchant poétique, les mêmes sympathies littéraires, le même amour du travail et de la gloire.][32]

The trick of the article is simultaneously to imply that Sainte-Beuve and Hugo are boyfriends while also maintaining the proposition that "Greek" friendship is here being used merely as a metaphor for a shared set of literary commitments. Part of the pretentiousness of which the article is accusing Sainte-Beuve is that he lays claim to a discourse to which he has, by virtue of his status, no right. Yet what makes the rhetoric of this passage seem so unstable is that the same-sex male relations explicitly referred to here, by way of their association with "Greece," are in no way themselves subject to ridicule or disgust. They are or are not ridiculous based on their cultural location and on the mutual positionings of the persons observing them and the persons enacting them.

One finds similar circumstances, and a similar combination of openness and the potential for ridicule, evinced in some of the short stories from 1848 that went into Henry Murger's *Scènes de la vie de bohème*. Murger's two stories "Un Café de la bohème" and "Une Réception dans la bohème" introduce the character of the oddly named twenty-four-year-old Carolus Barbemuche, "homme de lettres et philosophe platonicien" (man of letters and Platonic philosopher). There is some question as to whether he should be admitted to the bohemian circle of friends who form Murger's cast of characters. Unlike them, Barbemuche seems to have money all the time (they therefore refer to him as a "capitalist") and seems to hold steady employment. He writes intensely boring historical chivalric novels where the men are named Don Lopez and Don Alvar and the maidens have names like Inésille. Still, Barbemuche likes fine wine and has nice clothes, and his clothes and shoes are more or less the same size as those of the four needy men he is courting. Somehow he manages to seduce them one by one into agreeing to have him as part of their group. At one point during the discussions about Barbemuche, one of the girls the bohemians frequent asks "What does it mean to be a Platonician?" To which another girl, Mimi, replies, "It's a sickness of men who dare not kiss women . . . I had a lover like that and he lasted two hours." A few pages earlier, the narrator had observed: "Carolus had taken special note of Colline, and already felt for this Socrates—whose Plato he would later become—an attractive sympathy."[33]

In Parisian literary circles of the 1830s and 1840s, then, one finds a number of different social forms within which same-sex relations between men can take shape, and a variety of discourses for referring to them. Some seem to originate in and partake of an aristocratic ethos; some might be thought of as part of a bourgeois morality growing in predominance that will find ever new ways of justifying disgust at these relations; some are tied to a bohemian milieu, a particularly unstable one, through which people often pass with varying degrees of speed, but which seems to sustain the possibility for a nonjudgmental attitude toward these relations, and even a frank curiosity about them. Practices that originate in one cultural locale are available to be borrowed from other locales, but at the risk of ridicule. We can understand a little more about these various cultural possibilities by looking at some reactions to Custine by his contemporaries.

CUSTINE

After the failure of the Polish uprising against Russian rule in 1830–1831, numerous Polish exiles made their way to Paris. One of them was Count Ignace Gurowski. He was eighteen years old when he arrived in France, and he apparently started earning a living teaching horseback riding in a Parisian riding school. By 1835, Gurowski had moved in with Custine and Sainte-Barbe. The household (*notre trio,* Custine would call it) would remain together more or less until 1841.[34] Gurowski enjoyed a luxurious lifestyle, and his flamboyance and appeal were attractive to men and women alike, and, it appears, were rather costly to Custine. In 1841, Gurowski eloped with an infanta of Spain, Ferdinande-Isabelle de Bourbon, who was still underage at the time, causing a diplomatic scandal that finally ended in a quiet wedding in Dover in June of that year. One of Custine's biographers refers to Gurowski as "this Rubempré."[35]

The reference is not entirely anachronistic. Balzac's character, Lucien de Rubempré, the protagonist of *Illusions perdues,* did indeed exist in 1841. The first two parts of that novel as we know it ("Les Deux Poètes" and "Un Grand Homme de province à Paris") had already been published in 1837 and 1839. But the third part, "David Séchard ou les souffrances d'un inventeur," in which Lucien meets Vautrin and strikes some kind of sexual bargain with him, would only appear in 1843. The first installment of the various segments that for us are united together as the sequel to *Lost Illusions, Splendeurs et misères des courtisanes,* the novel in which Lucien is shown living in Paris at Vautrin's expense and in which Vautrin's love for him is revealed, would appear in 1838. Remaining segments would appear in 1843, 1846, and 1847. (The whole novel as we know it would only be assembled after Balzac's death, see chapter 4.)[36] If another of Custine's biographers wrote an article titled "Custine, héros de Balzac: Comment l'auteur de *La Russie en 1839* entra dans *La Comédie humaine* et fut un peu Vautrin" (Custine, a Balzacian Hero: How the Author of *Russia in 1839* Became Part of *The Human Comedy* and Took on a Little of Vautrin), it is doubtless due to the sense that Balzac's cognizance of all that was going on in Custine's life must have contributed to his ability to elaborate the Vautrin-Rubempré pair, and their complicated and interlocking sexualities.

Designating people's sexuality by reference to a literary character or text is a gesture worth wondering about. The editor of the Pléiade edition of *La Comédie humaine* provides a further example. When, in 1846, Balzac republished his 1830 short story "L'Auberge Rouge" ("The Red Inn"), he added a dedication to Custine. The Pléiade editor provides the following information about Custine: "The Marquis belonged to that 'race on whom a curse weighs,' evoked by Proust in *Sodom and Gomorrah*" (11:1245).[37] Muhlstein, Custine's most recent biographer, felt no need for circumlocutions, simply declaring that "Astolphe de Custine was homosexual."[38] Yet these taxonomic hesitations perhaps have a good deal to tell us about the varied perceptions of sexuality by people at different moments in time, and also about the different social positioning of the people doing the perceiving. In the case of the editor of "L'Auberge Rouge" we are probably dealing with an example of decorous euphemism rather than some implicit argument about the history of sexuality. Yet the readiness to hand of the literary example, and the ability to have recourse to Proust for the euphemistic phrase, provides some evidence of the important privileging of sexuality in modern French literature.[39] Referring to Gurowski as "a Rubempré" is slightly different—not a case of euphemism but one in which the namer sees literature as providing a repertory of types, and in which the type is not exclusively determined by sexual behavior. Rather, it is formed out of an interlocking set of sexual proclivities, economic exchanges, and class or status affiliations and ambitions.

Stendhal provides another interesting example of this. In 1830, Custine published a volume of travel writings, elaborately titled *Mémoires et voyages, ou Lettres écrites à diverses époques, pendant des courses en Suisse, en Calabre, en Angleterre, et en Écosse*. On January 10, 1830, Stendhal writes to Sutton Sharpe, telling him that Custine's book had just appeared the day before and that it is the best travel book on England yet to appear. Stendhal then adds: "People say that the author is *a member of the clergy of the R R bishop of Klogher*. He has a refined and aristocratic mind, he is 36 years old, and has 60,000 francs of yearly income."[40] The bishop of Clogher, Percy Jocelyn, a third son of the aristocratic family of Roden, to whose clergy Stendhal assigns Custine, had been caught in a hotel room in London with a young soldier on July 19, 1822.[41] In the mid-1830s, when working on *Lucien Leuwen,* a novel he did not complete, Stendhal came up with the character of an exiled Englishman, Lord Link, with whom his protagonist would strike up an acquaintance. In his notes for the novel, Stendhal wrote: "Lord Link, *a sardonic character.* Milord Link is a *bishop of Clogher,* but do not say this. [Lord Link, *personnage sardonique.* Milord Link est un *évêque de Clogher,* mais ne pas le dire]."[42] Stendhal is creating a category, bishops of Clogher, in which class or status as well as sexuality seem important components. He is also, in imagining a sexual secret for Link that he does not intend to reveal, creating an enigma where there is no necessary call for one. Custine sometimes longed for a certain enigma or "ignorance" to be allowed to surround "secrets" like his.[43] Custine and his secret seem to have provoked the novelistic curiosity of both Stendhal and Balzac, but in rather different ways.[44] Stendhal would link together the sexual behavior and aristocratic background of "people like" Custine and Percy Jocelyn to the end of producing an enigmatic and perhaps vaguely pathologized type. Balzac does something different.

I endeavor here to make clear the ways in which people's perceptions not just of Custine but of same-sex erotic behavior in general can reveal at least three separate things: a culture's extant models for comprehending that behavior, relative class positionings of the perceiver and the perceived, and also the various epistemologies that go along with various class positionings. The difference between Stendhal and Balzac is instructive in this light. Stendhal, however much he might have approved of Custine's account of England, was willing to typify and pathologize the marquis. Balzac was, as we shall see below, and again in chapter 4, inspired to a different kind of activity.

Balzac is much less catty in his correspondence about Custine than are many of his contemporaries. He writes to Madame Hanska of the Gurowski affair: "So Gorowski [*sic*] runs off with an infanta! And then marries her! How much better it would be to be an idiot like Gorowski than the intrepid worker that I am! [Et Gorowski (*sic*) enlève une infante! Et il l'épouse. Oh! qu'il vaut mieux être un sot comme Gorowski qu'un intrépide travailleur comme moi!]." In another letter he says, "Custine has fled to Italy after having helped *his friend,* the Polish fellow Gurowski, run off with the Infanta of Spain."[45] He then moves on matter-of-factly to other news items. Given the amount of venom with which people often refer to Custine in semiprivate written contexts, Balzac's restraint seems remarkable.

It apparently struck others around him as remarkable as well. In a memoir that has been ascribed to a certain Victor Felicien Lambinet, *Balzac mis à nu* (*Balzac Undressed*), Balzac's *failure* to be offended by Custine is remarked on. After a particularly nasty paragraph about all the high-society women who, encouraged by Custine's wealth, tried to convince him to marry them despite their knowledge of his household arrangements, the writer of this memoir then tells us that the duchess d'Abrantès, one of Custine's suitors and a great friend of Balzac's, introduced the writer to the "vile" (*immonde*) marquis:

> His friends tried without success to put up obstacles, to emphasize the turpitude of M. de Custine; Balzac was unmoved. He claimed not only indifference, but rather absolute tolerance where mores were concerned; that is what his classical studies had taught him. People could say what they would, the Marquis had a noteworthy name, a townhouse in Paris, a country estate at Saint-Gratien, a welcoming table and an open hand, and also a short memory as far as debts were concerned. What was there to hold against such a likable fellow? He dedicated *The Red Inn* to him, without being under any obligation to do so, merely because he liked the Marquis.[46]

Without imagining this memoir to be absolutely trustworthy, we can at least consider it as providing evidence that not everyone was drawn to pathologizing typologies, that a draw to them or a resistance to them was part of the project of claiming a social position for oneself, that the formation of an attitude toward sexual behavior is part of seeking out a particular positioning within a given social field.

Compare, in this light, the attitudes of Sainte-Beuve and Prosper Mérimée both toward Custine and toward Théodore Leclercq, another minor nineteenth-century literary figure who lived openly with his male partner. Sainte-Beuve evoked Sodom and Gomorrah in relation to Custine long before the modern editors of Balzac would do so. In a letter of 1844, Sainte-Beauve commented: "[M. de Custine] has here such a bad reputation for his mores, and one so richly deserved: how could people not know that where you are? People read him, and find him nice enough, but no one holds him in any esteem: he almost had to leave the country. His beautiful house in the Montmorency valley was a pure Sodom and Gomorrah."[47] Yet, in March 1851, writing an article upon the death of Théodore Leclercq, Sainte-Beuve could write:

> Following the Terror, there was a group of golden royalist youths, elegant dandies, who struggled energetically and courageously on behalf of an elegant and civilized way of life. It was among them, the *club de Clichy,* in this time of reaction around the 18 Fructidor, that for the first time he [Leclercq] met M. Fiévée, who was a few years older. They began together an enduring union that would last more than 40 years, and that only death was able to bring to an end. . . . Before accompanying M. Fiévée to Hamburg, M. Théodore Leclercq had accompanied him to England in 1802; he also accompanied him when he became Prefect of Nièvre (1813–1815); everywhere, at home or abroad, while those around him made observations about politics and governments, he enjoyed watching society, taking it gayly and lightly, finding in it the subjects of his *Proverbs,* which he would stage whenever he was able.[48]

How is it that Sainte-Beuve is able to write publically with such favor about the same-sex couple formed by Leclercq and Fiévée, whereas in his private correspondence he is so scornful of Custine?

One finds a similar set of divergent rhetorics in reading Prosper Mérimée, who at the moment of the Gurowski scandal writes a gossipy letter to the countess de Montijo to give her all the details. He notes that Custine has just joined the newlyweds in Brussels:

> M. de Custine is with them and announces that he is going to take a trip to the Indies. He was, in any case, having some trouble with the villagers in the town outside Paris where he lived because of certain liberties he had taken. They were ready to do him in, and he had to clear out in very short order.
>
> What do you think of that? Some end for the race of Louis XIV, one of his great-nieces marrying a Polishman who was being kept by another man! M. de Custine, or rather his friends, say that he is

Gurowski's father, but that is a clear lie. Were he his father, he'd be no better than Lot, of Biblical fame.[49]

Consider, in comparison, an excerpt from the article he wrote upon Leclercq's death in 1851:

> No one had better preserved those distinguished traditions of urbanity and politeness of French 18th-century society, which are perhaps incompatible with the development of constitutional customs and mores; but manners such as those of M. Théodore Leclercq are not learned, are not those of just anybody. They were the expression of a lively and delicate spirit, of a warm and caring heart. Add to that a graceful spirit of play, a certain natural coquettishness, and above all, a desire to please—a disposition that has nothing to do with a desire to be noticed. . . . In the final years of his life, M. Leclercq suffered from cruel losses. The death of his sister, and also of M. Fiévée, his childhood friend, from whom he had never separated, were terrible blows for him. He remained kind, likable, and witty; but his good spirits in front of his guests took an effort, and one could tell the effort was painful.[50]

The kindness to Leclercq reminds us once again of the availability of the option to be reasonably open and neutral—not to say favorably inclined—when referring publicly in print in mid-nineteenth-century France to two men living together. The contrasting hostility toward Custine obviously reminds us of the more easily available possibility of hostility toward same-sex relations. One might also speculate that the divergence between hostility and kindness has as much to do with class positioning as with sexual behavior. Leclercq and Fiévée seem marked by a certain bourgeois respectability and hospitality. In any case, they are not aristocrats; they are genteel and monied men of letters, whereas Custine is marked by aristocratic arrogance, however generous a host he might have been. We might remember in this regard the ironic comments about journalism in Custine's "Les Amitiés littéraires en 1831": "In this century of increased publicity, indiscretion is permitted and even demanded. A secret would be a privilege: no more privileges! That is today's call to order . . . or to disorder!" The link Custine suggests between noble status and freedom of sexual expression seems clear, as does the implication that he finds the direction of nineteenth-century French society to be detrimental to both. (The hostility toward journalism and journalists is also hard to miss.) This passage resonates with another from Custine's book on his travels in England. He was in fact in Dover when the Clogher scandal appeared in the English papers in 1822, and he wrote:

> Another cause of the stiffness and awkwardness that strikes us in English worldly relations is the publicity with which the press—entirely free—threatens the action of every individual: a ball, a walk, a conversation, and many other things, this or that offense against custom, against received usage, any attack on the established order will be broadcast the next day in the kingdom's numerous newspapers. . . . These people's civilization is carried to such extremes that one can truthfully say that what they lack today is *ignorance;* there is a innocent quality to imaginations, a charming naivete that depends on what one does not know: but who here is allowed not to know anything, in a country where the tiniest circumstances of life are written up and published? . . . where good as well as bad actions are judged, explained, analyzed by men of almost any class; where even those offenses whose bizarre nature should dictate that they be kept secret, are described and published, without regard for pure and innocent souls?[51]

This somewhat arrogant stance is perhaps not likely to endear a queer aristocrat to someone making a living writing journalism. What Sainte-Beuve and Mérimée's journalism shows is that the privilege of avoiding denunciation would be, for them, acquired differently. People such as Custine, with his amazing ability to put his foot wrong in print, would not be placed to good advantage. It is not only what one says in print and how one says it, it is also the position from which one speaks. That *position* speaks as loudly as the words.

In a passage from a book devoted to his travels in Spain in 1831, Custine wrote: "From the entire eighteenth-century, there is, to my eyes, no one but Rousseau who, in deeds as well as in words, gave witness to the greatness of the sacred calling that is literature; instead of making a living by writing, instead of selling his thought, he copied music, and this traffic served to meet his needs."[52] A few lines later, Custine lambasts "those merchants of ideas who are today called writers," before continuing, somewhat inconsistently:

> These businessmen of the book, these authors/booksellers, have turned our literature into a rented-out field, as lucrative, but also as dusty and muck-filled, as a field of beets or of rape. I, like anyone else, would love to traffic in whatever talent I might have, find out what it is worth in gold; I would love to sell, and at a high price, even my correspondence; I would even value myself according to their price more than according to what my conscience tells me. But I would never lie to raise my price, even were it to be necessary to acquire basic things in life. Still, without falsifying my mind's works, I would do my best to sell them for as much as I could get. (153–54)

Custine's *L'Espagne sous Ferdinand VII,* in which this passage is found, was published in 1838. Balzac read the book, noted the passage, and cited it in a preface to a work he published later in 1838, *La Femme supérieure,* which was later titled *Les Employés* (*The Bureaucrats*). His polemic with Custine in that preface begins with a rather unkind characterization of Custine as "an author almost as well known because of his name as because of the refined views that characterize his talent [un auteur presque aussi illustre par son nom que par la finesse de vues qui caractérise son talent]" (7:884). The preface continues in the annoyed voice of an author who is struggling to make a living in a difficult economic environment upbraiding another author of independent means: "A dithyrambic passage such as this would have better come from another pen than that of M. le marquis de Custine, whose hereditary fortune allows him to turn up his nose at the fortune his pen might win. . . . The sacred calling of which M. de Custine speaks requires a well-established life free of material cares and worries (7:888). In particular, Balzac points out, the world of journalism and the world of bookselling are what make it possible for an author to earn a living. And Balzac uses the occasion to complain both about the way taxes are arranged to hinder the expansion of journalism and the way Belgian booksellers flood the French market with editions of French books on which they pay no royalties to the authors. As Balzac puts it: "One of the many inconvenient facts of the miserable situation in which literature finds itself, and from which it will be unable to extract itself for some time, is the theft—one of the shames of nineteenth-century Europe—perpetrated by Belgium on French writers, and which would quickly be done away with, with all due respect to M. de Custine, if it were a question of bales of cotton" (7:891).

Were one to judge by the letter Custine wrote to Balzac after reading that preface, Custine was not at all displeased. The letter in question is one of the most ingratiating in the correspondence:

> I cannot help but to thank you, my dear Balzac, for the importance you give me, even in my own eyes, in your preface. . . . You are entirely correct in everything you say. . . . The more I read you, the more I see a secret analogy between the small sphere in which my mind is able to move, and that of your great mind. We see social life in the same way: we have the same desire to challenge prejudices without losing sight of truths; we have the same hatred of lies, the same need of independence. Where I merely scratch the surface, you penetrate the depths of the social body.[53]

If Custine does not mind being upbraided by Balzac, it is perhaps because being so involves simply being recognized as an interlocutor by one of the serious literary practitioners of the time—and being recognized without any reference being made to past or present sexual scandals.

Throughout all these materials one sees Custine consistently trying to retain his aristocratic demeanor and status, to lay claim to being both a literary figure and a patron of the arts, an honorary bohemian, and to find authorization for that claim through his association with established literary figures. The balancing of the various class tensions involved in such a project is rather difficult, and is made only more so by the knowledge in circulation regarding his sexuality.

Consider, as an example of the lability of class and sexual allegiances and hostilities, a few excerpts from another catty memoir writer of the time, the count Horace de Viel-Castel. No friend of Custine, Viel-Castel early on in his memoirs refers to the marquis as "that *Ganymede* who was not expelled by society because of his 150,000 francs of independent income [ce *Ganymède* que la société n'a pas chassé, parce qu'il a 150.000 fr. de rentes]." He also calls him "that being without, to our knowledge, a name one can mention [l'être sans nom avouable que nous connaissons]."[54] Yet later in the memoirs Viel-Castel recounts an episode that causes him to take a different point of view. It is in an entry for 1855, in which he is noting how sexual mores matter little when it comes to one's receivability in the world: "Mme la marquise de Beaumont, née Dupuytren, the most manly of our modern Sapphos, was caught last year in a brothel, going at it with the girls. This peccadillo has done her no harm. She is invited everywhere [Mme la marquise de Beaumont, née Dupuytren, la plus hommasse de nos Saphos modernes, a été surprise l'an dernier dans une maison de filles, s'exerçant à la *fricarelle.* Cette peccadille ne lui fait aucun tort, tout le monde la reçoit]" (229). He then settles into his topic with a further story about Custine:

> The abbé Coquereau, who insinuates himself everywhere these days, was at the Princesse Mathilde's three days ago, where Nadaud was singing. The songs were becoming a little risqué, so he prudishly moved off to a neighboring room, from which he could still hear everything. The Marquis de Custine, teasing him about his prudishness, said "I am surprised to see a Christian Silenus frightened off by so little." The abbé, in an attempt at being witty, replied, "*Monsieur, someone like you, who sins by the backside* [a difficult pun to translate: *fondement* means both foundation and anus] *is not well situated to call anyone else Silenus.*"
>
> [L'abbé Coquereau qui se fourre partout était, il y a trois jours, chez la Princesse Mathilde, où Nadaud chantait. Comme les chansons devenaient un peu grasses, il se prudifia au point de se retirer dans un salon voisin, d'où il pouvait tout entendre. Le marquis de Cusine [*sic*], voulant le plaisanter sur sa pruderie, lui dit: "Je m'étonne qu'un Silène chrétien s'effarouche de si peu de chose." L'abbé, pour faire de l'esprit, lui répondit: "*Ce n'est pas quand on pèche comme vous par le fondement, Monsieur, qu'il est permis de traiter les autres de Silène.*"] (229–30)

One might expect that Viel-Castel, given the pleasure he took earlier in expressing his homophobia, would relish this shaming rejoinder; to the contrary, he takes severe umbrage at the priest's response:

> The abbé said that aloud, in front of twenty people. We see what has become of French urbanity, we see what has become of the respect due to imperial royalty.
>
> A common priest dares say, in her presence, to a man she has invited to her house: "*You are a f. . . .*"

> [L'abbé fit cette réponse tout haut, au milieu de vingt personnes. Voilà où en est l'urbanité française, voilà où en est le respect que l'on doit à une Altesse Impériale.
>
> Un méchant abbé ose dire en sa présence à un homme qu'elle reçoit: "*Vous êtes un p. . . .*"] (230)

A public act of denunciation of sexual perversity is thus ruled as being out of line based on an allegiance to a particular aristocratic ethos that the accusation fails to respect. Both Proust and Balzac, as it turns out, are interested in the ways this particular facet of the aristocratic ethos renders possible a link between certain aristocrats and certain bohemians in their shared opposition to the growing predominance of prudish bourgeois sexual mores. Balzac clearly references this side of the aristocratic ethos in the worldly advice he has Henri de Marsay give to Paul de Manerville in *Le Contrat de mariage*, regarding Paul's plan to marry: "I will forgive you for that ridiculous idea only if you promise to marry in the way a great lord would, to entail your fortune, to use the honeymoon to sire two legitimate children, to give your wife a house completely separate from your own, to see her only out in the world, and never to return from a trip without advance warning" (3:532). Proust links this worldly ethos more directly to the question of same-sex sexual practices in a scene in *La Prisonnière* (*The Captive*) in which Charlus has arranged for a concert by his protégé Morel in the Verdurin salon, a concert to which he invites all his noble connections. The bourgeois Verdurins plan to use the occasion to orchestrate Charlus's downfall by publicly revealing Charlus's same-sex sexual proclivities to Morel (as if he didn't already know!). (Charlus's interest in Morel is, of course, both sexual and artistic.) Once the concert is over, Charlus's aristocratic guests (the narrator specifically focuses on the female ones) take their leave of him without bothering to notice the Verdurins:

> The most noble ladies were those who showed the most fervour in congratulating M. de Charlus upon the success of a party of the secret motive for which some of them were not unaware, without however being embarrassed by the knowledge, this class of society—remembering perhaps certain epochs in history when their own families had shown a similarly brazen effrontery—carrying their contempt for scruples almost as far as their respect for etiquette.

> [Les plus nobles étaient celles qui félicitaient avec le plus de ferveur M. de Charlus de la réussite d'une soirée dont certaines n'ignoraient pas le ressort secret, sans en être embarrassées d'ailleurs, cette société —par souvenir peut-être de certaines époques de l'histoire où leur famille était déjà arrivée à une identité pleinement consciente—poussant le mépris des scrupules presque aussi loin que le respect de l'étiquette.][55]

It is worth pausing over the translator's odd way of dealing with Proust's equally odd phrase, "par souvenir peut-être de certaines époques de l'histoire où leur famille était déjà arrivée à une identité pleinement consciente." More literally translated, the phrase would read "remembering perhaps certain epochs in history when their family had already attained a fully conscious identity."[56] Certainly it is meant to indicate something about the longstanding memory of diverse sexual practices within these families, and, in context, to imply that a set of protocols was available for dealing with the knowledge of them, apparently mostly by overlooking them with some degree of tolerance as long as family interests were protected. That set of protocols comes under attack in a bourgeois system devoted to what Proust here labels "scruples," which, for the bourgeoisie, are to be placed higher than etiquette, and which involve the castigation of nonconformist sexualities.

If Custine often seems a Balzacian or a Proustian type, it is because the two novelists are, in their sociological way, particularly drawn to liminal figures, figures with divided allegiances between divergent social groups, figures whose historical makeup causes them to seem out of place in their time (sometimes seeming to look both forward and backward), figures who attempt to construct a hybrid and unstable social space for themselves, creating social networks out of people who can only with difficulty be expected to be grouped together. Because Balzac and Proust are both attentive to figures whose liminality arises in good measure from their sexual practices, they show us in their writings the clash of divergent discourses and cultural practices around questions of nonnormative sexual practices, and they illustrate and analyze the interweaving of discourses and practices of and about sexuality with other ones having to do with social status and social power. Balzac and Proust are thus both remarkable in their awareness and demonstration of the ways in which what we recognize today as homophobia is slowly being rendered possible, plausible, and unremarkable in the world around them. The fact that someone like Balzac lets us notice this process has to do with his remarkable awareness of the ways the parameters governing the perception of sexuality were shifting in his moment, and his curiosity about the variety of interests at stake in, and wielding influence over, these shifts. It is in the context of this awareness that I would like to situate the remaining readings of this book, of *Le Cousin Pons* and *La Cousine Bette* in chapter 3, and of *Illusions perdues* and *Splendeurs et misères des courtisanes* in chapter 4. Before proceeding to those readings, however, I would like to make a few observations about Balzac's well-known works, *La Fille aux yeux d'or* (1834–1835), with its frank awareness of same-sex relations between women, and, briefly, about *Sarrasine* (1830), with its representation of a castrato. It will be worth the trouble to imagine the works as they might have been received by different groups of people in the 1830s: aristocratically identified ones such as Viel-Castel and Custine; those identified with bohemia, say, Eugène Sue, Henri de Latouche, and George Sand in the 1830s; and finally those either a bit taken with the nascent possibilities of the pathologizing typification of same-sex desire (Stendhal, for instance, or perhaps Vidocq) or with the scruples of bourgeois morality—Sainte-Beuve might sometimes fall into this category, or perhaps even George Sand later in life.

THE POSTFACE TO *LA FILLE AUX YEUX D'OR*

La Fille aux yeux d'or ends with the bloody spectacle, witnessed by Henri de Marsay, of the death of the beautiful Paquita at the hands of her aristocratic lover Euphémie, the marquise de San-Réal. There was a postface to the first edition of *La Fille aux yeux d'or* (1835) which unfortunately is missing from many modern editions. In it the author claims that the events of the preceding tale are mostly true and were told to him by the protagonist of the story. He adds that one of the most difficult things to believe about the story would doubtless be the incredible "half-feminine" beauty of the male hero (Henri de Marsay) at age seventeen, although traces of it were still apparent in the man of twenty-six who told the story to the author. The passage then continues:

> If there should be anyone interested in the *Girl with Golden Eyes,* they can see her again after the curtain has come down on the play, like an actress who, to receive her ephemeral crown of glory, rises up in perfect health after having been publicly stabbed. Nothing ends poetically in nature. Today, the *Girl with Golden Eyes* is thirty years old, and her beauty has faded. The marquise de San-Réal, who has rubbed elbows with certain readers of this tale this very winter at the Opera or at the Bouffes, is now of an age that women do not admit to, but which can be surmised from the frightful hairdos that certain foreigners allow themselves to display in the front rows of certain theater boxes, much to the dismay of the younger folk seated behind them. This marquise was raised in the tropics, where Girls with Golden Eyes are accepted by custom to such an extent that they are practically an institution.
>
> [Si quelques personnes s'intéressent à la *Fille aux yeux d'or,* elles pourront la revoir après le rideau tombé sur la pièce, comme une de ces actrices qui, pour recevoir leurs couronnes éphémères, se relèvent bien portantes après avoir été publiquement poignardées. Rien ne se dénoue poétiquement dans la nature. Aujourd'hui, la *Fille aux yeux d'or* a trente ans et s'est bien fanée. La marquise de San-Réal, coudoyée pendant cet hiver aux Bouffes ou à l'Opéra par quelques-unes des honorables personnes qui viennent de lire cet épisode, a précisément l'âge que les femmes ne disent plus, mais que révèlent ces effroyables coiffures dont quelques étrangères se permettent d'embarrasser le devant des loges, au grand déplaisir des jeunes personnes qui se tiennent sur l'*arrière*. Cette marquise est une personne élevée aux îles, où les mœurs légitiment si bien les Filles aux yeux d'or, qu'elles y sont presque une institution.] (5:1111–12)[57]

The passage is ambiguous and enigmatic while still being forthright about the presence of a lesbian subculture in Paris in the 1830s. Rose Fortassier has suggested Balzac is making a slightly veiled reference to Marie Dorval, the lead actress in Alexandre Dumas's play *Antony,* in which she appeared regularly in Paris from 1831 to 1834, and throughout the rest of France even longer.[58] At the end of the play, in order to protect her reputation, she is stabbed by her lover as her husband breaks down the door. The lover then declares to the husband, "I killed her because she resisted me."

Rumors were circulating regarding an affair between Dorval and George Sand. Alfred de Vigny, with whom Dorval was involved, wrote in the margins of one 1833 letter from Sand to Dorval, "I have forbidden Maria to reply to this Sappho who is pestering her."[59] It is also often suggested that the relationship between Lélia and Pulchérie in Sand's novel *Lélia* draws on Sand's relationship with Dorval. Rather like the correspondence between Balzac and Sue or Balzac and Latouche, the correspondence between Sand and Dorval provokes a wide range of critical speculation. Lillian Faderman refers indecisively to "a very sensual but not unambiguously sexual relationship between them." The editor of a 1950 edition of *La Fille aux yeux d'or,* on the other hand, declares that "some of Sand's texts leave no doubt as to the intimacy of their relation, nor as to the vice that they shared."[60] Arsène Houssaye, a contemporary of Sand, gives a long description in his *Les Confessions* of the passionate and intimate relation of a dark-haired woman novelist and a blond actress, without ever giving names: "It was more than a libertine affair of the heart; it was an oriental, an Indian, a Japanese passion. The two bacchantes would finally take their leave of each other at daybreak, still drunk on the paleness of the dreams they had lived out. And the woman of eloquence would be more eloquent on that day, just as the woman of the theater would have more caresses in her voice, more fire in her eyes, a wilder passion."[61] Houssaye also refers to the rumors circulating about the same-sex liaisons of the Princess of Belgiojoso. He notes that she was extremely fond of George Sand. "Why did they enjoy seeing each other so much? Doubtless in order to emancipate women and the people" (3). Houssaye also remarks that around this time Balzac was finishing *La Fille aux yeux d'or*—making clear that Balzac's contemporaries associated the story with a culture of same-sex relations between women that they knew to exist around them (3). In a letter to Sand, written on January 27, 1833, Gustave Planche, an aspiring suitor, warns her of Dorval's reputation:

> One of my friends who is close enough to J——te to be able to judge her truthfulness impartially has assured me that Madame A. D. [Allan Dorval] had for her a passion of the same nature as

> the passion Sappho had for the young Lesbians—it's terrible that I tell you such an ugly thing, isn't it? Perhaps it's disrespectful. But I don't think so. Between now and February 15, if by chance you find yourself alone with Madame A. D., you could easily find out if I have been misled. In any case, please burn this letter, and cover these preceding revelations in deep silence and forgetfulness. I don't care much about public opinion, yet I would still not like to be known as a stool pigeon.[62]

Doubtless, many letters such as Planche's were in fact burned. Yet enough testimonials remain to indicate not only the reigning curiosity about the Sand/Dorval connection, but a general awareness of and interest in same-sex relations between women.

It is thus not surprising that Balzac's postface should refer relatively openly to a subculture of women sexually interested in other women in Paris. (The sentences from the postface cited above are ostentatiously constructed with the feminine substantive *personnes* and its corresponding pronoun *elles* in order to suggest that women in particular among his readers may be interested in knowing the current whereabouts of Paquita and Euphémie.) The postface further suggests that it suffices to be sufficiently well-informed in order to be able to see members of this subculture all around.

At the same time, the postface deflates the spectacular violence marking the end of the story just told. It reveals both female participants in the story's bloody final scene to be still alive, and also unkindly notes how much less attractive they have become with the passage of time. The ridicule attached to the older marquise de San-Réal is particularly noteworthy. Why would the postface be so carefully constructed as to force us to recognize the artifice of the spectacular ending of the tale that has just been told?

The concluding pages of *La Fille aux yeux d'or* are themselves tonally rather unstable or even incoherent. One finds in them an excessive use of melodrama (bordering on camp), as an unknowing brother rides through Paris to the mansion in which he plans to kill a woman who is already in the process of being murdered by the sister that the brother does not even know he has. There is a somewhat ironic reference to the stylized representations of murder in the gothic novel that would shortly be taken up with gusto in France with the appearance of the *roman feuilleton* (serial novel): one of Henri's accomplices is pleased to note that the marquise has forgotten to soundproof the chimney, thus allowing the noise of her crime to be perceptible from the street, a mistake the men would not have made. The tabloid sensationalism in effect as brother and sister head for the shocking revelation that they have been sexually involved with the same woman suddenly gives way to a startlingly detailed painterly description (the tale is dedicated to Eugène Delacroix) of a room in bloody disarray due to the successful attempt of one woman to kill another after having sex with her. The very tonal instability of the passage (camp and the portrayal of intense violence) might indicate a certain indecisiveness on Balzac's part as to what sense to make of same-sex relations involving two women. It is nearly reduced to nothing but the material for a spectacular display.[63]

In my next chapter, I return to the question of Balzac's interest in and ways of thinking about same-sex couples. The novels I consider there, *Le Cousin Pons* and *La Cousine Bette,* date from 1846 and 1847, more than a decade later. In the interval, Balzac will have filled out his understanding of same-sex relations with a great deal more sociological content. That content, fascinating in its own right, will not ultimately prove sufficient to restrain the novelistic impulse to bring same-sex couples to a melodramatic end. Again in *La Cousine Bette,* Balzac will reserve a particularly sensational and mostly gratuitous violence for the end of the female couple, thereby furthering the kind of masculinist dissymmetry already apparent in his treatment of couples of women and couples of men a decade earlier. In *La Cousine Bette,* Balzac will, in speaking of Bette's feelings for Valérie, refer to "the most violent sentiment we know of, the friendship of one woman for another [le sentiment le plus violent que l'on connaisse, l'amitié d'une femme pour une femme]" (7:433, 424). As we will see more fully in the next chapter, that statement itself has several aspects. It is, on the one hand, a recognition of the ways in which women are at a disadvantage in the economic system that governs marriage and family formation for most people in France at the time: to escape from or to revolt against that system requires an immense effort for a woman. On the other hand, Balzac's pronouncement is also a kind of pop-psychological justification for the melodramatic treatment of same-sex eroticism between women.

Anne-Marie Meininger, who edited *La Cousine Bette* for the Pléiade edition of *La Comédie humaine,* annotates that sentence on the violent sentiment found in female friendships by recalling the violence of the conclusion of *La Fille aux yeux d'or.* She then reminds us that Balzac, in a letter to Madame Hanska, named the poet Marceline Desbordes-Valmore as one of his models for Bette:

> The passionate friendship of Marceline for Pauline Duchambge, who had been mixed up in the twists and turns of Marie Dorval's affair with Vigny, might have given Balzac some reason to wonder about the possible existence of a network of singular feminine friendships in Paris.
>
> [L'amitié passionnée de Marceline pour Pauline Duchambge, laquelle avait été mêlée aux péripéties de la liaison de Marie Dorval et de Vigny, a pu donner à Balzac quelques raisons de s'interroger sur l'existence d'un réseau de singulières amitiés féminines à Paris.][64]

The unnecessarily tentative quality of the claim regarding what Balzac *may* have known is unfortunate. The ideological constructs that produce that hesitant mode of expression are both tenacious and intellectually frustrating. Of course Balzac, moving in the circles he moved in and friends with the people he was friends with, and author of *La Fille aux yeux d'or* and its postface, as well as of *La Cousine Bette,* did more than wonder about the possible existence of same-sex relations between women. He knew of them, thought about the social forms through which they were enacted, theorized them (sometimes in sexist ways), and historicized them, just as he did with same-sex relations between men. I now turn to examine more closely how he does this within *La Fille aux yeux d'or.*

LA FILLE AUX YEUX D'OR

In 1900 the New York publishing house of P. F. Collier brought out a work titled *Honoré de Balzac in Twenty-Five Volumes: The First Complete Translation into English,* which was a reprint of the edition prepared by George Saintsbury and first published in England in 1895. When, however, in the "complete" Collier edition one reaches page seven of volume twelve, one finds a note from the editor that states: "In its original form the 'Histoire des Treize' consists—or rather, it was originally built up—of three stories: 'Ferragus' or 'the Rue Soly,' 'La Duchesse de Langeais' or 'Ne touchez-pas a la hache,' and 'La Fille aux Yeux d'Or.' The last, in some respects one of Balzac's most brilliant effects, does not appear here, as it contains things that are inconvenient."[65] So much for the completeness of the edition. Indeed, *La Fille aux yeux d'or* itself seems to foreshadow this reticence on the part of what the French call the Anglo-Saxon world. The protagonist of the story, Henri de Marsay, is the illegitimate son of a certain Lord Dudley, of wide-ranging sexual proclivities. The story tells us that in 1816 Lord Dudley "came to seek refuge in Paris in order to escape legal proceedings in England, where, of all things Oriental, only merchandise is protected" (5:1058, 331).[66] Just in case that reference is not clear, the narrator continues by recording Lord Dudley's reaction on catching sight of his son, whom he has apparently never before seen, and on whose extraordinary beauty (at twenty-two going on twenty-three, he barely looks seventeen and is as handsome as a spring morning) the narrator had just been expatiating: "On hearing his name, he said, 'Oh! He's my son! How unfortunate!'" (5:1058, 331).[67]

The prudery that gives rise to the legal situation from which Lord Dudley flees—the prudery testified to by the first "complete" English translation—is also inscribed in the novel in interesting ways. When Henri de Marsay receives a morning visit from his friend Paul de Manerville, who asks him to lunch, Henri in turn asks if Paul will be shocked if he gets ready to go out in front of Paul. (His toilet is going to take two and a half hours.) Paul says he will not be shocked, and Henri expresses ironic relief: "We are taking on so many English things at the moment that we are in danger of becoming as hypocritical and prudish as they are [Nous prenons tant de choses des Anglais en ce moment que nous pourrions devenir hypocrites et prudes comme eux]" (5:1071, 347). Yet, Paul *is* shocked by watching Henri and his servant in the elaborate process of getting Henri dressed. As we have seen, this same duo of Paul de Manerville and Henri de Marsay had also been used by Balzac in *Le Contrat de mariage,* published the same year. They made the same contrast there as here: Henri's well-maintained aristocratic dandyism contrasts with Paul's slow slide into bourgeois subjectivity. The contrast between these two ways of being—indeed, two ways of perceiving—structures the story in more profound ways as well.

La Fille aux yeux d'or opens with a prologue that apparently has little to do with the plot that follows. The prologue is one example of the endless pop-sociological descriptions of Paris popular at the time. It had been published separately elsewhere by Balzac before being roped into service for this story.[68] One of its functions is to construct the image of a reader objectively different from all of the Parisian types described in the preface and, in particular, from those images described in several passages at the prologue's end, as the presentation of Henri de Marsay and his family approaches:

> Is not seeking after pleasure a sure way of finding boredom? Society people have warped natures from an early age. Having nothing to do but to invent ways of enjoying themselves, they have been quick to misuse their senses, as the working man misuses alcohol. Pleasure is like certain medicaments: in order to keep on obtaining the same effects one has to double the doses, and death or besottedness is contained in the last one. (5:1050, 323)

> One finds, in the feminine world, happy little colonies which live after the Oriental mode and are able to preserve their beauty; but these women are rarely seen out in the streets on foot. They lie hidden, like rare plants which only unfold their petals at certain times of day and really are exotic exceptions. (5:1053, 326)

> In Paris, in high aristocratic circles, may sometimes be seen, here and there, a few ravishing young faces, the fruits of educations and mores that are quite exceptional. (5:1053, 326)

As the narrator strives to tie the almost hackneyed, stereotypical "analysis" of Paris with which the tale opens to the plot of the story he has to tell, he does so by referencing what we might think of as a tabloid-level set of prejudices about the perverse sexual mores of the aristocracy. It is as if he invites us to become prudish (English or American?) in order to relish the shock to our bourgeois sensibilities that may be coming, to be ready to feel outraged at the queer spectacle that is to follow.

On the other hand, or perhaps at the same time, the narrator assumes that the reader is savvy enough to figure out the ending of the story long before it happens, and so to take a different form of (French?) pleasure in watching the sophisticated Henri de Marsay be a dupe where the reader is not. Shortly after introducing the stunning de Marsay and his profligate father, the narrator comments:

> To make this story comprehensible, we must at this point add that Lord Dudley not unnaturally found many women ready enough to strike a few copies of so delightful a portrait. His second masterpiece of this kind was a girl called Euphémie, the daughter of a Spanish lady, brought up in Havana, conveyed back to Madrid with a young creole girl from the Antilles, both of them burdened with the ruinous tastes customary in the colonies. But she was luckily married to an old and phenomenally rich Spanish hidalgo, Don Hijos, Marquis of San-Real. . . . As much out of unconcern as through respect for youthful innocence, Lord Dudley gave his children no information about the relationships he was creating for them here, there and everywhere. Such situations are one of the inconveniences in civilization, though the latter has so many advantages that we must shut our eyes to its defects in view of the benefits it brings. (5:1057–58, 331)

The hint the narrator gives is hardly subtle: Henri has a half-sister, Euphémie. They don't know of each other's existence, and their ignorance will be important in the story. The sentences that follow the passage cited show Lord Dudley entranced by the gorgeous vision of his son, and disappointed, on learning of their rather close family relation, to feel obliged to remove him from consideration as a sexual object. Watch out! The incest train is coming.

A few pages later, Henri forms an attraction to a beautiful and mysterious girl with golden eyes who is walking in the Tuilerie gardens. He recounts his meeting with her to Paul de Manerville, as follows: "I found myself face to face with a woman . . . who, if she refrained from throwing her arms round my neck, did so . . . through one of those paralysing shocks which robs your arms and legs of movement" (5:1063, 337). Paul de Manerville, on hearing the girl described, tells Henri that everyone calls her "the girl with golden eyes," and that she has been seen in the garden previously with another young woman, more beautiful than she, whom Paul begins to describe before exclaiming, "Why now, upon my word, she takes after you!" (5:1064, 338).

On making inquiries as to where the girl lives, Henri finds that she lives in a palace belonging to Don Hijos, marquis de San-Réal (5:1067,

343). When Henri finally, fifteen or twenty pages later, makes it into the girl's presence, she comments to herself, "He has the same voice!" (5:1083, 361). Even before publishing the story, Balzac had, as a postface to *La Duchesse de Langeais,* announced that the story that was on its way would deal with "a terrible passion, one which our literature has never dared face up to [une passion terrible, devant laquelle a reculé notre littérature]" (5:1038). That sentence was published in 1834, which makes it in fact a bit inexact. George Sand's *Lélia* was published in 1833, and it included a character named Pulchérie whose same-sex interests were clear, and whose relation with her sister Lélia was affectively very charged.[69] (Balzac had been friends with Sand in the early 1830s, but in 1833–34 had little to do with her after she broke up with Jules Sandeau, with whom Balzac sided; indeed, Sandeau would move in with Balzac for about a year in late 1834. Balzac says nasty things about *Lélia* and Sand in a letter to Madame Hanska in October 1834, wondering why a woman with children would have been interested in characters who are *inféconds.*)[70]

Lélia successfully provoked outrage among critics. Leyla Ezdinli points to the reaction of a certain Alphonse du Valconseil, who expresses particular outrage at the enthusiasm with which Pulchérie "lost her innocence among the infamies of Sodom complicated by incest [perdit son innocence dans les infamies de Sodome compliquée d'incestes]."[71] Ezdinli also cites an article that appeared in *Le Figaro* on August 24, 1833, titled "Il ou Elle: Énigme" ("He or She: Enigma") that, without explicitly mentioning Sand, made clear what a stir she was making in literary circles: "They say that *she* writes books and that *he* smokes, that *she* left her husband and that *he* (this woman) drinks rum and punch; they maintain that she shaves. She requires her male lovers to call her/him sir and her female lovers, in the midst of the sweetest hugging and kissing, to call her/him miss [On dit qu'*elle* écrit des livres et qu'*il* fume, qu'*elle* a quitté son mari et qu'*il* (cette femme) boit du rhum et du punch; on assure qu'elle se rase. Elle exige que ses amants l'appellent monsieur, et que ses amantes, dans les plus doux embrassements, l'appellent mademoiselle]."

Any informed literary reader in Paris in the mid-1830s would thus have found nothing particularly enigmatic about *La Fille aux yeux d'or,* unless they willfully cast themselves in the role of the bourgeois prude feigning ignorance as to the existence of same-sex relations between women or between men. The story seems to be structured to allow readers to be perfectly "in the know" while they simultaneously try out what it would feel like to be surprised and shocked by the denouement. This particular situation—knowing while pretending not to know in order to see what kind of sensation might arise from that pretense—perhaps encapsulates a certain specific historical confrontation, the clash of several cultures, each with different epistemologies.

If there were not necessarily anything enigmatic about the story in the 1830s, it is not clear why there should be anything particularly enigmatic about the story for anyone who reads it carefully today. It is therefore somewhat surprising to find it so often read precisely as an enigmatic text. Shoshana Felman, for instance, writes:

> I remember that the textual ambiguity I was attempting to decipher was entirely baffling and astonishing to me: it took me time and labor even to understand it literally, to figure out that what the text was so elliptically narrating was the story of a triangular affair, of a woman loving both a woman and a man, and that the story's ambiguities derived, primarily, from the confusion, the misreadings, the mistakes made by (experienced by) a man (a suitor) in his difficulty—and indeed his impossibility—of grasping the situation from his male perspective: a predominant, stereotypical perspective that puts men (himself included) at the center of women's lives and that cannot conceive of femininity except as subordinate to man (himself, or else a rival who must surely in turn be male) as its only center. The protagonist, Henri, thus fails to guess that his rival is in fact a woman, and tragic consequences ensue. Henri is deluded, and his reading of the sexes and of sexual difference is ironically demystified and subverted by the text. But are we not all, in fact, the cultural progeny—and cultural hostages—of this perspective? This is why it was a text so hard to read in the beginning: its interpretation had to go against the grain of universal sexual error.[72]

La Fille aux yeux d'or is filled with patriarchal discourse, misogyny, exoticizing discourse, racism, and brutal violence against women, and readings such as Felman's that critique this aspect of the story are much to the point.[73] Yet her claims about the "universal sexual error" that the story enacts in order to subvert seem hard to credit.

First, we might note that while Henri is more of a dupe than any reader of the story need be, he is not as thick-headed as Felman claims. He does figure out, slowly, that Paquita, the girl with the golden eyes, is having an affair with a woman for whom he is only a substitute, and this even before, in the midst of passionate lovemaking with him, she "lifts him vigorously into the air" and cries out "Oh! Mariquita!" (5:1102, 384). The first time he had slept with her, he had noted that she was "virgin," but "by no means innocent" (5:1091, 370).[74] The narrator admits that Henri is sometimes so attached to life in the present that it takes him a while to put two and two together, but notes that after having reflected on his first night of lovemaking he does add things up:

> At that moment then, de Marsay perceived that he had been deceived by the girl with the golden eyes, for now he could see the past night in perspective, beginning as it had done with a trickle of pleasures which in the end had swollen into a torrent of voluptuousness. By now he was able to read that page, so brilliant in its effects, and divine its hidden meaning. Paquita's purely physical innocence, the amazing quality of her joy, the few words, at first obscure but now clear, which had escaped her in the midst of that joy, everything showed him that he had posed for another person. Since no form of social corruption was a closed book to him, since he professed perfect indifference with regard to all kinds of moral deviation and believed them to be justified by the mere fact that they were capable of being satisfied, he took no umbrage at vice, being as familiar with it as one is with a friend; but he smarted at the thought of having provided it with sustenance.
>
> [En ce moment donc, de Marsay s'aperçut qu'il avait été joué par la *Fille aux yeux d'or,* en voyant dans son ensemble cette nuit dont les plaisirs n'avaient que graduellement ruisselé pour finir par s'épancher à torrents. Il put alors lire dans cette page si brillante d'effet, en deviner le sens caché. L'innocence purement physique de Paquita, l'étonnement de sa joie, quelques mots d'abord obscurs et maintenant clairs, échappés au milieu de la joie, tout lui prouva qu'il avait posé pour une autre personne. Comme aucune des corruptions sociales ne lui était inconnue, qu'il professait au sujet de tous les caprices une parfaite indifférence, et les croyait justifiés par cela

> même qu'ils se pouvaient satisfaire, il ne s'effaroucha pas du vice, il le connaissait comme on connaît un ami, mais il fut blessé de lui avoir servi de pâture.] (5:1096, 377)

The text is a little roundabout, but not that hard to decipher. Henri understands that Paquita has been given to the "vice" of same-sex love-making, and that his sexual penetration of her was the first time she had ever been penetrated. *Une autre personne* (another person) is thus precisely *une autre* (some woman). He is not bothered by the vice. He is bothered by the fact that he has been used as a stand-in for a woman. (Paquita actually dressed him up as a woman before taking him to bed, which didn't seem to bother him while it was going on.) He returns to her palace a few nights later, in fact, in order to see if he cannot somehow make love to her so passionately that she can no longer mistake him for anything but a man. He imagines himself to be doing precisely this at the moment she cries out "Mariquita," cruelly dashing his hopes, arousing his masculinist ire once and for all, and causing him to begin laying plans to return once more to kill her. When he arrives to kill her, and hears the noises of someone else already doing so, he assumes that the person is the marquise herself.

Henri is thus *not* a dupe regarding same-sex relations between women. He seems perfectly familiar with them—as would have been any number of readers in the 1830s. What he does not know is that the woman who is his rival is also his half-sister. But the attentive reader is aware of this before the plot is even underway, and thus should be waiting with little surprise for the final scene, in which Henri returns to kill Paquita, only to discover that his rival has beat him to it. Discovering that Paquita is no longer a virgin ("For the blood you have given over to him, you owe me every drop of yours! [Pour le sang que tu lui as donné, tu me dois tout le tien!]" [5:1107, 389]), Euphémie has stabbed her to death. The reader may not be surprised by the revelation, but certainly she or he may have eagerly been awaiting the tabloid conflagration that these decadent, perverted aristocrats were heading for.

Felman universalizes the final meeting between Henri and Euphémie into a lesson about the loss of the paternal function in post-Revolutionary French society. She does this based on the identical sentence uttered by the two half-siblings as they apprehend the full significance of the other's presence: "Is not Lord Dudley your father? [Lord Dudley doit être votre père?]" (5:1108, 390). Felman writes:

> The return of the lost *name of the father* in the dénouement therefore strips Henri of his (adoptive) proper name, de Marsay, leaving him, indeed, with *no name* that he can claim to be *his own,* that he can claim to be his *proper* name. The cultural procedure of name giving as insuring representative authority is no longer valid in the story: the (male) authority of name givers, customarily father and husband, is here disrupted: the father is no longer truly and legitimately *represented* by the son, in much the same way as the masculine is no longer truly and legitimately represented by the feminine.[75]

This is well and good, although one might want to substitute "always already not" for both of the occurrences of "no longer" in the citation, for the artifice of the social construction of paternity is, for Balzac, a historical constant, not a modern novelty. Yet I think there is something that may be a bit flat-footedly obvious about the meeting between murderous half-brother and half-sister that risks being forgotten via this sophisticated attention to the father's name. Both Henri and Euphémie immediately think of "blood" when they see each other. "She remained true to the blood [Elle était fidèle au sang]," Henri states. Euphémie replies, "She was as free of guilt as it is possible to be [Elle était aussi peu coupable qu'il est possible]" (5:1108, 390). Paquita's faithfulness to the bloodline compensates for her falling away from same-sex fidelity to the sister and for her implicit attack on the masculinity of the brother. That is, faithfulness to the bloodline here trumps anything we might think of as possessiveness regarding sexual identity.

Balzac may well have both a historical and an epistemological point to make. Regarding the historical point, it seems similar to the one Proust's narrator makes in *La Prisonnière* when the bourgeois Verdurins try to shame Charlus in front of his aristocratic friends for his sexual relations with the plebeian Morel. As Proust's narrator puts it, etiquette trumps scruples. There is a possible place for and a possible way of recognizing and assimilating same-sex practices within the aristocratic ethos, especially when the family (with its "identité pleinement consciente") is threatened from the outside. The bourgeois system for understanding sexuality (the one that Felman seems unwittingly to universalize) is not the only one at people's disposal. It is only slowly coming into being.

The epistemological point in *La Fille aux yeux d'or* has something to do with the rapidity with which brother and sister assimilate into something unremarkable the various sexual histories that meet in their confrontation. There is no surprise or self-consciousness or shame expressed about anything that anyone else might construe as a "vice," nor is there any narrative punishment meted out to either of them—they even get away with murder. In this regard, the tabloid sensibilities of one segment of the reading public might be less than satisfied. We might say of Henri and Euphémie (as of the story itself) that they are not fully heterosexualized. And this is the paradox of the story, as well as the paradox of the way it is read by someone like Felman: it is possible for some to be surprised at what is not surprising in the story; it is possible for some to be ignorant of what is not ignored in the story; different ways of knowing and not knowing the world and its sexual relations seem able to coexist without noticing each other. Here history and epistemology perhaps meet, for it will be the work of the rest of the nineteenth century to produce the surprise that Balzac's story does not fully offer—a surprise we have perhaps most clearly seen in the reaction of Heppenstall to the Balzac novel he translates, but a surprise that Felman claims to experience as well. Yet the *lack* of surprise of someone like Henri, who "ne s'effaroucha pas du vice, il le connaissait comme on connaît un ami [took no umbrage at vice, being as familiar with it as one is with a friend"] (5:1096, 377), if it was present in 1815 when the action of the story is set and was available to the story's readers in the 1830s, would surely be worth recovering for today.[76]

CHAPTER THREE

Balzac's Queer Cousins and Their Friends

The family misfit looms as a palpable presence in many nineteenth-century novels, including Balzac's final pair, *La Cousine Bette* (1846) and *Le Cousin Pons* (1847).[1] A number of recent readings of nineteenth-century novels caution us against celebrating too easily our own rediscovery of these queer misfits. Consider, for instance, the cogent central argument of Roddey Reid's *Families in Jeopardy: Regulating the Social Body in France, 1750–1910*. Reid writes: "I want to argue that the repeated occurrence of orphans, hysterics, masturbators, and other familial outcasts in familial discourse operates not so much as the return of the repressed in dominant discourse as the promotion of a sociopolitical agenda through the relentless tactic of inventing and defining sexual-social deviance, or, put another way, through the introduction into the social body of *a mobilizing perception of the lack* of normative familial and sexual relations."[2] Reid's argument follows from Foucault's observations in *The History of Sexuality, Volume 1*, on the modern European creation of a discourse on sexuality. "A censorship of sex?" Foucault scoffs. "There was installed rather an apparatus for producing an ever greater quantity of discourse about sex." A sentence earlier, he comments: "Discourse was connected to sex by a complex organization with varying effects, by a deployment that cannot be adequately explained merely by referring it to a law of prohibition."[3]

Foucault's argument is that this proliferating discourse on sexuality was linked to a disciplinary regime of power that was also proliferating:

> This form of power demanded constant, attentive, and curious presences for its exercise; it presupposed proximities; it proceeded through examination and insistent observation; it required an exchange of discourses, through questions that extorted admissions, and confidences that went beyond the questions that were asked. . . . The medicalization of the sexually peculiar was both the effect and the instrument of this. . . . And conversely, since sexuality was a medical and medicalizable object, one had to try and detect it—as a lesion, a dysfunction, or a symptom—in the depths of the organism, or on the surface of the skin, or among all the signs of behavior. The power which thus took charge of sexuality set about contacting bodies, caressing them with its eyes, intensifying areas, electrifying surfaces, dramatizing troubled moments.[4]

When, in Balzac's *Le Cousin Pons* and *La Cousine Bette,* the sexually dubious bodies of Bette or Pons are subject to scrutiny, it sometimes seems as if they were being caressed by those very disciplinary eyes of which Foucault speaks, being detailed in all their lack of normativity by a gaze whose goal is to assert the privilege of normativity by savoring its absence.

Faced with this gaze, part of Reid's project in *Families in Jeopardy* is to watch it function, to write its genealogy, in particular in relation to prose fiction: "Prose fiction had a particularly powerful role to play as a social actor in constructing a discourse that rewrote the social body and cast social relations of postrevolutionary France into a language of family and sexuality."[5] Reid's procedure continues those readings of the nineteenth-century novel that have worked to understand the place of the institution of literature in the elaboration of disciplinary structures. Notable among these is D. A. Miller's landmark *The Novel and the Police,* a book whose arguments also might encourage some hesitation about leaping to a discovery of the queerness all around us in the nineteenth century. In one concise formulation, Miller writes: "Insistently, the novel shows disciplinary power to inhere in the very resistance to it. At the macroscopic level, the demonstration is carried in the attempt of the protagonist to break away from the social control that thereby reclaims him. At the microscopic level, it is carried in the trifling detail that is suddenly invested with immense significance. Based on an egregious disproportion between its assumed banality and the weight of revelation it comes to bear, the 'significant trifle' is typically meant to surprise, even frighten."[6] Both of these levels, as we shall see, incontestably operate in Balzac's *Cousin* novels. On the microscopic level, for instance, we receive through these novels a training in the details that mark a person as odd. Such a training cannot simply demonstrate a preexisting oddity; it produces the oddity in all its particular consequentiality.

Miller has an even more pointed warning for the overly eager critic:

> It has become easy to show how the various decorums that determine a work of literature, from within as well as from without, are exceeded by the disseminal operations of language, narrative, or desire—so easy that the demonstration now proceeds as predictably as any other ritual. Whenever a text makes confident claims to cognition, these will soon be rendered undecidable, and whatever ideological projects it advances will in the course of their elaboration be disrupted. . . . So common have arguments along these lines become that, even if it were true that literature exercises a destabilizing function in our culture, the current consensus that it does so does not. Yet the point of remarking what one might call . . . the "subversion hypothesis" of recent literary studies cannot be to dispute the evidence of such subversion, which may well be literature's most definitive, powerful, and seductive effect. It is rather a matter of seeing how this effect tends to function within the overbearing cultural "mythologies" that will already have appropriated it.[7]

Miller's critique of what he calls the "subversion hypothesis" clearly references Foucault's critique of what he calls the "repressive hypothesis," the idea that power is exercised over sexuality in order to narrow its possible modes and moments of expression. In another passage from *The History of Sexuality, Volume 1,* Foucault writes:

> Nineteenth-century "bourgeois" society—and it is doubtless still with us—was a society of blatant and fragmented perversion. . . . Not because, having tried to erect too rigid or too general a barrier against sexuality, society succeeded only in giving rise to a whole

> perverse outbreak and a long pathology of the sexual instinct. At issue, rather, is the type of power it brought to bear on the body and on sex. In point of fact, this power had neither the form of the law, nor the effects of the taboo. On the contrary, it acted by multiplication of singular sexualities. It did not set boundaries for sexuality; it extended the various forms of sexuality, pursuing them according to lines of indefinite penetration. . . . It produced and determined the sexual mosaic.[8]

For critics such as Miller or Reid, literature is understood to be one of those "lines of penetration" by which a discourse of sexuality took hold of peoples' lives and by which "sexuality" both took on meaning and commanded attention, justified its claim to telling the truth about our existence. Of one of Balzac's novels, Reid writes "*Les Paysans*'s realist narratives inculcate a desire for the normative family."[9] And Balzac's novels have often been offered as an example of the genre at its most disciplinary. As Miller comments: "Balzac's fiction characteristically inspires a sense that the world is thoroughly traversed by techniques of power to which everything, anything gives hold. This world is not so much totally intelligible as it is totally suspicious." At another point, Miller writes:

> The novel's critical relation to society, much advertised in the novel and its literary criticism, masks the extent to which modern social organization has made even "scandal" a systematic function of its routine self-maintenance. From this perspective, the enterprise of the traditional novel would no longer (or not just) be the doomed attempt to produce a stable subject in a stable world, but would instead (or in addition) be the more successful task of forming—by means of that very "failure"—a subject habituated to psychic displacements, evacuations, reinvestments, in a social order whose totalizing power circulates all the more easily for being pulverized.[10]

Balzac's novels portray a world saturated in disciplines of enforced legibility and social control, and they participate in the project of helping us become subjects who accept the world as such. Or do they? Do those two projects—portraying and analyzing a world on the one hand, and helping suture us to it on the other—fit together without some necessary friction? Before turning to a reading of Balzac's two *Cousin* novels, I would like to tease out a bit a response to this question, implicitly querying the sense Miller and Reid sometimes convey of a successful, totalizing, and coherent project of hegemonic power that would itself entirely encompass the effects of a novel by someone like Balzac. I would like to ask what it might mean to be intrigued by, to identify with, and to pursue an identification with the representation of a family misfit, and to do this by means of a look at some of Foucault's own archival work. I would like, then, to think a bit more about what it means to consider Balzac as a critical analyst, as a kind of protosociologist, investigating the conflicting social forms of the world that is evolving around him.

FOUCAULT IN THE ARCHIVES

What might we make of Foucault's own practice as a historian and archivist, a practice in which he never assumed that the form of power he was investigating was totalizing; a practice in which his interest was clearly directed toward those moments when what might be revealed would rather be the potential failure of its totalization, as well as the failure of its hold on any given person at any particular moment? In another remark about the "repressive hypothesis" from *The History of Sexuality, Volume 1,* Foucault observes that the hypothesis is double-edged. It is not only a misunderstanding of power to imagine that one can simply liberate oneself from it; it is also a misunderstanding of power—a parallel one—to imagine oneself unable to escape it. Foucault critiques analyses of power that "[lead] to two contrary results: either to the promise of a 'liberation,' if power is seen as having only an external hold on desire, or, if it is constitutive of desire itself, to the affirmation: you are always-already trapped."[11] What are you, if you are not always-already trapped? What is the alternative to imagining power as constitutive of desire itself? I want to consider here several of Foucault's prefaces: the preface to *I, Pierre Rivière, having slaughtered my mother, my sister and my brother . . . ;* the preface to *Herculine Barbin;* and a text titled "The Life of Infamous Men," which was to serve as the preface to an anthology (which never materialized) of extracts from the archives of the Hôpital général de la Bastille.[12]

I am interested in dwelling on these prefaces in part because of the complexities they reveal—within the genre of a preface presenting historical documents—in the act of the rediscovery and representation of those documents. That is, the prefaces consistently mark the texts they would present as resistant in two ways: their representation is an effort at resistance at the moment of that representation (now), and they are *evidence* of resistance at an earlier moment (then). Foucault often uses poetic language to characterize this play between two moments. Consider his description of the series "Parallel Lives" ("Les Vies parallèles"), in which Foucault published the modern edition of the memoirs of Herculine Barbin:

> The Ancients liked to display lives of famous men in parallel fashion. One could hear these exemplary shades converse across centuries.
>
> Parallel lines, I know, meet at infinity. Let us imagine others, which would always diverge. No meeting point nor any place for them to be collected. Often their only echo is that of their condemnation. We would have to grasp them in the force of the movement that separates them; we would have to rediscover the dazzling, momentary wake left behind as they rushed into an obscurity from which "nothing more is heard," and where all "fame" is lost. This would be the opposite side of the coin from Plutarch: lives so parallel that no one could join them.[13]

Their wake is of their moment. We grasp it in ours—as best we can, since, in their queer parallelness, they remain beyond our grasp. As one might expect, then, the prefaces I want to look at here contain both analysis and hostility to analysis; they represent and try to grasp something of these documents, even as they imagine the documents as importantly ungraspable. The prefaces implicitly or explicitly reflect on the nature of the relation between different moments, and the varied possibilities revealed when moments are brought into confrontation.

In the preface to *I, Pierre Rivière,* for example, Foucault hesitatingly asserts that the case of this murderer and all the texts that surround it are exemplary in *not* being exemplary: "In their totality and their variety they form neither a composite work nor an exemplary text, but rather a strange contest, a confrontation, a power relation, a battle among discourses and through discourses. . . . I think the reason we decided to publish these documents was to draw a map, so to speak, of those combats, to reconstruct these confrontations and battles, to rediscover the interaction of those discourses as weapons of attack and defense in the relations of power and knowledge."[14] The belief being expressed here would appear to be that these documents, in their simple republication, could create the space in which (now) some kind of discursive analysis could happen. On the other hand, no interpretation is to be offered: "As to Rivière's discourse, we decided not to interpret it and not to subject it to any psychiatric or psychoanalytic commentary. In the first place because it was what we used as the zero benchmark to gauge the distance between the other discourses and the relations arising among them" (xiii). That is, the nineteenth-century murderer, Pierre Rivière, has already been interpreted (then), and along with his own memoir, Foucault and his team published every text they could find that contributed to the interpretive effort, all the while imagining that Rivière's own words would somehow reveal why so many people needed to subject them to interpretation and would reveal how they somehow resisted or exceeded that interpretive effort.

In the text Foucault wrote to follow the collection of documents (for, after all, eight people, including Foucault, get to comment on the assembled dossier, even if their goal is not to interpret Rivière himself) Foucault asserts: "After nearly 150 years Pierre Rivière's memoir strikes us as a text of singular strangeness. Its beauty alone would still suffice to protect it today [Le mémoire de Pierre Rivière nous revient, après bientôt cent cinquante ans, comme un texte d'une grande étrangeté. Sa beauté seule suffirait encore à le protéger aujourd'hui]."[15] The vocabulary of this particular citation—"strangeness," "beauty," and the "protection" that beauty affords to strangeness—seems initially quite odd. It is the same vocabulary that Foucault uses in "The Life of Infamous Men," where he speaks of "singular lives, transformed into strange poems through who knows what twists of fate [des vies singulières, devenues, par je ne sais quels hasards, d'étranges poèmes]," or when he names one of his principles of selection for these *vies infâmes:* "the shock of these words must give rise to a certain effect of beauty mixed with dread [que du choc de ces mots et de ces vies naisse pour nous encore un certain effet mêlé de beauté et d'effroi]."[16] Of the many qualities that could contribute to this fearful beauty, we might isolate two. The first would be that, as Foucault insists, we know of these lives only because they caught the attention of modern administrative, systematic power as it extended itself. Because they stumbled into that power's path, and caused it to stumble over them, the sudden stark chance of their exposure allows them to be seen (from the perspective of a later moment) precisely in confrontation with power, which is thereby forced to reveal the path of its progress as well:

> But in order for some part of them to reach us, a beam of light had to illuminate them, for a moment at least. A light coming from elsewhere. What snatched them from the darkness in which they could, perhaps should, have remained was the encounter with power; without that collision, it's very unlikely that any word would be there to recall their fleeting trajectory. . . .
>
> We may amuse ourselves, if we wish, by seeing a revenge in this: the chance that enabled these absolutely undistinguished people to emerge from their place amid the dead multitudes, to gesticulate again, to manifest their rage, their affliction, or their invincible determination to err—perhaps it makes up for the bad luck that brought power's lightning bolt down upon them in spite of their modesty and anonymity.[17]

But a second reason for this fearful beauty might be, as in the case of Pierre Rivière, that they constitute a more serious obstacle to the continual penetration of power along its habitual paths into the quotidian lives of anonymous people. Pierre Rivière's writing might have managed somehow to be unassimilable to the various medical, legal, social, and familial discourses of power. It might have attained some degree of illegibility that constituted its beauty and its protection. "We are having a hard time resisting the feeling," Foucault admits, "that it has required a century and a half of accumulated and transformed knowledges to enable us at last if not to understand, at least to read it—and, even so, to read it none too well and to grasp so little of it. How, then, in the course of a preliminary investigation and a court hearing in the 1830s, could such a memoir be taken in by doctors, lawyers and jury, who were supposed to use it to determine the grounds for deciding between madness and death?"[18] Such a passage is useful in noting the complexities of the back-and-forth motion between historical moments that interests Foucault, the mutual implication of two moments. Rivière's exemplarity depends both on his moment and on the moment of representation 150 years later, where his challenging illegibility in his own moment becomes legible in a challenging way within the moment at which Foucault and his team represent these materials.

Thus, when Foucault and his team produce a new "dossier" out of the materials surrounding the Pierre Rivière case, they must understand that "dossier" as importantly different from any similar construction put together at that time. Back then, it would seem, a disciplinary impulse governed the elaboration of the dossier. But now the dossier illustrates the confounding of that very impulse. Foucault hesitates interestingly as to the line linking then to now, in his odd assertion that "we are having a hard time resisting the feeling that it has required a century and a half of accumulated and transformed knowledges to enable us at last if not to understand, at least to read it—and, even so, to read it none too well and to grasp so little of it." It is because knowledge has shifted that a confrontation of Pierre Rivière's moment with our own can now be productive. The sense of a shift between moments seems to enable a relation of productive *contingency* between them; it suggests the possibility of keeping the moments parallel; it suggests an interest in avoiding what we might call a precursive relation between them, where that relation depends on running a particular course from one to the other.[19]

In the final pages of *The History of Sexuality, Volume 1,* Foucault issues a call for a new future, one where what he has been calling the *dispositif de sexualité,* the "apparatus of sexuality" (the various modalities of obsessive concern with sexuality being a particular instance of the expanding forms of administrative power observable in their effects around Pierre Rivière or their effects on those lives preserved in the Bastille's archives), will have lost its hold on our lives: "Moreover, we need to consider the possibility that one day, perhaps, in a different economy of bodies and pleasures, people will no longer quite understand [on ne comprendra plus bien] how the ruses of sexuality, and the power that sustains its apparatus [dispositif], were able to subject us to that austere monarchy of sex, so that we became dedicated to the endless task of forcing its secret, of exacting the truest of confessions from a shadow."[20] In the prefaces that interest me here it is this challenge of finding (and wielding) an exemplum of the way power enters and structures quotidian and, in particular, sexual lives that intrigues me—of finding an exemplum whose encounter with power in certain cases might also expose the way power works and even, through some queer form of illegibility, show the legibility of the discourse through which power is operating to be open to question. That is, a glance at the past might be meant to encourage us to *ne plus bien comprendre,* no longer to understand quite exactly how or why we are what we are, or the necessity of our being so.

In the particular instance of Foucault's preface to the American edition of the memoirs of Herculine Barbin, the difficulty inherent in the balancing act of holding two moments queerly juxtaposed has provoked some discussion. *Herculine Barbin* assembles the memoirs of and various documents concerning a person named at birth (1838) Adélaïde Herculine Barbin, and considered to be "a child of the feminine sex." In 1860, after various petitions and examinations, Barbin succeeded in being declared "of the masculine sex" and named Abel.[21] Barbin spent much of her/his childhood and adolescence in a school for girls. The edition of these documents published in the United States includes an introduction by Foucault not present in the French edition. That introduction helps one to see in these documents an illustration of Foucault's arguments in his *History of Sexuality, Volume 1,* about the precise ways the apparatus [*dispositif*] of sexuality and the older apparatus of alliance (a regulatory system producing certain acceptable forms of sexual union for the perpetuation of families, the transmission of wealth, and the consolidation of social power) came in the nineteenth century to be pinned together, to work in tandem, thereby altering possible relations to one's own body:

> Biological theories of sexuality, juridical conceptions of the individual, forms of administrative control in modern nations, led little by little to rejecting the idea of a mixture of the two sexes in a single body, and consequently to limiting the free choice of indeterminate individuals. Henceforth, everybody was to have one and only one sex. Everybody was to have his or her primary, profound, determined and determining sexual identity; as for the elements of the other sex that might appear, they could only be accidental, superficial, or even quite simply illusory. . . . It was no longer up to the individual to decide which sex he wished to belong to, juridically or socially. Rather, it was up to the expert to say which sex nature had

chosen for him and to which society must consequently ask him to adhere. (viii–ix)

Toward the end of that introduction, Foucault says:

> Alexina [one of the names used by Herculine Barbin] wrote her memoirs about that life once her new identity had been discovered and established. Her "true" and "definitive" identity. But it is clear she did not write them from the point of view of that sex which had at last been brought to light. It is not a man who is speaking, trying to recall his sensations and his life as they were at the time when he was not yet "himself." When Alexina composed her memoirs, she was not far from her suicide; for herself, she was still without a definite sex, but she was deprived of the delights she experienced in not having one, or in not entirely having the same sex as the girls among whom she lived and whom she loved and desired so much. And what she evokes in her past is the happy limbo of a non-identity, which was paradoxically protected by the life of those closed, narrow, and intimate societies where one has the strange happiness, which is at the same time obligatory and forbidden, of being acquainted with only one sex. (xiii)

Foucault brushes over a few complexities in his introduction. How do we account, for instance, for the fact that Alexina/Abel constructs the narrative of her/his life in such a way as to suggest that she/he "herself" asked to be "reclassified," imagining that such a reclassification would help her sort out her life and affective relations? And how do we understand "the happy limbo of a non-identity" that Foucault says Alexina "evokes" in remembering her past? Such a happy non-identity would have an unclear relation to the demand or desire for a specific gendered/sexed body that Foucault seems to suggest descends on her at only a certain moment in her life. Did she live outside of sexuality in that earlier moment? Judith Butler observes, for instance, that "[Foucault] appears to romanticize [Herculine's] world of pleasures as the 'happy limbo of a non-identity,' a world that exceeds the categories of sex and of identity."[22] A bit later Butler concisely states the central difficulty of Foucault's introduction:

> In editing and publishing the journals of Herculine Barbin, Foucault is clearly trying to show how an hermaphroditic or inter-

sexed body implicitly exposes and refutes the regulative strategies of sexual categorization. Because he thinks that "sex" unifies bodily functions and meanings that have no necessary relationship with one another, he predicts that the disappearance of "sex" results in a happy dispersal of these various functions, meanings, organs, somatic and physiological processes as well as in the proliferation of pleasures outside of the framework of intelligibility enforced by univocal sexes within a binary relation. The sexual world in which Herculine resides, according to Foucault, is one in which bodily pleasures do not immediately signify "sex" as their primary cause and ultimate meaning; it is a world, he claims, in which "grins hung about without the cat" (xiii). Indeed, these are pleasures that clearly transcend the regulation imposed upon them, and here we see Foucault's sentimental indulgence in the very emancipatory discourse his analysis in *The History of Sexuality* was meant to displace. (96)

The force of Butler's critique and her subsequent careful reading of Herculine Barbin's own text seem compelling to me. Foucault's archival work clearly means to render visible the "moments" at which power seizes on various individuals, and the introduction to the English translation of *Herculine Barbin* does suggest that that moment comes *in the middle* of Herculine Barbin's life, as if she could have avoided the structuring effects of power up to that moment.

In the French version of Foucault's text on Herculine Barbin (which only became readily available with the 1994 publication of his *Dits et écrits*), the "happy limbo" paragraph is longer than in the American version and is preceded by an entire paragraph omitted in the American text. (The French version was also published in 1980, under the title "Le Vrai Sexe" in the journal *Arcadie.*) Because these passages may not be well known to an English-speaking public, I cite here a few sentences from the paragraph preceding the "happy limbo" one, and then a few sentences from its continuation:

> In the art of directing consciences, the term "discretion" is often used. An odd word that indicates the capacity to perceive distinctions, to discriminate between feelings right down to the smallest movements of the soul. . . . By this same word, however, directors of conscience also understand an aptitude to keep things in balance, to know how not to go too far, to keep quiet about what

> must not be said, to leave in advantageous shadow that which might become dangerous in the light of day. We might say that Alexina was able to live in this chiaroscuro of the regime of "discretion," the regime of convents, boarding houses, of Christian and feminine monosexuality. And then—this is her tragedy—she moved into an entirely different regime of "discretion." That of bureaucracy, justice, and medicine. . . .
>
> And what she evokes in her past is the happy limbo of a non-identity, which was paradoxically protected by the life of those closed, narrow, and intimate societies where one has the strange happiness, which is at the same time obligatory and forbidden, of being acquainted with only one sex. . . . The other sex is not there with its demands of division and identity. . . . [Alexina] was not caught by the formidable desire, known to so many who feel betrayed by their anatomy or imprisoned in their identity, to join the "other sex." She was happy, I believe, within this single-sex world where all her emotions and loves were to be found, to be "other" without ever having to be "the other sex." Neither woman loving other women nor man hidden among women. Alexina was the subject without identity of a great desire for women; and, for these women, was a point of attraction of and for their femininity, without anything ever demanding that they step outside of their entirely feminine world.[23]

Butler states that "Foucault appears to think that the journals provide insight into precisely that unregulated field of pleasures prior to the imposition of the law of univocal sex."[24] Yet, taking into consideration the full version of Foucault's text, it might be possible to see him claiming not that the convent school is an *unregulated* field of pleasure *prior* to the law's imposition, but that it is a field regulated differently, and into which the power that produces sexuality penetrates by different paths, producing different effects. Butler suggests not that Herculine is "outside" sexuality, but that "Herculine's sexuality constitutes a set of gender transgressions which challenge the very distinction between heterosexual and lesbian erotic exchange, underscoring the points of their ambiguous convergence and redistribution" (101). This seems, in fact, rather like what Foucault is trying to describe when he writes: "Neither woman loving other women nor man hidden among women. Alexina was the subject without identity of a great desire for women; and, for these women, was a point of attraction of and for their femininity, without anything ever demanding that they step outside of their entirely feminine world." Two moments in Herculine's life seem to participate in two different social dispensations, in which different forms for sexual relations pertain. The juxtaposition of the two moments reveals the contingency of each.

Part of an explanation for Foucault's interest in the image of Herculine's different sexuality in the slightly protected place of the convent school surely also lies in the image he uses of the chiaroscuro that reigned there, enabling one to "leave in advantageous shadow that which might become dangerous in the light of day." That image resonates with his observation in "The Life of Infamous Men" that the lives he would present there also might have remained in darkness: "In order for some part of them to reach us, a beam of light had to illuminate them, for a moment at least. A light coming from elsewhere. What snatched them from the darkness in which they could, perhaps should, have remained was the encounter with power."[25] The paradoxical force of Foucault's imagery is clear: given the power being represented by a beam of light searching out figures in the anonymous darkness, it might be preferable to remain in the dark. But instead we find ourselves trying to shed light on places where light has already done its worst. Modern literature, Foucault further suggests (he seems to mean the modern novel in the West, and this is the hypothesis Miller is testing out in his book) is a powerful flashlight: "A kind of injunction to ferret out the most nocturnal and the most quotidian elements of existence . . . would mark out the course that literature would follow from the seventeenth century onward, from the time it began to be literature in the modern sense of the word. . . . Hence, literature belongs to the great system of constraint by which the West obliged the quotidian to enter into discourse" (173–74). But precisely because literature forces secrets into discourse, it has a paradoxical potential to do the very kind of work Foucault imagines himself doing in collecting lives of the "infamous": "Lives that are as though they hadn't been, that survive only from the clash with a power that wished only to annihilate them or at least to obliterate them, lives that come back to us only through the effect of multiple accidents—these are the infamies that I wanted to assemble here" (163). As it turns out, "more than any other form of language, [literature] remains the discourse of 'infamy': it has the duty of saying what is most resistant to being said—the worst, the most secret, the most insufferable, the shameless" (174). Having thus started out "The Life of Infamous Men" insisting that, as far as the stories that will be included, "the persons included must have actually existed" (159), Foucault concludes about the texts that are to follow: "Neither 'quasi-' nor 'subliterature,' they are not even the first sketch of a genre; they are the action, in disorder, noise, and pain, of power on lives, and the discourse that comes of it. *Manon Lescaut* tells one of the stories that are presented here" (174). Having seemingly denied literature a place in his archival inquiry at the outset of "The Life of Infamous Men," he concludes that preface with a literary reference—as if literature might itself have the potential to reveal power trying to take hold of everyday life in some other moment, and thereby produce for a later moment some exemplary evidence of its (power's) contingent dispositions.[26]

The readings I offer of *Le Cousin Pons* and *La Cousine Bette* are situated within a necessarily double vision that draws inspiration from Foucault's example: of nineteenth-century French literature as sometimes functioning within a complicated disciplinary apparatus, and soliciting our participation in that apparatus as well, yet also of that literature as a place of stories of "disorder, noise and pain," the working of "power on lives," on Bette and Pons as figures like Manon, revealed in a light that arbitrarily takes hold of them and crushes them, yet a light that, from our moment need not (need no longer?) seem to be the light of day.

BALZAC AND SOCIAL FACTS AND FORMS

Foucault provides a helpful reminder of, first, the need to appreciate the links between the institutions of literature and the forms of power that were being advanced in nineteenth-century French society and, second, of the ways in which both archival research and careful readings of literary texts can guide us to a sense of the contingency of present-day social forms. I hope that the readings of Balzac that I have given up to this point, as well as the ones that follow, establish that

Balzac was himself keenly aware of the contingency of social forms and that investigating this contingency was a recurrent interest for him.

As I suggested in my preface, Balzac had a sophisticated way of thinking about what Durkheim referred to as social facts. Critics have sometimes suggested that if Balzac had any sociological acumen it was in spite of himself. In writing about *Les Paysans,* for instance, Lukács commented: "Yet, for all his painstaking preparation and careful planning, what Balzac really did in this novel was the exact opposite of what he had set out to do . . . It is precisely this discrepancy between intention and performance, between Balzac the political thinker and Balzac the author of *La Comédie Humaine* that constitutes Balzac's historical greatness."[27] Perhaps Balzac, the sociological thinker, was more critically astute than Lukács is able to admit. Even work such as Miller's and Reid's, at its moments of greatest suspicion, sometimes puts up a barrier between literature and critical thought—as if the work of literature (in its specific authorial intentions or in its effects on its readers) could only be ideological, as opposed, say, to offering tools for sociological analysis. It seems worth allowing someone writing literature (which is, after all, more a disputed category than a coherent concept) other ambitions as well—thus the reason for my efforts throughout this book to notice the way Balzac in his novels always tangles up his sociological project with an ideological one. Reid, for instance, in discussing Fredric Jameson's reformulation (in *The Political Unconscious*) of Lukács' approach to Balzac, writes:

> He [Jameson] proposes that realist novels both decode—demystify—feudal literary and social forms and recode conventions suitable to the new bourgeois world; the novel in this view is a process that transforms the reader's subjective attitude and produces a new kind of objectivity. The realist novel then simultaneously unmasks old ideologies and discourses, explores the world of emergent capitalism, and reconstitutes a new discursively overdetermined "real." Traditional cultural values are shown to be irrelevant and social relations are presumably reduced to their self-interested economic core.[28]

It seems always important to take into account the political or cultural interests that any given act of interaction or communication or representation works to further, the way it shapes perception, the way it asks for participation in a certain reality.[29] Yet if, as Reid along with Lukács and Jameson concede, Balzac traces the disappearance of a given set of social forms, it is not too much of a stretch to imagine that Balzac was himself interested in the generalized notion of the evolution of social forms, an aspect of his thought and his novelistic practice that might temper his apparent allegiance to any given ideological position. Whatever ideological content and ideological efficacy one chooses to ascribe to Balzac's novelistic ambitions and achievements, it also seems worth paying attention to their critical sociological side, to the ways in which Balzac, roughly fifty years ahead of his time, seems to heed Durkheim's call, in *The Rules of Sociological Method,* to treat social facts as things.[30] Without such attention, one will, for instance, have difficulty perceiving the full extent of Balzac's interest in sexuality as a social form.

Part of my project in this chapter and in the interlude preceding it is to call attention to Balzac's analysis of the relations that exist between larger social changes and changes in the social forms that enable sexual interaction, including, in particular, same-sex interactions. As I said in the preface, it is part of Balzac's sociological analysis to inquire into the ways we might understand a set of shared practices coming to constitute a sexuality or a sexual identity, to inquire into the historical and social processes in which and through which such sets of practices, such social forms, become fixed or unfixed, are allowed to operate, or are violently dismissed, and so on. Consensus regarding the social forms enabling same-sex interactions is, Balzac shows, subject to a great deal of local variation.

It is with this kind of sociological and historical vision in mind that we will best be able to see the analysis of sexuality that Balzac undertakes in *Le Cousin Pons* and *La Cousine Bette.* Pons and Bette do not fit into the ways of acting, thinking, and feeling that are predominant in the circles in which they move. They also struggle to engage with alternative social forms of intimacy. They thus find strong acts of coercion directed against them from throughout their social world. In their variance from normative social forms, they serve to reveal something of the historical and cultural specificity of those normative forms.

PONS

One of the strongest field recollections of this writer was his meeting, among the Boróro of central Brazil, of a man about thirty years old: unclean, ill-fed, sad, and lonesome. When asked if the man were seriously ill, the natives' answer came as a shock: what was wrong with him?—nothing at all, he was just a bachelor. And true enough, in a society where labor is systematically shared between man and woman and where only the married status permits the man to benefit from the fruits of woman's work, including delousing, body painting, and hair-plucking as well as vegetable food and cooked food (since the Boróro woman tills the soil and makes pots), a bachelor is really only half a human being.—Claude Lévi-Strauss, "The Family"

"Allons, vous n'aussi, vous n'êtes sans héritiers, n'est-ce pas! Vous n'êtes venus comme des champignons sur cette terre [Go on now, I suppose you'll be telling me you've no heirs either! And that the pair of you just popped up like mushrooms]."—Mme. Cibot, to Schmucke and Pons, in *Le Cousin Pons*

It might seem that *Le Cousin Pons* cries out for psychoanalytic illumination. Sublimation and displacement, what other concepts to use in order to grasp the odd figure of Pons after whom this novel is named? Apparently a celibate bachelor, devoted to his male companion Schmucke, devoted to eating, and devoted to collecting art and bric-à-brac, what else would Pons be but a case of misrouted, detoured sexual energy? It has been for a while now a strong temptation (perhaps more in the United States than in France) to read Balzac through a Freudian lens. I would like to question a bit further here why the Freudian way of reading Balzac has been for some such a strong critical temptation, and what consequences this has had for an understanding of sexuality in his novels. I will ask this question by way of another: How does Balzac himself participate in the construction both of narrative systems and of the kinds of narrative psychologies that attract and confirm what will later be known as Freudian readings? And does he do so fully? In other words, instead of using Freud to read Balzac, how might we read Balzac and Freud (and recent criticism) together as part of a given, bounded historical moment? And what will the limits of that moment be?

The titles of Balzac's *Cousin* novels indicate some of what is at stake. Bachelor and spinster cousins, family misfits and remainders, are construed by Balzac as both productive and destructive social forces, forces parasitic on the family, yet also radically other to it. Analyses of these novels thus almost necessarily involve one in a discourse on what might be called perversion, its simultaneous relation to and refusal of the reproductive function of the family, its perceived utility, its perceived wastefulness, its alternate, queer ways of relating to society. But must an analysis of sexuality in *Le Cousin Pons* lead one inevitably to question the strange nature of Pons's difficultly legible sexuality? Must one parse the nature of his relation to Schmucke? The novel certainly encourages us to try. Psychoanalytic concepts such as sublimation and displacement certainly are temptingly near at hand—positively offered by the text itself—when under the impulse to explain Pons's gastronomy or his mania for collecting:

> *Gourmandise,* a sin to which even virtuous monks are addicted, opened its arms to him: he flung himself into them as he had flung himself into the worship of masterpieces and devotion to music. Fine food and bric-à-brac became for him the currency of women. . . . The digestive process brings all the human forces into play. It is a kind of inner combat which, for those who make a god of their bellies, gives as much enjoyment as sexual intercourse. . . . [Pons's] every ecstasy was centered upon his gastronomic activities. (7:495, 31–32)[31]

And why not notice the novel's further suggestion that Pons's gastronomy and his mania for collecting are possible covers for a latent homosexuality? The novel in fact both lends credence to this reading and yet denies it. Pons and Schmucke are as good as married, we are told, as good as lovers, at the same time that we are told that Pons could never find a woman, was necessarily unhappy in love, not because of his own desires but because he was ugly.

> Pons was a happy man . . . in so far as happiness was possible for a man of feeling and delicacy, whose ugliness debarred him from "success with the fair sex." (7:488, 24)

> In 1835, a lucky chance compensated Pons for the coldness of the fair sex, and gave him something to lean on in his old age. He had been an old man from the cradle, and friendship provided him with

> a prop: he contracted what was for him the only kind of marriage possible in his situation—wedlock with a man, an elderly man, a musician like himself. (7:496, 33)

> They conversed . . . like lovers. (7:498, 35)

> Pons took Schmucke's hand between his own, and the clasp contained a movement that communicated his entire soul. They remained thus for several minutes, like lovers meeting again after a long separation. (7:526, 67)

> "It was not God's will that I should have the life I dreamed of," Pons continued. "How I should have loved to have a wife, children, a family! That was my only ambition: to be cherished by one or two people, in some quiet spot." (7:703, 263)

By both proffering and denying the possibility of Pons's interest in men, the novel might make us question the very choices it offers us. In fact, we might well consider reading the novel as showing how an inquiry into what is not heterosexuality is done in the service of heterosexuality itself. Or perhaps the novel suggests an odd twist on even that important possibility: perhaps the novel *does* sketch out the possibility that there would be parties perfectly interested in Pons and Schmucke being queer, parties whose rather murky motivations might lead us to question this inevitable explanatory recourse to the concept of sexuality itself.

It is by accepting on some level the theoretical priority of a model of family romance as necessary to the construction of sexual subjectivities, I want to suggest, and by accepting perversions as the spin-offs, abjects, misfits of that model that we are led to the question: What is the nature of Pons's sexuality? And we are not the only ones led to such a question. Yet precisely such a question also needs to be considered not as abstract, not as theoretical, but as produced by and producing sets of ideological effects. What can be understood about the kinds of interests that lie behind the question "What is the nature of Pons's sexuality?"—about the impulses that produce that particular line of questioning?

Within the novel itself, for example, the person most notably interested in Pons's sexuality (aside from the narrator) is Madame Cibot.

Her "disinterested" inquiries into his private life are part of her effort to position herself favorably in order to gain access to his inheritance. Of the many things that provoke the crises that bring an end to Pons's life one, of course, is his own foolishness in trying to lend a helping hand to heterosexuality. In a final, disastrous effort to ingratiate himself with his distant cousins, the Camusots, Pons tries to arrange a marriage between his "cousin" Cécile and a rich German, and further offers his rooms as the neutral ground on which the prospective couple might meet. Given that marriage is for Balzac as much an economic transaction as anything else, Pons, failing as a matchmaker, nonetheless thereby begins willy-nilly to participate in an economic world he had hitherto avoided. For Brunner, the German, while in Pons's rooms appreciates the economic value of all the collecting Pons has done, and, although unimpressed with Cécile, nonetheless offers to enter into a transaction with Pons wherein he would buy Pons's collection of paintings. The offer is overheard by a certain Rémonencq, who later passes the information on to Madame Cibot, in order to set her scheming.

As Sharon Marcus puts it: "It is thus Pons' uncharacteristic engagement in the world of heterosexual commerce that proves his downfall as a collector. His attempt to arrange a marriage between his cousin Cécile and Schmucke's rich friend Brunner inadvertently enables Cibot to appropriate his collection, appetite and affections."[32] By entering the inheritance game, Pons opens himself to a scrutiny whose intensity he will be unable to resist. We can extend this point a bit further if we notice the actual exchange that Rémonencq overhears:

> "So you don't see any obstacle?" said Pons.
>
> "I don't know," replied Brunner. "The girl is nothing to get excited about, and the mother's a bit prim. We'll see."
>
> "A fine fortune in prospect," remarked Pons. "More than a million . . ."
>
> "We shall meet on Monday," interjected the millionaire, "and if you would like to sell your collection of pictures, I wouldn't mind giving you five or six hundred thousand francs for them."
>
> "Oh," said the good Pons, surprised to learn how rich he was, "I could never part with the things which bring me happiness. I would only sell my collection for delivery after my death."

"Well, we shall see . . ."

"That sets two transactions going," said the collector; but his mind was on the marriage project. (7:555, 99)

Brunner is already losing whatever interest he may have had in Pons's "cousin" Cécile, but we should notice that, in fact, his proposed deal with Pons is itself an allegory of "heterosexual commerce," if we understand by that a system in which women are used instrumentally to pass family wealth across generations. For Brunner envisions precisely such an instrumental use of "the Pons collection," called by the narrator "the heroine of this story" (7:763, 331). Buying it deliverable after Pons's death is, after all, rather like marrying someone and then waiting around for her father to die so you can collect on the initial investment. And the narrator is careful in any case to inform us at the outset that Pons came back from Rome around 1810 "as an avid collector, laden with pictures, statuettes, frames, wood and ivory carvings, enamels, porcelains, etc. While living in Rome on his Academic scholarships, he had used up the greater part of his paternal heritage either in paying for or in transporting his purchases. Likewise he had squandered [il avait employé] his mother's estate on a journey he made through Italy after his three statutory years in Rome" (7:488, 24). Thus for Brunner and for Balzac the difference in the nature of the transaction involved in marrying Cécile or in buying Pons's paintings seems slight. Both carry wealth across generations; both represent investments for Brunner.

For Pons himself, the difference between marriage and art collecting might seem greater; Pons's love for art seems based on kinds of aesthetic pleasure and connoisseurship not self-evidently linked to the reproduction of wealth. Yet the novel does not allow anyone—not even Pons—to separate aesthetic and economic realms so easily. It portrays him from the outset, for instance, as hypercathected to kinship. Cash poor, even if art rich, Pons, in order to dine well as his stomach requires, is forced to drag his palate around to "family" tables where one can only observe that he had "inordinately extended the meaning of the word 'family'" (7:503, 41). His need for fine food (a need which in itself blends material and aesthetic realms), combined with his bachelor status, dictates a deep concern for family relations, a concern that causes him to come to use and to understand art objects as economic objects. Because Pons dines, and wishes to continue to dine, regularly with Cécile's parents, he uses the value of his collection as economic bait.

Cécile, who is having difficulty finding a husband, is Pons's first cousin twice removed, or, to express the relation another way, Cécile is Pons's father's brother's daughter's son's daughter. Cécile's mother protected her own inheritance by investing it in Parisian real estate, so the family lives in a house the mother bought. Her father is, at the time of the novel, still waiting to inherit from his own father, and is currently cash poor, having spent what cash he had reconstituting an estate in Normandy that has yet to produce notable revenues. Cécile thus has great expectations (from her mother, her father, and her father's father), once she comes into the family's landed wealth. Perceiving Cécile's difficulty—she is not pretty and she is only potentially rich—and realizing, thanks to Brunner's offer, the economic power of his own collection, Pons imagines himself capable of enriching the pool of Cécile's expectations and thereby securing himself once and for all a place in the "family" bosom. He declares, sentimentally "persisting in his kinship," that "my heir is of course my cousin Cécile" (7:559, 103).

A few pages earlier, on the sudden revelation to him of his wealth, Pons had immediately managed to invent an economic strategy to secure his future: he could sell his collection deliverable after his death. And even though the narrator helpfully insists that Pons was really only thinking of one transaction (Cécile's marriage) even as he says to Brunner, "that sets two transactions going" (referring also to a possible deal about the collection), we might take the hint that for Pons there is some confusion between affect and kinship and inheritance that he cannot resolve. For clearly the ideal situation Pons imagines is this: sell the collection to Brunner deliverable after his death, and then have Brunner marry Cécile so that he has the sentimental satisfaction of seeing the collection remain in the "family." The extravagant collection would thus ultimately redeem the "squandering" (the translator's word, not Balzac's) of his own inheritance, bringing it back with interest to the family, and bringing Pons the satisfaction of an additional tidy income from the sale, too! " 'My collection or the price it fetches will always belong to your family, whether I do a deal with our friend Brunner or whether I keep it,' said Pons, as he informed the astonished family that he had such valuable assets" (7:559, 103). Pons thus imagines a perfect superposition of (1) his attachment to his art objects, (2) his desire to be attached affectively to his "kin," and (3) his own economic self-interest. Whatever degree of consciousness we assign to his imagination, it seems necessary to account for the suggestion that on some level he strategizes as regards his economic interests, and that his very emotions form a part, conscious or not, of that strategizing.

Brunner, because he is more interested in art objects than in Cécile, and because he is rich enough not to be tempted by the wealth she will obtain only eventually and is misogynistically inclined against her because she is a spoiled "only" child from a family where a woman rules financially (her mother apparently wears the trousers just as she owns the house the family lives in), takes sadistic pleasure in turning down the marriage, confounding the usual rules and reasons for marriage, as if capable of extricating himself from the kind of strategic superpositions in which Pons finds himself implicated. Financially, it is in principle an advantage that Cécile be an only child. Sentimentally, Brunner claims, it is an insurmountable obstacle. As Brunner explains to Cécile's grandfather:

> But an only daughter is a child whom her parents' indulgence accustoms to doing as she pleases and whose will has never been crossed. What goes on here is the same as in several families in which, some time ago, I was able to take note of the worship that is paid to these heavenly creatures: not only is your grand-daughter the idol of the household, but also Madame la Présidente wears the . . . you know what I mean! Monsieur, I saw my father's home turned into an inferno for this very reason. My stepmother, the cause of all my misfortunes, an only daughter, an object of worship, the most charming of fiancées, became a fiend incarnate. (7:561, 105)

This is an interesting moment in the novel, a moment that allows us to appreciate the function of the novel's earlier digression on Brunner's past life. That earlier digression takes on relevance in juxtaposition to this scene where Brunner explains his reasons for turning down what seems "rationally" like a good match: Brunner is rich but German and had a Jewish mother; Cécile would bring him—despite the social strikes against him created by his nationality and his Jewish mother—legitimacy and access to Parisian circles of power. This immediate gain in status should, in the eyes of Cécile's family and their circle, compensate for the substantial inconvenience of all her eventual assets being tied up for the foreseeable future. Why is Brunner able to refuse the force of the calculation that seems so self-evident to everyone else? The complicated figure of the "stepmother" enters here: a figure of a kind of monkey wrench in the affective/kinship workings of the family. In Brunner's case, his "hyena" (7:534, 76) of a stepmother sufficiently disrupts his desire to participate in normal inheritance strategizing to allow him to pursue purely masculine, amical forms of economic sharing with his friend Wilhem, giving him outright five hundred thousand francs when he comes into his father's estate to make up for what they had dissipated together in their earlier years,[33] and to imagine marrying "a penniless girl from a large family, who has been well brought up but has no money of her own" (7:562, 105)—perhaps less out of allegiance to romantic notions of marriage than out of a considered effort to protect his wealth from any new "hyenas" who might come his way. This might explain why buying art appeals to Brunner more than does using a marriage as a way of accumulating wealth. It seems surer and it cuts women out of the circuit. (Brunner's friendship with Wilhem also echos Pons's with Schmucke: the strong affect of their link seems to exist outside the usual familial channels, and to exist precariously because it occupies this outside position. Such an affective link thus will not be easily "recognized" within familially oriented structures of inheritance and sentiment. It is no accident, then, that Pons will use the pair of friends, Fritz Brunner and Wilhem Schwab, as witnesses to the will through which he ultimately attempts to install Schmucke as his heir. It is also no accident that Pons's attempt does not succeed.)

Let us go even a step further in noting the way various interests in the ultimate disposition of Pons's collection comes to be tied up with shifting distributions of affect and sexuality. For if the discussion of a hypothetical sale between Pons and Brunner, through being overheard, opens the competition for that collection—a competition the description of which forms the latter half of the novel—it is certainly worth noting that not all the scenarios envisioned by the competitors for the collection correspond to heterosexual allegories. Pons wants, in the end, to leave the collection to Schmucke; Madame Cibot brings together a whole gang of dispossessed, economically and legally marginal figures, who want a part in it (Fraisier, Poulain, Rémonencq); the Camusots end up wanting it as well; and finally there is Pons's fake will, to which we will turn in a moment, in which he pretends to leave it to the state. Clearly, Madame Cibot is not interested in Pons's heterosexuality. Indeed, one of the long, irritating interrogations to which she subjects the ailing Pons and his friend Schmucke has precisely as its goals to establish that they have no heterosexual inclination or history, and to ensure that such a possibility disgusts them.

> "Matame Cipot, you're makink him cross," cried Schmucke, noticing that Pons was writhing like a worm under his bedclothes.
>
> "You be quiet too! You're just a couple of old rakes [deux vieux libertins]. You aren't prize beauties, but as the saying goes: 'Ugly as sin, there's still a way in!' . . . You're a nice pair, you are! Come on now, you've had your bit of fun, and the Lord's taking it out of you for leaving your children in the lurch, like Abraham . . ."
>
> "Can't you leave me in peace?" Pons cried out. "I have never known what it is to be loved . . . I've never had any children. I'm alone in the world [Je suis seul sur la terre]."
>
> "Is that Gospel truth?" said the concierge. "You're such a kind man, and women, it's a fact, always fall for kindness; that's what draws them. I'd have sworn that when you were young and hearty . . ."
>
> "Take her away," whispered Pons to Schmucke. "She's driving me mad."
>
> "Anyway, Monsieur Schmucke, he's sure to have some children . . . You're all the same, you old bachelors [Vous n'êtes tous comme ça, vous autres vieux garçons]."
>
> "*I?*" cried Schmucke, springing to his feet. "Nefer haf I . . ."
>
> "Go on now, I suppose you'll be telling me you've no heirs either! And that the pair of you just popped up like mushrooms [Vous n'êtes venus tous deux comme des champignons sur cette terre]." (7:580–81, 126–27)

What is Madame Cibot's strategy here? To annoy by suggesting a participation in a sexuality they find repulsive, or to annoy by reminding them of their regrets? When she suggests they are "vieux garçons," "comme ça," "venus comme des champignons," what is the implication regarding their relation to reproductivity? La Cibot takes Pons's phrase "Je suis seul sur la terre" and transforms it to "Vous n'êtes venus tous deux comme des champignons sur cette terre." Leave aside the suggestive *champignons* and notice merely the *venus*. Pons's statement of a present condition (*Je suis seul*) becomes in la Cibot's version something more ontological (*Vous n'êtes venus comme des champignons sur cette terre*). Such an assertion would in fact be a reassurance *to her* (if not to Pons or Schmucke). For one need not, in fact, find any absolute consistency in her strategy or her innuendo to appreciate what is at stake. She would rather they—in their very being—have no usual relation to reproductivity, for if they do not, then a window of opportunity opens, an avenue of attack on Pons's fortune can be conceived, a dispersal of wealth among the disenfranchised of Paris can be envisioned thanks to a failure of heterosexual inclination.

Does the novel then understand heterosexuality primarily as a means for the preservation and transmission of wealth in an ordered way? And is the threat of queerness in the novel the threat of an unforeseen protocol for the redistribution of wealth? Pons does in the end manage to write a will leaving his wealth to Schmucke, who is, as we discover, unable to hold onto it for long.[34] When Pons's will is challenged Schmucke doesn't know how to play his cards, and he allows himself to be impoverished and insulted to death. "No family allows itself to be despoiled by a foreigner without offering some resistance, and we shall see, Monsieur, whether fraud and corrupt dealing or family claims will prevail!" (7:745, 311), says the crook Fraisier (now acting as the family lawyer) to Schmucke just after Pons's death. Is this despoiling of Schmucke then readable as a final revenge of heterosexuality on a queer attempt to wrest some of society's wealth to its own ends—a revenge that needs to forestall not only the possibility of Pons leaving everything to Schmuck but also the avid greed of figures such as Rémonencq and Madame Cibot, who try to twist queerness to their own ends? In considering such a reading it should not be forgotten that sexuality itself might then be conceived of as a ruse of inheritance structures, part of a template that brings affect, family, and certain channels of inheritance into a certain kind of proximity.

There is another piece to the complex puzzle elaborated in *Le Cousin Pons*. It has to do with the overelaborate pretense of a first will that Pons draws up merely in order to catch Madame Cibot trying to peruse it and thereby establish her treacherous nature. The *exact text* of this first will, not the one finally in effect when Pons dies, is given in the novel, whereas the second one, in which Schmucke actually inherits, is only paraphrased. Why? The first will exists only as a device by which Pons proves to Schmucke that Madame Cibot is untrustworthy. He makes up his true will shortly after Madame Cibot betrays herself. It would be enough plotwise to tell us that the terms of the will were unfavorable to Madame Cibot. To what end, then, does the novel provide us with the full text?

> This is my last will and testament. . . . I have always been impressed by the damage done by certain inconvenient circumstances to the masterpieces of painting, often resulting in their destruction. I have been pained to see beautiful pictures condemned to be for ever moving from country to country and never being housed in one place to which admirers of these masterpieces might travel to see them. I have always thought that the truly immortal productions of the great masters should be national property, perpetually accessible to visitors from every country, just as God's own masterpiece, the light of day, is accessible to all His children. . . .
>
> And therefore, with this intent, I give and bequeath to His Majesty the King, as an accession to the Louvre Museum, the pictures composing my collection, with this charge, that if the bequest be accepted, a life annuity of two thousand four hundred francs be paid to my friend Wilhelm Schmucke. (7:707, 267–68)

Pons has a notary help him draw up this will, and the notary advises him of certain legal facts, specifically concerning which kinds of wills are the surest:

> "Contestation is always possible, Monsieur," said the notary. "That is one of the drawbacks of human justice. But, as regards wills, certain kinds cannot be challenged."
>
> "What kinds?"
>
> "A will made before a notary in the presence of witnesses who can certify that the testator is of sound mind, and provided the testator has neither wife, children, father nor brother."
>
> "I have nothing like that. All my affections are centered on my dear friend Schmucke, whom you see here."

> Schmucke was weeping.
>
> "If then you have only distant collaterals, since the law allows you to dispose freely of your real and personal estate, provided that you do not bequeath them on terms of which public morality disapproves—you must have seen cases of wills disputed because of their eccentricity—a will signed in a notary's presence is unassailable. . . . All the same, a holograph will, if it is clearly and properly drawn up, is also fairly unexceptionable!" (7:697–98, 257)

Pons chooses to write this first ruse of a will "holographically," knowing that to be fairly unassailable. The subsequent will, written after Madame Cibot has fallen into the trap (and Fraisier has managed to steal the first one), is written in the presence of witnesses and a notary. Pons annuls the first will, and, using the notary and his two friendly witnesses, institutes Schmucke as his sole heir in the most "unassailable" way possible.

Of the first will, the notary lets slip to Madame Cibot that it is "a fine will, full of good sense; a public spirited [*patriotique*] testament of which I strongly approve" (7:698, 258). Fraisier, on the other hand, acting as lawyer for Cécile's family understands a will like this to be Pons's most effective arm against his "family," and so, when he gets his hands on the will, he has a rather different reaction: "'Your gentleman is a monster. He's leaving everything to the Museum, the State. We can't go to law against the State! . . . The will is unassailable . . . We are robbed, ruined, despoiled, done for!'" (7:708, 268). This suggestive virtual will, annulled the next day in favor of one that names Schmucke "his sole heir" and presented as merely a feint, seems in fact more interesting than the second. It allows, after all, the state to enter the scene, conceivably as the *protector* of Schmucke. It may not give Schmucke *everything,* but it gives him an unattackable something. It further apparently subtracts, or should we say, sublimates, the Pons inheritance from commerce and into a realm of aesthetic contemplation guaranteed by a "national" museum.[35] Fraisier certainly appreciates its astuteness. In fact, he purloins it, precisely because he could use it to blackmail Cécile's mother (7:711, 273), for whom he is working, because despite what the notary has told Pons it constitutes a surer threat to the family's desire to recuperate Pons's estate than does the second notarized will.

What new analysis would the presence of this first will enable? Why does Balzac redact the full text for us? Pons's disruptiveness seems to me to be understood by the novel as having to do with his radical position in a society based on structures for the transgenerational transmission of wealth. Sexuality is often the effect of reading these structures a certain way. And the novel does in some ways perform this sexualizing reading. Pons is, within the novel, a limit case in a legal sense. He evades all legal restrictions on what to do with his accumulated wealth: no parents, no brothers, no wife, no children. Just a friend. Much of the discourse of the novel, of Madame Cibot, has understood this structural problem as a problem of sexuality. This slip in some ways parallels the conceptual slip from Pons's "Je suis seul sur la terre" to Madame Cibot's "Vous n'êtes venus tous deux comme des champignons sur cette terre." Pons tries to arrive at a bare structural fact of family status through which he escapes sexuality itself. Madame Cibot prefers some metaphor for reproductive forms, some reading of sexuality. Neither, I would argue, succeeds, or should succeed in convincing us of the correctness of their position, or in providing a coherent reading of the novel. This is made clearest in the interference effect of the juxtaposition of the two wills. Pons's call to the sovereign in his first, fantastic, fantasmatic, will, for instance, is an extremely odd one, one that almost admits to a sexual culpability.[36] I will leave you my paintings on the condition that as a by-product my friend get something out of it. And perhaps the unattackable state would accept—sheltering a brief expression of queer friendship in its own "sublimatory" interest as art collector—a kind of high-level inheritance tax on queer couples. (We might also note that the first will might better have assured the modest Schmucke's happiness.) A state might then help out a rich fag here and there, when it is demonstrably in its interest to do so.

Pons is "free" to do what he wants with his goods, the notary tells him, "provided that you do not bequeath them on terms of which public morality disapproves." The second will, despite all its official precautions, would, we know, be challenged by Fraisier and Pons's "relations" on precisely such grounds. They use the threat of such an appeal in their successful effort at the end of the novel to scare Schmucke into accepting their terms. In the first, strategic, will, Pons thus plays the game of sexuality, strategically driving a wedge between family and state interests, conceptualizing his collection within an economy a state will understand, and claiming for his friend some of the scraps of that economy. In the first will Pons and Schmucke rather admit to being two mushrooms the *state* might manage to savor. In this first will, Pons himself, then, finds himself caught up in the tourniquet of the question, "What is the nature of Pons's sexuality?" In his second will, he perhaps imagines himself justly—through legal formalism—escaping that tourniquet, free to declare Schmucke his heir, free to accede to some unbounded act of pure friendship; perhaps he imagines himself acceding to that act by effacing or evading or rendering irrelevant the question of sexuality that the novel has consistently posed him. The novel makes clear, in Schmucke's sad fate, the brutal failure of that evasion.

Yet perhaps, on the other hand, the failure is not absolute. For perhaps the interference of the two wills, the false choice of evading or acknowledging sexuality, of escaping its relation to the economics of inheritance, does open up a different moment—a moment in which we can glimpse something about the contingency of the dilemmas Pons faces. It is an unstable sense of that moment that I have tried to reconstruct here.

BETTE

JERRY DURANCE (Paul Henreid): I don't even know yet whether it's Miss or Mrs.
CHARLOTTE VALE (Bette Davis): It's aunt. Every family has one you know.—*Now, Voyager,* 1942 (dir. Irving Rapper)

Of the relation between Lisbeth Fischer (Cousin Bette) and her friend Valérie Marneffe, the narrator of *La Cousine Bette* tells us:

> Lisbeth and Valérie presented the touching spectacle of one of those friendships so close and so unlikely between women that Parisians, always too clever by half, immediately make it the subject of malicious gossip. The contrast between the masculine stiff temperament of the peasant from Lorraine and Valérie's warm creole indolence helped the calumny along. Madame Marneffe, moreover, had unthinkingly lent weight to the gossiping tales by the trouble she took over her friend's appearance, with an eye to a certain mar-

riage, which was, as we shall see, to complete Lisbeth's vengeance. (7:195, 165)[37]

The narrator here makes a rhetorical move similar to one we have seen in *Le Cousin Pons,* acknowledging the general existence of same-sex sexual relations all the while leaving ambiguous their actual occurrence between specific pairs of characters. This effect can be created (as it is in the passage cited above) by pointing to a generalized social gaze that maliciously assigns a queer identity to various characters.[38] It can also be created, as in the following passages, by using too many different names to characterize a given relationship:

> Lisbeth . . . adored Valérie, moreover; she had made a daughter of her, a friend, her love. She found in her a creole docility, a voluptuary's yielding temper. She chatted with her all morning, with much more pleasure than she had taken in talking to Wenceslas. . . . In this new friendship, Lisbeth had indeed found an outlet for her energy much more rewarding than her foolish love for Wenceslas. (7:200, 170)

> "How lovely you look this morning!" said Lisbeth, coming over to put her arm round Valérie's waist and kiss her forehead. "I share in the enjoyment of all your pleasures, your good fortune, your dresses . . . I didn't know what it was to live until the day when we became sisters." (7:239, 211–12)

Sister, friend, lover, daughter, the proliferation of available categories, along with the palimpsestic considerations (to which we shall return shortly)—this relationship overwrites the previous one with Wenceslas—all suggest that Bette's relation to Valérie falls into no one identifiable modality. By failing to do so, it exercises a certain compulsion on us (or at least on the Parisian public and the Balzacian narrator) to become preoccupied with it.[39]

We can begin to see why Balzac's final two novels, *La Cousine Bette* and *Le Cousin Pons,* are almost necessarily always understood as a pair. Balzac says as much in his dedication to the pair (linked with the omnibus title *Les Parents pauvres* [*Poor Relations*]): "My two stories are therefore placed together as a pair, like twins of different sex" (7:54, 10). The two cousins are thus parallel and yet asymmetrical. Parallel in the near illegibility of their sexualities (which is, it would appear, only meant to spur one on to more furious attempts to render them legible), they are nonetheless not parallel in the way their various illegibilities are constructed.

Just as *Le Cousin Pons* both lends credence to a reading of Pons as homosexual and yet denies it, so *La Cousine Bette* suggests the possibility of lesbianism without confirming it. What is at stake in siding with the malicious Parisian gossip and making Bette a butch lesbian? What is at stake in the narrator's equivocation on the subject? The beginning of an answer to these questions might be found in the remarkable scene in which Bette transfers her affections from the artist Wenceslas to Valérie. But first, a few plot details: Bette is the poor spinster cousin of Adeline Hulot. Adeline began as a simple peasant girl like Bette but caught the eye of Hulot, named baron by Napoleon, and was carried off to a Parisian wonderland, in which Bette eventually joined her. But Hulot, by the time of the novel, has become a fat old lecher who has used up his fortune on mistresses and can no longer afford to support his family in the style to which they are accustomed, much less arrange an appropriate marriage for his daughter Hortense. Hortense realizes this, and by a particular set of Balzacian coincidences she manages to arrange her own marriage with an impoverished but artistically talented Polish count in exile in Paris. She learns of Wenceslas, this talented count, because he lives in the same boardinghouse as Bette, who prefers this kind of slumming to depending on and living with her relations. In the boardinghouse one night Bette smelled smoke, and she single-handedly saved Wenceslas from suicide, thereby becoming his protectress and task-master, and later enabling her to drop hints to Adeline and Hortense about her new "lover." Hortense makes sufficient fun of what she sees as spinster Bette's pretensions to having a lover that Bette finally brings proof one day, in the form of a beautiful silver seal crafted by the talented Polish count. Hortense falls in love with the artist sight unseen, and finds a way to "steal" him from Bette.

Valérie Marneffe (the illegimate child of a grand figure from the Napoleonic period) and her dissolute husband also live in the same boardinghouse as Bette and Wenceslas. One evening, as he drives Bette home, the lecherous Hulot catches sight of the sexy Valérie. On the market for a new mistress, he takes up with her. She is thus, via Hulot, privy to the family's plans to arrange a marriage between Hortense and Wenceslas—plans the family initially keeps secret from Bette. Valérie lets the cat out of the bag "by accident" one day in a scene that marks the beginning of the friendship between the two women. But what is most interesting about the opening of this scene is the difficulty Valérie apparently has in understanding the nature of the bond between Bette and Wenceslas. This is another of those bonds for which there appears to be no name. Before the scene even opens, we have realized that this odd relationship, too, has attracted the attention and commentary of certain Parisians. Valérie originally thinks that Bette and Wenceslas are a couple. Her husband disbelieves this: "'Mademoiselle Fischer living with a young man!' repeated the civil servant. 'That's just porters' gossip. Let's not speak so lightly of the cousin of a Councillor of State who makes the sun shine and the rain descend at the Ministry'" (7:102, 63). Valérie has indeed been gossiping with the *portière,* Mme. Olivier, who has noted and attempted to decipher the nature of the affection that binds Bette to Wenceslas. The narrator agrees with Valérie's husband, however—at least initially—and gainsays the *portière's* malicious gossip. As Bette happily enters her paramour's apartment, bringing him a bit of dinner, the narrator comments: "The most bitter-tongued of Mademoiselle Fischer's detractors, watching even the beginning of this scene, would have acknowledged that the scandalous suggestions of the Olivier pair must be false. Everything in the tone, the gestures, and the looks of these two beings declared the purity of their life together. The old maid evinced the tender feeling of a dictatorial but sincere maternal affection. The young man submitted like a respectful son to a mother's tyranny" (7:108, 70).

As one might expect, things are actually not quite so clear. Malicious Parisians appear to have as much right to the truth as the Balzacian narrator, for the difficulty Bette has in reconciling herself to the idea that Hortense could steal her love from her is explained by the narrator precisely by reference to her problematic sense of the "maternal" nature of her relation to Wenceslas:

> She loved Steinbock [Wenceslas] well enough not to marry him, and loved him too well to give him up to another woman. She could not resign herself to being only his mother, yet thought her-

> self crazy when the idea of playing the alternative role crossed her mind. These warring impulses: her fierce jealousy, her happiness in possessing a man of her own, kept this woman's heart in a state of inordinate agitation. She had been truly in love for the past four years, and she cherished the wild hope of making *this illogical way of life—one that was leading nowhere* [*cette vie inconséquente et sans issue*]—permanent, though its continuance must mean the destruction of the person she called her child. (7:118–19, 81–82; my emphasis)

It is worth remarking on the phrase "cette vie inconséquente et sans issue." Bette's relationship with Wenceslas forms part of a life without sequence, without consequence, without issue in several senses of the word. It falls out of sequence, or fits into no sequence. Bette's life story misplaces amorous relationships and maternal ones; it doesn't put them in any order. In a moment of crisis a bit further along in the novel, she will beg Wenceslas in a queerly imaginative way:

> Consider: we need not marry—I am an old maid, I know. I do not want to stifle the flower of your youth . . . but, without marrying, can we not stay together? Listen. I have a head for business. I can gather a fortune for you in ten years' work. . . . Well, Wenceslas, stay with me. . . . You know, I understand everything. You shall have mistresses, pretty women like that little Marneffe who wants to meet you, who will give you the kind of happiness you could not find with me. Then you shall get married when I have saved thirty thousand francs a year for you.

> [Songez que, sans nous marier, car je suis une vieille fille, je le sais, je ne veux pas étouffer la fleur de votre jeunesse . . . mais, sans nous marier, ne pouvons-nous pas rester ensemble? Écoutez, j'ai l'esprit du commerce, je puis vous amasser une fortune en dix ans de travail. . . . Eh bien! Wenceslas, reste avec moi . . . Tiens, je comprends tout: tu auras des maîtresses, de jolies femmes semblables à cette petite Marneffe qui veut te voir, et qui te donnera le bonheur que tu ne peux pas trouver avec moi. Puis tu te marieras quand je t'aurai fait trente mille francs de rente.] (7:167, 134)

The abrupt switch to the *tu* form in Bette's "Eh bien! Wenceslas, reste avec moi" indicates the strangely moving pathos of this passage, a subtle effort to claim some kind of kinship, a gamble with vulnerability. For a moment it seems as if the gamble might have paid off. Wenceslas weeps, and replies: "You are an angel, Mademoiselle, and I shall never forget this moment" [Vous êtes un ange, mademoiselle, et je n'oublierai jamais ce moment-ci]" (7:167, 134). Choosing not to hear any ominous echos in Wenceslas's deflection of the *tu* and his return to the *vous* form, Bette is able to occupy the summit of joy for the space of a paragraph: "So strong is vanity in us, that Lisbeth believed that she had triumphed. She had made such a great concession in offering Madame Marneffe! She experienced the keenest emotion of her life. For the first time she felt joy flood her heart. For such another hour she would have sold her soul to the devil" (7:167, 135). Wenceslas's next observation quells the ecstasy "like an avalanche of snow upon that blazing crater." For he insists on returning her to the purely maternal position she had been trying to edge her way out of: "I love a woman against whom no other can prevail. But you are and you will always be [*vous êtes et vous serez toujours*] the mother I have lost" (7:167, 135).

This is not the sole occasion on which volcanic imagery is used to describe Bette's case. She is a bit like a truckload of affect on the loose. That affect is usually structured as hate, and the novel has as one of its central subjects the excess of her affect, its profoundly asocial bent. Consider in this light the beginning of her relationship with Valérie. The inconsequential nature of Bette's relationship with Wenceslas is seemingly carried over into this relationship, even if, at least at the outset, Valérie doesn't seem that promising a queer partner, given that she appears to have no ability to comprehend Bette's inconsequentiality. When she tells Bette of Wenceslas's infidelity, she apparently has no categories through which to comprehend Bette's (again volcanic) reaction:

> "Listen, my dear little Cousin Bette," said Madame Marneffe graciously. "Are you capable of a devoted friendship, proof against anything? Would you like us to be like two sisters? Will you swear to me to have no secrets from me, if I'll keep none from you, to be my secret eye if I'll be yours. . . ."
>
> Madame Marneffe broke off this picador's attack, for Cousin Bette frightened her. . . . Her teeth were clenched to prevent them from chattering, and her body was shaken convulsively and hor-

> ribly. . . . She was on fire! The smoke of the conflagration that ravaged her seemed to issue from the wrinkles of her face, as if they were fissures opened by volcanic eruption. It was a sublime spectacle.
>
> "Well, why do you stop?" she said hollowly. "I will be for you all that I was for him. Oh! I would have given my life-blood for him!"
>
> "You love him, then?"
>
> "As if he were my child!"
>
> "Well," Madame Marneffe went on, breathing more easily, "if you only love him like that, you are going to be very well pleased, for you want him to be happy don't you?"
>
> Lisbeth replied by nodding her head rapidly and repeatedly, like a madwoman.
>
> "In a month he's going to marry your second cousin."
>
> "Hortense!" cried the old maid, striking her forehead and rising to her feet.
>
> "Well, now! So you are in love with this young man?" asked Madame Marneffe.
>
> "My dear, we are now sworn friends," said Mademoiselle Fischer. "Yes, if you have attachments, I will regard them as sacred. Your very vices shall be virtues to me, for indeed I have need of your vices!"
>
> "So you were living with him?" Valerie exclaimed.
>
> "No, I wanted to be his mother. . . ."
>
> "Ah! I can't make head or tail of it," returned Valérie; "for if that's so, then you haven't been deceived or made a fool of, and you ought to be very glad to see him make a good marriage." (7:145–46, 110–11)

The scene insists perhaps too much on the uncategorizable nature of Bette's attachment, its "none of the above" character—neither mother nor lover, yet both. There is perhaps no need for Valérie to be as dimwitted as she here seems to be. But what the scene *does* highlight is the novel's interest in what we might call the slack in the cord that links sentiment or affect or sexuality to family structure. Thus even though Valérie is hardly the novel's most obvious exponent of family values, she here expects the course—the sequence—of Bette's affectual currents to follow typical maternal or amorous patterns. Yet what Bette's relations to both Wenceslas and Valérie reveal is that (at least in the

Balzacian novelistic universe) sentiment and affect and sexuality, once produced, exceed the structures that are meant to contain them.

Thus in at least his last two novels it would appear that Balzac is theorizing the same problem that would later interest Foucault in the first volume of *The History of Sexuality,* where he pursues the question of the relation between *alliance* and sexuality: "'Sexuality' was taking shape, born of a technology of power that was originally focused on alliance. Since then, it has not ceased to operate in conjunction with a system of alliance on which it has depended for support. . . . The family is the interchange of sexuality and alliance: it conveys the law and the juridical dimension in the deployment of sexuality; and it conveys the economy of pleasure and the intensity of sensation in the regime of alliance."[40] Gayle Rubin makes a similar point in "The Traffic in Women," although she uses somewhat different language to do so. If we equate what Foucault calls a system of alliance with what Rubin calls kinship, and what Foucault calls sexuality with what Rubin calls the sex/gender system, then what interests Rubin in the following passage is not that sex/gender depends on kinship for support, but that sex/gender took form through kinship, yet now is constrained to that form which no longer functions:

> The organization of sex and gender once had functions other than itself—it organized society. Now, it only organizes and reproduces itself. The kinds of relationships of sexuality established in the dim human past still dominate our sexual lives, our ideas about men and women, and the ways we raise our children. But they lack the functional load they once carried. One of the most conspicuous features of kinship is that it has been systematically stripped of its functions—political, economic, educational, and organizational. It has been reduced to its barest bones—sex and gender.[41]

When Valérie suggests that Bette's emotions should conform either to those of a proud mother or those of a jilted lover, she suggests that sexuality and its affects should overlap exactly with kinship structures and structures of marital exchange even in those cases where there is no chance of kinship or marriage. The novel itself presents Bette as an instance in which sexuality rests uncomfortably both inside and outside systems of kinship and inheritance. Valérie, too, operates within the novel as a disrupter of systems of inheritance and/or kinship (or perhaps it would be better here to stick with Foucault's word, *alliance*), almost causing family fortunes to disappear, destabilizing even *state* finances, wreaking havoc precisely with the smooth functioning of *alliances.* Her union with Bette, whatever its nature, is thus clearly the locus within the novel for thinking about a disruption in alliance. *Cousin Bette* might then have an interest not only in the family's relation to sexuality, but further in the possibilities for sexuality's continuance outside the system of the family. What would sexuality be if it were not related to inheritance? the novel might hesitantly ask.

Hesitantly, because it's not clear that such a relation could, for Balzac, ever be effaced.[42] Foucault insists that sexuality depended on alliance to elaborate itself, that the two are distinct but interdependent, and that, even though one might imagine that the "deployment of sexuality" as a social distribution of power would eventually have replaced the "deployment of alliance," such is not the case. He suggests, further, that psychoanalysis has done some of the cultural work of keeping them pinned together:

> Psychoanalysis, whose technical procedure seemed to place the confession of sexuality outside family jurisdiction, rediscovered the law of alliance, the involved workings of marriage and kinship, and incest at the heart of this sexuality, as the principle of its formation and the key to its intelligibility. The guarantee that one would find the parents-children relationship at the root of everyone's sexuality made it possible—even when everything seemed to point to the reverse process—to keep the apparatus of sexuality pinned to the system of alliance [de maintenir l'épinglage du dispositif de sexualité sur le système de l'alliance]. . . . The apparatuses of alliance and sexuality were involved in a slow process that had them turning about one another until . . . their positions were reversed. . . . With psychoanalysis, sexuality gave body and life to the rules of alliance by saturating them with desire.[43]

It is perhaps the double work of novels like *La Cousine Bette* that they both analytically reveal this strange pinning, and work on us to blind us to its force.

If we were to try to read *La Cousine Bette* as a novel about the pinning together of alliance, affect, and sexuality, our sense of who is at the center of the novel might change. The central character of the novel might become Célestine Crevel-Hulot. Her father, Crevel, is to be Valérie's prime catch, and catching him means depriving Célestine, his only daughter, of her father's estate—an eventuality Célestine's husband, Hulot's son, thanks to something we might call filial devotion, has every interest in preventing. In terms of this analysis, the novel would have three key points. The first, the opening gambit, would be Crevel's remark that, unlike his friend Hulot, he knows what mistresses are for and what they are not for. You don't squander your estate on them. "I love Célestine too well to ruin her" (7:66, 23) he insists in the book's opening pages, showing kinship duties and affective structures well aligned. By the novel's midpoint Valérie has them halfway unpinned: "Valérie, I love you as much as I love Célestine," Crevel admits (7:227, 198–99). And the crisis point that leads to the novel's denouement arrives when the opening kinship/affect relationship has been totally overturned and reinstated differently. As Bette reports the conversation to the "family": "'With Valérie as my wife, I'll be a Peer of France! I'll buy an estate I have my eye on—Presles. Mme de Serizy wants to sell it. I'll be Crevel de Presles. I'll be a member of the Council of Seine-et-Oise, and a Deputy. I'll have a son! I'll be anything in the world I want to be.' 'All very well,' I said to him; 'and what about your daughter?' 'Bah, she's only a daughter!' was what he answered. 'And she's become far too much of a Hulot, and Valérie can't bear that lot'" (7:369, 353–54). It is pretty clear that Valérie has no interest in this slightly crazed vision of an alternative family that Crevel elaborates. She wants him to die quickly after she marries him so that she can lay her hands on the estate. The forces of order magically intervene to prevent all this, of course, and Célestine does end the novel as the appropriately filled receptacle for wealth that she was always marked out to be.

And what of Bette? The novel understands her to be produced by and ruthlessly excluded from the system of alliance, and it carefully presents her hate—directed at representative kin—as another byproduct of the system:

> Lisbeth Fischer, five years younger than Madame Hulot although she was the daughter of the eldest of the Fischer brothers, was far from being as beautiful as her cousin. . . . The family, who lived as one household, had sacrificed the plebeian daughter to the pretty

> one, the astringent fruit to the brilliant flower. Lisbeth worked in the fields while her cousin was cosseted; and so it had happened one day that Lisbeth, finding Adeline alone, had done her best to pull Adeline's nose off, a true Grecian nose, much admired by all the old women. (7:80–81, 38–39)

Family matrimonial strategies, beauty taking pride of place over family hierarchy, a well-planned vengeful effort to sabotage the family's strategy: this passage indicates to what an extent Bette's vengeful affects can be read as a response to an experience of kinship/matrimonial strategy. A major goal of her revenge is to overturn this primal insult: she strategizes toward a marriage with the Baron Hulot's (Adeline's husband's) *older* brother, the Marshal Hulot. She would thereby displace Adeline in the family hierarchy, and, were she successfully to outlive the marshal and inherit his wealth after the baron had squandered his, she might have the additional satisfaction of seeing Adeline obliged to work for a living (7:205–6, 176–77). Bette miscalculates; the marshal dies before her plans can mature. Moreover, the kinship system has a few more lessons to teach her. For even a marriage to the marshal would have been *sans issue* (without offspring), and a family (understood, among other things, as a unit for reproducing and increasing wealth and social power) knows how to take things like this into consideration. Shortly after the marshal's death, we read:

> Lisbeth went to weep with rage to Madame Marneffe's, for she no longer had a place to live, the Marshal's lease of his house terminating with his death. Crevel, to console his Valérie's friend, took her savings and considerably increased them, and invested this capital in five-per-cents in Célestine's name, giving Lisbeth the life interest. Thanks to him, Lisbeth possessed an annuity of two thousand francs. When the inventory of the Marshal's property came to be taken, a note from the Marshal was found addressed to his sister-in-law, his neice Hortense, and his nephew Victorin, charging them with the payment, between them, of twelve hundred francs a year to Mademoiselle Lisbeth Fischer, who was to have been his wife. (7:353–54, 336–37)

What these "consolations" actually show is that it would never occur to anyone to allow Bette to inherit, or even possess for any length of time, any substantial *capital.* The marshal understands Adéline, her son, and her daughter to be the proper people for this task. Bette gets a little *interest,* thanks to what they inherit. Crevel's consolation prize for Bette is in some ways even more brutal. He, too, guarantees her an income, but seems, apparently without thinking about it, to appropriate some capital that had been hers for his own heir (still Célestine at this point), leaving Bette (only) her interest (however substantial) to live on.

This is not the first time such familial economic arrogance has surfaced in the novel. Adeline felt some remorse when her daughter stole Bette's paramour from her, and so to include Bette's happiness in the general happiness around the event of her daughter's wedding, she makes Bette a proposition:

> "We don't want you to work any longer," said the Baroness. "I suppose that you may earn forty sous a day, not counting Sundays: that makes six hundred francs a year. Well, how much have you put away in savings?"
>
> "Four thousand five hundred francs."
>
> "Poor Cousin!" said the Baroness.
>
> She raised her eyes to heaven, she was so moved to think of all the hardships and privations that that sum of money, gathered together through thirty years, represented. Lisbeth misunderstood the nature of the Baroness's exclamation, saw in it the contempt of a woman who has succeeded, and her hatred acquired a new intensity of bitterness, at the very moment when her cousin was abandoning all her mistrust of the tyrant of her childhood.
>
> "We will add ten thousand five hundred francs to that," Adeline continued, "placed in trust, the interest to go to you, the principal to revert to Hortense; so that you will have an income of six hundred francs a year."
>
> Lisbeth's cup was full, or so it seemed. (7:171–72, 139)

We need cast no aspersions on the sincerity of Adeline's emotions to see the way they float on top of an (unconscious?) devotion to familial strategy and a classist ideology that encourage her to dispossess Bette of her savings in the family's favor without even conceiving that she is doing so, without seeing any of the irony with which the narrator so carefully burdens this scene. Cousins are just more naturally suited to interest than to capital. Capital belongs to the family. Some concessions to queer cousins can be made in the distribution of interest. But the family will not hesitate to appropriate even the capital those cousins have accumulated through their own labor. Needless to say, it remains equally unclear to what degree Bette is ever conscious of the role of "kinship" itself in either her material or her affective affliction. Nor is it clear to what extent her relation to Valérie could have helped her lift herself out of that system.

For Foucault, friendship was one of the concepts that conceivably provided a way to begin thinking about sexuality separately from the system of family inheritance. The project of understanding friendship became for Foucault one way of loosening the pin linking sexuality and alliance.[44] We might pursue this concept a bit, because the narrator of *La Cousine Bette* finally arrives at the word friendship to label what exists between Valérie and Bette. Two interesting uses of this word come at the moment when Bette, who has been ill and confined to bed, hears that Valérie is on her own deathbed, with little time left to live. Hearing the news, Bette has a reaction as physical as her reaction on hearing of Wenceslas's betrayal:

> Cousin Bette's teeth chattered, she broke out in a cold sweat. The terrible shock she experienced revealed the depth of her passionate friendship [la profondeur de son amitié passionnée] for Valérie.
>
> "I must go to her," she said. (7:430, 421)

Finding Valérie rotting away, smelling quite foul, and spouting newly espoused truisms of family values, Bette is unable to stick it out to the bitter end with the nuns at the deathbed. As the narrator has it: "The most violent sentiment we know of, the friendship of one woman for another [Le sentiment le plus violent que l'on connaisse, l'amitié d'une femme pour une femme], had not the heroic constancy of the Church. Lisbeth, stifled by the noxious exhalations, left the room" (7:433, 424).

Why is it that the friendship of a woman for a woman would be the most violent sentiment known within the world of the Balzacian narrator? Why would we imagine the sentiment Bette has for Valérie, for instance, as more violent than that of Pons for Schmucke? Clearly because alliance and sexuality are pinned together in such a way that two men being "friends" creates different kinds of short-circuits than two women. (The large sums of money that change hands between the two friends Brunner and Schwab, for instance, apparently do not occasion any negative commentary or punitive impulses.) Foucault mainly speaks of friendship between men, but he acknowledges gendered dissymmetries in the concept on a number of occasions in the early 1980s by making reference to Lillian Faderman's *Surpassing the Love of Men*. What follows is the passage where he refers to that book in his 1981 interview, "Friendship as a Way of Life":

> There is a book that just appeared in the U.S. on the friendships between women. The affection and passion between women is well documented. In the Preface the author states that she began with the idea of unearthing homosexual relationships but that she perceived that not only were these relationships not always present but that it was uninteresting whether relationships could be called homosexual or not. And by letting the relationship manifest itself as it appeared in words and gestures other very essential things also appeared: dense, bright, marvelous loves and affections or very dark and sad loves. The book shows the extent to which woman's body has played a great role, and the importance of physical contact between women: women do each other's hair, help each other with make-up, dress each other. Man's body has been forbidden to other men in a much more drastic way.[45]

Foucault is ascribing to himself and to Faderman a position with certain resemblances to the position of the Balzacian narrator. That is, he acknowledges a social impulse to provide a label and a sexual content to these "friendships" from another time, and then resists making the label stick. The reasons Foucault might do this are of course different from the reasons a Balzacian narrator might do it. Foucault does it as part of his effort to move *contemporary* sexual practices into a new conceptual space. As he says most concisely in another interview: "I will say that we must use our sexuality to discover, to invent new ways of relating. To be gay is to be in the process of becoming and I would add . . . we must not be homosexual, we must work tenaciously to be gay [Je dirai, il faut user de sa sexualité pour découvrir, inventer de nouvelles relations. Être gay, c'est être en devenir et . . . j'ajouterais qu'il ne faut pas être homosexual mais s'acharner à être gay]."[46]

Foucault's desire to move into a new conceptual space that would leave "sexuality" behind is perhaps not on the agenda of the Balzacian novel, which, as we have seen, is to some extent interested in producing "sexuality" in its characters. Balzac's twin novels might, however, help us keep more firmly in mind than does Foucault the force of gendered dissymmetries in friendship (at least in nineteenth-century France). The friendship between Bette and Valérie is not the same as the friendship between Schmucke and Pons. Not that Schmucke holds on to the wealth Pons has queerly redistributed any better than Valérie or Bette hold on to theirs, but he does inherit, if only for a brief instant. *Le Cousin Pons* also imagines that first will, noticing a way of using the state to help two queer *men* be friends. In *La Cousine Bette,* it is Victorin Hulot who imagines a state intervention (help from the police in doing away with Valérie, that is), who pays for it as if it were a tax, so that the family can be saved.[47]

Both *La Cousine Bette* and *Le Cousin Pons* have ruthlessly violent endings, ensuring that *in fact* there is no inheritance possible for the queer friendships they haltingly sketch out, no disruption to the system of alliance. Yet as Balzac understands it, Bette and Valérie have by structural necessity constituted the greater threat to alliance in their pursuit of their own ends, and consequently are luridly punished in ways the men are not. Although Bette dies with a rather lighter technicolor touch than does Valérie, Balzac has carefully and cruelly figured her inevitable punishment throughout by always insisting, through the image of a yellow cashmere shawl, on the nonautonomy of Bette's own queer desires.

The shawl was given by the baron Hulot to his wife and by Adeline to her daughter Hortense. As the narrator says: "Cousin Bette, victim since her arrival in Paris of an admiration for cashmere, had been fascinated by the idea of possessing this yellow cashmere given by the baron to his wife in 1808, and which, according to the custom of certain families, had passed from mother to daughter in 1830" (7:89, 50). Bette wins the shawl from Hortense by proving that her constant talk about her lover, Wenceslas, is not a fiction. By proving Wenceslas to be real, she wins her shawl (a token of the system of alliances), but loses her lover/son to that same system. (We might think of Pons here, inadvertently opening his museum to heterosexual commerce.) The shawl reappears at all the queerest moments, as if repetitively to repin Bette to the system of alliance from which she would escape if she could; a kind of straitjacket she can't shake. Even when she moves in with

Valérie, and Valérie revolutionizes the way she dresses, she is nonetheless "still wearing the yellow cashmere" (7:196, 165); as she runs to Valérie's deathbed, she stops to put on "her famous yellow cashmere shawl" (7:430, 421). Tenacious and threadbare at once, the shawl clings in its effort to keep queerness abject. One might well wish she could have thrown it away.

IN HIS *History of Sexuality, Volume 1,* Foucault mentions not only psychoanalysis but also ethnology as one of those forms of knowledge that both has been part and parcel of the apparatus of sexuality and also has ensured that the apparatus of sexuality remain pinned to the apparatus of alliance. For instance, Foucault notes that the incest taboo would function differently in the two different "apparatuses": "It may be [il se peut bien]," he says ambiguously (perhaps a bit doubtfully), "that in societies where the mechanisms of alliance predominate, prohibition of incest is a functionally indispensable rule." In the domain of sexuality, the prohibition of incest functions differently; it "occupies a central place; it is constantly being solicited and refused; it is an object of obsession and attraction, a dreadful secret and an indispensable pivot."[48] In the case of alliance, the prohibition of incest would be formal, a rule; in the case of sexuality it is a spur, a topic of endless—if sometimes hushed or displaced—discussion, richly productive of psychological effects. Ethnology, in being a major locus of this discussion, has served the deployment of sexuality, but in the terms of its discussion it has also sustained a certain way of keeping the apparatuses of sexuality and alliance pinned together:

> If for more than a century the West has displayed such a strong interest in the prohibition of incest . . . perhaps this is because it was found to be a means of self-defense, not against incestuous desire, but against the expansion and the implications of this deployment of sexuality which had been set up, but which, among its many benefits, had the disadvantage of ignoring the laws and juridical forms of alliance. By asserting that all societies without exception, and consequently our own, were subject to this rule of rules, one guaranteed that this deployment of sexuality, whose strange effects were beginning to be felt—among them, the affective intensification of the family space—would not be able to escape from the

> grand and ancient system of alliance. Thus the law would be secure, even in the new mechanics of power. . . . By devoting so much effort to an endless reworking of the transcultural theory of the incest taboo, anthropology has been the loyal servant of the whole modern deployment of sexuality and the theoretical discourses it generates [L'ethnologie, en réélaborant sans cesse depuis si longtemps, la théorie transculturelle de l'interdiction de l'inceste, a bien mérité de tout le dispositif moderne de sexualité et des discours théoriques qu'il produit]. (109–10)

What has been most helpful to me in my efforts to read *Le Cousin Pons* and *La Cousine Bette* has been to think about the historic specificity of the pin holding alliance and sexuality together in the social world that Balzac is analyzing. One of the particularities of that post-Napoleonic, French Restoration world is the intense attention paid to alliance by the bourgeoisie as it tries to create itself as the legitimate locus of social power. It seems as if this return to alliance is in part an effort to repudiate, or to check, the seemingly free-wheeling fluctuations of social power felt to characterize the period of the Revolution as well as the subsequent Napoleonic period. One might choose to see the Restoration as thus merely a retrograde moment in the ongoing modernization of French social structures. This would be equivalent to supposing that we should imagine a story where alliance is slowly being left behind by sexuality, whatever hesitations that process involves.[49] If we think *instead* about rendering historically and geographically specific the pin that holds the deployments of sexuality and alliance together,[50] we might see the benefits of constructing a different (less historically reductive) relation between the two modalities of power. This might allow us to understand in the concentration on alliance we find in Balzac's world not so much a temporary step back in a grand historical narrative but rather a given, contingent, historical configuration whose contours we can trace not just in Balzac's novels but in, for instance, the Napoleonic Code, as well as in a variety of other discourses both reflective of and productive of the material conditions of mid-nineteenth-century France.[51] We might in this light begin to imagine Pons and Bette and their troubles with sexuality not in some ancestral relation to ourselves but in some "parallel" moment that might nonetheless provoke in some of us a tremor of recognition.

CHAPTER FOUR

The Shadow Economy of Queer Social Capital: Lucien de Rubempré and Vautrin

Le Cousin Pons and *La Cousine Bette* perhaps represent Balzac's most detailed thinking about the interrelation of the economic, social, and sexual aspects of the subjectivities of sexual misfits in his historical moment. Yet arguably his most influential portrait of a sexual misfit is the character Vautrin, who was first introduced in *Le Père Goriot* in 1834 and later reappeared in the novels *Lost Illusions* and *Splendeurs et misères des courtisanes,* as well as in the play bearing his name, *Vautrin.* And certainly the pairing of Vautrin with Lucien de Rubempré, begun in the final pages of *Lost Illusions* and continuing throughout *Splendeurs et misères des courtisanes,* has been immensely suggestive for later writers interested in thinking about or portraying male same-sex relations.[1] In *Lost Illusions, Vautrin,* and *Splendeurs et misères des courtisanes,* Balzac, among other projects, takes up an analysis of the shifting sociological significance in the various forms of sexual relations between men in his world. In particular, as I hope to show in this chapter, Balzac, by way of characters such as Lucien and Vautrin, investigates the kinds of economies (social and cultural as well as economic) in which intimate relations between men assume various kinds of value.

Balzac's play *Vautrin* is almost never read nowadays. His novel *Splendeurs et misères des courtisanes* is often read as if it were written after *Lost Illusions.* Yet the three works were conceived and elaborated in close chronological proximity to each other. Considering them in their proximity can help us to a better understanding of Balzac's project in developing the character of Vautrin. I would like here to spend a few pages discussing the composition of the novels and the play in order to help us see Balzac at work developing his ideas about both Vautrin and Lucien de Rubempré.

What is known today as the single novel *Lost Illusions* (made up of three parts) would have been known to Balzac's contemporaries as three separate novels. The first, published in 1837, was called *Illusions perdues,* and corresponds to the first division of the novel as it is published today. In it, we meet David Séchard and his father, who quarrel over how to run a printing firm and who face increasing competition in this endeavor from the wily Cointet brothers. We also meet Lucien Chardon, whose deceased father was a chemist who somehow managed to marry an aristocrat whom he saved from the guillotine. His wife, from the Rubempré family, is still alive (and impoverished) and works in Angoulême as a midwife. Her son, Lucien, is an aspiring poet who longs after both celebrity and his mother's aristocratic name. In the course of the novel, David Séchard dreams of making a fortune by revolutionizing the manufacture of paper in France. He also marries Lucien's sister, Eve. Lucien starts an affair with a local aristocrat, Mme. de Bargeton, and runs off to Paris with her. This section of *Lost Illusions* was given its current title, *The Two Poets,* in 1843, in what is known as the Furne edition of *La Comédie humaine,* where the three parts of the novel as we know it were first brought together. The second part, *An Important Man from the Provinces Goes to Paris* (*Un Grand Homme de province à Paris*) was first published separately in 1839. It tells of the ups and downs of Lucien's Parisian adventure, his meeting with a group of serious intellectuals known as the Cénacle, and his seduction by the world of journalism, where—for a brief moment—he achieves easy success. Yet by the end of the novel, he and his girlfriend Coralie have lived too high and too fast. Coralie dies, and Lucien is forced to return to Angoulême in rags, having forged David Séchard's signature on a number of bills in order to make ends meet. In the minds of Balzac's contemporaries and many subsequent critics, this section of *Lost Illusions* was a novel in its own right. One therefore sees frequent references to *Un Grand Homme de province à Paris* as a freestanding work.[2] (An interesting contemporary variation on this phenomenon is provided by Franco Moretti, who, in *Atlas of the European Novel,* writes a bit inaccurately that "*Lost Illusions* . . . begins in the Parisian West End." The novel begins in Angoulême; the *second part* of the novel begins in Paris. For Moretti, Paris is "where the great novels of the *Comédie humaine* take place," which perhaps explains his forgetfulness as to the exact location of the opening of *Lost Illusions.*)[3]

The third and final part of *Lost Illusions* was variously titled *David Séchard, or the Tribulations of an Inventor* (in its serial publication in 1843), *David Séchard* (when it was published on its own in 1844), and *Eve and David* (when it was collected with the other two parts in the Furne edition). Today it is called *An Inventor's Tribulations* (*Les Souffrances de l'inventeur*) based on a correction Balzac made to his copy of the Furne edition. In it, Lucien achieves a momentary brilliance in Angoulême after his return home, and holds out briefly the hope that he can redeem himself and his family fortunes. He fails to do so, unwittingly allowing himself to be used as a pawn by the Cointet brothers and their agents, who want to swindle David out of his new discovery of a cheaper means of manufacturing paper. Lucien, in disgrace, sneaks out of town, thinking to kill himself. Just as he is about to do so he meets a mysterious Spanish priest, who claims to be named Carlos Herrera but who is, in fact, Vautrin, the brilliant criminal already familiar to readers of *Le Père Goriot.* Vautrin offers to pay Lucien's debts and then take him to Paris and make a success of him if Lucien will agree to perform an unnamed service for him—a "proof of obedience"—in a hotel in Poitiers, where they will arrive shortly. Lucien agrees. They head off to Poitiers and then to Paris together. The money Lucien earns in Poitiers by doing Vautrin's bidding arrives too late to do his sister and brother-in-law much good. The Cointets successfully swindle David's secret out of him, although David nevertheless manages to retire to the country with his wife and children and a decent amount of money on which to live.

Balzac's play *Vautrin,* which was given a single performance on March 14, 1840, before being banned by the censors, was written in between the writing of the second and third parts of the novel we know as *Lost Illusions.* (Vautrin, of course, only appears in that novel in the third part.) In the play, Vautrin is protecting a handsome young man by the name of Raoul de Frescas; there is no character named Lucien de Rubempré.

Long before finishing *Lost Illusions*, and before writing the play *Vautrin*, Balzac had already begun writing *Splendeurs et misères des courtisanes*. The first part of that novel to be published was called *La Torpille* and appeared in 1838, even before *Un Grand Homme de province à Paris* was published (*La Torpille*'s title would shift a few times before becoming *The Way Working Girls Love* [*Comment aiment les filles*]). The novel concerns Lucien and Vautrin in Paris, and tells both the story of Lucien's passion for a prostitute named Esther and the scheming Lucien and Vautrin do (having already attained a royal decree granting Lucien the name de Rubempré) to arrange a socially advantageous marriage between Lucien and Clotilde de Grandlieu. Vautrin makes sure that Lucien's passionate love for Esther is lived out entirely in secret so as not to interfere with their marriage schemes. By chance, however, one night the extremely rich Baron Nucingen catches a glimpse of Esther in the woods at Vincennes, and he is so taken with her beauty that he spares no expense to discover the identity and whereabouts of the mysterious woman. This opening to the story of Lucien's *second* set of Parisian adventures was thus begun before the story of the first trip had been penned or published.

The continuation of *Splendeurs et misères des courtisanes* appeared serially in the journal *Le Parisien* under the title *Esther ou les Amours d'un vieux banquier* in 1843, a few months before *David Séchard ou les Souffrances de l'inventeur* would begin appearing serially in *L'État*. Whereas we tend to think of *Lost Illusions* and *Splendeurs et misères des courtisanes* as a long novel and its sequel, they were in fact composed in tandem. Lucien and Vautrin were conniving in Paris in *La Torpille* and in *Esther ou les Amours d'un vieux banquier* before they had ever met on the banks of the Charente at the end of *Lost Illusions*. And if we consider the play that received one performance in 1840, we know that Vautrin had met the handsome, homeless youth Raoul on a road in Italy before he ever met Lucien in France.

Splendeurs et misères des courtisanes has four parts, whose titles evolve in even more complex fashion than the titles of the three parts of *Lost Illusions*. The second part, known today as "What Love May Cost an Old Man," tells how Vautrin uses Nucingen's passion for Esther to extort money from him for use in the campaign to conquer the hand of Clotilde de Grandlieu. After many convolutions of the plot, things turn out badly. Esther, who truly loves Lucien, kills herself after finally having claimed a huge sum in order to sleep with Nucingen. On discovering her death, Nucingen, suspecting foul play, calls in the police. The money has mysteriously disappeared, and Lucien and Vautrin are arrested. They had, in any case, already been denounced to the Grandlieu family, who had ceased receiving Lucien.

At least until 1845 Balzac intended the fourth and final part of his novel *La Dernière Incarnation de Vautrin* to stand as a book in its own right. The third part, which finally came to be called *Where Evil Ways Lead* (*Où mènent les mauvais chemins*) was published as part of *Splendeurs et misères des courtisanes* in the Furne edition in 1846. On his copy of that edition, Balzac wrote at the end of the third part: "Fourth and final part: *The Last Incarnation of Vautrin.*" On that basis, the four-part novel we read today was assembled after Balzac's death.[4] The third part tells of the interrogation of Lucien and Vautrin by the magistrate Camusot. Vautrin successfully staves off a revelation of his true identity during the interrogation, but due to a complicated series of badly timed events, Lucien comes to believe that their plans and the nature of their relationship have been fully discovered, and so he hangs himself in a prison cell. The fourth part, first published separately in 1847, tells how Vautrin, at first overcome by Lucien's death, discovers that an old love of his, a convict named Théodore Calvi, is in the same prison and about to be executed. This reinvigorates Vautrin, who through a series of canny negotiations manages to save his old lover and, reunited with him, negotiates his way into being guaranteed a position as a chief of police in return for certain services rendered and certain secrets protected.

The publication history of these works, the relative simultaneity of their conception, and the overlapping periods of their completion, encourage us to see them all as in part different aspects of the same project of reflection—a project that comes increasingly over time to focus on forms of relations between men, and the possibilities for and consequences of the public recognition of those relations. Yet Balzac's intensifying attention to the diversity of forms for male same-sex intimacies is rarely commented on.

Franco Moretti sees in *Lost Illusions* (or at least in its middle section) Balzac's greatest novelistic and sociological feat. "Most urban novels *simplify* the urban system by turning it into a neat oppositional pattern," Moretti writes. "An over-complicated environment requires a symbolic form capable of mastering it."[5] Balzac, in *Lost Illusions,* complicates the structures usually used by novels set in urban environments, and thereby creates a new novelistic form. Balzac "revels in the complications of Paris" and replaces "a binary structure with a plurality of agents" (107). Yet for Moretti, this innovative narrative and sociological vision disappears from *Splendeurs et misères des courtisanes:*

> *Harlot* is *Lost Illusions'* continuation, of course, but in a deeper sense it is its drastic *simplification,* which returns Balzac's narrative structure from the new policentric model to the old binary matrix: field, and anti-field; Parisian West End, and City of Crime. It is a turnaround, a retreat, that shows how difficult the novel of complexity could be. . . . Even its inventor may well miss its deeper structural logic. No wonder, then, that Balzac yields to simplification, and reverts to that binary paradigm that *Lost Illusions* had so memorably overcome. (113)

Moretti is unquestionably one of the most provocative and helpful commentators on Balzac in recent years, but there are many reasons for not accepting his evaluation here. A first rather mundane correction needs to be made: given that the opening part of *Splendeurs et misères des courtisanes* was written *before* the Parisian section of *Lost Illusions,* it is a bit inaccurate to refer to the relation of the former to the latter as one of retreat or reversion.

One might also wonder on another level about an evaluation of *Splendeurs et misères des courtisanes* that finds it to be lacking in narrative or sociological complexity. What notion of sociology would be required to sustain such an evaluation? Given that so much of the final two parts of the novel takes place on only one site, the architectural complex including the Hall of Justice and the prison of the Conciergerie, is it fair to fault the novel for not demonstrating the same rambunctious relation to urban space that one finds in the middle section of *Lost Illusions?* In *The Way of the World,* Moretti claims that Balzac "subordinates sociology itself to narration." He expands on this point a bit later:

> If, therefore, when reading Balzac we are first struck by the breathtaking broadening of the sociological domain of the novel—the truly revolutionary innovation of the *Comédie* is its subordination

> of this incredibly vast and full universe *to narrative form*. . . . There comes into being, with Balzac, a new attitude, a vision of reality hostile to *analysis,* and literally bewitched by *pure narration.* Try to "discuss" the novels of the *Comédie:* you will end up merely retelling them. It is no longer possible to break free from this complex and enthralling narration: instead of being an instrument of knowledge, it has turned against knowledge. . . . The *Comédie Humaine* appears to have taught us to view the way of the world very attentively, with a previously unthinkable involvement: *but without asking any more what it "means."*[6]

These are odd assertions, especially for anyone familiar with the incredibly digressive structure of, say, the last section of *Lost Illusions,* with chapter titles such as "A glance at paper-making," or "A free public lecture on dishonored bills for those unable to meet them," or "How in the provinces being imprisoned for debt almost never happens," or "A history lecture for the ambitious—by a disciple of Machiavelli," or "The history of a business venture." If one turns to the third section of *Splendeurs et misères des courtisanes,* one finds chapters such as "Criminal law for the man in the street," with vocabulary lessons and information on the structure of the court system, or "A historical, archeological, biographical, anecdotal and physiological history of the Palais de Justice," or "The functions of an examining magistrate."[7] The various digressions—whether providing sociological detail, historical background, ideological commentary, or seemingly unrelated anecdotes—all require an effort of analytic attention to establish their function. One is constantly required to ask what the digressions are meant to bring to the novel. The problem, in these sections of Balzac's novels, is not that one cannot "break free" from an enthralling narration, but that often one cannot seem to hold onto the narration by which one is meant to be enthralled. Moretti's oddly selective vision of *La Comédie humaine* seems a result of his intent to see in Balzac a novelist whose sociological interest was entirely focused on the forms of mediation that govern human relations in a capitalist metropolis. For Moretti, Balzac seems simply to have *represented* in the plots of his urban novels the social relations occurring within a capitalist market or metropolis. Balzac is "trying to write the story of the city-as-market." Within the portrait Balzac is painting, "mediation itself *becomes the true pro-*

tagonist of the Comédie Humaine."[8] In these assertions from *Atlas of the European Novel* Moretti builds on his argument in *The Way of the World,* to the effect that "Balzac's great innovation lies in shifting the origin of plot from an *individual volition* to a *superindividual mechanism:* the mechanism of *competition,* which with the unification of the national markets, in the first half of the nineteenth century, ceases to be an exception to become the *norm* of social relations."[9]

It is, of course, crucial for any critical reading of Balzac to understand part of the point Moretti is making here: that the novels are more about the interaction *between* individuals and social facts or social forces than they are about individuals themselves. To recall Henry James's term, the novels are about people being "built-in." And there is no doubt that Balzac's sociological interests encompass the issues on which Moretti concentrates: the ways the "city-as-market" structured human relations. But why should we imagine this to be the entire extent of Balzac's sociological interests, especially if to do so we are required to dismiss a large portion of Balzac's output?[10] And why would one choose to imagine that Balzac—in the way his plots enact competition and mediation within the context of urban social mobility—only *represented* (and never analyzed) certain sociological phenomena? What of Balzac's curiosity about the ways in which given psychologies represent sedimented historical interests and produce reactions and calculations that may or may not serve agents well at any given moment? Balzac's sociological curiosity about the relations between given individual psychologies and social and political history runs throughout his novels and is certainly not limited to those set in Paris. *Lost Illusions,* for instance, foregrounds again Balzac's interest in the ways individual psychological formations can cause certain persons to enact (often by way of their sexuality) interests that need not be thought of as their own, and thereby even act to their own disadvantage.

Balzac also has an ongoing critical interest in the ways social forms such as families or friendship or other relationships between individuals interact with social forces and institutions such as the law and the state. In an earlier essay on Balzac, "Homo Palpitans: Balzac's Novels and Urban Personality," Moretti comments that "it has been difficult for *the state* to acquire prominence in the narrative of the last centuries: bourgeois culture is fundamentally a culture of private life, which is reluctant to identify and resolve itself entirely in great collective institutions."[11] Yet the state is incredibly prominent in Balzac's novels, as are the state's instruments (such as the Civil Code) and the state's agents: lawyers, magistrates, attorneys general, notaries, legislators, police agents, spies, and so on. The last two sections of *Splendeurs et misères des courtisanes* take place almost entirely in the Conciergerie—part prison, part courthouse, part police headquarters—for a reason. Aristocratic attorneys general, their friends, their wives, and the noble friends of their wives there interact with ambitious bourgeois magistrates, their bourgeois wives, and their clerks, as well as with police agents of dubious social provenance, with the criminal Vautrin, and with his protégé, Lucien de Rubempré. In the various legal and paralegal negotiations the novel recounts, they all enact different relations to the law and to the state. Moreover, it is precisely within this complex sociological framework that Balzac takes the occasion to think about the social forms of male same-sex relations. In October 1846 (shortly after the publication of part three of *Splendeurs et misères des courtisanes*, but before the composition of the fourth part), in a letter to the editor of the newspaper *La Semaine*, in which an article had just been published that reproached Balzac for the glamour found in his portraits of Vautrin and Lucien, Balzac denies any attempt to glamorize such characters and he adds a comment that Vautrin is very closely based on a real person: "Everything that Vautrin is, this man was, except for the passion I have assigned to Vautrin."[12] This is reasonably clear evidence that the analysis Balzac was elaborating in the final two sections of *Splendeurs et misères des courtisanes* has something to do with Vautrin's passion, his sexuality. I will try to elucidate this part of Balzac's analysis in the pages ahead.

One needs, then, to broaden Moretti's sense of Balzac's sociological achievement in order to be able to take into account Balzac's interest in sexuality and its links to socio-historical change or to evolving state interests. In the complexly interlocking set of writings that make up *Lost Illusions*, *Vautrin*, and *Splendeurs et misères des courtisanes*, Balzac sets himself the task (among many others) of investigating same-sex male sexuality from a variety of perspectives. His interests include the way family structure, historical change, and sexuality interrelate; the way people who are excluded from normative family structures create structures of their own; the ways those alternative structures relate to normative ones. In particular, in *Splendeurs et misères des courtisanes* he will investigate the way certain previously normative forms—forms losing prestige due to large processes of historical change—can sometimes ally themselves with the abject forms being produced by the new normativity in order to arrive at productive oppositional allegiances. Before turning to the final two sections of *Splendeurs et misères des courtisanes,* however, I wish to examine the construction of the character of Lucien de Rubempré within *Lost Illusions,* and the analysis his character enables of the ends of sexuality.

"A RUBEMPRÉ"

> Les Français, quand y débarquent chez nous, cherchent bien les Indiens et Maria Chapdelaine, pourquoi je partirais pas, moi, à la recherche de Gervaise ou de Lucien de Rubempré! [When the French come over here, they go around looking for Indians and Marie Chapdelaine. Why shouldn't I set off over there in search of Gervaise or Lucien de Rubempré?]—Michel Tremblay, *Les Nouvelles d'Édouard*

When one of the marquis Astolphe de Custine's biographers referred to Custine's young companion and housemate, Gurowski, who would eventually run off with a Spanish infanta, as "a Rubempré," that biographer was apparently referring to a conjunction of qualities: a willingness on the part of a younger man to be supported by an older one, an apparent openness to sex between men as part of the bargain, and a simultaneous openness to, not to say active pursuit of, sex with women.[13] One can easily imagine the concern expressed by conservative or moralizing critics on finding that such a figure as Lucien was achieving popularity with readers, and even attracting imitators. Flaubert himself takes note of the phenomenon in a letter to Louise Colet from 1853: "Balzac's perverse heroes have, I believe, turned many a head. The feeble generation that is currently out there seeking after power and fame has gained from reading these books a silly admiration for a certain kind of bourgeois immorality after which it now strives. I've been told stories about this privately. It is no longer Werther or Saint-Preux whom they want to be; it is Rastignac or Lucien de Rubempré."[14] Lucien's popularity has proved enduring. A few decades after Flaubert, Oscar Wilde, writing an article on Balzac in 1886, would comment: "Who would care to go out to an evening party to meet Tomkins, the friend of one's boyhood, when one can sit at home with

Lucien de Rubempré?"[15] One can also imagine, given Lucien's popularity, the interest people took (and still take) in knowing on whom he may have been modeled. In January 1837 Jules Sandeau would write with some concern to Balzac (with whom he had lived in 1834 and 1835) to inquire about Balzac's soon-to-be-published novel: "Tell me about *Lost Illusions*! I've been told in letters from Paris that it tells my story with you-know-who." By March, having received and read the novel, Sandeau seems reassured, and he writes to Balzac: "I do in some way resemble Lucien's bad side. But as for my story with Mme Dudevant, it is not to be found in your pages."[16] Sandeau had been concerned that he might find in *Lost Illusions* an account of his affair with George Sand, about which he was himself in the process of composing a novel. Relieved on this particular front, he seems rather amused to find that Balzac has found a way to include some kind of critique of his weaknesses in the portrait of Lucien. Balzac's and Sandeau's period of living together a few years earlier had ended abruptly, with Sandeau secretly fleeing while Balzac was away, leaving behind debts and a tear-soaked letter: "I have felt for quite a while that the life I was leading was without dignity. I had access to a level of luxury that did not correspond to the work I did, and my debts were growing day by day. . . . You have always been the best of brothers to me so I hope you will approve of my action."[17]

When critics look for models of Lucien, they frequently look for beautiful, charismatic young men of questionable masculinity and little willpower. Sandeau seems to have had much the same image of himself. Critics who chastised Balzac for creating such characters frequently did so in the service of orthodox masculinity. Indicating that someone is a potential model for Lucien is usually to suggest something negative about both that person's masculinity and his sexuality. Consider, in this light, the case of Hippolyte Auger, a now little-known man of letters of roughly the same age as Balzac. Auger recounts in his memoirs a scene in which he and Henri de Latouche, another one-time housemate of Balzac's, helped Balzac wallpaper a room in his apartment in a shiny blue calico that resembled silk: "Et vraiment tous trois nous faisions merveille"—the three of them made a wonderful spectacle doing it.[18] That would have been in 1829, Auger having met Balzac the previous year when he was looking for a publisher for a small review, *Le Gymnase,* that he and a group of Saint-

Simonians wanted to publish. Balzac at the time owned a publishing firm—although it was about to go bankrupt—and for a few months in 1828 his firm published several issues of Auger's review. Auger recounts in his memoir that for one of the issues he had written a historical sketch titled "Le Bouillon de Saint-Mégrin." In the meeting of the editorial board on that issue, Auger notes a certain dubious expression on the face of one of his collaborators, and he comments that on noticing this attitude in someone in whose taste he placed some trust he began to have doubts about the value of his sketch. He then recounts how, while correcting the proofs for the issue in question at the printers, he runs into Balzac, who brusquely asks him the name of the author of "Le Bouillon de Saint-Mégrin." Unsure of himself, Auger hides behind the policy of anonymity that governed the publication of articles in *Le Gymnase,* but offers to pass on any comments Balzac might have to the author. To which Balzac replies, as Auger tells it: "Well, what could I have to offer except congratulations? I find the sketch, written without any pretentious archaisms, to have been artfully spun." Auger claims to have laughed with relief and to have resisted the temptation to reveal to Balzac that he had himself written the piece (362–63).

Auger neglects—and this was doubtless intentional on his part—to say anything about the content of his historical sketch. Anyone in the know about queer French history might have grasped the coded reference and surmised Auger's ulterior motives in describing this scene between himself and Balzac. Henri III, king of France during a period of religious warfare in the sixteenth century, was known for his feminine airs as well as for the favors he lavished on the handpicked and handsome male courtiers who were known as his *mignons* (minions)—and with whom the nature of his relations provoked scandalous commentary. Saint-Mégrin was one of the *mignons* of Henri III, and in 1829 Alexandre Dumas would write and produce a historical drama called *Henri III and His Court,* one of the first successes of French Romantic theater, in which Saint-Mégrin would also figure. But while Dumas's drama would make some reference to the opprobrium surrounding Henri and his relations with his *mignons,* in that play the drama centered instead on political intrigue and on the infidelities of the *wife* of the duc de Guise with Saint-Mégrin. Auger's brief sketch, on the other hand, leaves politics pretty much entirely to the side, and instead coyly dwells on a scene in which Henri III, depressed and in mourning for the recently deceased princesse de Condé, is restored to interest in life at the moment in which he first forms an affectionate attachment to the extremely attractive young Saint-Mégrin, who with a bowl of bouillon had been sent to him by his mother Catherine de Medici to cheer him up.[19]

It could perhaps be said that what Auger's sketch lacks in seriousness it makes up in a kind of camp charm. The sketch certainly contrasts sharply with the usual serious intellectual tone that characterizes the writings in *Le Gymnase,* which was filled, as one might expect from a Saint-Simonian publication, with serious discussions of foreign policy and domestic social reforms.[20] The vague flippancy of Auger's sketch, combined with the confusing rhetorical position it occupies within the context of the seriously intellectual *Le Gymnase* (are we meant to disapprove of, laugh at, or be trained into Saint-Simonian tolerance for Henri III's penchants?) at least caused it to stand out. Small wonder it caught Balzac's eye. Auger's intent in his *Mémoires* in drawing his reader's attention to Balzac's interest in the sketch merits comment. The *Mémoires* contain, in somewhat coded fashion, a good deal of information about various queer subcultures throughout Europe (in particular in France, England, and Russia), and Auger seems to have meant to implicate Balzac in those subcultures.[21]

In his essay "Balzac et les saint-simoniens" Bruce Tolley suggests that while Auger's sketch might have attracted Balzac's attention because he was himself interested in writing about Catherine de Medici, it more likely drew Balzac's attention for what it suggested about Auger's "tendencies," about which certain other Saint-Simonians apparently expressed certain knowledge.[22] Tolley suggests we see in Auger a model for Lucien, and he has two reasons for making the suggestion. First, critics have often noted that the Cénacle, the group of Parisian artists, writers, thinkers, and activists that Balzac describes befriending Lucien in *Lost Illusions,* seems based on a group of Saint-Simonians, with D'Arthez being modeled on a prominent Saint-Simonian named Philippe Buchez.[23] Second, to find a model for Lucien one usually looks for someone with loose sexual morals, a feminine air, and a flippant and easy writing style, located in proximity to a group of more serious men whose masculinity seems less open to question.[24]

I wish to consider one final possible model for Lucien, a person who shares one of his names and who helps us appreciate the links between Lucien and the same-sex subcultures of his time that Balzac must have had in mind. Lucien's desire in *Lost Illusions,* fulfilled in *Splendeurs et misères des courtisanes,* is to trade in his common father's family name, Chardon, for that of his noble mother, Rubempré. On December 14, 1834, the soon-to-be-famous criminal (and poet) Lacenaire and his accomplice, Avril, brutally murdered a man called *la tante* Chardon along with his mother in their home during a robbery. Lacenaire's murder trial was a much-publicized event in Paris in mid-November 1835, and was covered in great detail in many newspapers, such as the *La Gazette des Tribunaux, Le Constitutionnel,* and *Le Charivari. Le Charivari* even published lithographs of both Lacenaire and Avril, as well as the text of a number of Lacenaire's songs. In *La Gazette des Tribunaux* for November 14, a man Avril had tried to recruit as an accomplice recounts that Avril tried to convince him to join them by saying that "we're going to kill *a fairy* [il s'agissait de tuer *une tante*]." When Avril was asked how such a fellow could have garnered enough money to be worth killing, he recounted that Chardon obtained his money by dressing up as a priest and going door-to-door in affluent neighborhoods selling fake religious artifacts and asking for money for religious causes.[25] Rumors circulated about Lacenaire's sexuality as well. He had met Chardon a few years earlier when they were in prison together—they had a common friend in another convict named Bâton. One contemporary observer noted that Bâton had been accused of being Lacenaire's "more than intimate friend."[26]

Lacenaire himself makes his way into *La Comédie humaine* on at least three occasions. In *La Muse du département* (1843), Mme. de La Baudraye collects autographs in an album. One of the high points of the album is a page on which she has included a signed poem by Lacenaire, "whose autograph was much sought after" (4:673).[27] At a certain moment in the first part of *L'Envers de l'histoire contemporaine* (1844), we are told that "all of Paris was taken up with the denouement at the Barrière Saint-Jacques [the location of the guillotine] of one of those horrible criminal trials that stand out in the annals of our criminal courts" (8:280), most likely the trial of Lacenaire and Avril. More relevant to our purposes, Lacenaire makes an unnamed appearance in *Splendeurs et misères des courtisanes.* At the opening of the third section (first published in 1846), the narrator is explaining why it is that the police vehicles that transport criminals from place to place in Paris are known as "salad baskets," and adds information about how the journey to one's execution at the Barrière Saint-Jacques now happens in much greater comfort than used to be the case when those to be executed were carried in a cart to the Place de Grève. "Without this explanation," the narrator adds, "it would be impossible to understand the witticism of a famous condemned criminal to his accomplice as they got into the salad basket: 'Now it's all up to the horses!' It is impossible to travel in better circumstances to one's ultimate punishment than one does these days in Paris" (6:698, 300). Why this digression was necessary in order to describe Lucien and Vautrin's arrival at the Conciergerie in their respective salad baskets is, at first glance, far from clear.

The famous condemned criminal mentioned (but not named) by the narrator was, of course, Lacenaire, whose remark was reported in *La Gazette des Tribunaux* on January 11, 1836. Balzac even named him in an earlier version of this part of his novel, but he corrected the proofs to leave out the name, substituting for it "un illustre condamné [a famous condemned criminal]" (see 6:1407). Pierre Citron, the editor of the Pléiade edition of *Splendeurs et misères des courtisanes,* adds in a note that Lacenaire was "primarily tried for the murder of a fellow convict named Chardon, but this is merely a coincidence" (6:1407). Perhaps not. Lacenaire seems to have been on Balzac's mind in the 1840s, and it seems more likely to imagine that if Balzac brought up Lacenaire in three separate works, and included the unnecessary digression as to Lacenaire's not particularly noteworthy remark about the horses at the outset of part three of *Splendeurs et misères des courtisanes,* it is because he had followed the case closely and saw some connection between Vautrin, Lucien, and Lacenaire. On the other hand, if he decided at the moment of correcting the proofs of that section of the novel to leave out Lacenaire's name, it might well be because its presence would have allowed an informed reader to make too quick and too easy a connection between Lucien Chardon and *la tante* Chardon. Male same-sex sexuality circles endlessly but elusively around Lucien. Lucien's sexuality is consistently held open to question; the novels about him clearly intend to provoke such questioning. But they seem written more in order to keep that questioning going than to provide specific and explicit answers to any questions. Balzac himself will use the word *tante* to refer to men who have sex with men in his novel, but not until Lucien is dead and Vautrin is put into a courtyard with the other male prisoners in an effort by prison officials to cause him to expose his true identity. The word *tante* will be applied by another prisoner to Théodore Calvi, one of Vautrin's old flames, and it will be applied to the male prisoners in general by a prison official (6:840, 453–54). Its direct application to Lucien Chardon remains carefully in suspension.

EATING LUCIEN

All columnists should be beaten into pulp and converted back to paper.—*Sabrina,* 1954 (dir. Billy Wilder)

Recent critics have not hesitated to speak of Lucien de Rubempré's "homosexuality." Lucette Finas refers to it as "highly probable."[28] Janet Beizer sees no need for even that qualification. Discussing Lucien and his friend David Séchard, to whom we are introduced in the opening pages of *Lost Illusions,* she writes: "While David stands for production and reproduction, Lucien figures destruction and sterility. His homosexuality is opposed to David's heterosexuality, and he becomes in every respect David's inverted counterpart. . . . If we are to understand Lucien's susceptibility to Herrera, it is imperative that we recognize his homosexuality as gradually emergent, inherent in his earliest attachments, latent in his narcissistic relational patterns."[29] Were Beizer's observations to be correct, *Lost Illusions* would be conceptually somewhat confused, and hopelessly homophobic as well. It would be conflating gender inversion with same-sex attraction; it would be making use of "homosexuality" to represent destruction and sterility; and it would be conceiving every sexual interest one man might have for another to be caused by the inhibited psychological development that Freud associates with a narcissistic personality disorder.

Beizer insists that "Balzac's 'case history' of Lucien . . . converges with Freud's theories about homosexual models of desire," and in support of her assertion she references the classic, and classically homophobic, Freudian discussions of male homosexuality in "On Narcissism" and in "Leonardo da Vinci and a Memory of His Childhood" (203 n.16). In "On Narcissism," Freud writes: "We have found, especially in persons whose libidinal development has suffered some disturbance, as in perverts and homosexuals, that in the choice of their love-object they have taken as their model not the mother but their own selves. They are plainly seeking themselves as a love-object and their type of object-choice may be termed *narcissistic*." In "Leonardo da Vinci," he writes:

> The boy represses his love for his mother: he puts himself in her place, identifies himself with her, and takes his own person as a model in whose likeness he chooses the new objects of his love. In this way he has become a homosexual. What he has in fact done is to slip back to auto-erotism: for the boys whom he now loves as he grows up are after all only substitutive figures and revivals of himself in childhood—boys whom he loves in the way in which his mother loved *him* when he was a child. He finds the objects of his love along the path of *narcissism*. . . . A man who has become homosexual in this way remains unconsciously fixated to the mnemic image of his mother. By repressing his love for his mother he preserves it in his unconscious and from now on remains faithful to her. While he seems to pursue boys and to be their lover, he is in reality running away from the other women, who might cause him to be unfaithful.[30]

Freud's tale of homosexual development has been retold many times within psychoanalytic circles. One retelling was in 1938 by Jacques Lacan in an article titled "La Famille" written for the *Encyclopédie française* (it has since been republished as a book under the title *Les Complexes familiaux dans la formation de l'individu*). In the final pages of this essay Lacan links the male homosexual to his mother in the same manner as does Freud. He goes even a step further and matter-of-factly blames the mother for the son's nonconformity:

> There is no need for analysts to dig very deeply to discover the clinical evidence that here too incriminates the mother, evidence concerning both the excesses of her tenderness towards the child and the virile traits within her own character. Inversion comes about, at least for the male subject, by way of a triple mechanism. There is, sometimes just at the edge of consciousness, almost always within the range of observation, an affective fixation on the mother, a fixation that implies the exclusion of all other women. There is, at a

deeper, but still accessible level, accessible if only to the poetic intuition, the narcissistic ambivalence according to which the subject identifies himself with the mother, and identifies the love object with his own specular image—the relation between him and his mother providing the form into which his mode of desire and his chosen object will always fit, his desire always motivated by tenderness and education, his love object reproducing his double at some particular moment. Finally, at the deepest psychic level, one finds the intervention—quite rightly called castrative—by which the mother has given expression to her own claim to virility.[31]

This is the same essay in which Lacan suggests a particular origin for psychoanalysis itself: "A great many psychological effects seem to us to be the result of a social decline in the paternal imago. . . . Perhaps it is even to this very crisis that one should ascribe the very appearance on the scene of psychoanalysis itself" (72–73). Lacan perhaps sounds here a bit like Balzac in some of his most conservatively programmatic moments—Balzac the spokesman for the virtues of a Catholic family within a monarchical state. This is probably not the best recommendation for imagining that Lacan, or Freud—when they indulge in this particular way of imagining the construction of the "homosexual" subject or the failings of the modern family—are of much use in *explaining* what goes on in a Balzac novel. Rather, the similarities might better serve to alert us to the presence of certain historically specific interests within certain strands of psychoanalytic discourse. As Michel Tort writes, in a helpful essay on the homophobia that runs through much psychoanalytic "theorizing," including that of Lacan and certain Lacanians, "in our present circumstances, our goal should not be to isolate some kernel of psychoanalytic truth that is protected from historically determined 'cultural' effects. Rather, we should figure out how certain elements within psychoanalytic theorizations have come into being within a certain historical situation that has conditioned them, and in which they attempt to intervene."[32]

While there is much within *Lost Illusions* that might resemble the reactionary family discourse that characterizes Lacan's essay, and while there are aspects in the portrayal of Lucien that correspond to Freud's ideologically complicated tale of homosexual development, there is a great deal more to the novel than that. There is, as we have seen elsewhere in Balzac, an investigation of the interests that motivate the very discourses for which the novel sometimes advocates. I think it would be fair, for instance, to argue that Balzac, in *Lost Illusions,* is making a point similar to Lacan's: that certain male subjects at certain moments in the history of the bourgeois family become arenas in which a mother's unacknowledged resistance to the family form in question plays itself out. Yet perhaps Lucien, with his doubtful sexuality, is not the only or even the best example of this. I would like here to look at the family situation of Lucien's friend David Séchard. This will help us to understand something of the place occupied by Lucien in the larger social field set out in the first part of the novel and something of the interests that press in on Lucien.

It is, after all, with David Séchard's encounter with his father that the novel opens, a scene in which David, freshly returned from Paris, lets himself be swindled by his father—swindled into buying his father's obsolete printing establishment and swindled further out of his maternal inheritance:

> He [David] drew his [father's] attention to the fact that he had never asked him to render an account of his mother's fortune. Even if this fortune could not be set off against the price asked for the printing-works, it should at least go towards the running of the new partnership.
>
> "Why," old Séchard replied, "all your mother owned was her brains and beauty."
>
> At this reply, David saw through his father completely, and realized that, in order to extract such a reckoning from him, he would have to take legal proceedings, and that these would be interminable, costly and discreditable. (5:135–36, 16)

In fact, the novel has already informed us, it was only because he was married that David's father escaped conscription into the Revolutionary army, and also during the Revolutionary period that he managed to buy the printing firm at half of its value, using the wife's savings. In short, legally, the printing firm probably to a great extent already belongs to David as his mother's heir. He pays his father for something that most likely he already owns.

This argument about money and maternal inheritance between a son and a dishonorable father suggests that David's relationship to production and to his home needs to be understood in relation to his deceased mother, whose ghost is never exorcized and whose inheritance is never properly passed on. The novel underscores this in the description of the Séchard living room, where David is negotiating with his father:

> The living-room had been modernized by the late Madame Séchard and shocked the eye with its appalling wainscots painted in wig-maker's blue; the panels were decorated with wall-paper depicting Oriental scenes in sepia on a white ground; the furniture consisted of six chairs with blue roan seats and backs in the shape of lyres. The two crudely-arched windows looking out on to the Place du Mûrier had no curtains; the chimney-piece was devoid of candelabra, clock and mirror. Madame Séchard had died when she was only half-way through with her plan for embellishment, and the "bear" [her husband], seeing no purpose in unproductive improvements, had abandoned them. (5:130, 10)

Madame Séchard's hand reveals itself through the bad taste it left behind, yet she is also present in the bare spaces that call to mind her uncompleted vision. She died before dispensing all the money she might have spent in pursuit of those commodities linked to her vision of modernization. The very idea of a project of modernization links her to her son, the modern printer, who could in this light be seen as picking up her fallen mantle. The lyres on the backs of the chairs in the opening pages hint at the commodification of poetry long before David—later in the novel—sends Lucien to Paris to enact in person that process of commodification for us.

Also interesting is the implicit disagreement between David's two parents over the concept of utility, a disagreement David will carry on in the next generation. What usefulness could there be in "unproductive improvements"? When, in the service of what, is expenditure waste? When are improvements useful, productive? How is one to understand the return expected from expenditures some might consider useless? Père Séchard imagines economy differently than do his wife and his son. The father lives in an economy based on hoarding, recycling, and a resistance to expenditure on anything as transient as fashion. David and his mother are more willing to spend on transient things, to improve, to renovate with the passing years; they are willing not to hoard money but to become susceptible to commodities, to accept a practice of obsolescence that challenges the father's faith in enduring value.

This struggle is figured initially in the contrast presented in the opening paragraph of the novel between, on the one hand, "wooden presses from which the now obsolete metaphor 'making the presses groan' originated," and on the other, "the devouring mechanical presses" that characterize recent technological innovation (5:124, 3). The two presses represent a movement from manual to mechanical labor, and they also represent the gradual loss of utility of the human body and the deracination of value from that body. The wooden presses are carefully linked to human agency and human speech. We are in their debt, the novel says, for an expression, "faire gémir la presse"—as if the presses themselves almost reached out for speech. Yet that very expression, like the wooden presses, is "now obsolete," and therefore also recalls the increasingly prevalent economy of obsolescence and of mechanical production, an economy as devouring as it is productive.

The mechanical presses (referred to here as Stanhope presses), with which David would want to replace his father's wooden ones, also seem to mark, as Père Séchard carefully points out, the death of the letter: "They cost two thousand five hundred francs apiece, almost twice as much as my three beauties put together, and they wear down the type because there's no give in them. I'm not educated like you, but bear this in mind: Stanhope presses may last longer, but they are the death of typeface characters [la vie des Stanhope est la mort du caractère]" (5:132, 12). These new presses that wear out their own typeface also effectively steal the value from Père Séchard's old but still perfectly *usable* characters: "Five thousand pounds of type from the Vaflard foundry." Valued by the father for their durability—"After a dozen years, the characters are as good as new. . . . The best founder is the one you go to least often"—it is precisely their durability that makes them worthless to the son. They have lasted too long, outlasted their value: "'Valued at ten thousand francs,' David continued. 'Ten thousand francs, father! But that works out at forty sous a pound, and Messrs Didot only charge thirty-six sous a pound for their new pica. Your old nail heads are only worth the metal they're cast in—ten sous a pound'" (5:132, 12). Barely worth the metal out of which they are formed, barely worth thinking about recycling, these perfectly usable characters become, in David's vision, waste. Almost magically, they appear later in the novel in the streets of Paris, at the conclusion of Lucien's first depressing visit to the offices of Finot's journal, where he is told that he has no value as a journalist. The old Giroudeau gives him a bit of friendly advice as they leave the office together: "There you go, like all rookies who want to be field-marshals! Take old Giroudeau's advice: left wheel in single file, quick march, go and pick up nails in the gutter like that fine chap over there: you can see he's been in the service by the way he moves. Isn't it a scandal that an old soldier who's looked straight into the cannon's muzzle a thousand times should be picking up nails in Paris?" (5:334, 237). The new economy of waste has already created a subsidiary economy of recycling thanks to which those human instruments for which the more general economy has no more important further use can find some desperately marginal utility. Those "old nail heads" worth so little to David, barely even worth taking the time to melt down, could perhaps provide a bare subsistence living to a homeless soldier, another waste product, whose time is worth so little that it can be worth his while to scour the gutters for scrap.

Literature, journalism, and the need of printers for material to print also confront each other within this economy of waste. Whether books or newspapers should or should not be considered commodities whose value has a limited life span is a question *Lost Illusions* is never done asking. The relation between David and Lucien is heavily overdetermined by this larger economic context. When David's father asks him how he managed to spend so much money in Paris, David replies, "Didn't I have living expenses, didn't I buy books?" To which his father answers: "Oh, you bought books, did you? You won't do well in business. People who buy books are hardly the right ones to be printing them" (5:135, 15). Yet, *pace* his father, David, however susceptible to books as commodities, is somewhat savvy about the economics of book manufacture. In this regard he is an interestingly divided character: devoted to literature on the one hand, yet on the other critically aware of the way people's relation to printed commodities can be exploited commercially. He is also finely attuned to the need of printers to innovate in using raw materials so as to maximize their profits. When he proposes marriage to Lucien's sister, Eve, he does so by way of a long lecture on paper making and the innovations he hopes for, innovations necessitated by the slow decrease in the quantity of linen rags available for paper manufacture. Linen, when used to make clothing, is more durable than cotton, and so linen clothes may represent long-term savings over cotton ones. They are, however, more expensive initially, which means more and more people are wearing cotton:

> In England, where four-fifths of the population wear cotton instead of linen, paper is now made out of scarcely anything but cotton rags. This paper, which in the first place has the drawback of tearing and breaking, dissolves so easily in water that a book made of cotton paper would be reduced to a mash after a quarter of an hour in water, whereas an old book would not be ruined if it stayed in it for two hours. An old book could be dried; it might turn yellow and fade, but the text could still be legible and the work would not be destroyed. (5:220, 110)

Here David sounds a bit like his father, favoring placing value in long-lasting items and counseling long-term investments. Books should be preserved, not thrown away on a whim: "What a disgrace it is that our era produces books that do not last! Ten years more, and Holland paper, that is to say paper made of linen rags, will be altogether impossible to use!" (5:222, 111–12). "Books that do not last" clearly refers as much to an economy of fashion—also understood in the novel as the struggle between journalism and literature—as to a manufacturing problem. David has a wide-ranging view of the problem. As a larger and larger market of readers develops, those readers are less wealthy in the aggregate and so need cheaper books. Cotton-based paper appears to be more economical. Also, paper made from linen is thick and heavy, and so produces large books. Yet the bookshelf footage available to common readers, as well as the decreasing average size of private and public libraries, is making smaller books more desirable. Not only is linen itself disappearing from the manufacture of clothing, and thus the price of linen rags rising, but the market value of linen paper is declining as its disadvantages become more significant in a world requiring smaller books. David's goal is thus to find a way to produce a paper that is cheap, long-lasting, and thin.

Books used to be luxury items—expensive and big. The private libraries of the nobility used to be located in mansions. But, as David notes, "the great mansions and suites of rooms in Paris will sooner or later be demolished, for soon private fortunes will no longer be on the same level as those that enabled the constructions of our forefathers" (5:222, 111). Another way of putting this would be to say that the wastefulness of an aristocratic economy of pomp and splendor used to be one of the material supports for the manufacture of books. As a new commodity form and a new mass-market for books come into place, the shape of literature, as well as the shape of books, is up for grabs.

In many different ways Lucien exists at the crossroads of these two markets—the old literary market of aristocratic pomp and splendor and the new literary market of disposable commodities. His father was a chemist who himself speculated on new ways to manufacture paper. His mother, the last member of an aristocratic family, was saved from the guillotine by the chemist, who in order to protect her life claimed that she was pregnant by him. The couple have two children, Lucien and Eve. But the chemist dies on the verge of an important medical discovery that would have rescued his family from the poverty into which they had fallen. After his death, his formerly aristocratic wife earns a small income as a midwife, and his daughter works as a laundress. They both invest their money in Lucien (as does David, once he is betrothed to Eve), in whose brilliant future they imagine their financial well-being to reside. "Tu sera notre aristocratie," David tells him—"You shall be our aristocracy" (5:184, 70). Lucien himself, once he has gained the protection of Mme. de Bargeton, Angoulême's leading aristocrat, and has quit the day job David had given him at the printing house and has left his family's humble lodgings, all the more readily conceives the dual project of dropping his father's name for his mother's and of earning a fortune through literature:

> By the beginning of September, Lucien was no longer a proofreader: he was Monsieur de Rubempré. . . . Assuredly, as he paced through his elegant sitting-room, his charming bedroom and his tastefully decorated study, he could forgive himself for levying thirty francs a month on the painfully earned wages of his sister and mother, for he could look forward to the day when the historical novel at which he had been working for two years—*The Archer of Charles the Ninth,* and a volume of verse entitled *The Marguerites*—would spread his renown through the world of literature and bring

> him enough money to pay his debt to his mother, sister and David. And so, feeling greater in stature, already hearing his name echoing down the corridors of the future, he was now accepting these sacrifices with a noble self-assurance. (5:233, 123–24)

One can understand that it might be tempting at this point to turn to psychoanalysis to invoke the weakening of the paternal imago in the post-Revolutionary moment, or to ponder the mother's way of implanting, through her excessive tenderness, her own virile protest against her fate within the bourgeois family.[33] Yet before deciding that his noble mother has successfully produced a homosexual son from within the confines of the bourgeois family (if that is what this is), one would have to take account of the problem posed by the fact that Lucien's love objects both at this point (the noblewoman Mme. de Bargeton), and once he arrives in Paris (the theater-girl Coralie), do not seem particularly to resemble him—especially as regards their biological sex. (Nor is it easy to see how, later in the novel, Vautrin could ever be imagined to be for Lucien, in Freud's words, a member of a series of "substitutive figures and revivals of himself in childhood—boys whom he loves in the way in which his mother loved *him* when he was a child.")

Clearly the novel shows that Lucien, on both psycho-social and allegorical levels, represents other people's interests—his mother's, Eve's, and David's to start with. One might add that the set of interests he represents throughout the novel is hardly internally coherent. To the extent that he seeks after his mother's name and an aristocratic tradition of ostentatious display, for instance, his interests are not modernizing ones, however much they might contribute to a weakening of the paternal imago. But let us pursue for a moment the way Lucien is shown to act to further the interests of the modernizing commodity economy that threatens the status and stature of literature itself. This strand of thinking in the novel passes through his patronymic.

It was Lucien who told David that Lucien's father had spent some time trying to find a new, plant-based material from which to make paper. Consider the fact that *chardon* means thistle. At a certain point in the third section of the novel, once the entire family has nearly been brought to ruin by Lucien's shenanigans in Paris, David is walking along chewing on a thistle (more precisely, on a nettle, an *ortie,* a close relative of a *chardon*) as he ponders how to invent a new kind of paste from which paper can be made. He spits the gob of chewed up nettle out onto his hand, and realizes that the action of *saliva* on thistles forms a perfect and inexpensive paste out of which to make a new kind of paper. We here find Lucien both in the mind and in the mouth of his friend:

> A prey to the vexations due to lack of money, a prey to the worry caused by his wife's state of mind—reduced to despair as she was by Lucien's infamous conduct—David was still pondering over his problem. It had so happened that, as he was on his way from his house to see Petit-Claud, he had absent-mindedly been chewing a nettle stalk which he had steeped in water as a means for somehow or other retting the stalks he was using as material for his pulp. He was trying to find a process equivalent to the various kinds of attrition effected by soaking, by weaving or by ordinary wear-and-tear on anything of which the end-product is thread, linen or rag-stuff. As he made his way home, quite satisfied with his talk with Petit-Claud, he realized that he had a ball of pulp in his mouth. He took it out, rolled it out in his hand, and found that it made a better pulp than any of the compounds he had produced hitherto; for the principal defect in pulps made from vegetable matter is that they lack adhesiveness. . . . He told himself that he would use a machine and a chemical agent to carry out the operation which he had just accomplished automatically [*machinalement*]. (5:603, 536–37)

A bit earlier, David had explained to his wife why it was probably best to find a way to use weeds to make paper: "But I intend to use nettles and thistles [*les orties, les chardons*] because, in order to keep down the cost of the raw material, recourse must be had to vegetable substances which grow in marshes and infertile soil and therefore are very cheap. The whole secret lies in finding a way to treat these plants" (5:583, 515).[34] Lucien's effaced patronymic thus links him to an economy of new low-cost primary resources being sought out by an ever more hungry industrial Europe. His displaced presence in the salivating mouth of his friend suggests that, if we wished, we could choose to ask questions about the characteristics of the objects of *David's* desire. On another level, we could simply ask to what extent David's financial interests in producing paper for mass-market literature necessarily require the production not only of cheap paper but also of expendable agents to write on that paper. Consider in this light some remarks made to Lucien by his friend Lousteau in Paris:

> It's always the same story, every year the same enthusiastic inrush of beardless ambition from the provinces to Paris: an equal, indeed an increasing number of young men who leap forward, with high head and lofty heart, to their wooing of Fashion. . . . They all fall into the pit of misery, the mire of journalism, the morass of the book-trade. These mendicants go round like gleaners, picking up biographical articles, "tartines," news-in-brief columns on the newspapers or else write books bespoken by the shrewd-minded pedlars of scrawl who prefer a piece of nonsense they can sell in a fortnight to a masterpiece which stays long on their hands. (5:346, 249)

Lucien, Lousteau, and their ilk are, in short, the nail collectors of literary Paris, produced by an economy of rapidly outdated commodities, an economy in which literature continually struggles to imagine itself as somehow different—thereby aiding in the production of deluded scribblers. David's desire for Lucien, tied to his desire for cheap paper, is complicit in Lucien's abjection as one such scribbler. Thus, when in the third part of the novel Lucien returns to Angoulême in rags and tatters, having "failed" in Paris, he has, by a certain logic, not failed at all. He has done his service through his writing, and he has even worn out his clothes, which can now be recycled. All of this has happened, in a certain way, *machinalement,* as a form of automatic behavior, just as David unwittingly used his own saliva to produce a solution to his industrial problem. We might think then that the novel portrays *David* as instrumental in producing Lucien as a subject subjected to waste, a disposable commodity. Of course, one cannot say that either David or Lucien has a particularly clear grasp of the interests they enact. Lucien may be marked by the moralizing discourse of the novel as a degraded producer, an abject consumer, and a distasteful waste product, but the novel has carefully laid out the complicity of everyone else's desires in making him so, and has shown that all the forms of desire *for* Lucien, as well as any form of desire Lucien exhibits, are deeply marked by conflicting historical interests that often do not directly further the personal interests of any particular agent. We shall see in what follows that this is as true of sexual desire within the novel as of any other form of desire.

In *Lost Illusions,* Balzac's sociological eye investigates different forms of capital and the possible methods of conversion between them. Lucien takes on the project of reestablishing the *social* capital that once would have been his mother's by virtue of her aristocratic position ("You will be our aristocracy"). Lucien's mother and sister invest their *economic* capital in the process of Lucien's cultivation, with the idea that their money will be converted into advantageous *cultural* capital and that a cultivated Lucien would be better equipped to win economic and social remuneration for the entire family ("He could forgive himself for levying thirty francs a month on the painfully earned wages of his sister and mother, for he could look forward to the day when the historical novel at which he had been working for two years . . . would spread his renown through the world of literature and bring him enough money to pay his debt to his mother, sister and David"). David imagines (or the novel imagines through him) a more complicated exploitation of Lucien—the economically and socially impoverished embodiment of a certain amount of cultural capital—as a second-order raw material for the production of economic capital by way of mass-market commodities made out of ink on paper ("I intend to use *orties* and *chardons*"). "The use or exploitation of cultural capital," Pierre Bourdieu writes, "presents particular problems for the holders of economic or political capital. . . . How can this capital, so closely linked to the person, be bought without buying the person? . . . How can this capital be concentrated—as some undertakings demand—without concentrating the possessors of the capital, which can have all sorts of unwanted consequences?"[35] On one level the novel may present David as a heroic inventor of a new kind of paper, thereby contributing to the greatness of the French nation. On the other hand, the novel also points out that the huge quantities of paper intended to be sold as newsprint or as the raw material for books require a labor pool of scribblers. The more poorly paid those scribblers are—the more deluded they are about the system of exploitation that profits from them—the better. This all enters into David's desire for Lucien.

True, the novel seems to redeem David in the end, creating in him the perfect family man. Having been swindled by the Cointets into selling them his immensely valuable industrial secret in return for an all-too-small fortune, he retires with wife and children to a country estate. But the novel reserves what is perhaps some of its bitterest irony for its concluding description of this new David: "He diverts himself by the cultivation of letters, but he leads the happy and lazy life of a landowner improving his estate [Il cultive les lettres par délassement, mais il mène la vie heureuse et paresseuse du propriétaire faisant valoir]" (5:732, 681). In "il cultive les lettres" one hears an echo of the exploitation of the *orties* and the *chardons* that are now busily being turned into newsprint and paper all over France, precisely to produce those books and journals that fill David's moments of leisure as he sits around (just as his father would have) slowly increasing the value of his estate. David the inventer has served his purpose and been put out to pasture, where he nonetheless continues to exercise the economically somewhat useful function of a consumer of "high-brow" culture.

THE VALUE OF BEAUTY

Lucien's fate in *Lost Illusions,* his relations with his mother, his sister, and his brother-in-law, and the forms of desire invested in him are all used to hammer home Balzac's point about the strategies that different groups develop for increasing their total capital by playing social, cultural, and economic capital off against each other. Lucien's beauty is much commented on throughout the novel, but the *value* of Lucien's beauty (much more fully investigated in *Splendeurs et misères des courtisanes*) only becomes thematized in *Lost Illusions* once Lucien meets Vautrin. The scene between Lucien and Vautrin at the end of *Lost Illusions,* a seduction scene involving two men, thus prepares the issues Balzac was to be studying in detail throughout *Splendeurs et misères des courtisanes,* especially in its third and fourth parts. In those two sections, the relation between Lucien and Vautrin becomes the focus of intense public and state scrutiny, and Vautrin will prove able to exploit competing interests within the state structure in order to capitalize not only on his own passionate relationship with Lucien but also on the passions of others for this male beauty, even after Lucien is dead.

Until the moment Lucien encounters Vautrin, the most explicit version of male same-sex desire we see in *Lost Illusions* is David's for

Lucien, most pithily condensed into the thistle stalk that David reduces to pulp with his saliva. As in the case of the masticated thistle, this male-male desire expresses itself mostly in rather displaced forms. The desire to use Lucien, to turn him into a cog within the machine of the literature industry, a cog soon to be worn down and spat out, doubtless also contains some awareness of the transience of Lucien's beauty—on which he and so many others are trying to capitalize. Yet the limited, displaced, sublimated expressions of David's desire for Lucien also indicate the culturally and historically specific difficulty David and Lucien apparently have in finding a form for the expression of sexual desire between them. They are not noble, nor are they particularly well educated about the forms of intimate relations possible within the nobility. They are not about to make use of the social forms that exist within prison culture—assuming they are even aware of them. Even though David has spent time in Paris, he and Lucien do not seem to share a bohemian set of cultural practices and attitudes. Doubtless Lucien's Parisian apprenticeship in bohemia in the second part of the novel is part of what prepares him for his encounter with Vautrin in the third part, by which time he seems fully ready to understand the nature of the sexual proposition Vautrin makes him.[36]

It is by way of the story of a paper-eating secretary told by Vautrin to Lucien that Lucien finds his place in Vautrin's plans and that Balzac connects together the agendas of the different parts of his novels. Vautrin tells Lucien of the Swedish baron de Goërtz, who was traveling and in need of a secretary. In a small village he came across the son of a goldsmith, "remarquable par une beauté qui ne pouvait certes pas valoir la vôtre" (5:692, 637). This could mean, simply, "remarkably handsome, though certainly not so handsome as you," but more literally it means, "remarkable for a beauty that was not of the same value as yours." The more literal translation in fact proves more germane to the context. The baron chooses to find the young secretary to be intelligent as well as beautiful, "comme moi je vous trouve de la poésie au front [just as I find poetry on your brow]" (5:692, 637). Vautrin does not care a fig for Lucien's literary aspirations, of course, just as the baron was probably not all that preoccupied by the cute young boy's level of intelligence. The poetry of Lucien's brow is a saleable commodity for Vautrin, not in terms of literary potential but in terms of the way beauty can be exploited in the search for economic and social capital. Vautrin's lesson to Lucien is that Lucien has not yet understood how to exploit the value of his physical beauty: "The priest looked at Lucien with a smile and said to him, with infinite grace and an almost ironical smile: 'A diamond has no idea of its value'" (5:691, 636–37).

Vautrin continues by recounting that despite the young secretary's physical appeal, the baron apparently demanded a great deal of him: "Once at Stockholm, he installed him as a secretary and put a great burden of work upon him. This young secretary spent his nights writing, and like all hard workers he contracted a habit: his was to chew paper. . . . Our handsome young man began with blank paper, but he grew tired of that and took to masticating manuscripts, which he found more tasty. . . . Finally the little secretary, passing from one flavor to another, acquired the habit of munching parchment" (5:692, 637–38). Clearly, the story Vautrin tells contains an echo of the image of the plant stem in David Séchard's mouth, linking David's desire for Lucien to Vautrin's seduction of him. Vautrin's effort is to convince Lucien to submit to Vautrin's expert exploitation of his physical beauty, a submission that in some ways parallels David's desire to exploit Lucien's literary delusions. Vautrin is also associated with David in that their economic desires are linked to their sexual desires—a desire Vautrin is much more capable of acknowledging than David ever was. Writing, slightly melodramatically, about the story Vautrin is telling Lucien, Christopher Prendergast suggests that we "link Vautrin's story with the general logic of production and consumption articulated around the theme of paper in *Illusions perdues* as a whole. In its peculiarly exotic way, it makes literal the informing metaphor of the society as voraciously consuming and self-consuming. . . . A society based on the ceaseless production, circulation and 'consumption' of bits of paper is a society that is fundamentally 'unsound', without a stable center, a society devoted to the dispersal and squandering of vital substance, including supremely language."[37] Vautrin's story certainly picks up on the thematics of the consumption of paper that runs throughout the novel—but perhaps not in the service of some moralistic concern with "vital substances." Rather, the story allows Balzac to return to his concern with the various kinds of economies in which male beauty and male same-sex relations are caught up, once again linking that concern to his other sociological interests.

Implicitly, Vautrin tells Lucien that all of his literary obsessions with paper and its value were red herrings. A better investment strategy would have been to rely on his beauty, not his literary aspirations. He insists repeatedly on the beauty of the secretary in his story: "le joli petit secrétaire," "ce beau secrétaire," "le bel enfant," "la beauté du jeune commis." At a certain point the overworked but beautiful paper addict unconsciously eats an important treaty between Russia and Sweden, and he is sentenced to death as a result. However, because of the young man's *beauty,* the king of Sweden and the baron let the "joli petit secrétaire" escape to the court of Kurland, and the baron even gives him a recommendation to the duke there. The duke is forewarned about the young fellow's dangerous habit, yet still employs him as a secretary. The young lad inevitably repeats his errors and, in the middle of the night, hard at work,

> the little paper-eater discovered that he was masticating a receipt for a considerable sum of money, signed by the Duke himself. Panic-stricken, he stopped before he had eaten his way through the signature, ran and flung himself at the feet of the Duchess, explained his mania to her and implored his sovereign lady to shield him—what's more, this took place in the middle of the night! The young clerk's beauty made such an impression on Her Grace that, when she became a widow, she married him. Thus, right back in the eighteenth century, in a country where armorial bearings were all that mattered, a goldsmith's son became a sovereign prince! (5:694, 639)

Vautrin is giving Lucien a lesson in how to turn one's weaknesses to one's own advantage. The secretary exploits both his beauty and the pity occasioned by his paper-eating disability (and also a certain sexual lability) to accumulate social capital. Why should Lucien not do the same? Vautrin thus understands Lucien's literary aspirations as a disability and also as a kind of mechanical, obsessive habit, but one from which perhaps value can be extracted. If one knows how to play the courtier, and has the advantage of beauty, there are ways to rise socially.

The title *Splendeurs et misères des courtisanes* designates courtiers in the feminine: courtesans. For some readers this has meant that the title refers only to the splendors and miseries of Esther, the prostitute whose passion for Lucien is recounted in the first two parts of the novel. According to this reading, it would only be for convenience's sake that the title is applied to the last two parts of the novel, which concern Vautrin and Lucien and which take place after Esther's death. In French, *courtisan* can refer either to a male courtier or to a man with obsequious manners, whereas in the feminine form, *courtisane,* the word refers more specifically to women of dubious sexual morals but operating within the highest social circles. The social dissymmetry between the masculine and feminine forms of the word is part of what is at issue in the novel. In its first two parts, Lucien and Vautrin capitalize on Esther's beauty in order to finance their campaign to capitalize on the beauty of Lucien. What is the negotiability of masculine, as opposed to feminine, beauty? Under what market conditions can one exchange masculine beauty for economic and social capital? How are the rules that govern the market in beauty different in the case of masculine beauty than in the case of feminine beauty? What are the historical specificities that govern that market in Lucien and Vautrin's moment? These are the questions to which the second half of *Splendeurs et misères des courtisanes* turns, suggesting that the omnibus title serves equally well for both halves.[38]

In "Balzac's Illusions Lost and Found," D. A. Miller suggests that if Vautrin fails in his project to turn Lucien from the son of an apothecary into someone rich, famous, and of the highest social position, his failure has something to do with the way he is drawn to Lucien: "The desire to be, to have Lucien, fatally attaches [Vautrin] to a specific object rather than to social processes themselves. . . . For though Vautrin is able to see and manipulate 'the arbitrariness of the sign' at most other levels, when confronted by a Rastignac or Lucien, he is entirely willing to grant the appearance all the erotic authority of the reality. A semiotician, as such, can never fall in love. . . . To the extent that Vautrin is enamoured, he abdicates his semiotic competence, not because he misreads the signs, but because in this domain he fails to understand them as signs at all."[39] This seems to me both right and wrong. Vautrin exploits Lucien's beauty with as much savvy as he can muster. His savvy may be limited by the fact that his desire turns out to be an intense form of love. But I think that Vautrin's failure to assure Lucien's fame might be more helpfully linked to what we might call Vautrin's anachronistic vision of the world. Balzac knows that some people are better readers of the world than others, not *in general* but *at a given point in time.* Semiotic competence is not, for Balzac, some abstract talent that some have and others do not. It is a talent that some people have to a greater or lesser extent within given delimited spheres of action and given time frames. Vautrin, for all of his intense, cynical, visionary nature, is as subject to handicapping as anyone else in this arena—not only by the vagaries of love but by his very historically overdetermined makeup. Miller understands as much when he refers to Vautrin's "inaptly ancien régime understanding of paternity."[40] Vautrin's understanding of paternity is complex and antinormative, as we shall see. But there is a way in which his very relation to the world, despite the power and successes he reveals in the novels, is belated. This historically produced incapacity of vision will be carefully revealed by his failures within *Splendeurs et misères des courtisanes.* But before turning to an analysis of the conclusion of that novel, I would like to look briefly at the play *Vautrin* to gain a fuller understanding of Vautrin's relation to the noble classes.

VAUTRIN'S FANS

Car les héros de l'Iliade ne vont qu'à votre cheville, ô Vautrin, ô Rastignac, ô Birotteau . . . et vous, ô Honoré de Balzac, vous le plus héroïque, le plus singulier, le plus romantique et le plus poétique parmi tous les personnages que vous avez tirés de votre sein! [For the heroes of the *Iliad* barely come up to your ankles, Vautrin, Rastignac, Birotteau . . . And you, Honoré de Balzac, the most heroic, the most singular, the most romantic, the most poetic of all the characters that emerged from your heart.]—Charles Baudelaire, *Salon de 1846*

Lu hier le stupéfiant *Vautrin* de Balzac. L'avais-je lu déjà? Mais alors, de quel œil distrait, pour ne point encore m'être rendu compte que c'est là, bien plus encore que dans *Le Père Goriot* ou dans les *Illusions,* qu'il le faut surprendre et qu'il s'y confesse bien plus significativement. [Yesterday I read Balzac's amazing *Vautrin.* Had I read it before? If so, not very attentively, for I did not realize that it is only here, more than in *Le Père Goriot* or in *Illusions perdues,* that one can discover who he is, here that he reveals himself more significantly.]—André Gide, *Journal,* April 26, 1918

The marquis de Custine was in the audience for the one and only performance of *Vautrin* in 1840. "He was superb," Balzac wrote to Madame Hanska. "He had a box and was applauding to beat the band."[41] It was a big event, sold out long in advance. The famous actor

Frédéric Lemaître was to play the title role, and Custine made a special trip back to Paris from Versailles, where he was serving as a juror, to attend the performance. After seeing it, he wrote to Balzac:

> You have seen society from a very poetical point of view and you present it to us in a new and original form: this is a great achievement. The comic and the pathetic are both present, struggling for the upper hand in this one-of-a-kind play at which one laughs and cries at the same time. . . . Frédéric is wonderful; but the women actresses didn't help matters any. . . . We shouted ourselves hoarse calling for the author. . . . I would like to see you, and speak about all this, but I have to return to my galley. Would that I could meet a Vautrin there, given that I am unable to return tomorrow to your Parisian penal colony.[42]

Custine seems to have been unaware when he wrote the letter that the play was about to be closed down by the censor.

Balzac had already had problems getting authorization from the censors to produce the play. The character Vautrin, who would already have been known to Balzac's readers from *Le Père Goriot* and from the first parts of *Splendeurs et misères des courtisanes,* was found too immoral. The censors, in reading earlier versions of the play, had objected to various parts of the characterization of Vautrin, including the closeness of his relations with a family of aristocrats to whom he renders certain services—notably returning to them their long-lost son. Balzac made various changes to the play, which appear not to have modified anything about Vautrin in any significant way but which gained him permission to have the play performed. The censors intervened again after the first performance of the play, forbidding any further performances. It would not be performed again until shortly before Balzac's death in 1850. Many theories exist as to why it was banned. One that has received wide circulation, although it is not universally accepted, is that Frédéric Lemaître in one scene chose to wear a wig that made him resemble King Louis-Philippe, and the censors retaliated for this offense to the royal person.[43]

The play and the scandal surrounding it would have helped to draw attention to Balzac's central character. The nature of the reaction to Vautrin, both the character and the play, can be judged from a defense of Balzac written by his friend Delphine de Girardin a few days after the performance, for the column she published in the *La Presse* under the name of le vicomte de Launay:

> The subject of all conversations this week is M. de Balzac's play. What have you to say of it?
>
> "It's abominable."
>
> "It's detestable."
>
> "It's execrable."
>
> "It's deplorable."
>
> "It's miserable."
>
> "It's pitiful."
>
> "It's a sorry spectacle."
>
> "It's disgusting."
>
> "It's revolting."
>
> "But have you seen it?"
>
> "No."
>
> "And you, Madame?"
>
> "No, I couldn't get a box."
>
> "And you, my dear?"
>
> "That evening, my dear aunt, I was at the Opera."
>
> "Well then, how do you know that it was so frightful?"
>
> "I read it in the newspaper."[44]

Vautrin's sexual desires are not referenced in the play with anything like the specificity with which they are treated in the already published works in which he had appeared: *Le Père Goriot* and the first two sections of *Splendeurs et misères des courtisanes.* That specificity only increases, of course, in the later works: the final part of *Lost Illusions* and the final two parts of *Splendeurs et misères des courtisanes.* It seems likely, given the series of derogatory adjectives that Girardin provides, that the sexuality of the character formed one of the subtexts of the reception of the play.

The play recounts the story of the dashing young Raoul de Frescas, who is, without knowing it, the son of the duke and duchess Montsorel. Because Raoul was born a few months prematurely, only seven months into his parents' marriage, the jealous duke chose to believe that Raoul's real father was not himself but a friend of his, who loved the duchess and was subsequently executed during the Revolution. He told his wife that if she did not admit her guilt he would kill the child.

His wife falsely admitted to being guilty of adultery in order to save her son's life. The duke promised to let the child live but disposed of it in a way unknown to the mother. To avenge himself further, he has forced his wife to raise in their household, as her son, a child whom he produced adulterously with a Spanish courtesan. Vautrin discovers Raoul as a handsome and homeless child who understands himself to be an orphan. The criminal is taken with him strongly enough to raise him and promise him a great future. They have recently arrived in Paris, and Vautrin is introducing Raoul into noble circles. The duke and duchess have thus met him, though they remain unaware of who he is (their son was named Fernand). The duchess, however, has been troubled by certain family resemblances she imagines seeing in the handsome young fellow. Meanwhile, the duke is hoping to marry off his other son, Albert, to Inès de Christoval, the daughter of a Spanish duchess whose husband has been banished to Mexico. Yet Inès and Raoul have fallen in love. Unless Raoul can establish a pedigree for himself there is no hope for their love. Vautrin, who is also unaware of Raoul's true background, has, out of devotion to his "creation," promised to concoct a suitable pedigree for Raoul so as to allow him to follow his heart: "Your family? We are busy putting one together for you right now" (81). Vautrin is not impressed by the authentic sentiment Raoul seems to feel for Inès, yet he still finds her to be a good match for Raoul. She is "an adorable strong-box, with the prettiest eyes in the world, a shapely dowry, a svelte, delicious cash-box, as elegant as a white-sailed corvette leading back the galleons from America for which we are all impatiently waiting, offering all the joys of life, just as does the image of Fortune painted above the doors of the Lottery offices" (80).

Vautrin has always been interested in families formed outside of normative heterosexual reproductive practices. In *Le Père Goriot,* in his odd patriarchal fantasy of owning a slave plantation in the United States, he was interested in slaves because they were "children ready-made [des enfants tout venus]" (3:141, 131), an expression that recalls Mme. Cibot's words about Schmucke and Pons: "Go on now, I suppose you'll be telling me you've no heirs either! And that the pair of you just popped up like mushrooms [Allons, vous n'aussi, vous n'êtes sans héritiers, n'est-ce pas! Vous n'êtes venus comme des champignons sur cette terre]" (7:581,127). In *Le Père Goriot,* he also speaks to Rastignac of his desire for devotion: "Mais je vous aime, moi. J'ai la passion de me dévouer pour un autre" [But I am fond of you. My passion is to devote myself to another man]" (3:186, 182). (Although here the translator has chosen the decorous "But I am fond of you" for "Mais je vous aime," there is much more play within *aimer* than this translation allows for.) Vautrin will, of course, make similar declarations to Lucien. When in *La Cousine Bette* the narrator endeavored to characterize Bette's relationship to Valérie, he used a list of possibilities, "she had made a daughter of her, a friend, her love" (7:200, 170), and adds the word "sister" a few pages later. He also showed Bette's relation to Wenceslas to be a nearly illegible combination of mother and lover. Similarly, Vautrin understands that the intimate relation he wishes to construct with another man will be difficult to name, as it will involve not only love, desire, and sex, but also complex transgenerational and transgender components. Of Raoul, he says, "he is my creation. I am his father and his mother" (66). Raoul refers to him as "this man that can only be understood as part of a fairytale, a guardian angel, almost a fairy god-mother [cet homme qui ne s'explique que par la féerie, cette providence, je puis dire maternelle]" (76).

Through the various twists and turns of the play's plot, Vautrin nearly fails at his project of assuring Raoul's success. He learns in the nick of time of Raoul's true parentage, and he is able to gamble with that information to assure his protégé's future. But his first reaction on learning the true facts of Raoul's past is one of despair: "He has a father, a family, a mother. This is a disaster! Now in whom will I be able to take an interest? Who can I love? Twelve years of paternity is not easily repeated" (117). It would seem that a prerequisite for Vautrin's love is precisely that it exist in counterdistinction to normative families. Yet *Vautrin* ends with Vautrin sacrificing himself to Raoul and his "real" family, as a final act of devotion to his love object. This earns him the devotion of Raoul's mother: "You are not a criminal, and in any case all mothers would absolve you of your crimes," she tells him. "He loves him as would a mother," she observes to herself (118, 119). In the end the duke himself, while it is not in his power to have Vautrin pardoned, treats him respectfully and with gratitude, an attitude that Vautrin reciprocates. Even Raoul, on learning that his protector is a criminal who has returned illegally to France, remains loyal to him, completing the poignant sentimental reconciliation with which the play concludes.

Perhaps it was this representation of generous complicity between a powerful family and a sordid, seemingly anarchical criminal that allowed the bourgeois moralists of the day to take offense. At the end of the play the criminal, so drawn to beautiful young men and so hostile to normative categories for intimate relationships, finds recognition from within an aristocratic family that has had its share of hidden alternative family relationships. Both the criminal and the nobles recognize a shared code of devotion and loyalty in each others' actions. What Balzac begins to investigate here is the presence of a certain aristocratic ethos within Vautrin that is intricately interwoven with his same-sex desires. Vautrin's scorn for the bourgeois ideology of family, and the way it uses sentimentality to obscure economic relations, leaves open a space for recognition of and by alternative forms of family relation, where economic interest and duty on the one hand, and loving devotion on the other, might be structured differently. This odd conjuncture between Vautrin and certain members of the nobility—who recognize that as their social group loses dominance certain of their forms of intimate relation are being put at risk—is more fully developed in the final two parts of *Splendeurs et misères des courtisanes.*[45]

VAUTRIN'S PREDICAMENT

Previous critics have noted and commented on the odd sympathy that seems to exist between Vautrin and the attorney general, the count Grandville, in the final sections of *Splendeurs et misères des courtisanes.* Marguerite Drevon and Jeannine Guichardet speak of Grandville's "surprising indulgence" and of an "obscure solidarity" that is "indefinable but definite" between the aristocrat and the criminal. Philippe Berthier speaks of their "obscure connivance."[46] It is the sociological import of this connivance that I wish to study. Through it, Balzac weaves together his observations about shifting forms for relationships between men with his observations about the political history of early nineteenth-century France. There are certain impediments to the connivance between Vautrin and Grandville that interest Balzac—impediments embodied mostly by nonaristocratic agents of the state and its legal bureaucracy, in particular the bourgeois examining magistrate, Camusot, and a number of police agents—in particular the characters Bibi-Lupin and Corentin. In the fourth part of *Splendeurs et misères des courtisanes,* "The Last Incarnation of Vautrin," Vautrin will, in negotiations involving what we might call queer social capital, successfully parlay Lucien's attractiveness to men (in particular to the attorney general) into a new life for himself as a police chief. In the third part, "Where Evil Ways Lead," Vautrin is negotiating, but unsuccessfully, with social capital that is not quite as queer as that which rules in the final section of the novel. If his negotiations fail and Lucien kills himself, it is due, the novel asserts, to the efficacy of the state bureaucracy in shaping the actions of its own agents.

Vautrin's predicament, once he is brought to the Conciergerie for questioning by the magistrate Camusot, is how to get word to Lucien—who is also to be interrogated regarding the suspicious circumstances of Esther's death—to inform him that circumstances are not as dire as he might imagine and that he should not, out of despair, reveal anything incriminating about Vautrin's true criminal identity. Vautrin's disguise as the priest Carlos Herrera is the only thing that can excuse socially Lucien's relation to him. For Lucien to be known to have consorted with an escaped convict, to have lived with him, to have been supported by him, and who knows what else, would be social suicide. Vautrin has no doubts as to his own ability to outwit Camusot. His concern is that the bumbling, weak-willed Lucien will cave in under pressure. In order to bolster Lucien's morale and even perhaps to prevent his interrogation, Vautrin miraculously slips a message out of the prison to his right-hand woman, his aunt, Jacqueline Collin, whom he instructs to visit a pair of highly placed noblewomen, former lovers of Lucien's, to obtain their intervention on his behalf. The novel thereby becomes a tale of the struggles of aristocratic social capital to assert its value within and against a legal bureaucracy.[47] Can individual aristocrats exert enough authority to influence the machinery of justice? Have Lucien and Vautrin banked enough social capital, played his physical beauty (and apparently his erotic talents, as well) on the market in appropriate fashion and with sufficient savvy so as to be able to command the return on their investment that would cause certain aristocrats to exert themselves on Lucien's behalf?

Even before Vautrin sets his aunt in motion, Lucien has already become a stake in a battle being waged with aristocratic social capital for control of Camusot himself. As a nonnoble bureaucrat in the French justice system, Camusot owes his position and his hopes for advancement to various protectors. One of them, Madame d'Espard, hates Lucien and wants him disgraced and convicted. Another, the duchess Maufrigneuse, one of the pair of former lovers Vautrin plans to contact, has already let Camusot know of her desire that Lucien be set free in short order. The narrator tells us early on, with a degree of irony that will become increasingly apparent as the plot unfolds: "No human power, neither the King nor the Keeper of the Seals, nor yet the Prime Minister, can encroach on the authority of an examining magistrate, nothing can stand in his way, he cannot be given orders. He is subject only to his conscience and the law" (6:718, 322). "It is decisive for the specific nature of modern loyalty to an office," Max Weber writes, in describing modern bureaucracy, "that, in the pure type, it does not establish a relationship to a *person,* like the vassal's or disciple's faith in feudal or in patrimonial relations of authority." He continues: "Modern loyalty is devoted to impersonal and functional purposes. Behind the functional purposes, of course, 'ideas of culture-values' usually stand. These are *ersatz* for the earthly or supra-mundane personal master: ideas such as 'state,' 'church,' 'community,' 'party,' or 'enterprise' are thought of as being realized in a community; they provide an ideological halo for the master."[48] Camusot himself seems a hybrid rather than pure type of bureaucrat. He is loyal to his office at certain moments and, at others, hyperconscious of the patronage system that provides for his advancement. Thus the question he and his wife ask each other on receiving news of the competing wishes of Mme. d'Espard and Mme. de Maufrigneuse is: "Which of the two is the more powerful?" (6:722, 326).

Weber also notes that "mass democracy makes a clean sweep of the feudal, patrimonial, and—at least in intent—the plutocratic privileges in administration. Unavoidably it puts paid professional labor in place of the historically inherited avocational administration by notables" (224–25). Such an observation nicely captures the tension in Balzac's novel that inhabits both Camusot and his superior (the noble attorney general, the count Grandville, a friend of Lucien's two former mistresses), and sets the two against each other.

I have noted previously Balzac's awareness—as regards sexuality—of the particularized contours of the new bourgeois public sphere that was being constructed around him, a sphere that certainly differed from previous ones (in which aristocrats predominated) regarding the forms of same-sex intimacy that were tolerable. This same awareness is evident in *Splendeurs et misères des courtisanes,* where the multiple discrepancies between Camusot's ethos and that of both the aristocrats who surround him and of Vautrin become increasingly important. When, in the final two parts of the novel, we find Vautrin becoming the ally of aristocrats such as Grandville in opposition to agents of the new bureaucratic state such as Camusot, Bibi-Lupin, and Corentin, we find enacted for us a number of interrelated processes: the ever firmer institutionalization—the growing independence—of a primarily bourgeois state bureaucracy in France; the resentful efforts of a traditional aristocratic hierarchy to resist that same process; and, in and around those two parallel processes, a struggle regarding appropriate forms of intimacy, regarding the values assigned, the place afforded, and the public attention given to various forms of intimate attachment—including sexual relations between men.

In terms of public revelations of intimacy, there are two within Camusot's purview: the revelation—should his interrogations be successful—of Vautrin's true identity and of the truth of his relationship with Lucien, and also the public revelation of the apparently scandalously intimate letters exchanged between Lucien and three noblewomen: the duchess Maufrigneuse, the countess Sérizy, whose husband is very highly placed at court, and Clotilde de Grandlieu, to whom Lucien had been engaged. The intimacy between Lucien and Vautrin is linked to the aristocratic intimacies, for, as Mme. de Sérizy puts it, when told that Lucien has confessed Vautrin's true identity to Camusot: "For myself, I should not hesitate between death and the prospect of seeing a man whom everyone knew as my best friend, proclaimed at law the intimate of a convict . . . The King is very fond of my husband [Quant à moi, je n'hésiterais pas entre la mort et la perspective de voir un homme que le monde a regardé comme mon meilleur ami, déclaré judiciairement le camarade d'un forçat . . . Le Roi aime beaucoup mon mari]" (6:782, 391). The social capital of an aristocracy that wishes to protect its honor and its codes of intimacy is pitted against the zeal of an independent justice system, and against the interest of the "state," which the novel understands to be both increasingly separate from the king, his court, and the nobility and invested in favoring different forms of intimacy.

Vautrin successfully passes through his interrogation with Camusot without his true identity being revealed, and the novel even almost hands him a victory when Camusot is given a letter that Esther, minutes before committing suicide, had mailed to Lucien, and which has only just been discovered. The letter clears Lucien of any suspicion in Esther's death and should pave the way for his immediate release. Vautrin even dares suggest to Camusot that an interrogation of Lucien is no longer called for. Yet, despite the disguised Vautrin's masterful performance during his own interrogation, Camusot retains suspicions about his true identity and so is unable to resist calling in Lucien for questioning: "In all lines of work, there exists a certain professionalism. Even absent any curiosity, Camusot would have questioned Lucien just as he had just questioned Jacques Collin [aka Vautrin], out of respect for the magistrature, employing all the ruses which a conscientious magistrate may properly employ. As for favors he might do, as for his own promotion, everything for Camusot was subordinate to a desire to know the truth, to figure it out, even if it could not then be revealed" (6:766–67, 374). By professional deformation Camusot takes an official deposition from Lucien and tricks him into revealing that Vautrin is not Carlos Herrera, as he claims, but the escaped convict, Jacques Collin. The interrogation was unnecessary but it produces a legal document—the deposition—that contains evidence of other kinds of crimes. Camusot then sends Lucien back to his cell where he takes the time to write a number of letters before hanging himself rather than having the nature of his intimacy with Vautrin publicly revealed.

Within seconds of sending Lucien back to his cell, Camusot receives a note from the duchess Maufrigneuse and the countess Sérizy, asking that he not interrogate Lucien and indicating that they are on their way to see him. As soon as he receives the note, Camusot becomes aware that his professional habits have served him ill: "Camusot understood that he had committed a gross blunder in setting traps for Lucien" (6:777, 386). He reveals what he has done to the attorney general, who backhandedly compliments him on being an excellent examining magistrate, thereby implying he will never advance to be anything else. Mme. de Sérizy arrives, and cannot understand that she is too late, declaring like a "despot": "It cannot be, it must not be too late yet" (6:781, 390). Her friend, the attorney general, makes a pointed observation about the modern justice system: "The King is without the slightest authority over the least examining magistrate in his kingdom or over the deliberations of a Court of Assize. Therein lies the greatness of our new institutions" (6:782, 391). He then leaves her alone with Camusot, not wanting to be party to any transaction that might take place between them. Still, Camusot cannot rise above his professionalism. When Mme. de Sérizy suggests that he suppress Lucien's deposition, Camusot is scandalized in true Weberian fashion: "That would be a crime which no magistrate would dare commit, a crime against society" (6:783, 392). When she tries to snatch the deposition from him and burn it, they enter into hand-to-hand combat over the burning document, both badly singeing their fingers. At this moment, the count Sérizy arrives and Attorney General Grandville, who is one of his closest friends, returns. For the sake of his intimate friendship with Sérizy, who is deeply upset to find his wife in this predicament, Grandville decides to "compromise his duty," to set Lucien free, and to forget about the burnt deposition. Camusot has no choice but to acquiesce. It almost seems that Camusot's "instincts" and honor as a magistrate have been stymied and that the social capital of the aristocracy has been well spent.

And yet Mme. de Sérizy is too late, for Lucien has just been discovered dead in his cell. Why does the novel show Mme. de Sérizy successfully subverting the justice system in order to save Lucien, and then have her success be only minutes, seconds, too late to do any good? I would like to suggest two reasons, the first having to do with the characteristics of social capital.

When Jacqueline Collin sets off to carry out her nephew Vautrin's orders to cash in some social capital and set in motion the duchess Maufrigneuse and the countess Sérizy to save Lucien, her first task is to visit the duchess, who is perhaps slightly easier to see and who is also a sure route of access to the more powerfully placed and more carefully protected countess, whose husband is a minister. But how is an unknown woman of dubious background to gain access to a duchess (and at a very early hour at that!)? The duchess keeps the unknown woman waiting an hour, but when Jacqueline convinces the duchess of the urgency of her mission they set off together to see the countess. Because Jacqueline is accompanied by the duchess they are admitted immediately, but it is already two in the afternoon, and at more or less exactly the same moment Camusot, having finished interrogating Vautrin, has Lucien brought in for his interrogation. This race against time, along with conforming to certain conventions of the nineteenth-century serial novel also, in Balzac's case, carries a sociological message. (We see here Balzac's skill at taking certain conventions of popular entertainment—suspense, being in the nick of time, being seconds too late—and deploying these devices in the service of a complex analysis of large movements of social transformation, innovation, or obsolescence.) One of the reasons Lucien is saved too late is because of the way social capital works. Because it is attached to a person it is very difficult to cash in by proxy. Thus part of Vautrin's failure is produced by the inherent inefficiency of his project, that of accumulating social capital through an instrument such as Lucien, who cannot easily transfer that capital to the strategically more wily Vautrin.

Yet perhaps the primary reason that Vautrin loses the battle with Camusot and that Lucien kills himself has to do with a more fundamental miscalculation. Vautrin underestimates his enemy, Camusot, not in underestimating his intelligence but rather in underestimating the efficacy of the bureaucratic system of which he is an agent and which has shaped him in its own interests. If interrogating Lucien is not in Camusot's own personal interest (if, in fact, it threatens to narrow his career opportunities substantially) and yet he does so anyway, it is because he has been shaped to his role by the judicial bureaucracy itself, and the judicial bureaucracy has an interest in being hostile to the exercise of social capital by the aristocracy. Even the aristocratic Attorney General Grandville feels this predicament, wanting to intervene earlier to protect his friend the count Sérizy by protecting his wife, but feeling compelled not to: "He was suffering. Here is why. The dignity of his position prevented him interfering in any way with the inferior magistrate's absolute independence, and yet this case involved the honour, the reputation of his best friend, one of his most zealous protectors, Count Sérizy, minister of State, member of the Privy Council, deputy prime minister" (6:779, 387–88). Grandville himself reflects a few lines later that "at one time the royal power allowed for the evocation of special cases . . . Our mania for equality will be the death of this age." That is, it used to be that the king could choose to remove a case that was before the courts from their jurisdiction and give it to the jurisdiction of his council. Such a convenient procedure is no longer allowed. Grandville *suffers* because he feels competing obligations. He knows the king's power is constrained, and what he feels as the "dignity" of his position is an implication of, an effect of, the constraints on that power. Yet Grandville also exists within the social world of his peers, a world of honor, patronage, and friendship out of which grows a profound sense of obligation to his best friend, one of the only two "intimate" friends he has, as the novel later informs us (6:888, 503). Grandville longs to exercise his power in accordance with those more "intimate" obligations, but he feels obliged to restrain himself from doing so. It is only after Mme. de Sérizy has burned her fingers in hand-to-hand combat with Camusot—and Camusot finds himself in a room with three counts, a countess, and a need to recover his own "dignity" in the face of those four people—that Grandville feels in a position to protect his friend Sérizy and "compromise" his duty in the diplomatic performance of exercising a certain authority over Camusot. For things to have reached such an extreme has taken time, the time necessary for Lucien to hang himself. Lucien is thus killed, in a certain way, by the "dignity of position" felt by both Grandville and Camusot. This particular force, the force of bureaucratic loyalty to one's profession rather than loyalty to a person, is what defeats Vautrin.

When in the fourth part of the novel Vautrin finds himself in a room with Grandville and Camusot, barely able to contain his rage, Grandville sends Camusot from the room, and Vautrin comments: "You did well to send Lucien's murderer away! . . . I could stand it no longer, I was about to strangle him" (6:897, 513). As if strangling a bureaucracy's agent would be an adequate act of vengeance against the bureaucracy itself. This is the scene in which the complicity between the two men begins to establish itself, and it does so out of a combination of frustration and rage at Camusot on the one hand and love for Lucien on the other. Vautrin continues: "Don't you realize that that idiot of a judge killed him for us; for you loved him, my Lucien, and he loved you! I know you inside-out, sir [Je vous sais par cœur, monsieur]. That dear child told me everything, every night, when he came in; I put him to bed, as a maid would her tiny charge, and I had him tell me everything. . . . He confided everything to me, down to the tiniest detail of his sensations" (6:898, 514). Here, along with the clear suggestion that Lucien proved seductive to men other than Vautrin, we see Vautrin's new game. He is beginning to play with what we might call his queer social capital. The novel performs the odd balancing act, in its final sections, of showing Vautrin sometimes sincerely overcome by his emotions for Lucien, but now also able to understand that in certain contexts the sincere performance of those emotions for another man can be valuable. Grandville provides one of those sympathetic contexts, for, as the narrator tells us on the next page in a heavily coded passage,

> the convict had profoundly moved the magistrate who was seized with divine pity for this unhappy man [*ce malheureux*], whose life and feelings he was able to divine. . . . A man who, moreover, had reached the age of fifty-three without ever having succeeded in inspiring love, Monsieur de Grandville admired tender natures, as do all men who have not been loved. It was perhaps that despair, the lot of many men to whom women grant only their friendship and their esteem, that formed the secret bond of intimacy between Messieurs de Bauvan, de Grandville and de Sérizy; for a shared misfortune [*malheur*], like a shared happiness, tunes souls to its own diapason. (6:899, 515)

The code used here is the same as the code, examined in the preceding chapter, used to describe Cousin Pons: "In 1835, a lucky chance compensated Pons for the coldness of the fair sex, and gave him something to lean on in his old age. He had been an old man from the cradle, and friendship provided him with a prop: he contracted what was for him the only kind of marriage possible in his situation—wedlock with a man, an elderly man, a musician like himself" (7:496, 33). Grandville and Vautrin share the same condition, the same *malheur.* The scene between Grandville and Vautrin asks to be read as a seduction scene between two men, just as was the scene between Lucien and Vautrin at the end of *Lost Illusions.* The commonalities between Vautrin and Grandville that Vautrin and the narrator call to our attention are their shared desire for intimacy with men, their shared attraction for Lucien, and their shared resentment at Camusot and the increasingly dominant and increasingly bourgeois bureaucratic system that he represents.

Vautrin's performance is so effective that Grandville is quickly won over. As the novel puts it: "Monsieur de Grandville was won over to the criminal's side. It remained to win over the Attorney General" (6:516, 900). That is, Vautrin wins over first the private man, and then he must win over the official. If it is his queer social capital that seduces the man, could that same capital have any effect on the official?

ASSIMILATING VAUTRIN

Tantes are everywhere in "The Last Incarnation of Vautrin," the concluding section of *Splendeurs et misères des courtisanes*. Balzac first introduces the word in a scene in which a prison official sends Vautrin out into the courtyard in which other prisoners are exercising, including some of Vautrin's former accomplices, in order to see if they will recognize him and thereby confirm his identity as an escaped convict. It turns out that Vautrin's former mate on the chain gang, Théodore Calvi, is also in the prison, awaiting execution. Once Vautrin's former accomplices recognize him, which they do without giving him away to the officials, they surmise that Vautrin is there to see Calvi, to whom he had formed a passionate attachment. As one of them says, "I know what the plan is! He wants to see his *tante* who's due to be executed" (6:840, 453). This gives rise to a digression in which the narrator takes it on himself to explain to the reader what this slang word, known to prisoners, police agents, and prison guards, means.[49] He does so by recounting a scene in which an English lord has come to take a tour of the French prison system:

> The governor, having shown him round the whole prison, the yards, the workshops, the dungeons, etc., pointed to one building with an expression of disgust.
>
> "I shan't take Your Lordship there," he said, "for that's the quarters of the *tantes* . . ."
>
> "Really!" said Lord Durham, "and what are they?"
>
> "That's the third sex, my lord." (6:840, 453–54)

Assuming that digression to have shed sufficient light on the matter and to need no further commentary, the narrator moves on, but once the word *tante* has been introduced into the text, it refuses to disappear. At one point Camusot is speaking to Grandville about the need to arrest Vautrin's aunt (*tante*) Jacqueline Collin, whom they believe to be in possession of the incriminating letters exchanged between Lucien and his aristocratic lovers. Camusot feels obliged to qualify his way of identifying her: "Jacques Collin has a *tante*, a natural *tante,* not an artificial one" (6:892, 507). When Vautrin himself enters the room a few pages later and surmises they are talking about his aunt, he interjects, "The person is my aunt, quite a convincing aunt [une tante vraisemblable], a woman, an old one" (6:897, 513). Vautrin thus makes clear that not all *tantes* are women and not all of them are old.

Given that everyone in the justice system knows this word, what it means, and how to use it, it is quite interesting to note how close people come to applying it to Lucien, without ever quite daring to do so. When Camusot tells Grandville that Vautrin has been put into contact with Calvi, he describes the relationship between the two as follows: "At the moment he [Vautrin] is with your condemned man [Calvi], who was formerly, at the penitentiary for him, what Lucien was in Paris . . . his protégé" (6:891, 506). Given that Camusot will, on the very next page, refer to Vautrin's "natural" *tante,* it is noteworthy that he does not employ the word here. (Grandville has already noted the similarities between Calvi and Lucien, describing Calvi as "a young man of twenty-seven years, as handsome as the one who died yesterday, and blond like him" [6:889, 504].) A bit earlier in the book, Camusot's wife had been trying to curry favor with the duchess Maufrigneuse by warning her that the monstrous Vautrin must still possess incriminating letters:

> "Monsieur Camusot knows for a certainty that that monster has put away in a safe place the most compromising [*compromet*tantes!] letters from the mistresses of his . . ."
>
> "Of his friend," interjected the Duchess quickly. (6:878, 493)

The ellipsis in both of these passages indicates the possibility that the vulgar expression *tante* might have been on the verge of escaping from the prison yard, moving from Calvi through Vautrin to Lucien, and finally ending up being pronounced in the world of the aristocracy itself. In both of these cases, that threat is warded off by translating the word into one drawn from the aristocratic ethos and lexicon, *ami* or *protégé.* Yet the complicity that is developing between Grandville and Vautrin is, in some ways, an acknowledgment that someone from the culture of *tantes* and someone from the culture of *amis* and *protégés,* might, in certain circumstances, make common cause.

During his interrogation by Camusot, Vautrin had tried to pass off the story that he was secretly Lucien's father, thereby explaining the extent of the intimacy between them. Lucien was so offended on hearing this that it shocked him into confessing. Vautrin's emotion, on seeing Lucien's corpse is so affecting, that a doctor, one of the witnesses to it, suggests it confirms the story that Vautrin truly is Lucien's father:

> "You will let me keep something of my dear child! . . . Be so kind, sir," he said to Dr Lebrun, "as to cut off one or two locks of his hair, I cannot . . ."
>
> "It is his son, that's certain!" said the doctor.
>
> "Do you really think so?" replied the governor with a meaningful look that left the doctor with something to think over. (6:818, 430–31)

Coded phrases such as the last—"d'un air profond qui jeta le médecin dans une courte rêverie"—are examples of the procedures of semi-censorship, euphemism, and innuendo that Balzac frequently employs in referring to same-sex relations. Indeed, this seems to have been the increasingly standard way, in the 1830s and 1840s, of doing so. That standard gives way to more explicitness than one usually finds, especially in a novel, once the word *tante* is made available. Yet the novel shows clearly that the usage of that word is regulated: it is not to be applied in just any social context.

Vautrin has it in his power to make public the sexually explicit letters exchanged between Lucien and the three noblewomen, thereby bringing down scandal on three noble families. What does it mean then, that Grandville, in order to save three noble families from the scandal that could be called down on them, with the permission of the king, commutes Calvi's sentence and turns him over to Vautrin, whom he agrees to have succeed Bibi-Lupin as chief of police after a six-month probationary period? What does it mean, in other words, that through Grandville the state—or at least that part under the king's influence (as opposed to the infrastructure of the state, to which Camusot, Bibi-Lupin, Corentin, and the various prison officials all belong)—suddenly takes an interest in the well-being of Vautrin and Calvi, a same-sex male couple? (This fantasy of a benign state interest in a pair of male same-sex domestic partners was fleetingly brought up in *Le Cousin Pons* as well, as we saw in the previous chapter.)

Lucien's death occurs in the Conciergerie on May 15, 1830. This means that Vautrin's six-month probationary period as chief of police will include the days of the July Revolution. The narrator has already told us that even though the events surrounding Lucien's arrest were the talk of the town while they were going on, the memory of them was quickly effaced by the events of the July Revolution: "The tempestuous July days of 1830 caused so great an upheaval that what took place shortly before them has been forgotten. People were so concerned with politics during the last six months of the year, that scarcely anyone still recalls, however strange they may have been, what personal, judicial and financial catastrophes, the annual diet of Parisian curiosity, duly occupied them during the first six months" (6:699, 301). And when reason is given as to why the king and Grandville should be willing to allow a queer criminal to be named chief of police in order to protect the reputation of the threatened noble families, the answer, in the words of the general secretary of the Cabinet Office, is that: "We are on the eve of great things, and the King doesn't want, at this point, to see the peerage talked about, tarnished . . . It isn't a low criminal action now, it's an affair of State" (6:904, 520). In other words, the king is about to take those political actions that will provoke the public dissatisfaction that gives rise to the Revolution that displaces him. After the Revolution, a number of his most important government officials will themselves receive prison sentences. To put it another way, there will be a huge market correction regarding social capital. Who can tell what will be the fate of the players Balzac presents to us: Lucien may have just missed a chance at staying alive; Vautrin, on the other hand, has managed his final incarnation just under the wire. After the July Revolution, his negotiations with Grandville would no longer have been able to take place. Yet he apparently will assimilate easily to the state infrastructure both pre- and post-1830, and so survive his probationary period and longer with ease. "After having exercised his functions for some fifteen years, Jacques Collin retired in 1845 or thereabouts," the novel tells us in its final sentence (6:935, 554).[50] Yet if he and Theodore apparently do here begin some unremarkable assimilated life as domestic partners, quietly ensconced within a state bureaucracy, it is clear that they owe that fate to a very peculiar conjuncture of circumstances: in particular, to a sympathetic and aristocratic attorney general, willing to be swayed by Vautrin's queer social capital into an alliance that suits a king who does not yet know his days are numbered, an alliance that satisfies a certain animus shared between Vautrin and Grandville against a bourgeois examining magistrate whose professionalism brought so much grief to the main characters in the novel. As it wraps itself up in its final pages, the novel does not tell us of Camusot's future. Yet he is, of course, in more ways than one, the clearest representative of one aspect of what is to come: an increasingly independent and increasingly bourgeois judiciary, with extremely limited sympathy for sexual minorities.

That Camusot and his ilk successfully assume larger and larger shares of state power can be discovered from reading *Le Cousin Pons,* set in the 1840s. Mme. Camusot is, in that novel, Pons's greatest persecutor. Yet the whole time Camusot and his friends (including Anselme Popinot) spend accumulating power, Vautrin will go on being chief of police, an enduring symbolic challenge to the dominance of their social group and the dominance of the forms of sexuality that they favor and practice. Perhaps we might imagine that the people who will group together to form the social category that we today know as homosexual could be thought of not primarily as the descendants of Vautrin, Lucien, or Grandville but as, to a greater or lesser extent, the sons and daughters and the granddaughters and grandsons of Camusot and his wife, whose homophobia is, as Balzac shows, a form of class interest. Who knows if those children and grandchildren, when they find themselves confronted with some bit of the state apparatus, will find a Vautrin in some position of political power and convince him to identify with their interests, the way Vautrin found Grandville?

Imagine Vautrin and his boyfriend Calvi, in the 1830s, living in the same world as Grandville, Sérizy, and Bauvan; as Rastignac and Marsay; as Custine and Sainte-Barbe; as Fiévée and Leclercq; as *la tante* Chardon. They are all strangely liminal characters, tightly bound to their particular moment by that very liminality. Many of them defend themselves and their forms of intimacy more, it seems to me, by looking back for permissions to social forms from the immediate past than they do by any relation to a future. As for the present they inhabited, it was one in which the hostility of the bourgeois social order would be experienced every day but held at a distance more easily, the more social, cultural, and economic capital one possessed. Balzac's own novels could often be the vehicles of that very hostility. Yet the novels were and are more than that, mostly thanks to their sociological sophistication. There was, for Balzac, no *one* model in which to capture Lucien, Vautrin, Calvi, Grandville, Custine, Gurowski, Pons, Schmucke, Schwab, Brunner, and all the others. Balzac saw multiple forms for male same-sex desire in the world around him, open to multiple meanings and susceptible to appropriation by various social groups. He saw historical and social forces producing and favoring certain forms for certain people and not others. He was curious about the forces and the forms and about the processes by which people came to inhabit them. There is something intimidating about Balzac's vision of sexuality. Sexuality, for Balzac, is not in any primary way a place of selfhood or identity, rather it is more an impression that no individual could master or even successfully read. Indeed, the interests being enacted by that impression often seem, subjectively speaking, nearly illegible. Yet it seems to me that it is in his effort to objectify those forms so that they and the interests they carry achieve some legibility that Balzac has so much to offer, both as a historian and as a sociologist of sexual forms.

EPILOGUE

Vautrin's Progeny

"Vautrin is all the rage," writes Robert de Montesquiou to Proust on April 17, 1921, after having read part one of Proust's *Le Côté de Guermantes,* which had been published in August 1920. He is struck, in particular, by the scene in which Charlus, having offered to lend direction to Proust's narrator's life by taking him under his wing, then hails a handsome and drunk young cab driver and rides off with him into the night. From the letter it is also clear that Montesquiou has noticed the title, *Sodome et Gomorrhe,* that Proust had announced for the volume that would follow *Le Côté de Guermantes.* The short first section of *Sodome et Gomorrhe* would in fact first be published together with part two of *Le Côté de Guermantes* a few weeks after the date of Montesquiou's letter. He writes there, with the malicious wit of a true dandy:

> Vautrin is all the rage. Your Charlus is related to him, and, from an article by Régnier that I have just read, I see that Rachilde too has just resurrected him. The reincarnation you are daringly performing promises us some tasty *otia* [diversions] (if your scene with the cab driver is any indication), and promises you *numerous printings,* under the cover of the two biblical towns that you plan to discover. For everyone will buy a copy, some in order to delight in what you do, others in order *to wax indignant,* but in every case in order to see *what you are up to,* under that *repugnant and titillating* label, that *no one else has yet dared employ,* unable to furnish themselves ahead of

time with the *sacer esto* that allows one to *say everything* and to draw *large dividends.*

[Vautrin est à la mode, votre Charlus en tient et j'ai lu, dans un feuilleton de Régnier, que Rachilde venait, elle aussi, de le remettre en scène. La réincarnation que vous en risquez nous promet de piquants *otia* (si j'en juge par le *fiacre du quartier*) et, à vous, de *nombreux tirages,* sous le couvert, et le découvert des *deux villes bibliques,* car tout le monde achètera, les uns pour se délecter, les uns *pour s'indigner,* et chacun pour voir de quoi il *retourne,* sous l'étiquette *repoussante et aguichante,* que *nul n'a encore osé employer,* faute de s'être fait revêtir d'avance du *sacer esto* qui permet de *tout dire* et de toucher *le gros dividende.*] [1]

The article Montesquiou refers to by Henri de Régnier was published in the literary supplement of *Le Figaro* on March 27, 1921. It reviewed Rachilde's 1921 novel, *La Souris japonaise* (*The Japanese Mouse*), and included the following observation: "Father Armand de Sembleuse, whose troubling figure is evoked by Mme Rachilde at the outset of her strange story, is a priest of the same family as Balzac's Carlos Herrera."[2] The first part of *La Souris japonaise* is made up of a first-person narration by the handsome, blond, dissolute Henri de Dormoy of his education as an adolescent by the slightly more handsome priest Armand de Sembleuse, who attempts to save him from the horrors of female sexuality by way of the exalted homoerotic yet platonic passion that grows up between the two of them. It would thus seem clear that in Parisian literary circles in the 1920s references to Vautrin were one means of referring to eroticized or sexualized relations to men. This is confirmed by a review of *Sodome et Gomorrhe* from the *Revue de France* on June 15, 1922, in which Fernand Vandérem writes: "Here, for example, we come upon a newcomer, a little musician by the name of Morel, discovered by poor M. de Charlus. The nature of the affection he feels for Morel is much more clearly specified than is that of Vautrin for the young Rubempré."[3]

Some literary reviewers of the 1920s were thus willing to admit openly the sexualized nature of the Vautrin/Rubempré relation. Literary scholars of differing social persuasions have not always been so willing to make that admission. In an article on Henri de Latouche from 1899, for instance, Raoul Deberdt speaks of "passionate friendships that are entirely cerebral, such as that of Lucien and Vautrin," and in a book on Balzac first published in 1924 André Bellessort clearly hedges his bets. Speaking of Vautrin, he writes: "One finds in him, along with a dubious [*équivoque*] feeling that Balzac fortunately leaves covered in shadow, a kind of monstrous paternal instinct comparable to Goriot's."[4]

The variety of extant opinions about the nature of Vautrin's relation to Rubempré at any number of historical moments—the 1850s, 1890s, 1920s, 1970s, or even today—is a good reminder of how difficult it is to take any one opinion as indicative of general attitudes toward same-sex sexuality at any particular moment. Every such opinion has to be understood as the statement by one particular social agent in a social field rich in possibilities for beliefs about and attitudes toward same-sex sexuality. A given statement can be taken as indicative of where a given person is positioned within the social field, but also should be seen as forming part of a given person's strategies for establishing a personal trajectory within that field. Montesquiou, for instance, understands Proust as carefully constructing a rhetorical position from which one can "say everything," yet also wickedly implies that Proust is in part interested in the commercial gains possible in the 1920s via the portrayal of same-sex subjects. Proust, in his reply to Montesquiou's letter, defends himself precisely against any commercial intent: "My dear sir, what a strange idea you must have of my life! The expression 'large dividends' made me smile ruefully, for my books earn me nothing."[5]

In a letter from about a year later, after having read the rest of *Le Côté de Guermantes* and the beginning of *Sodome et Gomorrhe,* Montesquiou writes in a kinder and more admiring vein: "You are trying to *broaden the field of literature,* to open to it the immense territory of *inversion* that, up until today, had been under embargo, and that has the potential to furnish, *in terms of art,* perilous and beautiful works."[6] In this letter, Montesquiou no longer mentions Balzac and Vautrin, yet from the outset of the reception of Proust's *Recherche,* they were understood to be important precursors in this project of enlarging the field of literature. Proust clearly felt this relation not just in terms of *what* literature allowed itself to represent; he also understood Balzac to be his precursor in terms of the reasons for representing certain rarely touched subjects. That is, he understood that Balzac's interest, like his own, in representing a wide range of different forms of sexual relations involved a commitment to a sociological understanding of the varied forms of sexual culture within a given society. This is clear from a passage from the "Sainte-Beuve et Balzac" section of *Contre Sainte-Beuve:*

> This reality of the life shown in Balzac's novels means that they give a sort of literary value to countless things in life which had hitherto seemed to us too contingent. But it is precisely the *law behind these contingencies* that is revealed in his work. . . . He shows delicate truths, cut from the superficial cloth of society life, all sufficiently generalizable so that a long time later one can still say: how true that is! . . . There are also profounder truths, such as Paquita Valdès falling in love precisely with the man who resembles the woman she lives with, such as Vautrin, supporting the woman who is able to see his Sallenauve, his son, on a daily basis; such as Sallenauve marrying the daughter of Mme de l'Estorade. There we see circulating, underneath the evident exterior action of the drama, mysterious *laws* of the flesh and of feelings. (emphasis added)
>
> [Cette réalité selon la vie des romans de Balzac, fait qu'il donnent [*sic*] pour nous une sorte de valeur littéraire à mille choses de la vie qui jusque-là nous paraissaient trop contingentes. Mais c'est justement la loi de ces contingences qui est dégagée dans son œuvre. . . . Il a de ces fines vérités cueillies dans la superficie de la vie mondaine et toutes à un degré de généralité assez grand, pour qu'après très longtemps on puisse se dire: comme c'est vrai! . . . Il en est de plus profondes comme Paquita Valdès aimant précisément l'homme qui ressemble à la femme avec qui elle vit, comme Vautrin entretenant la femme qui peut voir tous les jours son Sallenauve, son fils; comme Sallenauve épousant la fille de Mme de l'Estorade. Là, sous l'action apparente et extérieure du drame, circulent des mystérieuses lois de la chair et du sentiment.][7]

By mentioning "laws" Proust seems to be making reference to the way in which material that might otherwise be seen as anecdotal, or only of sensational interest, could, in the hands of a gifted novelist, become the matter for psychological and social analysis.[8] Clearly his own novelistic ambitions resemble Balzac's in this area. There is, however, an oddity about this passage. One could read any recent edition of Balzac's *La*

Comédie humaine from beginning to end without finding any page on which Vautrin is to be found keeping a woman who has the ability to see a son of his named Sallenauve. Similarly, one will be hard pressed to find any account in *La Comédie humaine* of a marriage between the daughter of Mme. de l'Estorade, one of the correspondents in Balzac's epistolary novel, *Mémoires de deux jeunes mariées,* and someone named Sallenauve. The solution to this puzzle is an interesting one, and has something to tell us about the cult status Vautrin quickly assumed for many of his fans, among whom Proust must surely be counted.

CHARLES RABOU

Les jours où il était tout à fait mis sur Balzac, il citait aussi des oeuvres qui à vrai dire ne sont pas de Balzac, mais de Roger de Beauvoir et de Céleste de Chabrillan. Mais il faut dire à son excuse que la petite bibliothèque . . . était pourvue à la fois des oeuvres de Balzac, d'Alphonse Karr, de Céleste de Chabrillan, de Roger de Beauvoir et d'Alexandre Duval, tous reliés pareils. [On those days when he set to talking about Balzac, he would also cite works that, if truth be told, were not by Balzac but by Roger de Beauvoir or Céleste de Chabrillan. In his defense, we should note that his small library . . . was furnished with the works of Balzac, of Alphonse Karr, of Céleste de Chabrillan, of Roger de Beauvoir, and of Alexandre Duval, and they all had been bound in the same materials.]—Marcel Proust, "Le Balzac de M. de Guermantes," *Contre Sainte-Beuve*

When Balzac died in August 1850, he left a number of unfinished projects, including the beginning of two novels, *Le Député d'Arcis* and *Les Petits Bourgeois.* I will address here *Le Député d'Arcis,* of which Balzac had published the first segment in *L'Union monarchique* in spring 1847. Balzac's widow (whom he had married only a few months prior to his death) had the idea to make some money by having someone finish some of her husband's projects so that she could sell them to publishers. Her first choice was the novelist Champfleury, who writes to his mother on April 11, 1851: "I am to concern myself with her husband's unfinished novels and his notes. She wants me to continue work on them under her direction. But this is a delicate question." A few months later, he writes: "Mme. de Balzac has been very kind to me. She is the one who suggested I take a rest, for I am working to bring her husband's miscellaneous works into some kind of order so that we can publish them." A month after that, he writes that Mme. de Balzac has helped him out of a delicate financial situation, noting to his mother that "fortunately Mme de Balzac came to my rescue by paying me quite well for the work I am doing for her." Yet by November of that year, he has to admit that "I am no longer on good terms with Mme de Balzac; we have had a falling out."[9] Later in life he apparently told a friend that Balzac's wife "proposed that I finish the novels he had started. I refused categorically, and gave her a list of names of those I thought better suited to such work, of which I disapproved."[10]

In fact, he seems, in a letter of June 28, 1851, to have given her only one name, that of Charles Rabou, novelist and journalist.[11] In the early 1830s, Rabou, Balzac, and Philarète Chasles had published together a volume of stories called *Contes bruns.* It would seem that Rabou and Balzac fell out of touch in the mid-1830s. Once assigned the task by Balzac's widow in the early 1850s, he undertook to finish Balzac's novels with gusto, and he had no problem producing large quantities of text. His extended version of *Le Député d'Arcis,* which ended up appearing as a series of three differently titled novels, first appeared in 1853 in *Le Constitutionnel,* before appearing in book form in 1854 and 1855. *Le Député d'Arcis* was published in four volumes in 1854, continued by the five volumes of *Le Comte de Sallenauve,* also 1854, and completed by the four volumes of *La Famille Beauvisage* in 1855. All thirteen volumes were published as works of Honoré de Balzac, "finished by M. Ch. Rabou." Of the thirteen volumes, only the first volume, and a quarter of the second, were written by Balzac, although no official indication is given of the point at which Balzac left off and Rabou began.

One of the earliest Balzac scholars, Charles de Spoelberch de Lovenjoul had ascertained who had written what by at least the 1880s, and had published his findings in his *Histoire des oeuvres de H. de Balzac.* Yet the same publishers of Lovenjoul's volume would, at least as late as 1892, publish a compact two-volume edition of *Le Député d'Arcis,* that, while it did not publish the whole of Rabou's extension, included a considerable amount of it in a volume credited to Balzac that no longer even mentioned Rabou's participation. Similarly, many of the editions of Balzac's *Oeuvres complètes* right into the early twentieth century included parts of Rabou's text with no indication that the editors were aware they were doing so.[12]

Proust knew the whole of Rabou's extended version, and he seems to have been quite devoted to believing it to be Balzac's work.[13] In a letter from 1898, he refers to "the Rastignac who sets up meetings with Vautrin in distant suburbs," which appears to be a reference to an episode at the end of volume 2 of *La Famille Beauvisage*. In a letter to Lucien Daudet in 1901, he specifically asks Daudet, "Have you read *Le Comte de Sallenauve* and *La Famille Beauvisage?*" In another letter to Daudet, in 1916, he notes that Balzac seems to have taken some of his characters' names from the *Historiettes* of Tallemant des Réaux, "notably Madame de Sallenauve." Yet the name Sallenauve only occurs in Rabou's sections of the novels.[14]

Proust's determination to see Balzac in Rabou might seem incredible to someone reading the novels today, the stylistic differences between the two authors being so evident. Balzac's *Le Député d'Arcis* sets out to be an examination of how a family with a considerable but extremely bourgeois fortune can rise, across three generations of planned marriages, from provincial obscurity to an important socio-political position in Paris. The family's final ascent is to take place during the July Monarchy. The novel seems to have been intended to be an occasion for an in-depth look at the way social prestige and economic capital interacted during the July Monarchy (thereby continuing the project we see being carried out in *Le Cousin Pons* and *La Cousine Bette*). It would also be an occasion to critique the corruption of electoral politics in the same period and, given the cast of repeating characters that Balzac had developed in his years of working on *La Comédie humaine,* a chance to revisit some friends from long ago. For example, Henri de Marsay, after a successful political career leading to a stint as prime minister, has recently died. His friend Rastignac, the protagonist of *Le Père Goriot,* now married to the daughter of his then mistress, Delphine de Nucingen, has evolved into a government minister trying to hold on to his office in the rocky political waters of the 1830s and early 1840s. Maxime de Trailles, the infamous rake present in a number of tales, now aged fifty, would like to be married in order to pay his debts—and he is willing to trade on his title and his prestige in order to attract bourgeois capital.[15]

The intent and outline of the project of *Le Député d'Arcis* are clear in the short section Balzac did write and publish during his lifetime. Once Rabou takes over, all pretensions to socio-political or psychological analysis disappear. The novel becomes a somewhat second-rate *roman feuilleton,* a melodramatic grab bag of mistaken identities, increasingly far-fetched coincidences, innovative psychiatric inventions for suicidal aristocrats, rescue missions in South American rainforests, shipwrecks, duels, dramatically timed cardiac arrests, crafty uses of elaborate poisons, endless discoveries of illegitimate children, cross-generational marriage, and so on. Rabou's contribution to the novel begins with the introduction of a new character, the sculptor Dorlange, who has never known his parents and who suddenly and mysteriously hears that he is in fact the son of a forgotten aristocrat named Sallenauve, who wishes now to recognize his son and to launch him on a political career. All the wishes of the mysterious absent father rapidly come true, and Dorlange, the new comte de Sallenauve, quickly finds himself both rich and successful, elected as the Député d'Arcis.

All of the characters in Rabou's novel seem to have read every other Balzac novel, and the novel itself is continually reminding us of the titles of the other novels—encouraging us to run out and buy them to complete our own knowledge of this novelistic universe. Thus at one moment Sallenauve, suddenly finding what is happening to him to be incredible, stops to think:

> Hold on! What if this man is not my father? What if he is not even the Marquis of Sallenauve, as he claims to be? What if, just like the unfortunate Lucien de Rubempré (see *A Great Man from the Provinces in Paris* and *A Harlot High and Low*) whose story made such a splash, I have been caught up in the coils of some serpent similar to that counterfeit priest, Carlos Herrera, and am facing a similar rude awakening?
>
> But are the situations at all similar? Carlos Herrera had a reason to exercise his fascination on Lucien de Rubempré; but given my firm principles, and my life of steady, quiet work, what hold could someone get on me? What could they want from me?

> [Mais, dis donc! si cet homme n'était pas mon père, s'il n'était pas même le marquis de Sallenauve, pour lequel il se donne; si, comme le malheureux Lucien de Rubempré (Voir *Un Grand Homme de Province à Paris* et *Splendeur et misère des Courtisanes* [*sic*]) dont l'histoire a eu un si effroyable retentissement, j'étais enlacé par

quelque serpent à la façon du faux prêtre Carlos Herrera et exposé à un si terrible réveil?

Quelle vraisemblance? vas-tu me dire: Carlos Herrera avait un intérêt à fasciner Lucien de Rubempré; mais sur toi, homme de principes solides, qui t'es fait une vie de recueillement et de travail, quelle prise pourrait-on avoir, et enfin que te voudrait-on?] [16]

Given that Rabou has already, at this early point in the novel, managed to introduce a number of the juiciest sexual figures of *La Comédie humaine* (including la Zambinella, whose funeral Sallenauve managed to see in Rome, after which he also received a commission to make a copy of Sarrasine's sculpture of the castrato, during the making of which he also falls in love with Marianina de Lanty, who will later, for secretive reasons, flee to a convent, and who will also later be revealed to be the illegitimate child of the father of Madame de l'Estorade, to whom she bears an astonishing resemblance, and so on) we might well be wondering if Vautrin is not lurking somewhere out in the wings.

We will have to read pretty much all the way to the end of Rabou's many volumes to discover that this mysterious marquis of Sallenauve in fact *really is* the marquis of Sallenauve. But he is not really the father of Dorlange/Sallenauve. Sallenauve's *mother*—currently the mistress of a rich South American dictator—is paying the down-and-out aristocrat to provide her son with a name and a future. The novel meanwhile insists on having a number of people remark curiously on the resemblance between Dorlange/Sallenauve and Danton.

Yet Vautrin is, in fact, just around the corner. Sallenauve, by successfully winning the election in Arcis, has caused some difficulties to Maxime de Trailles, who had hoped that the election, by going to the candidate he favored (a certain Beauvisage) would advance his plan to marry Beauvisage's daughter, Cécile. Maxime thus vengefully decides to try to discover something about Sallenauve's true background. To do this he turns to friends who are friends with Vautrin, now chief of the criminal police force in Paris, to ask for his help.

Vautrin himself, it turns out, is tired of being chief of police and wants to become head of the intelligence services instead. He turns to Rastignac, his former tablemate at the Vauquer boardinghouse, for help. Here is the description Rastignac gives of the old criminal to another friend:

> I have been informed that beginning in 1830, when he was put in charge of the criminal police, he has given his life an entirely bourgeois appearance. I have only one reservation about that: it is too much of a disguise for him. . . . He is rich. . . . He has twelve thousand francs in income, the three hundred thousand francs he inherited from Lucien de Rubempré, and the income from a patent leather factory he founded near Gentilly, and that is very successful. His aunt, Jacqueline Collin, with whom he lives, is still engaged in shady dealings, which naturally earn her a lot, and I have every reason to believe that the two of them have been very successful playing the stock market . . . Every evening, in a café near police headquarters, below the Pont Saint-Michel, he plays dominos like a good bourgeois fellow, and on Sundays he goes out into a countryside populated by retired small businessmen, and calmly passes the time in a shack he bought not far from the Romainville forest, in the Saint-Gervais meadows.
>
> [J'ai su que, depuis 1830, époque où il a été placé à la tête de la police de sûreté, il a donné à sa vie une allure exactement bourgeoise, à laquelle je ne ferais même qu'un reproche, celui de le déguiser trop. . . . Il est riche. . . . Il a douze mille francs d'appointements, les trois cents mille francs qu'il a recueillis dans la succession de Lucien de Rubempré, plus le produit d'une fabrique de cuirs vernis, qu'il a établie du côté de Gentilly et qui rend beaucoup. Sa tante, Jacqueline Collin, avec la quelle il fait ménage commun, s'occupe toujours d'affaires un peu véreuses, où elle recueille nécessairement de très beaux bénéfices, et j'ai de fortes raisons de croire que tous deux ont joué avec bonheur à la Bourse. . . . Tous les soirs, dans un café situé près de la Préfecture, au bas du pont Saint-Michel, il fait bourgeoisement sa partie de dominos, et le dimanche dans la compagnie de petits commerçants retirés, il va philosophiquement passer sa journée à une bicoque qu'il a achetée non loin du bois de Romainville, dans les près Saint-Gervais.][17]

Reading this, one might well imagine Vautrin to be bored and looking to change jobs. Rastignac, with what we might call Rabousian logic—a logic hard to comprehend except insofar as one understands that it helps Rabou's plot along—suggests that if Vautrin wants to take over the secret intelligence services, he should in fact be creating a different public image for himself. He should try leading a more brazen and dissolute life: "All of this is much too bucolic ever to lead him toward the operation of the political police," Rastignac observes.

Fans of the demonic Vautrin of *Le Père Goriot* and *Splendeurs et misères des courtisanes* will not be disappointed to learn that Vautrin chooses to make some changes in his lifestyle in order to merit an appointment as head of the secret service. Rastignac sets out an odd program for Vautrin to follow: "If I were him . . . in order to really clean up my reputation, I would seek out a well-known actress much in view at the moment. Maybe I wouldn't ruin myself for her, but I would pretend to, giving the impression that I was victim of a crazed passion for her—one of those passions for which the public is, if not deeply sympathetic, at least highly indulgent."[18] Vautrin follows it out to the letter.

It just so happens that, a few days earlier, Vautrin had been on the trail of a counterfeiter, who had run into a crowded church in order to shake off his pursuer. There Vautrin heard the remarkable new singing talent, Luigia, giving a performance: "The beauty of her voice, of the song, of the words of that sacred hymn—words rendered perfectly distinct by the incredible skill of the performer—seemed to have a remarkable effect on [Vautrin]. . . . He went and stood in the shadow of one of the church's pillars, and remained standing there; but at the moment at which the final notes of the holy canticle faded away, he dropped to his knees, and anyone who could have seen his face would have noticed two large tears moistening his cheeks." When Vautrin recounts the experience to Jacqueline Collin, he describes Luigia's voice as "this voice that moved me so deeply, by which, suddenly fifty years younger, I was transported back to the day of my first communion with the Pères de l'Oratoire who raised me."[19]

I provide these details in part to demonstrate how strange it is, on one level, that Proust could have imagined this plot to be the work of Balzac. Yet this woman, who makes Vautrin weep with her voice, is the one to whom he will, disguised as the Swedish count Halpher-tius, choose to offer his patronage in order to carry out Rastignac's suggested program.[20] Luigia used to be Delange/Sallenauve's housekeeper and model. This is thus the moment to which reference is made in *Contre Sainte-Beuve,* one of those moments in which, for Proust, Balzac's mastery reveals itself: "Vautrin supporting the woman who is able to see his Sallenauve, his son, on a daily basis." For, yes, the story has a few more twists and turns to it: if Sallenauve resembles Danton, it is because Danton is his maternal grandfather, having had an illegitimate daughter who later ran off to Paris, only to be taken up by the sordid Jacqueline Collin, thereby meeting Jacques Collin, who fell in love with her and got her pregnant. Vautrin is thus Sallenauve's father.

Vautrin becomes the patron of Luigia without knowing any of this. He discovers it quite late in the thirteen-volume set, but soon enough for us to witness enough paroxysms of paternal devotion to imagine him resembling Goriot in ways *Le Père Goriot* would never have led us to believe possible. Lest we think his queer history is forgotten, his aunt reminds us of it. When he accuses her of bad faith for having hidden the existence of his son from him for many years, especially when she knew how deeply he cared for the mother, she succinctly comments, "What's this? . . . Now you are interested in women?"[21] This is an interesting rejoinder, for the novel has also insisted on the similarities between Vautrin's sentiments for his son and his sentiments for Lucien. The narrator comments that one can easily understand the strength of his feelings for Sallenauve "if only one takes the trouble to recall the prodigious paternal instinct that appeared in this man at the moment of Lucien de Rubempré's death, the death of his son, as he called him, a son he had claimed for himself against all the laws of nature and without having had much at all to do with the facts of his birth."[22]

Proust admired in Balzac what he called "the law behind these contingencies." What Proust means by the presence of "laws" in Balzac's novels is perhaps the possibility of reading into the anecdotal details of a story an allegory of a social process through which sexuality assumes a form. We here see him to be an incredibly generous reader of Rabou, finding, in the twists and turns of Rabou's tabloid plot, matter for speculation about the way queer sentiments can be housed inside paternal ones or protectively heterosexual ones—thereby in some way showing a refined appreciation for the sociological project Balzac had set himself in creating the character of Vautrin, and in developing him in different ways across three novels and a play. Even if we do not choose to read Rabou with the same generosity Proust shows, we can respect his double reading practice here: he reads simultaneously as an avid fan of Vautrin, eagerly awaiting any new installment in the story of his queer life, and as a student of Balzac the sociologist interested in the evolving social forms through which sexuality comes to expression.

Balzac and Proust, by way of their novelistic projects and by way of the multiple relations between them (Proust as fan, Balzac as precursor, both of them as critical sociologists with an interest in the social forms of sexuality) have much to teach us about the history of sexuality. They are, of course, both actors in that history, but they are also both critical analysts of it as well: the history of sexuality as a history of social forms. They both show how useful it is to remember that at any given cultural moment there is likely to be a rich variety of extant forms: forms that compete, evolve, borrow from each other; forms that succeed and fail in various ways and for various reasons. They both show there to be no easily recountable, unilinear, or progressive history of sexuality that can account for the evolution of these forms, and they are both aware of the necessarily reductive critical procedure (even though they both sometimes engage in it) that consists in looking to the past expecting to find in it this or that sexual form of one's own moment, or in using a contemporary form as a paradigm for understanding sexual relations of an earlier moment. They both understand there to be an ongoing struggle between official, or dominant, or hegemonic forms that seek out institutional means to broadcast themselves, perpetuate themselves, impose themselves and alternative forms that exist without much recognition from large institutional structures such as the law, the state, psychiatry or psychoanalysis, the family—and that necessarily experience resistance in their efforts at expression or self-perpetuation. These misfit forms nonetheless subsist and create traditions for themselves. This is finally the most compelling lesson to be learned from Proust's loyalty to Vautrin—even to the Vautrin perpetuated by Rabou. Such loyalty was a cultural practice of resistance, the compelling gesture of a misfit protecting and preserving the culture that protects and enables him in his nonnormative cultural efforts. Here again, Proust followed in Balzac's footsteps.

NOTES

Preface

1 Georg Lukács, *Studies in European Realism,* trans. Edith Bone (London: Merlin, 1972), 51.

2 Throughout this book I will cite novels from Balzac's *La Comédie humaine* from the Pléiade edition (Honoré de Balzac, *La Comédie humaine,* ed. Pierre-Georges Castex, 12 vols. [Paris: Gallimard, 1976–1981]) by volume and page number: for example, in this case, 5:312–13. If there is a second page number it refers to a readily available English translation: in this case Honoré de Balzac, *Lost Illusions,* trans. Herbert J. Hunt (Harmondsworth: Penguin, 1971), 213–14. When necessary for the sake of accuracy or to bring out a particular nuance I will modify "silently" the cited translation. When no English translation is cited translations are my own.

3 See Balzac, 5:1241–42. Margaret Cohen's *The Sentimental Education of the Novel* (Princeton: Princeton University Press, 1999) is immensely helpful in describing the differing ambitions of French novelists in the 1830s. See in particular her introduction on how, around 1830, the novel genre "became an authoritative form of social and cultural analysis imbued with the highest literary prestige" (3). Cohen's project is to ask "how the modern novel in France took shape in response to the local conflicts of literary production as well as sweeping social transformation, returning Balzac and Stendhal to the literary contexts of their time" (4). Her comments on and her contextualization of Balzac throughout the book are remarkable. My project here is in some ways less wide-ranging. I want to explore some of the particular currents of social and cultural analysis within Balzac that have as yet perhaps not received sufficient attention. On sociological and gender issues in Balzac's writing from texts earlier than those I examine here, see Sharon Marcus's introduction to Balzac's *The Physiology of Marriage* (Baltimore: Johns Hopkins University Press, 1997),

and also Catherine Nesci, *La Femme mode d'emploi: Balzac, de la "Physiologie du mariage" à "La Comédie humaine"* (Lexington, Ky.: French Forum Publishers, 1992).

4 James, for instance, wrote a number of essays on Balzac tracing his own richly ambivalent relation to his precursor. See Henry James, *Literary Criticism: French Writers. Other European Writers, The Prefaces to the New York Edition*, ed. Leon Edel (New York: Library of America, 1984), 31–151. He comments that "the greatest thing in Balzac . . . is the whole attempt—it is the method" (66); he observes that "the novel, the tale, however brief, the passage, the sentence by itself, the situation, the person, the place, the motive exposed, the speech reported—these things were in his view history, with the absoluteness and the dignity of history" (110); and he states that he himself "can only speak, as a man of his own craft, an emulous fellow-worker, who has learned from [Balzac] more of the lessons of the engaging mystery of fiction than from any one else, and who is conscious of so large a debt to repay that it has had positively to be discharged in instalments, as if one could never have at once all the required cash in hand" (121). On Faulkner and Balzac, see the chapter titled "Vautrin's Hundred" in Edward J. Ahearn's *Marx and Modern Fiction* (New Haven: Yale University Press, 1989), 119–63. On Proust and Balzac, see the epilogue to this book and also my "Proust's Queer Metalepses," *MLN* 116, no. 4 (September 2001): 795–815.

5 For brevity's sake, along with Lukács I'll just mention here Pierre Barbéris, *Balzac et le mal du siecle: Contribution à une physiologie du monde moderne* (Paris: Gallimard, 1970), and his *Mythes balzaciens* (Paris: A. Colin, 1972); and Fredric Jameson, *The Political Unconscious: Narrative as a Socially Symbolic Act* (Ithaca: Cornell University Press, 1981). Further examples will be cited in later chapters.

6 See, for example, David Bellos, "Reconnaissances: Balzac et son public feminin," *Oeuvres et Critiques* 9, no. 3 (1986): 253–62; and Juanita Helm Floyd, *Women in the Life of Honoré de Balzac* (New York: Holt, 1921). See also, David Bellos, *Balzac Criticism in France 1850–1900: The Making of a Reputation* (Oxford: Clarendon, 1976), 9, 69, on the way Balzac was sometimes denigrated for his popularity with and attention to women. Feminist critics have varied quite a bit in their claims about Balzac. Arlette Michel does not hesitate to speak of "le féminisme balzacien" in the chapter of that title in her *Le Mariage chez Honoré de Balzac: Amour et féminisme* (Paris: Les Belles lettres, 1978), 209–24. Margaret Cohen gives an interesting analysis of Balzac's "animosity" toward women writers in "A Compromised Position: French Realism and the *Femme Auteur*," in *The Sentimental Education of the Novel* (163–95). In *Literary Criticism* Henry James gives a nice statement of the paradox when he writes: "It is the opinion of many of Balzac's admirers, and it was the general verdict of his day, that in all this the greatest triumphs are the characters of women. Every French critic tells us that his immense success came to him through women—that they constituted his first, his last, his fondest public. . . . Balzac's superior handling of women seems to us to be both a truth and a fallacy. . . . His reader

very soon perceives, to begin with, that he does not take that view of the sex that would commend him to the 'female sympathizers' of the day. There is not a line in him that would not be received with hisses at any convention for giving women the suffrage, for introducing them into Harvard College, or for trimming the exuberances of their apparel. His restrictive remarks would be considered odious; his flattering remarks would be considered infamous" (61).

7 I will be citing many of them in the pages ahead. Along with Margaret Cohen's *The Sentimental Education of the Novel,* mentioned above, let me mention here the inspiring work by Sharon Marcus, *Apartment Stories: City and Home in Nineteenth-Century Paris and London* (Berkeley: University of California Press, 1999). The volume edited by Michal Peled Ginsburg, *Approaches to Teaching Balzac's "Old Goriot"* (New York: Modern Language Association, 2000), contains articles by two important feminist critics of Balzac: Margaret Waller ("A Feminist Approach: Realism and Its Others," 98–108) and Dorothy Kelly ("Between Bodies and Texts: A Psychoanalytic Reading of *Le Père Goriot,*" 109–17).

8 To take one more quotation from Henry James, writing in the 1870s: "Afraid of nothing as he was, he attacked all the deepest things in life and laid his hand upon every human passion. He has even—to be complete—described one or two passions that are usually deemed unmentionable. He always deals with a strong feeling in preference to a superficial one, and his great glory is that he pretended to take cognizance of man's moral nature to its deepest, most unillumined and, as the French say, most *scabreux* depths—that he maintained that for a writer who proposes seriously to illustrate the human soul there is absolutely no forbidden ground" (*Literary Criticism,* 58). See also Lawrence R. Schehr, "A Queer Theory Approach: Gender and Genre in *Old Goriot,*" in Ginsburg, 118–25.

9 My usage of the word *queer* never implies anything in particular about anyone's sexual practices. It indicates, rather, a nonnormative social positioning often forced on someone, one that of course bears on that person's sexuality in some way, as it also bears on her or his emotional behaviors and relations to biological reproduction, economic production, and the reproduction of social forms such as the family—all of these other areas being inextricably implicated in the construction of anyone's sexuality, queer or otherwise.

10 It bears mentioning that my previous book, *Gide's Bent: Sexuality, Politics, Writing* (New York: Oxford University Press, 1995) made extensive reference to psychoanalytic materials by Freud, Klein, Lacan, and others. André Gide is unquestionably less sociological and more psychological a writer than Balzac, which may explain why his work resonated more with that of his near-contemporary Lacan than I could imagine Balzac's work doing. In the book on Gide I examine "the shape of [Gide's] sexual subjectivity" or the way Gide was "preoccupied" by sexuality—in the sense that it was a structural and structured part of him long before he came to writing. Thus Gide explored, mainly in psychological and stylistic terms, how sexuality could be expressive in its

own right, "beyond any intention of the writing or the sexual subject in question" (3–4). The continuity between my project on Gide and this one on Balzac has to do with tracing the shaping and expressive power of sexuality as a social institution, one that is "built-in" (to use a phrase from Henry James that we will encounter shortly) to any given subject. In this project on Balzac, my attention is perhaps more strongly drawn to the "building-in" process by which social institutions shape individuals, whereas the Gide project paid more attention to one individual's exploration of the particular way he was "built-in" sexually, to his literary exploration of the kinds of interventions that might be made into the shape, the form, of one's own sexuality.

11 Pierre Bourdieu, *The Logic of Practice,* trans. Richard Nice (Stanford: Stanford University Press, 1990), 56.

12 Émile Durkheim, *The Division of Labor in Society,* trans. W. D. Halls (New York: Free Press, 1984), 286–87.

13 Émile Durkheim, *The Rules of Sociological Method,* ed. Steven Lukes, trans. W. D. Halls (London: Macmillan, 1982), 39–40.

14 "Indeed some of these ways of acting or thinking acquire, by dint of repetition, a sort of consistency which, so to speak, separates them out, isolating them from the particular events which reflect them. Thus they assume a shape, a tangible form peculiar to them and constitute a reality *sui generis* vastly distinct from the individual facts which manifest that reality" (Durkheim, *The Rules of Sociological Method,* 54).

15 Again, Durkheim: "In order for a social fact to exist, several individuals at the very least must have given . . . rise to some new production. . . . There is one word which, provided one extends a little its normal meaning, expresses moderately well this very special kind of existence; it is that of *institution.* In fact, without doing violence to the meaning of the word, one may term an *institution* all the beliefs and modes of behaviour instituted by the collectivity; sociology can then be defined as the science of institutions, their genesis and their functioning" (*The Rules of Sociological Method,* 45).

16 James, *Literary Criticism,* 869, 870.

17 Pierre Bourdieu, *Pascalian Meditations,* trans. Richard Nice (Stanford: Stanford University Press, 2000), 137. Bourdieu is citing Michel Butor, *Répertoire,* vol. 2 (Paris: Minuit, 1964), 214.

18 Durkheim, *The Rules of Sociological Method,* 62.

19 James, *Literary Criticism,* 93.

20 I rely here on two helpful sources: Michelle Perrot, "Balzac et les sciences sociales de son temps," in *Balzac dans l'Histoire,* ed. Nicole Mozet and Paule Petitier (Paris: SEDES, 2001), 27–36; and Ian Hacking, *The Taming of Chance* (Cambridge: Cambridge University Press, 1990).

21 Perrot, "Balzac et les sciences sociales," 30.

22 Hacking, *The Taming of Chance,* 135.

23 Frédéric Le Play, *Instruction sur la méthode d'observation dite des monographies des familles* (Paris: Société d'économie sociale, 1862), 13.

24 Lukács, *Studies in European Realism,* 6.

25 Georg Lukács, "Healthy or Sick Art?" in *Writer and Critic and Other Essays,* trans. Arthur Kahn (London: Merlin Press, 1978), 106.

26 Elisheva Rosen, "Droit et roman: Le Modèle balzacien," in Mozet and Petitier, 50.

27 Elisheva Rosen, "Le Personnage et la poétique du roman balzacien," in *Balzac: Une Poétique du roman,* ed. Stéphane Vachon (Montreal: XYZ, 1996), 206–7.

28 The English translation cited here is *The Rise and Fall of César Birotteau,* trans. Ellen Marriage (New York: Carroll and Graf, 1989).

29 *Habitus* is a "system of structured, structuring dispositions" (Bourdieu, *The Logic of Practice,* 52) that "produces individual and collective practices. . . . It ensures the active presence of past experiences, which, deposited in each organism in the form of schemes of perception, thought and action, tend to guarantee the 'correctness' of practices and their constancy over time, more reliably than all formal rules and explicit norms" (54). It is "embodied history, internalized as a second nature and so forgotten as history" (56). Bourdieu does caution against thinking about habitus as a form of (conscious) calculation. It is "a socially constituted libido, not necessarily conscious of itself. It is not a calculation" (Pierre Bourdieu, *"Si le monde social m'est supportable, c'est parce que je peux m'indigner": Entertien avec Antoine Spire* [Paris: L'Aube, 2002], 51). I take it that when Balzac refers to a *"profound* calculation" or to an "arithmetic" of emotions, he understands calculation and arithmetic to be under most circumstances anything but conscious.

30 Bourdieu, *Pascalian Meditations,* 160.

31 Durkheim: "Despite the fact that beliefs and social practices permeate us in this way from the outside, it does not follow that we receive them passively and without causing them to undergo modification. In thinking about collective institutions, in assimilating ourselves to them, we individualise them, we more or less impart to them our own personal stamp" (*The Rules of Sociological Method,* 47 n.6). Bourdieu: "The principle of the differences between individual *habitus* lies in the singularity of their social trajectories, to which there correspond series of chronologically ordered determinations that are mutually irreducible to one another. The *habitus* which, at every moment, structures new experiences in accordance with the structures produced by past experiences, which are modified by the new experiences within the limits defined by their power of selection, brings about a unique integration, dominated by the earliest experiences, of the experiences statistically common to members of the same class" (*The Logic of Practice,* 60).

32 Bourdieu, *Pascalian Meditations,* 157.

Introduction: Balzac and Alternative Families

1 Jean-Étienne-Marie Portalis, "Discours préliminaire prononcé lors de la présentation du projet de la commission du gouvernement," in P. A. Fenet, *Re-*

cueil complet des travaux préparatoires du Code civil (1827–28; Osnabruck: Otto Zeller, 1968), 1:518.

2 Ibid.

3 Which explains why in France there exists a long and hearty tradition of living outside legal marriage. As Françoise Picq puts it: "A large part of the population lived outside the Code" (Picq, *Libération des femmes: Les Années-mouvement* [Paris: Seuil, 1993], 78).

4 Portalis, "Discours préliminaire," 1:465.

5 Xavier Martin, *Nature humaine et Révolution française: Du siècle des Lumières au Code Napoléon* (Bouère: Dominique Martin Morin, 1994), 263. See also Martin's: "L'Individualisme libéral en France autour de 1800: Essai de spectroscopie," *Revue d'histoire des facultés de droit et de la science juridique* 4 (1987): 87–144; and his "L'Insensibilité des rédacteurs du Code civil à l'altruisme," *Revue historique de droit français et étranger* 60 (1982): 589–618.

That families themselves would have some inkling that the law might need to be thought separately from the realm of feelings—that families themselves would understand that the two registers might in fact be conflictual—seems obvious. Of course, the scene of the negotiation of a marriage contract would be a prime moment in which the conflict would manifest itself. (In this light, it is hardly surprising that Balzac should have written a work called *Le Contrat de mariage*.) Consider also, in this regard, the incredibly detailed description of his father's marriage contract that Pierre Rivière obsessively provides (even though the contract would have been written before his birth) at the outset of the memoir in which he recounts how he came to murder his mother in his father's defense: "The clauses of this contract stipulated that husband and wife should have a joint estate comprising all movable property and immovable property present and future, that if one of the spouses predeceased the other and no children were living at that time, the survivor should enjoy the whole of the estate owned by the spouse during his lifetime, and if there were children, should enjoy his own properties only and the children the other half; that the father and the mother of the future wife shall contribute to the marriage settlement and that she herself shall contribute any movable and immovable property she may inherit from her father's and mother's estate; that the said properties shall be managed and administered by the husband in conformity with the law concerning the dowry system. The inalienability of these properties as specified in the civil code is also mentioned in the contract. It stipulated further that the husband's marriage portion was valued at 100 francs and the wife's portion consisted of linen and personal effects of several sorts, a cupboard with two doors, a bed, bed linen and several other articles mentioned, the whole valued at the sum of four hundred francs. That on the marriage day the said portion of the joint estate shall be deemed as constituting a receipt for the joint estate. That the said wife under the aforesaid authorization reserves the right to renounce the settlement in the form of joint estate at any time or in any manner should the dissolution of the said settlement occur and shall recover exempt from all debts and encumbrances her portion aforementioned as well as everything which she may inherit, of which she shall give a satisfactory inventory in evidence. That should the dissolution of the joint estate occur in the lifetime of the spouses, the survivor shall in no way be deprived of his rights aforementioned to enjoy the personal properties of the spouse during his lifetime. Such were the clauses of the contract" (Foucault, ed., *I, Pierre Rivière, having slaughtered my mother, my sister and my brother . . . : A Case of Parricide in the Nineteenth Century* [Harmondsworth: Penguin, 1978], 56–57). There were, in fact, some concessions to friendliness in the seemingly cold-hearted contract Rivière describes. The rights of a surviving spouse to enjoy the usufruct of a deceased spouse's property after the spouse's death were not granted as a matter of course; they had to be agreed to in the contract, otherwise the heirs (and the spouse could not be an heir) would receive both use and title of the property at the spouse's expense.

6 Again, it is worth noting that families—and not just aristocratic ones—were not always willing participants in this effort to manipulate their practices and their psychologies. Jacques Poumarède notes that heirs would sometimes, by mutual agreement, keep a family estate intact rather than divide it, and that notaries would be complicit in the attempt of families to get around the new laws (Poumarède, "La Législation successorale de la Révolution entre l'idéologie et la pratique," in *La Famille, la Loi, l'État: De la Révolution au Code civil,* ed. Irène Théry and Christian Biet [Paris: Éditions du Centre Georges Pompidou, 1989], 173). Margaret H. Darrow notes much the same thing in her *Revolution in the House: Family, Class, and Inheritance in Southern France, 1775–1825* (Princeton: Princeton University Press, 1989), 15–16. She also observes that the principle of equal inheritance remained controversial throughout the nineteenth century, some commentators believing it to be the root cause of "social atomization and the worst evils of modern life—selfishness, alienation, and rootlessness" (11–12). See also Pierre Bourdieu's analysis in "Land and Matrimonial Strategies," in *The Logic of Practice,* 147–61.

7 The situation was actually a bit more complicated. Originally in Revolutionary law all heirs inherited equally, but this was changed by the creation of what is known as the *portion disponible,* the part of an estate that a person is free to leave in any way whatsoever, including the decision that that portion could be used to advantage one heir over another. As Margaret Darrow puts it: "The Napoleonic Code endorsed the ideal of equal inheritance in intestate cases. However, the Code also retained and enlarged the portion disponible, which . . . a person could leave to anyone he or she chose by a written will. The portion disponible was an equal share in the succession. If its recipient were not among the legal heirs, he or she shared in the estate equally with them. If an heir, he or she received a double portion" (*Revolution in the House,* 9). Martin suggests that the *portion disponible* was also created with a particular practice of family in mind. By giving parents some testamentary freedom, it provided a form of "implicit blackmail intended to guarantee the docility of offspring

even after they would have reached their majority" ("L'Individualisme," 133). For a helpful contextualization of these legislative fluctuations, see Lynn Hunt, *The Family Romance of the French Revolution* (Berkeley: University of California Press, 1992), esp. 64–67, 161–63. For an interesting account of how different individuals and families tried to influence their legislators in the shaping of family law in the years prior to the adoption of the Civil Code, see Suzanne Desan, "Reconstituting the Social After the Terror: Family, Property, and the Law in Popular Politics," *Past and Present* 164 (August 1999): 81–121.

8 Cited in Pierre Antoine Perrod, "Balzac et les 'majorats,'" *L'Année balzacienne* (1968): 213. *Majorats* figure importantly in Balzac's *Le Contrat de mariage*. For a discussion of the legal details involved, see Adrien Peytel, *Balzac: Juriste romantique* (Paris: Ponsot, 1950), 157–76.

9 When, many years later, Michel Foucault was asked about possible new forms of relations between individuals, he stated: "We live in a relational world that institutions have considerably impoverished. Society and the institutions which frame it have limited the possibility of relationships because such a rich relational world be very complex to manage. . . . We should secure recognition for relations of provisional coexistence, adoption . . . of one adult by another. Why shouldn't I adopt a friend who's ten years younger than I am? And even if he's ten years older?" (Foucault, "The Social Triumph of the Sexual Will," in *Ethics: Subjectivity and Truth*, ed. Paul Rabinow, trans. Robert Hurley et al.; volume 1 of *Essential Works of Foucault, 1954–1984* [New York: New Press, 1997], 158). Foucault's point about institutions such as the Civil Code serving to legislate and manage a limited relationality is well taken, even if the historical complexities of the institution of adoption are more curious than he seems to realize. For a discussion of the use of the legal structure of adoption in the way Foucault imagines, see John Borneman, "Caring and Being Cared for: Displacing Marriage, Kinship, Gender, and Sexuality," *International Social Science Journal* 49, no. 4 (December 1997): esp. 574–80. For information on adoption in France prior to the Revolution, see Kristin Elizabeth Gager, *Blood Ties and Fictive Ties: Adoption and Family Life in Early Modern France* (Princeton: Princeton University Press, 1996).

10 Cited in Hughes Fulchiron, "Nature, fiction et politique: L'Adoption dans les débats révolutionnaires," in Théry and Biet, 214.

11 Ibid., 215.

12 Cited in ibid.

13 In a helpful article on the novel, Armine Kotin Mortimer notes the incredible frequency with which the word *héritier* occurs in *Ursule Mirouët*: "'Héritiers' is used 105 times in the 220 pages . . . by far the greatest number of occurrences among the 49 novels included in an electronic concordance of *La Comédie humaine* that I consulted" (Mortimer, "Balzac's *Ursule Mirouët*: Genealogy and Inheritance," *Modern Language Review* 92, no. 4 [October 1997]: 853 n.4).

14 There are at least two helpful accounts of Balzac and melodrama: Peter Brooks, *The Melodramatic Imagination: Balzac, Henry James, Melodrama, and the Mode*

of Excess (New York: Columbia University Press, 1985), 1–23, esp. pp. 3, 15–17; and Christopher Prendergast, *Balzac: Fiction and Melodrama* (London: Edward Arnold, 1978), esp. 3–16, 175–87.

15 The English translation cited here and elsewhere is *Ursule Mirouët*, trans. Donald Adamson (Harmondsworth: Penguin, 1976); note that I have made frequent adjustments to keep the translation closer to the French.

16 Legal scholars have developed numerous terms in their attempts to grapple with the differential forms of influence of the law on the lives of differently situated people within the same society: for example, "legal competence," "legal ideology," "legal culture," "legal consciousness." All the terms are wielded in an effort (similar to Balzac's) to understand how the law comes to matter in general or to matter to this or that person in a specific context: "It would be interesting to know if law matters in different ways when issues of legal consciousness involve divorces or commercial transactions or housing as contrasted with criminal or welfare law. The question is not simply one of social class, although class certainly figures differently in these different fields of law. Different substantive areas of the law represent different kinds of social relationships and interactions and involve different kinds of legal actors, procedures, and institutions. Law may matter more for consciousness associated with some of them than for others" (David M. Engel, "How Does Law Matter in the Constitution of Legal Consciousness?" in *How Does Law Matter?* ed. Bryant G. Garth and Austin Sarat [Evanston, Ill.: Northwestern University Press, 1998], 140.) Thanks to Mark Harris for this reference.

17 Nicole Mozet has even suggested that Désiré is not really his son. In *La Ville de province dans l'oeuvre de Balzac; L'Espace romanesque: Fantasmes et idéologie* (Paris: SEDES, 1982), she suggests that Désiré is a clandestinely illegitimate child, arranged for to compensate for his father's impotence (220). On bourgeois family practices of inheritance, see Robert Nye, *Masculinity and Male Codes of Honor in Modern France* (New York: Oxford University Press, 1993). Nye notes, for instance, "for a French bourgeois family that aspired to crown its rise to wealth with ennoblement, four things were required: an investment strategy that would permit the accumulation of wealth surely and not ignobly; an inheritance strategy that would maintain most of the wealth as a *bloc;* marital strategies that would enhance its growth and smooth transmission; and fertility strategies that would neither fragment the heritage nor arrest its progress. All these strategies were *family* strategies in the sense that they required family members to act as a unit and to sacrifice their individual interests in behalf of the prosperity of the group" (37).

18 "As long as I live," Désiré's mother says to him at one point, "I shan't let you ruin yourself in a foolish marriage" (3:845, 109). She plans to find him a wife, perhaps the mayor's daughter, who will both further his political career and enhance the family fortune.

19 Mortimer, for instance, notes: "My own response to such complexity is to draw the family tree," and she refers in this context to Balzac's "exercise in ex-

cessive, unreasonable writing" ("Balzac's *Ursule Mirouët,*" 855), which perhaps is not so unreasonable as all that if the *reason* was to get the reader to draw the family tree and thereby participate in understanding family as a calculation.

20 Adamson has translated the sentence as "have I any other family?" But family and heirs are not self-evidently synonymous; this is the essential lesson of the novel.

21 Note the careful dating of the novel. It begins with the beginning of the Restoration and ends with the July Monarchy in full swing. Balzac positions his plots carefully in time (discussed at greater length in chapter 2). Here it suffices to note that the avidity of the heirs is for Balzac tied to the spirit of the July Monarchy. Minoret himself married for love during the Revolution and actively earned his wealth during that period and during the Empire. His retirement, corresponding to the period of the Restoration, is the period in which the greed of his bourgeois heirs is growing. The denouement comes after the end of the Restoration, well into the July Monarchy.

22 Nicole Mozet has referred to Nemours in this novel as "the locus of a stunning redefinition of filiation conceived no longer in terms of blood but in terms of love" (*La Ville de province,* 219). See also her "La Question de l'origine à l'origine du roman balzacien," in *Balzac: Une Poétique du roman,* ed. Stéphane Vachon (Montreal: XYZ 1996), 285–94; and "*Ursule Mirouët* ou le test du bâtard," in *Balzac, Oeuvres complètes: Le Moment de "La Comédie humaine,"* ed. Claude Duchet and Isabelle Tournier (Saint-Denis: Presses universitaires de Vincennes, 1993), 217–28.

23 Along with exercising a kind of ruthless irony that often characterizes the voice of the Balzacian narrator when describing bourgeois culture, it would seem that the narrator of *Ursule Mirouët* has a theoretical point to make here as well: sentiments have their basis in interest, be it economic or symbolic. Sentiments may even be, to some unknown extent, the sediment of a long practice of furthering the economic or symbolic interest of some group or other. It is therefore also the case, as Balzac is fully aware, that any given emotional reaction may well be the product of a set of interests that no longer pertains. Thus the Balzacian interest in emotional structures that are out of sync with their historical moment (see chapter 1). On the relations between economic and symbolic interests, see Pierre Bourdieu, *Outline of a Theory of Practice,* trans. Richard Nice (Cambridge: Cambridge University Press, 1977), 172–73, 177–80.

24 For a discussion of the legal complexities of the novel, see Peytel, *Balzac,* 219–38.

25 Pierre Bourdieu, "Des familles sans nom," *Actes de la recherche en sciences sociales* 113 (June 1996): 4. Also helpful for understanding what is at stake in *Ursule Mirouët* is Bourdieu's distinction between practical and official kinship and the different situations in which they are visible and invokable (see *Outline of a Theory of Practice,* 30–43).

26 See Joan Wallach Scott, *Only Paradoxes to Offer: French Feminists and the Rights of Man* (Cambridge: Harvard University Press, 1996), 100.

27 My emphasis. See *Le Code civil: Textes antérieurs et version actuelle* (Paris: Flammarion, 1997).

28 In cases where someone is judged incapable of writing a will, relatives up to the twelfth degree still inherit. The degree of successibility was reduced from twelve to six in 1917 (see *Le Code civil,* article 755). The legal status of spouses was modified in 1957, 1958, and 1972 (see articles 731, 765, and 767). It was only in 1958 that article 731, which indicates who falls into the category of *héritier,* was modified to include spouses. On feminist struggles from the early twentieth century onward, see Picq, *Libération des femmes,* 76–80. See also the chapters on Hubertine Auclert and Madeleine Pelletier, and also the concluding chapter, "Citizens but Not Individuals: The Vote and After," in Scott, *Only Paradoxes to Offer.*

29 The story doesn't end there, because inheritance *taxes* vary widely according to the person to whom you leave your goods. There is, first of all, a variable amount that is nontaxable according to your status: when the PACS was adopted it was 330,000 francs for a spouse, 300,000 for a descendant, and 10,000 for someone not related by blood. According to the PACS legislation, the allowance for a member of a PACS was 300,000 francs. Not quite the equivalent of a spouse but as good as a son or daughter. There is one further step to take into account. Beyond the nontaxable allowance, tax rates vary according to category. Spouses are taxed progressively from 5 percent to 40 percent on increasing amounts, as are descendants. Unrelated people are taxed at 60 percent. According to the new law, a member of a PACS would be taxed 40 to 50 percent, progressively, a much worse situation than that of a spouse. It might also be worth mentioning, in this regard, that partners must have been in a PACS for at least two years before the death of one of the partners for these fiscal advantages to take effect. The same is not true for marriages. The legislation for the PACS was published in *Le Journal Officiel: Lois et Décrets,* no. 265 (November 16, 1999): 16959. A dossier covering the debates leading up to the adoption of the law, and including many of the important texts, can be found on the Web site of the France Queer Resources Directory (www.france.qrd.org).

30 Cited in Remi Lenoir, "La Famille, une affaire d'État: Les Débats parlementaires concernant la famille (1973–1978)," *Actes de la recherche en sciences sociales* 113 (June 1996): 29.

31 Didier Eribon, *Papiers d'identité: Interventions sur la question gay* (Paris: Fayard, 2000), 151.

32 Cited in Élisabeth Zucker-Rouvillois, "L'Expertise familiale ou la perte du doute scientifique," in *Au-delà du PaCS: L'Expertise familiale à l'épreuve de l'homosexualité,* ed. Daniel Borrillo, Éric Fassin, and Marcela Iacub (Paris: PUF, 1999), 125. There are those in France who write as if to suggest that gays and lesbians would lose their radicalness by achieving legal recognition for some of their forms of relationality, to suggest that they *belong* outside the norm. Conceivably some of Heritier's remarks could be assimilated to that kind of rhetorical position. Judith Butler provides a succinct counter to such arguments:

"We are all supposed to be satisfied with this apparently generous gesture by which the perverse is announced to be essential to the norm. The problem as I see it is that the perverse remains entombed precisely there, as the essential and negative feature of the norm, and the relation between the two remains static, giving way to no rearticulation of the norm itself" (Butler, *Antigone's Claim: Kinship Between Life and Death* [New York: Columbia University Press, 2000], 76).

33 Françoise Héritier, *Masculin/Féminin: La Pensée de la différence* (Paris: Odile Jacob, 1996), 258. One of Héritier's more notorious declarations in the recent debates was the assertion that the "difference between the sexes" is "the basis of the creation of the fundamental opposition that allows us to think" (cited in Sabine Prokhoris, *Le Sexe prescrit: La Différence sexuelle en question* [Paris: Aubier, 2000], 145). Prokhoris's book is an interesting dissection by a psychoanalyst of some of the recent French statements about sexual difference (see esp. 142–84).

34 In *Antigone's Claim* Judith Butler has many insightful passages addressing this theoretical problem. She comments concisely at one point, "the very description of the symbolic as intractable law takes place within a fantasy of law as insurpassable authority" (30).

35 Héritier, *Masculin/Féminin*, 254.

36 John Borneman, "Until Death Do Us Part: Marriage/Death in Anthropological Discourse," *American Ethnologist* 23, no. 2 (1996): 229.

37 Bourdieu, "Des familles sans nom," 5.

38 That the doctor in his will leaves money to the noble Savinien de Portenduère, who is in love with Ursule, and not to Ursule herself, could perhaps be taken as an indication that even alternative families are often organized in patriarchal and antifeminist ways. Claudie Bernard comments: "This paradoxical family is thus simultaneously perfectly patriarchal and yet modern" ("La Dynamique familiale dans *Ursule Mirouët* de Balzac," *French Forum* 24, no. 2 [May 1999]: 189).

39 "The Code started from the idea that movable goods were quite secondary, and so it failed to show much concern for them. This way of considering matters had its consequences; various drawbacks quickly made themselves apparent to all concerned" (Barthélemy Terrat, "Du régime de la propriété dans le *Code civil,*" in *Le Code civil, 1804–1904: Livre du centenaire* [Paris: Arthur Rousseau, 1904] 1:342).

40 Those who live "outside the Code" would thus seem to have a particular interest in gaining an understanding of modern financial instruments and in learning to exploit them. The doctor is a good example of someone who has done this. Cousin Pons, as we will see in chapter 3, could have used a few lessons. Other "alternative" or "queer" Balzacian characters will have varying degrees of success in this regard.

41 Mortimer, "Balzac's *Ursule Mirouët,*" 858–59.

42 The English translation cited here is *Old Goriot,* trans. Marion Ayton Crawford (Harmondsworth: Penguin, 1985).

43 There are many influential psychoanalytic readings of Balzac, and my readings would be impossible without them. They are also extremely varied in their approaches and conclusions. (More than counseling against psychoanalytic readings [far from it], I am suggesting here a caution about certain ways of understanding "normal" family structure and "normal" gender and sexuality that I often find perhaps unwittingly invoked in psychoanalytic accounts of Balzac's novels.) Here is just a sample of psychoanalytically inflected work on Balzac that I have learned from, in spite of whatever disagreements I may note in this volume: Janet L. Beizer, *Family Plots: Balzac's Narrative Generations* (New Haven: Yale University Press, 1986); Leo Bersani, *A Future for Astyanax: Character and Desire in Literature* (New York: Columbia University Press, 1984); Peter Brooks, *Reading for the Plot: Design and Intention in Narrative* (New York: Vintage, 1984), and *Body Work: Objects of Desire in Modern Narrative* (Cambridge: Harvard University Press, 1993); Shoshana Felman, *What Does a Woman Want? Reading and Sexual Difference* (Baltimore: Johns Hopkins University Press, 1993); Jameson, *The Political Unconscious;* and Naomi Schor, *Breaking the Chain: Women, Theory, and French Realist Fiction* (New York, Columbia University Press, 1985).

44 Beizer, *Family Plots,* 132.

45 Roddey Reid's *Families in Jeopardy: Regulating the Social Body in France, 1750–1910* (Stanford: Stanford University Press, 1993), especially the introduction and the first chapter, offers a helpful analysis of the ideological uses of family panic.

46 In a nuanced reading of *Le Père Goriot,* Sandy Petrey observes that "the degree of kinship in kinship denominations has nothing to do with a fact, everything to do with an attitude" (Petrey, *Realism and Revolution: Balzac, Stendhal, Zola, and the Performances of History* [Ithaca: Cornell University Press, 1988], 95). Petrey, too, however, exhibits the same habit of analytical thought we have seen elsewhere, of returning to the *nom de Père* as somehow once having provided a center to the field of kinship relations, which is only in the moment of the novel becoming open to challenge. He cites Lacan on the way the *nom du Père* has supported the "Symbolic function"—"from the dawn of time" (87). He also associates Balzac's moment with a point of crisis, "when *père* no longer means *père*" and therefore a moment when "the words for the relationships the Father institutes lose their self-identity as well" (88). Yet perhaps Petrey—in his simultaneous effort to show that the enactment of kinship relations is *always* a performance aimed at reproducing social power relations *and* to claim (melodramatically) that in Balzac's moment we find a sudden crisis in the "paternal function" with "deadly implications" for human society (90)—simply replicates a rhetorical confusion we also see in Balzac in his less analytical, more polemical, moments.

47 On Michonneau and Vautrin, see Lawrence R. Schehr, *Rendering French Realism* (Stanford: Stanford University Press, 1997), 94–104.

48 Michonneau is also performing one of the endless acts that continually strive to construct the "public sphere" as heterosexual. Rastignac will have, within *La Comédie humaine,* an important future as a government official. He will therefore always be haunted by this queer moment at the outset of his Parisian career (see chapter 4 and the epilogue for more on this topic). Balzac's understanding of the way the bourgeois public sphere is establishing itself as heterosexual, and thereby inflecting the sexual choices of certain social agents, is clear here, as well as in other works such as *Splendeurs et misères des courtisans.* Eric Clarke gives a helpful overview of the large process, particular elements of which we see in the exchange between Rastignac and Michonneau: "Historically, the greatest impediments to queer public sphere inclusion have been twofold: first, the heterosexist tenor of the bourgeois familial morality defining proper civic personhood and universal humanity; and second, the relegation of erotic experience, which has largely shaped a queer sense of self and collective belonging, to the proprietary privacy of the intimate sphere. Acting together, these two impediments have meant that even as the public sphere both draws upon and legitimates specific forms of intimacy and erotic experience—indeed is saturated by spectacles of intimacy—those that do not conform to a heteronormative standard are demonized and repudiated" (Clarke, *Virtuous Vice: Homoeroticism and the Public Sphere* [Durham: Duke University Press, 2000], 5). On Rastignac in *Le Père Goriot,* see also D. A. Miller, "Body Bildung and Textual Liberation," in *A New History of French Literature,* ed. Denis Hollier (Cambridge, MA.: Harvard University Press, 1989), 681–87.

49 The importance of the work of Michel Foucault for my project will perhaps be clearest in chapter 3. At times it has seemed to me that thinkers such as Bourdieu or Durkheim better help to highlight the sociological aspect of Balzac's interest in sexuality; that is, sexuality as a set of institutions, a set of social forms—coagulated bits of history—exterior to an individual and yet also inevitably incorporated in any individual. Yet Foucault's work on the disciplining of sexuality in nineteenth-century France and his work on the particular sets of institutions and discourses through which that particular disciplining is implemented (perhaps the most sociological parts of his work) provide powerful models as well for understanding the aim of some of Balzac's analysis and also for understanding the role novels can play in the implementation of forms of discipline.

Chapter One. Legal Melancholy: Balzac's Eugénie Grandet *and the Napoleonic Code*

1 Translations from *Le Contrat de mariage* are my own.

2 Pierre Bourdieu, "On the Family as a Realized Category," *Theory, Culture, and Society* 13, no. 3 (1996): 21–22.

3 The English translation cited here and elsewhere is *Eugénie Grandet,* trans. Sylvia Raphael (Oxford: Oxford University Press, 1990). As in the case of the passages cited elsewhere, I have made silent adjustments to the translation.

4 For discussions of *habitus* and *hexis,* see Bourdieu, *The Logic of Practice,* esp. chaps. 3, 4, and 9 of book 1. Bodily *hexis* "is political mythology realized, *embodied,* turned into a permanent disposition, a durable way of standing, speaking, walking, and thereby of feeling and thinking" (69–70).

5 Not that all Balzac's contemporaries took this conservative posturing seriously, nor that it made them think of his novels as providing the moral uplift they might seem to be claiming to offer. For information on the right-wing condemnation of Balzac's negative influence on morals, see Bellos, *Balzac Criticism in France,* 32–33, 37–41, 113–15.

6 I don't think that the melancholy that Balzac is presenting needs to be read as identical to the well-known melancholy of numerous male protagonists of romantic narratives: René, Adolphe, Octave, etc. As Margaret Waller has shown, the crisis of masculinity represented by these protagonist's melancholy is a clear spur to narration. And as Kari Weil shows, the romantic melancholy of these kinds of tales has a lot to do with an attempt to recuperate a relation to a troubled past. The Balzacian difference, it seems to me, has something to do with the difference between romantic and realist narrative; in Balzacian realism, melancholy is much more explicitly tied to the material, economic, and (as we shall see) legal structures within which bourgeois life is conducted. The Balzacian realist novel itself depersonalizes melancholy, making it less a symptom of an individual psyche than a social form produced out of material conditions. See Margaret Waller, *The Male Malady: Fictions of Impotence in the French Romantic Novel* (New Brunswick: Rutgers University Press, 1993); and Kari Weil, "Romantic Exile and the Melancholia of Identification," *differences* 7, no. 2 (1995): 111–26.

7 The presence of the Civil Code in Balzac's novels is detailed in Peytel, *Balzac;* and Marie-Henriette Faillie, *La Femme et le Code civil dans "La Comédie humaine" d'Honoré de Balzac* (Paris: Didier, 1968).

8 Sigmund Freud, "On Narcissism: An Introduction," trans. Cecil M. Baines, in *General Psychological Theory: Papers on Metapsychology,* ed. Philip Rieff (New York: Collier, 1963), 60–61.

9 Sigmund Freud, "Mourning and Melancholia," trans. Joan Riviere, in *General Psychological Theory,* 170.

10 Schor, *Breaking the Chain,* 102.

11 Schor returns to the concept of melancholy in *One Hundred Years of Melancholy* (Oxford: Clarendon Press, 1996), in which she surveys a number of other nineteenth-century French literary works in order to consider the place of melancholy in them. Helpful critical readings of the Freudian conceptual deployment of narcissism, melancholy, and homosexuality can be found in Judith Butler, "Freud and the Melancholia of Gender," in *Gender Trouble: Feminism and the Subversion of Identity* (New York: Routledge, 1990), 57–65, and "The

Lesbian Phallus and the Morphological Imaginary, in *Bodies That Matter: On the Discursive Limits of "Sex"* (New York: Routledge, 1993), 57–91; and Diana Fuss, "Fallen Women: 'The Psychogenesis of a Case of Homosexuality in a Woman,'" in *Identification Papers* (New York: Routledge, 1995), 57–82.

12 Freud, "On Narcissism," 73.

13 Schor, *Breaking the Chain,* 92.

14 Freud, "On Narcissism," 69–70.

15 Schor, *Breaking the Chain,* 106.

16 The novel makes explicit the extent to which Grandet's financial fortunes have been intimately linked to his wife's family's wealth from the beginning of the marriage. Grandet married his wife at about the same moment in the Revolutionary period that the state started selling off church lands. Thanks to his own ready cash, his wife's dowry, and a bribe to the Revolutionary official paid by his father-in-law, Grandet was able to buy some farms, some choice vineyards, and an old abbey (3:1030, 31, 6–7). His (and his wife's) wealth only increased in 1806, with the death of his wife's three relatives, but any new wealth accrued during the marriage would have been part of the community property of the marriage. Each spouse in theory possessed half of the value realized via community property during the marriage. With the dissolution of the marriage at the point of the death of one of the spouses, half of all of the value added to the community property during the marriage would be inherited by the deceased spouse's heirs. Suppose Mme. Grandet to have died without a will: "In the event of intestate succession the Code allowed collateral kindred to succeed up to the 12th degree, while it simultaneously excluded from intestate succession the surviving spouse. Though the widow was to receive one half of the community fund, and thus of the property acquired by the husband during the marriage and all his movables, she was excluded, as a stranger to the blood, from any share in his inherited lands, which were thus to be kept within the group of the kindred" (Max Rheinstein, "The Code and the Family," in *The Code Napoleon and the Common-Law World,* ed. Bernard Schwartz [New York: New York University Press, 1956], 156). Rheinstein speaks of a widow, but the same holds for a widower. Eugénie would inherit from her mother half of the community property at the time of marriage, half of all the accrued value of the community property, all of the lands and buildings belonging to her mother at the time of marriage, and all of the lands and buildings her mother inherited during the marriage. Eugénie's mother could legally have given or willed to her husband no more than half of her estate: by law, half of her estate had to go to Eugénie. One sees here the potential—one Eugénie and her mother were probably unaware of during the mother's lifetime—to unite together and wield influence over Grandet.

17 Paul Gide, *Étude sur la condition privée de la femme,* 2nd ed. (Paris: Larose et Forcel, 1885), 415.

18 It was not until 1907, for instance, that a French woman would have the legal right to dispose of assets acquired by her own work during marriage. Starting

in 1907, such earnings were set aside in a "reserved fund" (separate from the community property of the marriage) that was to be both used and managed by the wife. Consider the comments of one scholar from 1956: "Altogether, the changes in the French law of marital property . . . have been modest. Even the most far-reaching, *i.e.* the establishment of the wife's free enjoyment and management of her reserved fund, seems to be limited in its effect by the cautious attitude of banks and business circles in general, which, before honoring a married woman's transaction, are wont either to require strict proof that the asset in question is part of her separate fund, or, even more generally, will not act unless her act is countersigned by her husband" (Rheinstein, "The Code and the Family," 153).

19 Both Eugénie and her father, then, are examples of the uneven distribution of "legal consciousness" in everyday life, the uneven distribution of the mindset necessary to make use of the law to one's own advantage. For an interesting discussion of the relations of law to everyday life, see Austin Sarat and Thomas R. Kearns, "Beyond the Great Divide: Forms of Legal Scholarship and Everyday Life," in *Law in Everyday Life,* ed. Austin Sarat and Thomas R. Kearns (Ann Arbor: University of Michigan Press, 1993), 21–62. See also, in that same volume, Hendrik Hartog, "Abigail Bailey's Coverture: Law in a Married Woman's Consciousness," 63–108, which discusses the case of an eighteenth-century American woman who finds a way to use the law to protect herself against her husband, but without giving up a traditional practice of femininity.

20 Another way of understanding Eugénie's actions would be to take seriously her inheritance of the "nobility" of her mother's soul. Her nobility, apparent in her almost arrogant refusal to concern herself with matters of money, could represent an ideological resistance to a bourgeois ethos, a resistance that draws its inspiration from an idealized image of an aristocratic ethos, an image perhaps transmitted to women by the church. Here again, we could see parallels between Paul de Mannerville and Eugénie, both of whom experience a link between sentimentality and a nobility of soul—an odd mixture and resignification of specific bourgeois and aristocratic practices. (I owe some of these insights to an exchange with Remi Lenoir and Marcela Iacub.)

21 Jean-Louis Halpérin, *L'Impossible Code civil* (Paris: Presses Universitaires de France, 1992), 15.

22 This would be another example of Pierre Bourdieu's "Don Quixote effect," which I mention in my preface and which he describes in *Pascalian Meditations:* "Habitus is not necessarily adapted to its situation nor necessarily coherent . . . Thus it can be observed that to contradictory positions, which tend to exert structural 'double binds' on their occupants, there often correspond destabilized habitus, torn by contradictions and internal division, generating suffering. Moreover, even if dispositions may waste away or weaken through lack of use (linked, in particular, to a change in social position or condition), or as a result of heightened consciousness associated with an effort of transformation (such as the correction of accents, manners, etc.), there is an inertia (or

hysterisis) of habitus which have a spontaneous tendency (based in biology) to perpetuate structures corresponding to their conditions of production. As a result, it can happen that, in what might be called the Don Quixote effect, dispositions are out of line with the field and with the 'collective expectations' which are constitutive of its normality. This is the case, in particular, when a field undergoes a major crisis and its regularities (even its rules) are profoundly changed" (160).

23 See, for example, this passage from near the end of Balzac's *La Rabouilleuse* (translated by Donald Adamson under the rather different title *The Black Sheep* [Harmondsworth: Penguin, 1970]), in which Philippe Bridau is awaiting the death of the woman he married for money so that he can marry an aristocrat:

> "What fortune would I need to marry one of the Grandlieu daughters?" Philippe inquired of de Marsay.
>
> "You? You wouldn't get the ugliest of the six for less than ten million francs," de Marsay answered insolently.
>
> "But with a private income of 200,000 francs a year, you could get Mademoiselle de Langeais, the Marquis's daughter," Rastignac butted in; "she is an ugly woman aged thirty, with nothing in the way of a dowry; that would fit your bill." (4:538–39, 336–37)

24 About this scene, Dorothy Kelly comments: "Yet despite her inheritance of Grandet's fortune and ideology, she keeps the grain of a revolt. When she marries, she does not give herself completely to her husband because she refuses to have sexual relations with him. . . . She succumbs to the law, all the while showing marriage for what it is in her world: the exchange of commodities. Curiously, by her decision, her husband becomes her slave: " 'Je serai votre esclave!' lui dit-il" (p. 1194) (" 'I will be your slave!' he said to her"). In pointing out the laws that govern the exchange of women, she has shown that the "master" is in fact another slave of this economic family system" (Kelly, *Fictional Genders: Role and Representation in Nineteenth-Century French Narrative* [Lincoln: University of Nebraska Press, 1989], 71.) References to slavery and the slave trade punctuate Balzac's novels. Vautrin's plantation fantasy, mentioned earlier in the introduction, is another famous instance. Bonfons's somewhat disingenuous metaphorical declaration of his enslavement is obviously meant to resonate in some way with the information that Charles has made his recent fortune in the slave trade. We might qualify Kelly's observation about the enslavement of the master a bit by noting that Eugénie, her mother, and Nanon have a much closer experience of dispossession of their own labor than Bonfons ever will, and that it may well be part of Balzac's analytic project for us to notice this.

25 Balzac has his finger on a hot topic here. As Caroline Ford notes in an article on Restoration France: "The many cases involving women who entered religious communities without parental consent resulted in demands for legislation limiting the property rights of 'women religious,' who had the right

to equal inheritance under the Napoleonic Civil Code, and fanned the flames of anticlericalism throughout the nineteenth century" (Ford, "Private Lives and Public Order in Restoration France: The Seduction of Emily Loveday," *American Historical Review* 99, no. 1 [February 1994]: 22). Ford's argument in that essay is that "female religious communities potentially threatened family, state, and the principle of paternal authority, on which the postrevolutionary civil order was based. . . . While a separate identity and organization for women within the church certainly did not call existing gender roles into question, it implicitly undermined public order by destabilizing the juridical notion of paternal authority on which that order was based, until new laws governing female religious communities in 1880 and 1901 heralded their legal demise" (43). Seeing a Balzacian priest trying to dissuade a rich woman from entering a religious order reveals clearly how complex and conflicting simultaneous allegiances to a patriarchal civil order and to the church could be. Similarly, one sees clearly how someone like Eugénie could see in a religious community a space securely outside the civic order she finds so repressive.

Chapter Two. On Not Getting Married in a Balzac Novel

1 Lynn Hunt mentions this same legislative fact in her *The Family Romance of the French Revolution,* 163–64. The law Hunt cites dictates that unmarried people over the age of thirty would pay a 25 percent supplement on their personal and sumptuary taxes. Translations from *Pierrette* are my own.

2 For information on nineteenth-century French phobic discourse about single people, see the introduction to Takao Kashiwagi, *La Trilogie des "Célibataires" d'Honoré de Balzac* (Paris: Nizet, 1983), 11–20. See also Jean Borie, *Le Célibataire français* (Paris: Le Sagittaire, 1976). Kashiwagi also discusses the links between *Eugénie Grandet* and the *célibataire* novels (see 55–65).

3 Borie, *Le Célibataire français,* 7, 91.

4 The work in question is *Le Député d'Arcis,* which Balzac never finished—so Maxime was never married off by Balzac. See my epilogue for a discussion of *Le Député d'Arcis.*

5 Richard Terdiman sees hostility to a bourgeois order as lying at the heart of the development of what he calls "counter-discourse": "The open and virulent anger felt by the antibourgeois for the bourgeois can rarely have been more evident or more focused [than it was in the nineteenth century]. It was all the more corrosive because typically it was driven by the personal guilt of a conflicted class identity, by personal implication in the detested formation itself. Alienated middle-class writers may have cherished alienation, but they *hated* an irretrievably middle-class identity. The anger generated out of such a crux provides the subjective dynamism of the counter-discourse; its virulence becomes the principle of the counter-discourse's social importance" (Terdiman, *Discourse/Counter-Discourse: The Theory and Practice of Symbolic Resistance in Nineteenth-Century France* [Ithaca: Cornell University Press, 1985], 66).

6 Jacques Mulliez, "Révolutionnaires, nouveaux pères? Forcément nouveaux pères! Le droit révolutionnaire de la paternité," in *La Révolution et l'ordre juridique privé: Rationalité ou scandale? Actes du colloque d'Orléans, 11–13 septembre 1986,* ed. Michel Vovelle (Paris: PUF, 1988), 375.

7 Ibid., 384, 386. On these questions of "private marriages," of adoption, of "la recherche de la paternité," as they evolved from the most liberal legislative moments of the Revolution to the reactionary Napoleonic Code, see also Halpérin, *L'Impossible Code civil,* 112, 123–27, 165–67, 252–54, 280–83.

8 Martin, "L'Individualisme libéral en France autour de 1800," 100.

9 Pierre Bourdieu's concluding comments to his chapter "Land and Matrimonial Strategies" in *Logic of Practice,* where he discusses strategies used by certain small landholders to keep together their patrimony, capture much of the complexity of Balzac's own demonstration: "Here, as elsewhere, the agents obey the impulses of feeling or the injunctions of duty more than the calculations of interest, even when, in doing so, they conform to the economy of the system of constraints and demands of which their ethical and affective dispositions are the product. . . . Faced with the dangers that every marriage presents for the patrimony and therefore the lineage, owing to the fact that the compensation due to the younger brothers could force the break-up of the patrimony—which the privilege of the eldest son was precisely intended to avoid—families respond with a range of actions designed to overcome this specific contradiction of the system. . . . The superficially very different solutions—birth control, emigration or celibacy of younger sons, etc. . . . have their common origin in the *habitus,* which is the product of the structures that it tends to reproduce and which implies a 'spontaneous' submission to the established order and to the orders of the guardians of that order. Marriage strategies are inseparable from inheritance strategies, fertility strategies, and even educational strategies, in other words from the whole set of strategies for biological, cultural and social reproduction that every group implements in order to transmit the inherited powers and privileges, maintained or enhanced, to the next generation. Their principle is neither calculating reason nor the mechanical determinations of economic necessity, but the dispositions inculcated by the conditions of existence, a kind of socially constituted instinct which causes the objectively calculable demands of a particular form of economy to be experienced as an unavoidable call of duty or an irresistible impulse of feeling" (160–61).

10 See, for instance, Jameson, *The Political Unconscious,* 164–66, 174.

11 The 1830 Revolution is often concisely understood as the moment at which the conservative branch of the royal family that came back to power in the 1815 Restoration and that favored the interests of the landed aristocracy was deposed in favor of a branch of the royal family more willing to back the interests of industrial and banking capital. Republicans who would have participated in the 1830 Revolution to encourage political reform would thus not see their interests given much support by the new "Citizen-King," Louis-Philippe. One recent account of the 1830 Revolution does insist, however, that "the elite of

the July Monarchy remained principally one of landowners. . . . While there can be little doubt that 1830 did not bring a capitalist bourgeoisie to power—their numbers were too small and most entrepreneurs were not over-eager for an active political role—1830 was self-consciously and assertively a bourgeois revolution. Louis-Philippe was hailed as a bourgeois king, however silly that may sound; the hereditary peerage was abolished; the new rulers gloried in the idea of bourgeois power. . . . The rule of the bourgeoisie meant the dominance of a traditional landed and professional middle class" (Pamela Pilbeam, *The 1830 Revolution in France* [New York: St. Martin's Press, 1991], 194). See also David H. Pinkney, *The French Revolution of 1830* (Princeton: Princeton University Press, 1972). Numerous studies of Balzac's own sense of political history and his own political evolution exist. See, for example, Bernard Guyon, *La Pensée politique et sociale de Balzac* (Paris: Colin, 1967); Ronnie Butler, *Balzac and the French Revolution* (London: Croom Helm, 1983); René-Alexandre Courteix, *Balzac et la Révolution française* (Paris: PUF, 1997). See also the articles and discussions in the special issue of the journal *Europe* 43 (1965) devoted to Balzac, history, and politics.

12 At a certain point the narrator offers a general reflection on the lives of certain odd shopkeepers, who do not seem to participate in ordinary life: "No passerby could understand the motivation behind the cryptogamic existences of certain shopkeepers. Looking at them, one is forced to ask: why do they live? what do they live for? what do they turn in to? where do they come from?" (4: 46–47). Cryptogams are plants such as ferns or mushrooms, without seeds or flowers—somehow sexually dubious. We will see, in the pages ahead, the Marquis de Custine referred to as a cryptogam by Philarète Chasles. Cousin Pons and his friend Schmucke will be referred to as mushrooms by their *portière* (female porter). The character of Jean-Baptiste Molineux in *César Birotteau*, another odd *célibataire*, is also described by the narrator as a cryptogam when he is first presented (6:105–8, 81).

13 Nye, *Masculinity and Male Codes of Honor*, 44–45. Nye is citing Foucault, *The History of Sexuality. Volume 1: An Introduction*, trans. Robert Hurley (New York: Vintage, 1990), 123.

14 On chlorosis, see Moïse Le Yaouanc, *Nosographie de l'humanité balzacienne* (Paris: Maloine, 1959), 212–20; and Jean Starobinski, "Sur la chlorose," *Romantisme* 31 (1981): 113–30.

15 Portalis's observations can be found in his presentation of the proposed articles on marriage for the *Civil Code* to the legislature: "Présentation au corps législatif, et exposé des motifs, par le consieller d'état Portalis," in Fenet, *Recueil complet*, 9:145.

Interlude: Balzac and Same-Sex Relations in the 1830s

1 Honoré de Balzac, *Correspondance*, ed. Roger Pierrot (Paris: Garnier, 1960–1969), 2:207. There are only a handful of letters from Sue to Balzac in the

Correspondance, but they do show Sue's obsession with body parts. One from early 1832 concludes: "A vous d'orteil si vous pouvez, sinon à vous de glande pinéale" (1:681). In January 1833, Sue signs off, "A vous de périnée" (2:221). These are expressions modeled on the standard conclusion to a friendly letter: "A vous de cœur," meaning roughly, "to you from the heart." Sue sends his letters to Balzac from his big toe (*orteil*), pineal gland, and perineum.

2 Balzac, *Correspondance,* 1:345.

3 See Pierre Citron, *Dans Balzac* (Paris: Seuil, 1986), 85–101. He reprises there some of the material from his earlier essay, "Sur deux zones obscures de la psychologie de Balzac," *L'Année balzacienne* (1967): 3–27.

4 Citron, "Sur deux zones obscures," 12.

5 Graham Robb, *Balzac: A Biography* (New York: Norton, 1994), 154; see also 153–159, 261.

6 These include a tumultuous friendship with Latouche and another with Jules Sandeau. For a description of Balzac, Auger, and Latouche merrily wallpapering Balzac's apartment, see Frédéric Ségu, *Un Maître de Balzac méconnu: H. de Latouche* (Paris: Belles-Lettres, 1928), 34–38. Some have speculated that Auger was a possible model for Lucien de Rubempré (more on this in chapter 4).

7 Suzanne Jean Bérard, *La Genèse d'un roman de Balzac: "Illusions perdues," 1837* (Paris: Colin, 1961), 1:203 (see, in general, 1:193–207).

8 Rayner Heppenstall, in the introduction to his translation of Balzac's *A Harlot High and Low* (Harmondsworth: Penguin, 1970), ix–x.

9 More information on Custine is given in forthcoming pages. David Halperin's essay, "How to Do the History of Male Homosexuality," *GLQ: A Journal of Lesbian and Gay Studies* 6, no. 1 (2000): 87–124, is helpful on historiographical issues. Halperin writes: "The history of discourses pertaining to forms of *male* intimacy . . . condense a number of the crosscutting systems of thought at whose intersections we now find ourselves. . . . The very incoherence at the core of the modern notion of homosexuality furnishes the most eloquent indication of the historical accumulation of discontinuous notions sheltered within its specious unity. . . . What *homosexuality* signifies today is an effect of [a] cumulative process of historical overlay and accretion" (89–91). Eve Kosofsky Sedgwick earlier wrote of "relations enabled by the unrationalized coexistence of different models" (*Epistemology of the Closet* [Berkeley: University of California Press, 1990], 47). Both Halperin's and Sedgwick's formulations are useful for thinking about the French material from the 1830s that I present here.

10 Eugène-François Vidocq, *Mémoires; Les Voleurs,* ed. Francis Lacassin (1837; Paris: Laffont, 1998), 823–24.

11 Rumors circulated about Lacenaire's sexuality as well. This seems apparent in even a twentieth-century representation of Lacenaire, from Marcel Carné's 1945 film *Les Enfants du paradis,* where both Lacenaire and his accomplice Avril are characterized by a certain sexual ambiguity. About Chardon, we can note the following from an account by one of Lacenaire's contemporaries: "Chardon, the son, usually also called 'auntie,' was well known for his *anti-*

physical penchants. It is thus only natural that the first suspects in the case of his murder were all from the group of abject beings to which he belonged. Several of these vile men were arrested, and later released for lack of evidence. Others were simply put under surveillance, without anything worthwhile being discovered" [Le fils Chardon, généralement surnommé *la tante,* était bien connu pour ses goûts *antiphysiques,* et ce fut naturellement sur les êtres abjects dont il faisait partie que l'accusation publique tomba tout d'abord. Parmi ces hommes immondes, plusieurs furent arrêtés, puis relâchés faute de preuves. D'autres furent simplement surveillés, sans que cette surveillance produisît de meilleurs résultats]" (cited in Lacenaire, *Mémoires, poèmes et lettres,* ed. Monique Lebailly [Paris: Albin Michel, 1968], 193).

12 Louis-Mathurin Moreau-Christophe, "Les Détenus," in *Les Français peints par eux-mêmes: Encyclopédie morale du dix-neuvième siècle* (Paris: Carmier, 1841–1850), 4:89–90.

13 The last three citations are taken from a novel written in 1833 by one of Henri de Latouche's protégés, Arnould Fremy, titled *Les Deux Anges* (Paris: Gosselin, 1833), 1:109–11. There was a spate of writings about "unearthly" creatures of unclear sexuality in this period, of which Fremy's novel would be a minor instance. More-celebrated examples are Latouche's own *Fragoletta* (1829) and Balzac's *Sarrasine* (1830) and *Séraphîta* (1835). George Sand used angels as well to figure a love that somehow exceeded human limits. In a passage from her *Journal intime,* written in 1834, when she was in the final days of her relationship with Alfred de Musset, she writes: "Quel mal avais-je fait aux anges du ciel pour qu'ils descendissent sur moi et pour qu'ils missent en moi pour châtiment, un amour de lionne? pourquoi mon sang s'est-il changé en feu, et pourquoi ai-je connu au moment de mourir des embrassements plus fougueux que ceux des hommes? [What wrong did I do to the angels of heaven that caused them to come down and punish me by inflicting on me a lioness's love? Why has my blood turned to fire, and why, on the brink of death, have I known kisses more ardent than those of men?]" (Sand, *Journal intime,* in *Oeuvres autobiographiques,* ed. Georges Lubin [Paris: Gallimard (Pléiade), 1971], 2:964).

14 For a look at the way various critics do their best to avoid seeing the relationship between Vautrin and Lucien de Rubempré as in any way sexualized, see Philippe Berthier, "Balzac du côté de Sodome," *L'Année balzacienne* (1979): 152–54.

15 Barbéris, *Balzac et le mal du siecle,* 1:194–95.

16 Cited in ibid., 1:191.

17 One is reminded of Eve Kosofsky Sedgwick's droll characterizations of scholarly dismissals of questions about sexuality, such as: "Passionate language of same-sex attraction was extremely common during whatever period is under discussion—and therefore must have been completely meaningless"; or, "The author under discussion is certified or rumored to have had an attachment to someone of the other sex—so their feelings about people of their own sex must have been completely meaningless" (*Epistemology of the Closet,* 52).

18 Halperin, "How to Do the History of Male Homosexuality," 101. There is an immense body of work available on the category of male friendship. It includes Sedgwick's *Epistemology of the Closet* and also her earlier book, *Between Men: English Literature and Male Homosocial Desire* (New York: Columbia University Press, 1985). On France, see Anne Vincent-Buffault, *L'Exercice de l'amitié: Pour une histoire des pratiques amicales aux XVIIIe et XIXe siècles* (Paris: Seuil, 1995). George Rousseau and Caroline Warman discuss some of Custine's friendships in: "Made from the Stuff of Saints: Chateaubriand's *René* and Custine's Search for a Homosexual Identity," *GLQ: A Journal of Lesbian and Gay Studies* 7, no. 1 (2001): 1–29. Some recent work on eighteenth-century England has provided me with a helpful counterpoint as I have thought about the French nineteenth-century materials: Raymond Stephanson, " 'Epicoene Friendship': Understanding Male Friendship in the Early Eighteenth Century, with some Speculations about Pope," *The Eighteenth Century* 38, no. 2 (1997): 151–70. Stephanson's methodology has been interestingly critiqued by George Haggerty in his book *Men in Love: Masculinity and Sexuality in the Eighteenth Century* (New York: Columbia University Press, 1999), 16–20. Yet Haggerty's own methodology seems inappropriate to the materials I am considering. Haggerty disdains "the constant insistence that we look for the 'genital' in erotic relations." He likens it to "searching for keyhole testimony in a sodomy trial." That characterization does not seem to me sufficient reason to say one cannot or should not be interested in the presence or absence of "genital" behavior. It is not clear to me what is to be gained by limiting one's curiosity in this way. Haggerty opts for the term "love," in all its intentional vagueness, concluding: "What the monstrous figure of the sodomite has so often excluded is the love he shares with the men with whom he is sexually intimate. The 'love' cannot be expressed–'dare not speak its name'—because that is what is really threatening. Two men having sex threatens no one. Two men in love: that begins to threaten the very foundations of heterosexist culture" (20). Such generalizations seem untenable to me. When, in 1827, the marquis de Custine set up a rendezvous with a guardsman, it seems unlikely he was much interested in love. He already had a male partner at home. When the guardsman brought along a couple of buddies to the rendezvous and beat up Custine, leaving him naked on the road, it would certainly seem that someone was threatened, whatever was happening to heterosexist culture.

19 Sand, *Histoire de ma vie,* in *Oeuvres autobiographiques,* 2:125–26.

20 Historians of sexuality in France often understand the early part of the nineteenth century as a relatively open period as compared to the conservatism that sets in around mid-century. In an essay in *Homosexuality in Modern France,* for instance, Michael David Sibalis writes: "the Revolutionary and Napoleonic era was a time of relative freedom for pederasts and sodomites, especially when compared to the years before 1789 and after 1840 or 1850" ("The Regulation of Male Homosexuality in Revolutionary and Napoleonic France, 1789–1815," in

Homosexuality in Modern France, ed. Jeffrey Merrick and Bryant T. Ragan Jr. [New York: Oxford University Press, 1996], 96). In an article in the same volume, Victoria Thompson comments: "While during the July Monarchy (1830–48), a period of tremendous social upheaval, sexuality and gender often appeared as fluid, by the 1850s and 1860s sexuality and gender were increasingly organized into rigidly defined categories" ("Creating Boundaries: Homosexuality and the Changing Social Order in France, 1830–1870," 103). This may be too large a generalization, however. Different cultural locations would have experienced any such process at different rates, and certainly in some cultural locations there may never have been much experience of "relative freedom" or "fluidity" at all. For examples of violence and legal action against expressions of male same-sex sexuality in this period, see Sibalis, "Regulation of Male Homosexuality," 88–92; and also Jean-Paul Aron and Roger Kempf, *Le Pénis et la démoralisation de l'Occident* (Paris: Grasset, 1978), 26–28, 41–44, 103–56. More discussion on Sand and female same-sex culture in the period follows toward the end of this interlude. See also Lillian Faderman, *Surpassing the Love of Men: Romantic Friendship and Love between Women from the Renaissance to the Present* (New York: Quill, 1981), 254–76; Joseph Barry, *Infamous Woman: The Life of George Sand* (New York: Doubleday, 1977); and Marie-Jo Bonnet, *Les Relations amoureuses entre les femmes du XVIe au XXe siècle* (Paris: Odile Jacob, 1995), 211–24. Rose Fortassier's introduction to *La Fille aux yeux d'or* (5:771–77), which portrays a relationship between two women, gives information on Balzac's possible sources for his story, as does the earlier introduction by Pierre-Georges Castex to his edition of Balzac's, *Histoire des treize* (Paris: Garnier Frères, 1966), esp. 355–61. A helpful set of methodological considerations can be found in Sharon Marcus, "Quelques problèmes de l'histoire lesbienne," trans. Jean-Yves Boulard, in *Les Études gay et lesbiennes: Colloque du Centre Georges Pompidou, 23 et 27 juin 1997,* ed. Didier Eribon (Paris: Centre Pompidou, 1998), 35–43. I am also indebted to the unpublished work by Leyla Ezdinli, "Rumor and Reputation: George Sand's Transvestism and the Literary Star System."

21 See Sand, *Histoire de ma vie,* in *Oeuvres autobiographiques,* 2:128–31, 1333.

22 Ibid., 129. Balzac, too, can play with lists of male friends in ways that imply something about the nature of the intimacy found in the friendship. In *Le Cousin Pons,* while describing the pair of friends, Wilhelm Schwab and Fritz Brunner, who in some ways mirror the pair made by Pons and his dear friend Schmucke, Balzac writes: "Put the names of Fritz and Wilhelm beside those of Damon and Pythias, Castor and Pollox, Orestes and Pylades, Dubreuil and Pemjah, Schmucke and Pons. . . . Add these two fresh names to all these examples, and you will be doing them justice" (7:536, 78).

23 On acts of cultural appropriation involving the bourgeoisie and the nobility in this time period, see Nye, *Masculinity and Male Codes of Honor,* 35–46. On the relative social position of the bohemians, see Pierre Bourdieu, "The Field of Cultural Production, or: The Economic World Reversed," trans. Richard Nice,

in *The Field of Cultural Production,* ed. Randal Johnson (New York: Columbia University Press, 1993), 29–73; and Bourdieu, *The Rules of Art: Genesis and Structure of the Literary Field,* trans. Susan Emanuel (Stanford: Stanford University Press, 1996), 54–60.

24 Sand, *Histoire de ma vie,* in *Oeuvres autobiographiques,* 2:47.

25 Lubin's speculations can be found in the editorial matter of Sand, *Oeuvres autobiographiques,* 2:1316. On the event in 1824, see Julien-Frédéric Tarn, *Le Marquis de Custine, ou: Les Malheurs de l'exactitude* (Paris: Fayard, 1985), 69; Pierre de Lacretelle's introduction to Custine's *Souvenirs et portraits* (Monaco: Éditions du Rocher, 1956), 25–27; Anka Muhlstein, *Astolphe de Custine, 1790–1857: Le Dernier marquis* (Paris: Grasset, 1996), 172–74, 186–92; and A. de Luppé, *Astolphe de Custine* (Monaco: Éditions du Rocher, 1957), 96–101. See also the discussion of Custine in relation to Stendhal in James Creech, *Closet Writing/Gay Reading: The Case of Melville's "Pierre"* (Chicago: University of Chicago Press, 1993), 19–27; and Rousseau and Warman, "Made from the Stuff of Saints."

26 Muhlstein, *Astolphe de Custine,* 174.

27 Ibid., 192. It is from Muhlstein that I learned of the cryptic passage in Sand's *Histoire de ma vie.* On Custine's celebrity as a host, see the contemporary account of his home at Saint-Gratien by Delphine de Girardin, writing under her pseudonym, le vicomte de Launay, in the "Courrier de Paris" in *La Presse* on July 6, 1837. See also A. de Luppé, "Custine, héros de Balzac: Comment l'auteur de *La Russie en 1839* entra dans *La Comédie humaine* et fut un peu Vautrin," *Le Figaro littéraire* (June 11, 1955): 5–6. Luppé also suggests that Custine was no longer welcome in purely aristocratic salons after the scandal and therefore sought out more mixed salons. He also created a brilliant mixed salon of his own, which included the literary, theatrical, musical, and artistic stars of the time. For a sense of how willingly and frequently certain members of Parisian literary circles dined at Custine's, see (by one of the frequent diners) Antoine Fontaney, *Journal intime,* ed. René Jasinski (Paris: Les Presses francaises, 1925).

28 Some scholars have suggested that Custine, while admiring Sand's talent, did not care for her (see Luppé, *Astolphe de Custine,* 203). Custine was friends with Chopin first; Sand apparently asked Chopin to arrange for her to meet Custine. (This would have been in about 1836; see Thérèse Marix-Spire, *Les Romantiques et la musique: Le Cas de George Sand, 1804–1838* [Paris: Nouvelles éditions latines, 1954], 527.) One of Chopin's biographers suggests that Custine was explicitly trying to seduce Chopin, a possibility that may have influenced Custine's attitude toward Sand, and hers to him. See William G. Atwood, *Fryderyk Chopin: Pianist from Warsaw* (New York: Columbia University Press, 1987), 109, 114. In a letter to Varnhagen d'Ense from 1840, Custine describes his somewhat ambivalent reaction to Sand's recent novel, *Le Compagnon du Tour de France.* But in an 1848 letter to the same person, he describes reading Sand's *La Mare au diable* with tears in his eyes. In the 1840 letter he also describes with some interest Sand's reaction to hearing Pauline Viardot sing (accompanied on the piano

by Chopin): "An ecstatic Mme Sand took Mme Viardot's head between her hands, kissed it, gazed at it with admiration and adoration; then she sat down in her lap!" (Custine, *Lettres à Varnhagen d'Ense,* ed. Roger Pierrot [Geneva: Slatkine, 1979], 387–98, 500).

29 Custine, "Les Amitiés littéraires en 1831," in *Paris; ou, Le Livre des cent-et-un* (Paris: Ladvocat, 1831–1832), 5:126. The 1830s saw a series of articles on literary friendships between men, often written by a member of one literary camp, attacking the professional and personal morals of an opposing camp. Henri de Latouche perhaps began the trend with his article "De la camaraderie littéraire" in the *Revue de Paris* in October 1829, an attack on the Romantics—Hugo, Sainte-Beuve, and their circle. Two notable contributions to the trend were later made by the literary critic Gustave Planche, who would be the model for Balzac's character Claude Vignon. Planche published "De la haine littéraire" in the *Revue des deux mondes* on December 1, 1831, and "Les Amitiés littéraires" in the same journal on September 1, 1836.

30 Custine, "Les Amitiés littéraires en 1831," 104.

31 It begins: "Mon Ami, ce petit livre est à vous; votre nom s'y trouve à presque toutes les pages; votre présence, ou votre souvenir s'y mêle à toutes mes pensées. Je vous le donne, ou plutôt je vous le rends; il ne serait pas fait sans vous." It continues, a bit later: "L'amitié, ô mon Ami, quand elle est ce qu'elle doit être, l'union des âmes, a cela de salutaire qu'au milieu de nos plus grandes et de nos plus désespérées douleurs, elle nous rattache insensiblement et par un lien invisible à la vie humaine, à la société, et nous empêche, en notre misérable frénésie, de nier, les yeux fermés, tout ce qui nous entoure." A bit later, still: "La plupart des amitiés humaines, même des meilleures, sont donc vaines et mensongères, ô mon Ami; et c'est à quelque chose de plus intime, de plus vrai, de plus invariable, qu'aspire une âme dont toutes les forces ont été une fois brisées et qui a senti le fond de la vie. L'amitié qu'elle implore, et en qui elle veut établir sa demeure, ne saurait être trop pure et trop pieuse, trop empreinte d'immortalité, trop mêlée à l'invisible et à ce qui ne change pas [My Friend, this small book is yours, it has your name on almost every page; your presence, or the memory of you, lingers in my every thought. I offer it to you, or better, I return it to you; without you, it could not have been. . . . Friendship, o my Friend, when it is all it should be, a union of souls, quietly and invisibly reattaches us to human life and to society, thus having a salutary effect in the midst of our moments of deepest, most painful despair. It prevents us, in our miserable frenzied states, from denying blindly all that surrounds us. . . . Most human friendships, even the best of them, are vain and filled with lies, o my Friend; a soul that has been broken and sunk to the depths of life aspires to something more intimate, truer, invariable. The friendship of that soul's desire, in which it seeks a home, cannot be too pure or pious, cannot be too marked by immortality, too mixed with the invisible and all that is not subject to change]" (Sainte-Beuve, *Les Consolations,* 3rd ed. [Brussels: Hauman Cattoir et comp., 1837], v, ix, xiv).

32 *Le Figaro,* April 29, 1830. Leyla Ezdinli kindly brought this article to my attention.

33 Henry Murger, *Scènes de la vie de bohème* (Paris: Gallimard [Folio], 1988), 171–203 (citations from 171, 191, 181).

34 See Muhlstein, *Astolphe de Custine,* 233–38; Luppé, *Astolphe de Custine,* 173–80, 183–86, 204, 210, 214, 216, 220–23.

35 Pierre de Lacretelle, in his introduction to Custine's *Souvenirs et portraits,* 49 (see, on the Gurowski episode, 46–63). For a nonchalant description of some of the bits of this episode by Custine himself, see his three letters to Varnhagen d'Ense from 1841 in *Lettres à Varnhagen d'Ense,* 407–34.

36 In addition to my discussion in the opening pages of chapter 4, on the publication history of the two novels, see 5:1119–30 and 6:1309–15.

37 The editor for the story in question is Anne-Marie Meininger.

38 Muhlstein, *Astolphe de Custine,* 12.

39 Cf. the comments of Michel Foucault: "Hence, literature belongs to the great system of constraint by which the West obliged the quotidian to enter into discourse. But literature occupies a special place within that system: determined to seek out the quotidian beneath the quotidian itself, to cross boundaries, to ruthlessly or insidiously bring our secrets out in the open, to displace rules and codes, to compel the unmentionable to be told, it will thus tend to place itself outside the law, or at least to take on the burden of scandal, transgression, or revolt" (Foucault, "The Life of Infamous Men," in *Power,* ed. James D. Faubion, volume 3 of *Essential Works of Foucault, 1954–1984,* series ed. Paul Rabinow [New York: New Press, 2000], 174).

40 Stendhal, *Correspondance générale,* ed. V. Del Litto, et al. (Paris: Honore Champion, 1999), 3:743. Italicized phrase is in English and italicized in the original.

41 See Pierre de Lacretelle's introduction to Custine's *Souvenirs et portraits,* 23–24. Mention of the incident can be found in the London *Times* on July 25, 26, and 31, 1822, as well as on August 3. The bishop, who had apparently previously had someone jailed for threatening to reveal his sexual life, fled the country and did not attend his trial, the accounts of which can be found in the *Times* on November 8, 12, and 13, 1822. More details can be found in Jacques Birnberg, "Stendhal, l'Évêque de Clogher et l'Irlande en 1822: Marginalité sexuelle et marginalité beyliste," *Australian Journal of French Studies* 26, no. 2 (1989): 148–75, esp. 160–63. See also Louis Crompton, *Byron and Greek Love: Homophobia in Nineteenth-Century England* (Berkeley: University of California Press, 1985), 300–11.

42 Stendhal, *Romans et nouvelles,* ed. Henri Martineau (Paris: Gallimard [Pléiade], 1952), 1:1534. The editor adds: "Faut-il dévoiler au lecteur que pour Beyle être un évêque de Clogher signifie avoir des mœurs spéciales [Needless to say, for Beyle, to be a bishop of Clogher was to be given to peculiar habits]" (1:1534). There are also passages in Stendhal's *Vie de Henry Brulard* that link "l'amour socratique" to Clogher (see Birnberg, "Stendhal, l'Évêque de Clogher et l'Irlande en 1822," 149).

43 Rousseau and Warman cite an 1818 letter by Custine to his friend La Grange, where Custine writes: "Depuis que je suis au monde, mon être est une énigme qu'aucun coeur n'a devinée [Since my arrival in this world, my being has been an enigma that no heart has penetrated]" (14–15). For Rousseau and Warman, this kind of writing is evidence of the way Custine used the romantic discourse codified and typified in Chateaubriand's *René,* of a self with a dark, hidden secret (incestuous desire in René's case), in the construction of his self-image. They are convincing on this point. My sense is that this romantic discourse would have been only one of a number of discourses available over the course of Custine's lifetime, as he constructed a set of practices that enabled him to live with a man and to seek out sexual relations with men. Some of the available discourses may have had more or less appeal to him at different moments in life—or to have had variably apparent advantages or disadvantages. One need not imagine him as exclusively attached to any of them; rather one might think of him as making strategic use of a number of them across his lifetime.

44 See Birnberg, "Stendhal, l'Évêque de Clogher et l'Irlande en 1822," for a full treatment of this question. On the possibility that Balzac and Stendhal were each reading the other as part of an effort to craft ways of writing about male same-sex sexuality, see C. W. Thompson, "Stendhal connaisseur de l''improper': De Byron à William Courtenay, Lord Link et Balzac," *Stendhal Club* 29, 40. 114 (January 1987): 113–39, esp. 128–32.

45 Balzac, *Lettres à Madame Hanska,* ed. Roger Pierrot (Paris: Robert Laffont, 1990), 1:532, 570.

46 [Victor Felicien Lambinet], *Balzac mis à nu et les dessous de la Société romantique d'après les Mémoires inédits d'un contemporain,* ed. Charles Léger (Paris: C. Gaillandre, 1928), 68. In another volume ascribed to Lambinet and edited by Léger, Lambinet provides mean-spirited and detailed portrayals of Custine openly and successfully cruising a cute, young German musician during an aristocratic dinner party, and seducing in other circumstances another cute, young, second-rate Italian musician (see Lambinet's *Madame Récamier, la reine Hortense, et quelques autres: La Société mondaine et littéraire sous la Restauration et le Second Empire,* ed. Charles Léger [Paris: Mercure de France, 1941], 116–17, 170–73).

47 Sainte-Beuve, *Correspondance générale,* ed. Jean Bonnerot (Paris: Stock, 1947), 5:732.

48 C.-A. Sainte-Beuve, "M. Théodore Leclercq," in *Causeries du lundi,* 3rd ed. (Paris: Garnier Frères, 1858), 3:529–31. Fiévée's biographer tells us that their contemporaries discreetly referred to their relationship as an "amitié à la grecque" (Jean Tulard, *Joseph Fiévée: Conseiller secret de Napoléon* [Paris: Fayard, 1985], 59). Hippolyte Auger's memoirs contain a wonderfully evocative description of a few days spent with Fiévée and Leclercq at their country estate near Tours (Auger, *Mémoires,* 293–309).

49 The letter was written on May 22, 1841 (Prosper Mérimée, *Correspondance générale,* ed. Maurice Parturier [Paris: Le Divan, 1943], 3:56–57).

50 *Revue des deux mondes* (March 1, 1851): 981.

51 Custine, *Mémoires et voyages, ou Lettres écrites à diverses époques, pendant des courses en Suisse, en Calabre, en Angleterre, et en Écosse* (Paris: Vézard, 1830), 2:88–89.

52 Custine, *Souvenirs et portraits,* 153.

53 Balzac, *Correspondance,* 3:459–60.

54 Horace de Viel-Castel, *Mémoires sur le règne de Napoléon III (1851–1864),* ed. Pierre Josserand (Paris: Guy Le Prat, 1942), 1:43.

55 Marcel Proust, *A la recherche du temps perdu,* ed. Jean-Yves Tadié, (Paris: Gallimard [Pléiade], 1987), 3:777; *Remembrance of Things Past,* trans. C. K. Scott Moncrieff, Terence Kilmartin, and Andreas Mayor (New York: Vintage, 1982), 3:275.

56 Earlier published versions of the *Recherche* gave the phrase slightly differently: "Arrivée à une identité d'impudeur [of immodesty] pleinement consciente" (Proust, *La Prisonnière* [Paris: Gallimard (Folio), 1972], 328). But neither of the two recent scholarly editions I have consulted includes the additional word *impudeur*. Clearly, Moncrieff translated the sentence to include *impudeur.*

57 The translation from the postface is my own.

58 Fortassier, introduction to *La Fille aux yeux d'or,* 5:771–72.

59 George Sand, *Correspondance inédite George Sand—Marie Dorval,* ed. Simone Andre-Maurois (Paris: Gallimard, 1953), 27. Editors of *La Fille aux yeux d'or* also often point to source material in *Souvenirs et mémoires* by the countess Merlin, whose salon Balzac frequented and whose maiden name was Maria de las Mercedes. She was born in Havana, and she mentions in the memoirs (which were published starting in 1836, but which Balzac may have read in manuscript or heard read in a salon) an aunt she had named Paquita, as well as another relative in Madrid named Mariquita (see 5:775 of *La Comédie humaine;* see also Castex's comments in his edition of Balzac's *Histoire des treize,* 362–64). Merlin's memoirs have recently been republished as: *Souvenirs et mémoires de madame la comtesse Merlin: Souvenirs d'une créole,* ed. Hector Biancotti and Carmen Vásquez (Paris: Mercure de France, 1990): Paquita is found on p. 48; the devout, patriotic, and unmarried Mariquita on pp. 246–53. The countess Merlin was also good friends with Custine. Later in the 1840s, she would compose a book that was both a travelogue and a sociological analysis of the colonial situation in Havana, *La Havane;* sections of which were dedicated to Custine, George Sand, and others. Carmen Vásquez suggests that Merlin was helped in the composition of *La Havane* by the intellectual with whom she was involved at the time, Philarète Chasles (see *Souvenirs et mémoires,* 12–13). Later in life, Chasles would publish a particularly perfidious set of memoirs that found ways to discuss the sexual deviance of several of his acquaintances. Those memoirs contain a particularly virulent description of Custine: "Chez la comtesse Merlin, je vis entrer un jour, annoncé comme marquis par le laquais, sans que je saisisse parfaitement son nom, un homme . . . qui s'assit après avoir serré la main de la comtesse. . . . La comtesse avait retiré promptement, mais non vive-

ment sa main, sans presser celle du marquis. La nuance était légère; car dans les mouvements des personnes bien élévées de ces régions il n'y a jamais une brusquerie anguleuse ou une véhémence trop accentuéé. . . . Une heure se passa comme une minute; et il prit congé sans bruit, comme les gens du dix-huitième siècle. La comtesse regardait sa petite main et la secouait légèrement. 'Ce pauvre marquis, me dit-elle, il est charmant. Mais je ne peux pas le toucher, sa main me répugne.—Pourquoi?—Elle ne serre pas, elle colle. . . . C'est Custine!—Ah! lui dis-je.' Cette exclamation la fit sourire. Je n'ai connu que depuis lors la véritable vie de cet être extraordinaire et malheureux, problème et type, phénomène et paradoxe, que le vice le plus odieux à mon tempérament chevauchait, domptait, opprimait et ravalait; qui, au vu et au su de toute la société française, y pataugeait, y vivait comme Fiévée avec son ami Théodore Leclerc, qui subissait, tête basse, le mépris public; et qui d'autre côté était, sans se racheter, loyal, généreux, honnête, charitable, éloquent, sprituel, presque philosophe,—distingué, presque poëte. Ces mélanges d'éléments compliqués et contradictoires, fondus dans un même type unique sont fréquents aujourd'hui. Mais jamais je n'ai rien vu de tel que Custine. Mon irrépressible curiosité me poussa donc à connaître ce caractère unique. Mon herbier de cryptogames, ma collection de phénomènes sociaux, mon répertoire de nosologie monstrueuse, n'auraient pas été complets, si ce catholique fervent, ce sensuel mystique, ce talent subtil, poétique, élévé,—perdu dans un vice,—cette conscience austère pliant sous le fardeau de sa honte; cette maladie et cette misère du paria social, tout en pleurs, devant une société qui valait peut-être moins que lui,—avait manqué à mon grand musée d'originaux. Je l'étudiai donc très-attentivement; je le plaignis beaucoup; et je rêvai souvent avec tristesse sur les effets que les vieilles civilisations produisent, sur ce gentilhomme déchu, et sur certains organismes exténués et avachis qui se développent comme les lichens chez les peuples qui finissent [One day at the Countess Merlin's a man whose name I did not catch entered and was announced as a Marquis . . . who sat after taking the countess's hand. The countess had promptly (but not overly quickly) withdrawn her hand without holding onto his. It was a slight nuance, for in the movements of people in these elevated spheres nothing is jarring or overly accentuated. . . . An hour flew by, and he took his leave unostentatiously, like someone from the eighteenth-century. The countess looked at her hand and gave it a little shake. 'The pour Marquis,' she said, 'is a charming fellow. But I cannot bear to touch him; his hand revolts me.' 'But why?' 'It does not take hold of yours; it sticks to you. . . . He's Custine!' 'Ah ha!' I replied. At that she smiled. It was only after this time that I learned the true details of this extraordinary and unhappy fellow's life. He was a type, a problem case, a phenomenon and a paradox, hounded, overtaken, oppressed and swallowed whole by what is for me the most odious vice. In full view of all of French society, he wallowed in this vice, as did Fiévée and his friend Leclerc [*sic*]. He lowered his head and endured the public's scorn. In his own way, he was, without in any way redeeming himself, loyal, generous, honest, charitable, eloquent, witty, philosophical, even,—distinguished, practically a poet. These odd complicated and contradictory mixtures are common nowadays. But I had never seen a case like Custine. I was led on by my irrepressible curiosity to get to know this unique fellow. My herbarium of cryptogams, my collection of social phenomena, my repertory of monstrous nosologies would have been incomplete had this fervent Catholic, this sensual mystic, this subtle, elevated, poetic talent, lost in vice, this austere conscience weighed down by shame, this sick and miserable social pariah, tearfully facing a society that was perhaps less worthy than he, not been included in my museum of originals. I therefore studied him extremely closely. I felt sorry for him. I often sadly thought of the effects produced by aged civilizations, about this fallen gentleman, about the extenuated and shapeless organisms that develop like lichens among peoples that are coming to an end]" (Chasles, *Mémoires* [Paris: Charpentier, 1876], 1:308–11).

60 Faderman, *Surpassing the Love of Men,* 456 n.6. Albert Prioult, ed., writing in *La Comédie humaine* (Paris: Hazan, 1950), 11:620. Others who share Prioult's position are Antoine Adam, in *Le Secret de l'aventure vénitienne: La Vérité sur Sand et Musset* (Paris: Perrin, 1938); and René Jasinski, in *Les Années romantiques de Théophile Gautier* (Paris: Vuibert, 1929), esp. 289–326.

61 Arsène Houssaye, *Les Confessions: Souvenirs d'un demi-siècle, 1830–1880* (Paris: Dentu, 1888), 2:13–14.

62 Maurice Regard, *Gustave Planche, 1808–1857: Correspondance, Bibliographie, Iconographie* (Paris: Nouvelles éditions latines, 1955), 71.

63 On the function of melodrama in *La Fille aux yeux d'or,* see the helpful pages in Prendergast's *Balzac,* 63–68. Prendergast concludes his analysis by commenting: "The extension, by way of the analogical play of the text, of the sexual and familial intrigue into the social, and specifically urban, domain of modern life, with its tentative gesture at the comprehension of a whole social structure, marks the first stage in a literary intinerary that will result in deeper and more complex realizations" (68).

64 Balzac's letter to Madame Hanska is from June 28, 1846, *Lettres à Madame Hanska,* 2:232. (Two days earlier he had had dinner with Custine at Madame Merlin's.) Meininger's comments are from *La Comédie humaine* 7:1366–67. (see also 7:24–26). Pauline Duchambge was a composer who set to music poems by, among many others, Desbordes-Valmore and Custine. In an article written shortly after her death, Pierre Hédouin comments ambiguously: "Dans sa première jeunesse, la calomnie, ce fléau des grandes et des petites villes, qui fait la proie de tout ce qu'il y a de distingué, n'a point épargné Mme du Chambge. . . . Tendre rêveuse, un peu romanesque, elle a pu se laisser entraîner par excès de sentiment et de pitié, mais son cœur est resté pur de toute action pouvant torturer sa conscience [In her early youth, she was not spared calumny, that scourge of both small and large towns that attaches itself to anyone of any distinction. . . . Perhaps, being a tender-hearted dreamer, and taken with novels, she let herself be drawn to certain excesses of feeling and of pity, but her heart remained unsullied by any action that might have tortured her

conscience]" (Hédouin, *Mme Pauline du Chambge* [Paris: Mourgues, 1858], 5). Hédouin also recounts that Duchambge kept many souvenirs from old friends in her apartment, including a model of the spiral staircase from the set of the first production of Vigny's *Chatterton,* a play that starred Marie Dorval, and which included a famous bit of acting in which Dorval's character, Kitty Bell, in a moment of profound emotion, slid down the staircase.

65 Balzac, *Honoré de Balzac in Twenty-Five Volumes: The First Complete Translation into English* (New York: Collier, 1900), 12:7. Harper and Row apparently also published an American version of Saintsbury's edition of Balzac around the same time. That version did include a translation of *La Fille aux yeux d'or,* and excised the sentence about its inconvenience from the preface. On the English reception of Balzac, see the helpful work of Sharon Marcus, "Comparative Sapphism," in *The Literary Channel: The Inter-National Invention of the Novel,* ed. Margaret Cohen and Carolyn Dever (Princeton: Princeton University Press, 2002), 251–85.

66 The English translation cited here is *The Girl with the Golden Eyes,* in *History of the Thirteen,* trans. Herbert J. Hunt (Harmondsworth: Penguin, 1974). I will often have silently modified the translation.

67 The idea of English prudery was a commonplace in nineteenth-century France, and French writers such as Balzac or Gautier poked fun in particular at the prudery regarding male same-sex relations. It was, in fact, more than prudery. Balzac and Gautier both make plain that men risked their lives in England by having sex with other men. In *La Maison Nucingen,* Balzac writes of a "well-known English lord" who had to fire the handsome young groom to whom he was deeply attached because a journalist wrote an article that suggested there might be something "improper" (not to say inconvenient) in their relationship. From "improper" to the gallows, the narrator of the story notes, is only a short step (6:344–45). Gautier, in his pornographic *Lettre à la Présidente,* about a trip to Italy in 1850, writes of coming across a bottle of oil in the restroom of an inn where a handsome young male servant worked. He deduces that "this oil served to lubricate the behind of this pretty boy, highly sought after by the Englishmen who go to Italy to satisfy their pederastic tastes, which are punished by a rope on their friendly island—a touching attentiveness on the part of their government, which thereby guarantees a few fucks to some Englishwomen who wouldn't get them otherwise [cette huile servait à lubrifier le derrière de ce joli garçon, fort recherché des Anglais qui vont en Italie satisfaire leur goût de pédérastie, punie de la corde dans leur aimable île; attention touchante du gouvernement, qui procure ainsi quelques vieux coups aux Anglaises, qui ne seraient jamais baisées sans cela]" (Gautier, *Lettre à la Présidente: Voyage en Italie, 1850* [n.p.: Les Perspective, n.d.], 13). As we have seen, Stendhal was aware of this situation, and the migrations it caused. See Birnberg, "Stendhal, l'Évêque de Clogher et l'Irlande," esp. 150–51. See also Crompton, *Byron and Greek Love.*

68 Rose Fortassier, the editor of the story for the Pléiade edition, tells us that

"Balzac also recycled in *La Fille aux yeux d'or* the text of a 'physiologie' that he offered at the same time to Mme Béchet for her *Nouveau Tableau de Paris au XIXe siècle*" (5:781). Chantal Messol-Dedoin informs us that part of the material had even been published in 1830 in *La Caricature* (Messol-Dedoin, "La Charade et la chimère: Du récit énigmatique dans 'La Fille aux yeux d'or,'" *Poétique* 89 [February 1992]: 32). There are endless examples of this genre at the time, such as *Les Français peints par eux-mêmes* (1840–1842) or *Paris; ou, Le Livre des cent-et-un* (1831–1832). See Judith Wechsler, *A Human Comedy: Physiognomy and Caricature in Nineteenth-Century Paris* (Chicago: University of Chicago Press, 1982).

69 One could profitably compare the kiss between brother and sister at the end of *La Fille aux yeux d'or* with the kiss between two sisters at the end of part 2 of *Lélia*.

70 Balzac, *Lettres à Madame Hanska,* 1:196.

71 Valconseil, *Revue analytique et critique des romans contemporains* (Paris: Gaume frères, 1845), 90; cited by Ezdinli, "Rumor and Reputation." Ezdinli suggests persuasively that this 1845 volume collects articles published much earlier in the press.

72 Shoshana Felman, *What Does a Woman Want?* 18. See also Messol-Dedoin, who in "La Charade et la chimère" states that "the point of departure for the story is a mysterious situation that requires clarification" (35).

73 See also Owen N. Heathcote, "The Engendering of Violence and the Violation of Gender in Honoré de Balzac's *La Fille aux yeux d'or,*" *Romance Studies* 22 (autumn 1993): 99–112.

74 It seems unlikely that Balzac actually imagined sex between women to be nonpenetrative, if only given the evidence that he was a reader of Sade (to whom de Marsay makes an oblique reference within *La Fille aux yeux d'or*). Yet it serves his purpose to portray the sex between Paquita and Euphémie as nonpenetrative, because to do so provides a mechanism for dropping hints about the sexual relation between the two women (as in the sentence about Paquita being a virgin, but not an innocent one). Moreover, it also allows him to link Euphémie's possessiveness about Paquita's virginity to an aristocratic ethos concerned with blood lines; allows Euphémie to ascertain physically from Paquita's body that she has been "unfaithful"; and allows for an ending to the story that is all the more lurid.

75 Felman, *What Does a Woman Want?* 60.

76 A similar kind of reading of the story *Sarrasine,* written a few years before *La Fille aux yeux d'or,* can be offered. *Sarrasine* was, of course, transformed into one of Balzac's most well-known texts by Roland Barthes, who reprinted it and subjected it to a bravura line-by-line analysis in *S/Z: An Essay* (trans. Richard Miller [New York: Hill and Wang, 1974]). Like *La Fille aux yeux d'or, Sarrasine* shows an analytic as well as a melodramatic interest in sexual forms that are passing into obscurity, and in the effects of the uneven distribution

of knowledge that remains about those increasingly little-known forms. As is the case with *La Fille aux yeux d'or,* it is possible melodramatically to overread the story's emphasis on *enigma* ("the mystery of the Lantys [l'histoire énigmatique de la maison Lanty] presented a continuing source of curiosity, rather like that contained in the novels of Ann Radcliffe" [6:1046; *S/Z,* 224]), and so miss the story's interest in the ways the enigma experienced by certain characters (Sarrasine and Béatrix Rochefide, to whom his story is narrated) is not a generalized or a generalizable one but is produced by the social and historical forces bearing on their specific persons. *Sarrasine,* like *La Fille aux yeux d'or,* can be read as a story investigating the social distribution of ideologies and epistemologies of sexuality, of historical knowledge about sexuality's evolving forms. It performs a demonstration of the way that distribution shifts over time and thereby affects our abilities to perceive and act in the world.

Sarrasine is, of course, filled with clues to the "shocking revelation" at the story's end, just as is *La Fille aux yeux d'or.* At the party at which the story opens, Marianina sings the cavatina from Rossini's *Tancrède,* one of Rossini's most famous contralto trouser roles—the kind of role that would, in an only slightly earlier period, have been sung by a castrato. Within certain circles in Balzac's moment (within even narrower circles in our moment) this reference would have been clear. Gautier's poem "Contralto," in *Émaux and Camées,* which explicitly links the question of that kind of voice to sexual indeterminacy, makes clear that this frame of reference was active and available to Balzac's readers. When Prince Chigi finally forces Sarrasine to notice what Zambinella is, the prince understands Sarrasine to be astonishingly ignorant: "Where do you come from? Has there ever been a woman on the Roman stage? And don't you know about the creatures who sing female roles in the Papal States?" (6:1072; *S/Z,* 250). As Roland Barthes puts it, "ignorant of the code of Papal customs, Sarrasine dies from a gap in knowledge" (*S/Z,* 185). Yet Barthes's analysis moves toward the psychoanalytic rather than the historical or sociological: "To make *being-castrated,* an anecdotal condition, coincide with *castration,* a symbolic structure, is the task successfully carried out by the performer (Balzac), since the former does not entail the latter" (*S/Z,* 163–64). This allows a universalizing conclusion that might recall Felman's: "*Sarrasine* represents the very confusion of representation, the unbridled (pandemic) circulation of signs, of sexes, of fortunes" (*S/Z,* 216). Yet such universalizing is only possible by implicitly insisting that the single critical point of view on the story somehow coincide with a particular point of view within the story: that of Sarrasine, or that of a reader not sufficiently informed (i.e., not having had a particular formation), or that of a reader drawn to melodramatic scenes of what we have learned to think of as castration anxiety, a form of social policing that usually functions in the service of very precise historical interests. Those historical interests are invested in certain aspects of Balzac's oeuvre, without, however, having a monopoly over it.

Chapter Three. Balzac's Queer Cousins and Their Friends

1 It may not be entirely exact to call them the final pair. His projects in these years also included *Les Paysans* and *Le Député d'Arcis,* neither of which he would complete, and also *La Dernière Incarnation de Vautrin,* which we know as the final section of *Splendeurs et misères des courtisanes.* He worked on all these projects simultaneously. See Donald Adamson, *The Genesis of "Le Cousin Pons"* (Oxford: Oxford University Press, 1966), 3–8, 41–46.

2 Reid, *Families in Jeopardy,* 52.

3 Foucault, *The History of Sexuality,* 23.

4 Ibid., 44.

5 Reid, *Families in Jeopardy,* 3.

6 D. A. Miller, *The Novel and the Police* (Berkeley: University of California Press, 1988), 27–28.

7 Ibid., x–xi.

8 Foucault, *History of Sexuality,* 47.

9 Reid, *Families in Jeopardy,* 190.

10 Miller, *The Novel and the Police,* 29–30, xii–xiii. Balzac's novels were fairly consistently denounced as immoral and inimical to family values by proselytizers for the normative family among his contemporaries, which does not in any way disprove Reid's claim but does calls attention to the difficulties in gauging the effects of any particular representation of an ideological discourse on an audience likely to receive that representation in widely divergent ways. See Bellos, *Balzac Criticism in France,* 13–14, 21–26, 32–42.

11 Foucault, *History of Sexuality,* 83.

12 The importance and interrelation of the *Herculine Barbin* preface and "The Life of Infamous Men" are pointed out by Eribon in *Michel Foucault et ses contemporains* (Paris: Fayard, 1994), 265–87.

13 Two volumes appeared in the "Vies parallèles" series published by Gallimard, *Herculine Barbin dite Alexina B.,* presented by Foucault in 1978, and *Le Cercle amoureux d'Henri Legrand,* presented by Jean-Paul Dumont and Paul-Ursin Dumont in 1979. The two paragraphs cited in the text are on the back cover of both volumes. Judith Butler mentions these sentences in *Gender Trouble,* (102), suggesting an interpretation of their relevance to *Herculine Barbin* and to Foucault's own life.

14 Foucault, ed., *I, Pierre Rivière,* x–xi.

15 Foucault, ed., *I, Pierre Rivière,* 199. The French citation is from Foucault, ed., *Moi, Pierre Rivière, ayant égorgé ma mère, ma soeur et mon frère . . . : Un cas de parricide au XIXe siècle* (Paris: Gallimard, 1973), 265.

16 Foucault, "The Life of Infamous Men," 157, 159. The French citations are from Michel Foucault, "La Vie des hommes infâmes," in *Dits et écrits 1954–1988,* ed. Daniel Defert and François Ewald (Paris: Gallimard, 1994), 3:237, 239.

17 Foucault, "The Life of Infamous Men," 161–63.

18 Foucault, ed., *I, Pierre Rivère,* 199.

19 I have in the back of my mind here the final sentences of Foucault's essay "Friendship as a Way of Life": "We have to dig deeply to show how things have been historically contingent, for such and such reason intelligible but not necessary. We must make the intelligible appear against a background of emptiness, and deny its necessity. We must think that what exists is far from filling all possible spaces. To make a truly unavoidable challenge of the question: what can we make work, what new game can we invent?" (Foucault, "Friendship as a Way of Life," in *Ethics: Subjectivity and Truth,* 139–40).

20 Foucault, *History of Sexuality,* 159.

21 Michel Foucault, ed., *Herculine Barbin. Being the Recently Discovered Memoirs of a Nineteenth-Century French Hermaphrodite,* trans. Richard McDougall (New York: Pantheon, 1980), 150–51.

22 Butler, *Gender Trouble,* 94.

23 Michel Foucault, "Le Vrai Sexe," in *Dits et écrits,* 4:120–21. ["Dans l'art de diriger les consciences, on utilise souvent le terme de 'discrétion.' Mot singulier qui désigne la capacité de percevoir les différences, de discriminer les sentiments et jusqu'aux moindres mouvements de l'âme. . . . Mais, par ce même mot, les directeurs de conscience entendent aussi l'aptitude à garder la mesure, à savoir jusqu'où ne pas aller trop loin, à se taire sur ce qu'il ne faut pas dire, à laisser au bénéfice de l'ombre ce qui deviendrait dangereux à la lumière du jour. On peut dire qu'Alexina a pu vivre pendant longtemps dans le clair-obscur du régime de 'discrétion' qui était celui des couvents, des pensions, et de la monosexualité féminine et chrétienne. Et puis—ce fut son drame—, elle est passée sous un tout autre régime de 'discrétion.' Celui de l'administration, de la justice et de la médecine. . . . Ce qu'elle évoque dans son passé, ce sont les limbes heureuses d'une non-identité, que protégeait paradoxalement la vie dans ces sociétés fermées, étroites et chaudes, où on a l'étrange bonheur, à la fois obligatoire et interdit, de ne connaître qu'un seul sexe. . . . L'autre sexe n'est pas là avec ses exigences de partage et d'identité. . . . Elle n'était pas traversée de ce formidable désir de rejoindre l' 'autre sexe' que connaissent certains qui se sentent trahis par leur anatomie ou emprisonnés dans une injuste identité. Elle se plaisait, je crois, dans ce monde d'un seul sexe où étaient toutes ses émotions et tous ses amours, à être 'autre' sans avoir jamais à être 'de l'autre sexe.' Ni femme aimant les femmes ni homme caché parmi les femmes. Alexina était le sujet sans identité d'un grand désir pour les femmes; et, pour ces mêmes femmes, elle était un point d'attirance de leur féminité et pour leur féminité, sans que rien les force à sortir de leur monde entièrement féminin."]

24 Butler, *Gender Trouble,* 98.

25 Foucault, "The Life of Infamous Men," 161.

26 Foucault offers another version of a relation to literature in a 1970 interview, in which he contrasts Pierre Guyotat's *Éden, Éden, Éden* (a book published in France in 1970 that was placed under various forms of legal interdiction until 1981) to Flaubert's *Madame Bovary* (subject to its famous trial in 1857). Foucault is perfectly willing to call Guyotat's book "transgressive": "No one, be-

fore Guyotat, had spoken of what he evokes in his book. Since the limits of what is expressible at the heart of our lexicon and our language are surpassed in Guyotat's text, one can say quite precisely that this text is transgressive" ("Folie, littérature, société," in *Dits et écrits,* 2:117). The book's representation of sexuality, of homosexuality, exceeds for Foucault all previous literary representations, whereas the adultery and suicide represented in *Madame Bovary* were "common currency" at the time. Here is the lesson Foucault draws: "When *Madame Bovary* was published, literature possessed in and of itself sufficient transgressive force: it was enough, to create a scandal in a given work, to reconstruct the day-to-day reality of a bourgeois family. Today, on the contrary, literature doubtless says more than what homosexuals actually practice in Paris. But the book [*Éden, Éden, Éden*] was not condemned [it could be sold, but not to minors; nor could it be published—or reviewed, or even displayed in bookstores], whereas homosexuals are punished without fail. So far has the transgressive force of literature been lost" (2:117–18). If we were to try to align these observations from 1970 with his 1977 "Life of Infamous Men," we might ascertain that precisely from *Manon Lescaut* to *Madame Bovary* Foucault is willing to see in literature not merely the deployment of power, but, in fact, the betrayal of power.

27 Lukács, *Studies in European Realism,* 21.

28 Reid, *Families in Jeopardy,* 189.

29 Erving Goffman's work comes to mind, as in *The Presentation of Self in Everyday Life,* where he writes, "When we allow that the individual projects a definition of the situation when he appears before others, we must also see that the others, however passive their role may seem to be, will themselves effectively project a definition of the situation by virtue of their response to the individual and by virtue of any lines of action they initiate to him. . . . Together the participants contribute to a single over-all definition of the situation which involves not so much a real agreement as to what exists but rather a real agreement as to whose claims concerning what issues will be temporarily honored" (Goffman, *The Presentation of Self in Everyday Life* [New York: Anchor, 1959], 9–10).

30 For another approach to Balzac's sociology in the *Cousin* novels, see Per Nykrog, "La Révélation de la société invisible chez Balzac," in *Balzac et "Les Parents pauvres,"* ed. Françoise van Rossum-Guyon and Michiel van Brederode (Paris: SEDES, 1981), 11–19.

31 The English translation cited here and elsewhere is *Cousin Pons,* trans. Herbert J. Hunt (Harmondsworth: Penguin, 1968).

32 Marcus, *Apartment Stories,* 68. Marcus's entire insightful discussion (64–71) of Pons and Cibot is germane to my topic.

33 Cécile's reaction on hearing this indicates a typically Balzacian cynicism in the face of altruism: "Fancy giving five hundred thousand francs to his companion in misfortune! Oh, Mamma, I shall have a carriage and a box at the *Italiens*!" (7:550, 92). She has, unfortunately, failed to perceive the misogyny or the homophilia motivating Brunner's "altruism."

34 When the marquis de Custine died in September 1857, roughly a decade after *Le Cousin Pons* was written, the acuity of Balzac's analysis was borne out by real events. Custine had named his friend Sainte-Barbe his *légataire universel* (sole heir). Custine's distant relatives immediately began legal proceedings against Sainte-Barbe. The proceedings themselves were still ongoing in October 1858, when Sainte-Barbe himself died, "disgusted, saddened, and worn out," as one of Custine's biographers puts it. While the proceedings would eventually vindicate Sainte-Barbe, his chosen heir would concede to the court's judgment that Custine's papers, letters, family portraits, and the like could not be understood as part of Custine's legacy to Sainte-Barbe, and so remained the property of his "natural heirs." The fate of Custine's papers is unknown. See Tarn, *Le Marquis de Custine*, 708–14.

35 Of course, the novel understands that this realm does not escape from economic considerations entirely. The state would need to value the Pons bequest enough to agree to pay the required annuity to Schmucke. Earlier in the novel, there's another intriguing reference to the "value" of museums. The novel opens with Pons offering a fan he has scavenged, painted by Watteau and once owned by Madame Pompadour, to Cécile's mother as a sort of peace offering. It takes Cécile and her mother roughly half the novel to realize the "value" of the gift, and when Cécile makes a condescending remark to the effect that she might have to concede to Pons some expertise as far as these "silly trifles" go, her father is shocked: "Why, the State is about to pay a hundred thousand francs for the late Councillor Dusommerard's collection and to go halves with the City of Paris in spending nearly a million on the purchase and repair of the Hôtel de Cluny for the housing of such 'silly trifles'. Such 'silly trifles', my dear child, are often the only relics we have of vanished civilizations. An Etruscan jar, a necklace, sometimes worth forty or fifty thousand francs respectively, are 'silly trifles' which reveal the perfection that had been reached by the arts at the time of the siege of Troy, and prove that the Etruscans were Trojans who had taken refuge in Italy!" (7:540, 82). The whole novel constitutes a diffuse reflection on national inheritance, of course, and on what Restoration society is to make of the inheritance of the *ancien régime*, of the Revolution, of the Napoleonic Empire. The displacement of attention to the Trojans and the Etruscans thus cannot be understood merely as a disinterested, scientific appeal to the value of archeology. It is more an appeal to a network of institutions that would cement a conservative, transmissable, national identity in the face of (and even making use of) a mountain of evidence of ongoing social disruption and violent appropriation.

36 For an analysis of "processes of voluntary affiliation: processes of caring and being cared for," and of the ways in which legal devices are "stretched to fit and made to serve the practical goals and situations of actual people" precisely in order to compensate for the ways in which the dominant order enforces "the repression of care and the privileging of forms of communal reproduction," see Borneman, "Caring and Being Cared for," 573–84.

37 The English translation cited here and elsewhere is *Cousin Bette,* trans. Marion Ayton Crawford (Harmondsworth: Penguin, 1965).

38 Balzac's rhetorical technique resembles in some ways that of Arsène Houssaye, who in his memoirs seems to describe a possible liaison between George Sand and the princesse de Belgiojoso, and a few pages later (in the section of his memoirs entitled "Où il n'est pas question du rocher de Leucade") seems to describe a liaison between Sand and Marie Dorval without naming either of them. In a later portrait of Marie Dorval ("Les Larmes de Mme Dorval") Houssaye calls Dorval the *inséparable* of Sand, and shows Dorval lamenting the lack of attention she receives from Jules Sandeau: "If he loves me at all, it is because he knows I am the intimate friend of George Sand; it is because he discovers on my cheeks the kisses of his mistress" (Houssaye, *Les Confessions,* 2:1–5, 13–15, and 4:330–31).

39 For an earlier discussion of the critical difficulties in approaching the relationship between Valérie and Bette, see Diana Knight, "Reading as an Old Maid: *La Cousine Bette* and Compulsory Heterosexuality," *Quinquereme* 12, no. 1 (1989): 67–79.

40 Foucault, *History of Sexuality,* 108.

41 Gayle Rubin, "The Traffic in Women: Notes on the 'Political Economy' of Sex," in *Toward an Anthropology of Women,* ed. Rayna R. Reiter (New York: Monthly Review, 1975), 199.

42 Cf. Judith Butler's comments: "We might read the desire for a sexuality beyond kinship as a sign of a certain utopian strain in sexual thinking which is bound to fail, and which requires that our conceptions of kinship remain frozen in their most highly normative and oppressive modes. Those who imagine themselves to be 'beyond' kinship will nevertheless find terms to describe those supporting social arrangements which constitute kinship. Kinship in this sense is not to be identified with any of its positive forms, but rather as a site of redefinition which can move beyond patrilineality, compulsory heterosexuality, and the symbolic overdetermination of biology" (Butler, "Against Proper Objects," *differences* 6, nos. 2 and 3 [1994]:14). Butler reflects in interesting ways on links between Rubin and Foucault in this essay (11–15). Butler and Gayle Rubin's conversation in "Sexual Traffic" in the same issue of *differences* (62–99) also contains interesting and helpful reflections on Foucault and kinship (83–88), although they both conflate the term kinship (of which the usual French equivalent is *parenté*) and alliance. In the particular instance of the two novels I am investigating, I think there might be something to be gained from keeping a distinction between the two terms.

43 Foucault, *History of Sexuality,* 106–7, 113.

44 In "Friendship as a Way of Life," Foucault speaks of a "way of life" as something that "can be shared among individuals of different age, status and social activity. It can yield intense relations not resembling those that are institutionalized" (138). Of a relationship between an older and a younger man, he suggests: "They have to invent, from A to Z, a relationship that is still formless,

which is friendship: that is to say, the sum of everything through which they can give each other pleasure" (136).

45 Ibid., 138–39.

46 Foucault, "Entretien avec M. Foucault," in *Dits et écrits,* 4:295. Foucault does not seem to take very careful account of differences between his call for a present-day project and the historical work Faderman is doing (he refers to her book in this interview as well). Nor does he dwell for long on dissymmetries produced by gender oppression. He does in 1984 comment in yet another interview: "I should say, also, that I think that in the lesbian movement, the fact that women have been, for centuries and centuries, isolated in society, frustrated, despised in many ways and so on, has given them the real possibility of constituting a society, of creating a kind of social relation between themselves outside the social world that was dominated by males. Lillian Faderman's book *Surpassing the Love of Men* is very interesting in this regard. It raises the question: What kind of emotional experience, what kind of relationships, were possible in a world where women in society had no social, no legal and no political power? And she argues that women used that isolation and lack of power" (Foucault, "Sex, Power, and the Politics of Identity," in *Ethics: Subjectivity and Truth,* ed. Paul Rabinow, trans. Robert Hurley et al., volume 1 of *Essential Works of Foucault, 1954–1984* [New York: New Press, 1997], 168).

47 As Madame Nourrisson reminds him in suggesting a way of paying her for her murderous intervention on his behalf: "One day within the next three months a poor priest will come to ask you for forty thousand francs for a benefaction—for a ruined monastery in the desert, in the Levant! If you are pleased with the way things have fallen out, give the fellow the forty thousand francs. It's not any more than you'll pay, anyway, to the Inland Revenue [Vous en verserez bien d'autres au fisc!]" (7:388, 375).

48 Foucault, *History of Sexuality,* 109. Thus perhaps one reason Foucault does not often use the word kinship (*parenté*) in *The History of Sexuality, Volume 1* is precisely in order to differentiate his own (genealogical) project from the (nonhistorical, or at least only problematically historical) project of an ethnography theorized in books like Lévi-Strauss's *Les Structures élémentaires de la parenté,* a project whose own genealogy, Foucault is implying, needs investigation.

49 Both Butler and Rubin suggest the inadequacies of this kind of narrative of "supercession": see Butler, "Against Proper Objects," 12–14; and Rubin, "Sexual Traffic," 84–88.

50 Here are two pin (*épingle*) passages from Foucault's *History of Sexuality, Volume 1:* "This interpenetration [*épinglage*] of the apparatus of alliance and that of sexuality in the form of the family allows us to understand a number of facts" (108). "The guarantee that one would find the parents-children relationship at the root of everyone's sexuality made it possible—even when everything seemed to point to the reverse process—to keep the apparatus of sexuality coupled [de maintenir l'épinglage] to the system of alliance" (113).

51 Michal Peled Ginsburg nicely states a similar point about Balzac: "The par-

ticularity Balzac attempts to capture in his novels is not the particularity of an individual, product of a specific milieu (such particularity can always be subsumed within a universal), but rather the irreducible particularity of a historical reality, of a specific historical moment that cannot be 'seen' except through the life of individuals" (Ginsburg, *Economies of Change: Form and Transformation in the Nineteenth-Century Novel* [Stanford: Stanford University Press, 1996], 33). For relevant analyses of the Napoleonic Code and of its centrality to Balzac's imagination, see the introduction and chapter 1 of this book, and also André-Jean Arnaud, *Essai d'analyse structurale du Code civil français: La Règle du jeu dans la paix bourgeoise* (Paris: R. Pichon et R. Durand-Auzias, 1973); Nye, *Masculinity and Male Codes of Honor,* esp. 3–9, 47–57; and Faillie, *La Femme et le Code civil.*

Chapter Four. The Shadow Economy of Queer Social Capital: Lucien de Rubempré and Vautrin

1 For the importance of the pair to Wilde and to Proust, see the epilogue to this volume as well as my "Proust's Queer Metalepses." See also Philippe Berthier, "Marcel et Charlus Herrera," in *Balzac: Illusions perdues: "l'oeuvre capitale dans l'oeuvre,"* ed. Françoise van Rossum-Guyon (Groningen, Neth.: CRIN, 1988), 94–103; and Roger Kempf, *Sur le corps romanesque* (Paris: Seuil, 1968), 133–89. In 1962, Daniel Guérin published a modernized version of the relations between Vautrin and Lucien in his play *Vautrin: Du roman à la scène et à l'écran* (Paris: Plume d'or, 1962).

2 The Penguin edition of *Lost Illusions* (trans. Herbert J. Hunt [Harmondsworth: Penguin, 1971]), which I will be citing throughout this chapter, inexplicably translates *Un Grand Homme de province à Paris* as *A Great Man in Embryo.* I will also be citing in this chapter the Penguin translation of *Splendeurs et misères des courtisanes: A Harlot High and Low,* trans. Rayner Heppenstall (Harmondsworth: Penguin, 1970). I will refer to it here by its French title, which is more literally translated as *The Glories and the Miseries of Courtesans,* and in which the word "courtesan" has a much wider range of reference than does "harlot."

3 Franco Moretti, *Atlas of the European Novel, 1800–1900* (London: Verso, 1998), 87. The second citation from Moretti is from his book *The Way of the World: The Bildungsroman in European Culture* (London: Verso, 1987), 143.

4 The editorial matter of the Pléiade edition of *La Comédie humaine* gives a full account of the publication history. See, for instance, 5:3–7, 103–8, 1119–30, and 6:1309–15. Balzac's prefaces for the separate segments of *Lost Illusions* are also interesting. See 5:109–21. For further details on the chronology of Balzac's composition and publication of these works, see Stéphane Vachon, "Chronologie de la rédaction et de la publication d'*Illusions perdues,*" in Françoise van Rossum-Guyon, ed., *Balzac: Illusions perdues: "l'œuvre capitale dans l'œuvre,"* 1–11.

5 Moretti, *Atlas,* 107.

6 Moretti, *The Way of the World,* 157–58.

7 Many, though not all, editions of Balzac's novels drop the chapter titles. The digressive structure remains.

8 Moretti, *Atlas,* 109.

9 Moretti, *The Way of the World,* 147.

10 In some helpful comments on Moretti's work, Michal Peled Ginsburg notes how "in Moretti's scheme, historical context intervenes in the literary scene by 'selecting' a certain preexisting form as 'symbolic form,' suitable for performing certain functions within the culture. . . . But by shifting emphasis to the selection of symbolic form, Moretti is left without a historical explanation for the production of particular forms—for novelistic practice. . . . When abstract, formal models or categories become 'historicized,' as they do in Moretti's treatment of the Bildungsroman, they acquire a certain material density: we attribute to the model itself a reality that is appropriate only to particular texts and, as a result, the differences among the particular texts from which the model is derived recede from our horizon. . . . The specificity of each text as a particular articulation of a particular cultural context is lost" (Ginsburg, *Economies of Change,* 3–6).

11 Moretti, "Homo Palpitans: Balzac's Novels and the Urban Personality," trans. Susan Fischer, in *Signs Taken for Wonders: Essays in the Sociology of Literary Forms,* rev. ed. (London: Verso, 1988), 127.

12 Balzac, "Lettre à Hippolyte Castille," in *Œuvres complètes,* vol. 28 (Paris: Le Prat, 1963), 491.

13 See Pierre de Lacretelle's introduction to Custine's *Souvenirs et portraits,* 49. I discuss Custine and Gurowski in the interlude, this volume.

14 Cited in David Bellos, *Balzac Criticism in France,* 38 (see also 20–21, 37–39).

15 Oscar Wilde, "Balzac in English," in *The Artist as Critic: Critical Writings of Oscar Wilde,* ed. Richard Ellmann (New York: Random House, 1969), 30–31.

16 Cited in Bérard, *La Genèse d'un roman de Balzac,* 1:204 (on Sandeau and Balzac, see 197–206).

17 Cited in ibid., 1:201.

18 Hippolyte Auger, *Mémoires (1810–1859),* ed. Paul Cottin (Paris: La Revue rétrospective, 1891), 368.

19 "Le Bouillon de Saint-Mégrin" is in *Le Gymnase: Recueil de morale et de littérature* 1, no. 1 (May 8, 1828): 52–66. It is perhaps worth recalling that Vidocq, in his description of *tantes* and the marriage ceremonies they enacted in French prisons, compares them to Henri III and his *mignons:* "Henri III signed a marriage contract with Maugiron, the one of his mignons that he loved the best, and had all his other favorites sign it as well. This gave rise to a satiric pamphlet titled: *La Pétarade Maugiron.* I here provide a quatrain from that work. It was destined to serve as an epitaph for one of the noblemen in this monarch's court, as well as for his family: Here lies Turcis, his son, and his wife, / You, passerby, must judge who was the worst, / Tircis took his son as wife, / His wife had as a husband her son [Ci gist Tircis, son fils, sa femme, / Juge

passant qui fis le pis, / Tircis prit son fils pour sa femme, / Sa femme eut pour mari son fils]" (Vidocq, *Mémoires,* 824).

20 For more information on *Le Gymnase* and Auger, see Bernard Guyon, "Une Revue romantique inconnue: *Le Gymnase,*" *Revue de littérature comparée* 11, nos. 2 and 4 (1931): 314–21, 489–511. Auger was certainly capable of writing in a more serious (even plodding) vein, as in the prose drama he published in 1832, *Les Mœurs et les lois,* a clumsy combined denunciation of inheritance laws, class inequality, and the sexual oppression of women, all regular topics for the Saint-Simonians.

21 Auger describes in his memoirs his acquaintance with many of the major figures of Paris's queer male scene, not only Fiévée and Leclercq, but Custine and Sainte-Barbe as well. He uses the interesting word *commensal* to describe Sainte-Barbe's relation to Custine (*Mémoires,* 481).

22 Bruce Tolley, "Balzac et les saint-simoniens," *L'Année balzacienne* (1966): 62–64.

23 On models for D'Arthez and the members of the Cénacle, see Tolley, "Balzac," and also Osamu Nishio, *La Signification du Cénacle dans "La Comédie humaine" de Balzac* (Tokyo: France Tosho, 1980).

24 The attractiveness of Lucien as a model for many readers, along with the presence of figures such as Auger, Gurowski, Latouche, and Sandeau in Balzac's world, indicate the extent to which the rigors of heterosexuality as we know it failed to interest many men of the time. Indeed, it seems possible to understand Lucien, his models, and his imitators as in some way expressions of a resistance to a certain persistent effort at social ordering via enforcements of masculinity.

25 Details on Chardon, his swindles, his "most infamous habits," and his pierced ears can be found, among other places, in *La Gazette des Tribunaux* (November 14, 1835), *Le Constitutionnel* (November 13, 1835), and in Lacenaire, *Mémoires et autres écrits,* ed. Jacques Simonelli (Paris: José Corti, 1991), 348–49. One might remember here that Vautrin's disguise throughout *Splendeurs et misères des courtisanes* is that of the Spanish priest Carlos Herrera, just as one might remember the way in which, in *La Cousine Bette,* Madame Nourrison suggests that Victorin Hulot pay her and Vautrin for their help in getting rid of Valérie: "One day within the next three months a poor priest will come to ask you for forty thousand francs for a benefaction—for a ruined monastery in the desert, in the Levant! If you are pleased with the way things have fallen out, give the fellow the forty thousand francs. It's not any more than you'll pay, anyway, to the Inland Revenue" (7:388, 375).

26 See Lacenaire, *Mémoires, poèmes et lettres,* 330. On Lacenaire's sexuality, see also Nicholas Dobelbower, "*Les Chevaliers de la guirlande:* Cellmates in Restoration France," *Journal of Homosexuality* 4, no. 3/4 (2001): 131–47. For information on the culture in which Chardon and Lacenaire would have been circulating, see, in that same issue, Michael Sibalis, "The Palais-Royal and the Homosexual Subculture of Nineteenth-Century Paris," 117–29.

27 Théophile Gautier dedicated part of one of the poems ("Études de mains") in his collection *Émaux et camées* (1852) to a description of Lacenaire's hands. Dorian Gray stumbles across the poem shortly after killing Basil Hallward in Wilde's *The Picture of Dorian Gray.*

28 Lucette Finas, *Le Toucher du rayon: Proust, Vautrin et Antinoüs* (Paris: Nizet, 1995), 45. While I find the idea of gauging the "probability" of a fictional character's "homosexuality" to be somewhat odd, I have found Finas's discussion of Vautrin's relations with Rastignac, Rubempré, and Calvi, as well as her presentation of Proust's interest in those relations, very helpful.

29 Beizer, *Family Plots,* 146, 152.

30 Freud, "On Narcissism," 69, and *Leonardo da Vinci and a Memory of His Childhood,* trans. Alan Tyson (New York: Norton, 1964), 50.

31 Jacques Lacan, *Les Complexes familiaux dans la formation de l'individu* (Paris: Navarin, 1984), 109–10.

32 Michel Tort, "Quelques conséquences de la différence 'psychanalytique' des sexes," *Les Temps modernes* 55 (June 2000): 184.

33 Donald Adamson offers some helpful reflections regarding the situation of Lucien's mother and her name: "It is doubtful whether, in purely historical terms, a Rubempré even in Revolutionary times would have married a pharmacist and, when widowed, taken to midwifery. In Mme. Chardon Balzac describes a character whose way of life has certainly only been made possible by the exceptional historical circumstances through which she has lived: the turmoil of the French Revolution, and the confiscation of aristocratic estates, accounting—fictionally, at least—for her gradual decline from a privileged social elite to the lower levels of the working class. . . . As the only child of the last of the Comtes de Rubempré, she is, genealogically speaking, a heraldic heiress able to confer upon her son(s) the right to quarter the paternal arms with her own and to adopt her surname in addition to the father's; Lucien's father not having been armigerous, however, the *ordonnance* [royal approval] becomes necessary: this is no adoption of the maternal in addition to the paternal surname and arms, but the obliteration of the father's family by the mother's" (Adamson, *Balzac: Lost Illusions* [London: Grant and Cutler, 1981], 42–43).

34 For information on Balzac's sources for the history of paper making, for the history of the market in linen rags, and for the idea of finding cheap plants from which to make paper, see Anne-Marie Meininger, "'Illusions perdues' et faits retrouvés," *L'Année balzacienne* (1979): 47–75, esp. 62–63; and Claire Bustarret, "Balzac et le papier," *Balzac: Imprimeur et défenseur du livre* (Paris: Paris-Musées/Des Cendres, 1995), 81–104.

35 Pierre Bourdieu, "The Forms of Capital," trans. Richard Nice, in *Handbook of Theory and Research for the Sociology of Education,* ed. John G. Richardson (New York: Greenwood, 1986), 245.

36 I am referring in this paragraph to some of the considerations of the available forms for male same-sex relations that I looked at in the interlude. Foucault expressed a version of the same historical predicament that Balzac examines in

his interview "Sex, Power, and the Politics of Identity": "And one of my hypotheses . . . is that homosexuality became a problem—that is, sex between men became a problem—in the eighteenth century. We see the rise of it as a problem with the police, within the justice system, and so on. I think the reason it appears as a problem, as a social issue, at this time is that friendship has disappeared. As long as friendship was something important, was socially accepted, nobody realized men had sex together. You couldn't say that men *didn't* have sex together—it just didn't matter. It had no social implication, it was culturally accepted. Whether they fucked or kissed had no importance. Absolutely no importance. Once friendship disappeared as a culturally accepted relation, the issue arose: 'What is going on between men?' And that's when the problem appears" (171).

37 Christopher Prendergast, *The Order of Mimesis: Balzac, Stendhal, Nerval, Flaubert* (Cambridge: Cambridge University Press, 1986), 113.

38 D. A. Miller has provided a helpful analysis of the marketability of the male body in Balzac and Stendhal's writing in "Body Bildung and Textual Liberation," 681–87. Pierre Citron, in his introduction to the novel in the Pléiade edition also comments that the *courtisanes* of the title might well include Lucien (see 6:416).

39 D. A. Miller, "Balzac's Illusions Lost and Found," *Yale French Studies* 67 (1984): 176–77.

40 D. A. Miller, "Body Bildung," 681.

41 Balzac, *Lettres à Madame Hanska,* 2:515.

42 Balzac, *Correspondance,* 4:72–73.

43 For the play *Vautrin,* I will be citing volume 23 of the Club de l'honnête homme edition of Balzac's *Oeuvres complètes* (Paris: Guy Le Prat, 1961). Translations are my own. That edition's introduction to the play (5–13) helpfully recounts the history of its composition and production. For information on the reception of *Vautrin* in both 1840 and 1850, see Bellos, *Balzac Criticism in France,* 12, 23–34. For information about the excitement attendant on the play's production and the various speculations about why it was banned, see René Guise, "Un Grand Homme du roman à la scène," *L'Année balzacienne* (1966): 191–216.

44 Madame de Girardin, *Lettres parisiennes du vicomte de Launay,* ed. Anne Martin-Fugier (Paris: Mercure de France, 1986), 632.

45 In critical discussions Vautrin is often associated with some kind of modernity. D. A. Miller speaks, for instance, of "Vautrin's homosexuality as the advance guard of sexual modernism," where by sexual modernism he means various kinds of desublimated "sexual commerce" ("Balzac's Illusions," 177 n.11). I think that this position needs to be qualified. Balzac is always interested in how new social forms grow out of old ones and inherit aspects of those older forms, sometimes to their disadvantage. Vautrin's failures (including his erotic ones) within *Splendeurs et misères des courtisanes* arguably are due to his involvement in (and we might even say his unconscious predisposition to) older, aristo-

cratic forms. In this regard, it is surely no coincidence that three of his primary love objects—Rastignac, Raoul de Frescas, and Lucien—are all, at least in part, noble born.

Another version of the modernist claim for Vautrin comes from Charles Bernheimer in his *Figures of Ill Repute*. Bernheimer seems oddly unwilling to admit the possibility that Vautrin had sex with other men, or that Balzac took a serious sociological interest in sex between men. He prefers to see sex between men as a textual rather than a physical phenomenon. He speaks of "what critics have generally agreed to call Vautrin's homosexuality," and suggests that those critics have "too often ignor[ed] the implications of this sexual choice for the conduct of the narrative of which he is a guiding genius." A bit later, he writes: "Through no oversight or prudery does Balzac leave the reader in doubt as to whether or not Lucien's father-mother actually engages in homosexual acts with him. The issue is not so much carnal knowledge as representational function. . . . Homosexual desire . . . is imagined by Balzac as desire for the exchangeability of signs, including those of gender. It coincides with the creation and circulation of values in a capitalist economy, one of whose effects, as Balzac demonstrates in *Le Père Goriot,* is the destruction of the family and of paternal authority" (Bernheimer, *Figures of Ill Repute: Representing Prostitution in Nineteenth-Century France* [Cambridge: Harvard University Press, 1989], 55, 57–58). There are a number of errors in these assertions. It would be fair to say of sex between men and women in *Splendeurs et misères des courtisanes* that it is more explicitly pointed to than sex between men. This is due to certain complex forms of censorship operative in Balzac's representational context. For Balzac, however, men can have relations with each other that are just as carnal as relations between men and women or between women, even if references to them within the novels are more coded. Further, *pace* Bernheimer, Balzac often associates male same-sex forms of intimacy more fully with an *ancien régime* ethos and its remnants in nineteenth-century France than with the increasingly dominant bourgeois or capitalist ethos. Balzac suggests that the increasingly dominant bourgeois system of morality *hinders* the development of forms of intimacy between men in ways that earlier systems did not. Finally, as I have observed frequently throughout these chapters, Balzac understands that the discourse that vaunts *bourgeois* family values (there are other kinds of families, and other values) and that tries to shore up the power of men within those families—a discourse Balzac certainly indulges in regularly—is a ruse of power with little claim to say anything historically or sociologically accurate about changing family forms.

46 Marguerite Drevon and Jeannine Guichardet, "Fameux Sexorama," *L'Année balzacienne* (1972): 269; and Berthier, "Balzac du côté de Sodome," 173.

47 Pierre Bourdieu defines social capital as "the aggregate of the actual or potential resources which are linked to possession of a durable network of more or less institutionalized relationships of mutual acquaintance and recognition—or in other words, to membership in a group—which provides each of its

members with the backing of the collectivity-owned capital. . . . The volume of the social capital possessed by a given agent thus depends on the size of the network of connections he can effectively mobilize and on the volume of capital (economic, cultural or symbolic) possessed in his own right by each of those to whom he is connected. . . . The network of relationships is the product of investment strategies, individual or collective, consciously or unconsciously aimed at establishing or reproducing social relationships that are directly usable in the short or long term" (Bourdieu, "The Forms of Capital," 248–49).

48 Max Weber, "Bureaucracy," in *From Max Weber: Essays in Sociology,* ed. and trans. H. H. Gerth and C. Wright Mills (New York: Oxford University Press, 1946), 199. Weber's writing on bureaucracy forms a helpful counterpoint to the last two sections of *Splendeurs et misères des courtisanes.*

49 Both Philippe Berthier and Lucette Finas comment helpfully on this scene in the novel: see Berthier, "Balzac du côté de Sodome," 148–52; and Finas, *Le Toucher du rayon,* 67–89.

50 In the proofs, Balzac had actually written "and the readers of *La Comédie humaine* will be able to see the results of his underground duel with the famous Corentin" (6:1507), but apparently he reconsidered his intention to continue the story even further.

Epilogue: Vautrin's Progeny

1 Marcel Proust, *Correspondance,* ed. Philip Kolb (Paris: Plon, 1970–1993), 20:187.

2 Cited in Proust, *Correspondance,* 20:189 n.15.

3 Ibid., 21:299 n.10.

4 Raoul Deberdt, "Un Grand Exciteur d'âmes: Le Maître de Balzac et de George Sand," *Revue des revues* (May 1, 1899): 275; André Bellessort, *Balzac et son œuvre,* 10th ed. (Paris: Perrin, 1936), 335.

5 Proust, *Correspondance,* 20:195. On the strategies behind decisions to treat same-sex relations in literary works in the 1920s, see my "Practices of Posterity: Gide and the Cultural Politics of Sexuality," in *André Gide's Politics: Rebellion and Ambivalence,* ed. Tom Conner (New York: Palgrave, 2000), 47–71.

6 Proust, *Correspondance,* 20:337.

7 Marcel Proust, *Contre Sainte-Beuve,* ed. Bernard de Fallois (1954; Paris: Gallimard [Idées], 1979), 263–65.

8 Proust also doubtless has somewhere in mind Balzac's declaration in his famous *Avant-propos* to *La Comédie humaine:* "A writer could become a more or less faithful, a more or less successful, a patient and courageous painter of human types . . . the archeologist of social property . . . but in order to deserve the praise for which any artist longs, was I not obliged to study the reason or reasons behind social effects" (1:11).

9 Jules Troubat, *Sainte-Beuve et Champfleury: Lettres de Champfleury à sa mère, à son frère, et à divers* (Paris: Mercure de France, 1908), 124–26.

10 Pierre Dufay, "Champfleury et Mme Hanska," *Mercure de France* (April 1, 1908): 567.

11 See Mme. Honoré de Balzac [Eveline Hanska], *Lettres inédites à Champfleury (1851–1854),* ed. Lorin A. Uffenbeck and Élizabeth Fudakowska (Paris: Champion-Slatkine, 1989), 90. Madame Balzac herself claimed to her publisher that Balzac had indicated to her during his final illness that he wanted Rabou's help with *Les Petits Bourgeois,* and, although she apparently did not like the look of Rabou once she met him, she also told her publisher that she was going to communicate to him the ideas that her husband had left her regarding the conclusion to *Le Député d'Arcis.* Champfleury later denied the possibility that the idea to choose Rabou had come from Balzac himself (see *Lettres inédites,* 31, 32 n.8, 92 n.6, 94).

12 See Charles de Spoelberch de Lovenjoul, *Histoire des œuvres de H. de Balzac,* 2nd ed. (Paris: Calmann Lévy, 1886), 155–56; Honoré de Balzac, *Le Député d'Arcis,* 2 vols. (Paris: Calmann Lévy, 1892). This 1892 edition is particularly interesting in that it includes an index (2:265–68) indicating in which other works from *La Comédie humaine* the characters in this novel appear. The index is evidence of Rabou's effort to incorporate a good number of Balzac's most popular characters into his work, one way or another, and also of a publisher's interest in appealing to fans of given characters. English-language versions of Balzac's complete works from the late nineteenth and early twentieth centuries (including Saintsbury's edition) included parts of Rabou's work. Interesting evidence of the presence of Rabou's text in various editions of Balzac's *Oeuvres complètes* can be found in one of Henry James's essays on Balzac (from 1875) in which Balzac is criticized for the clumsy characterization of Madame de l'Estorade in *Le Député d'Arcis,* whereas the passage James is criticizing is in fact by Rabou (see James, "Honoré de Balzac," in *Literary Criticism,* 44).

13 Gide, on the other hand, claims not to have been fooled by the difference between the Balzac and the Rabou sections when he read *Le Député d'Arcis* in 1934 (he says he read it all out loud!). See André Gide, *Journal II: 1926–1950,* ed. Martine Sagaert (Paris: Gallimard [Pléaide], 1997), 477, 1095–97.

14 See Proust, *Correspondance,* 2:252, 2:459, 15:150. I am indebted to the helpful index to Proust's correspondence compiled by: Kazuyoshi Yoshikawa et al., *Index général de la correspondance de Marcel Proust* (Kyoto: Presses de l'Université de Kyoto, 1998).

15 Balzac discusses his plans to marry off this terrifying *célibataire* in his preface to *Pierrette* (see 4:22–23).

16 Honoré de Balzac and Charles Rabou, *Le Député d'Arcis* (Paris: Potter, 1854), 3:206.

17 Balzac and Rabou, *Le Député d'Arcis,* 4:207–9.

18 Ibid., 211–12.

19 Honoré de Balzac and Charles Rabou, *Le Comte de Sallenauve* (Paris: Potter, 1854), 2:10–11, 60.

20 As late as 1951, one commentator on Balzac continues the confusion between Balzac's work and Rabou's. In "Balzac et le troisième sexe," Patrice Boussel writes that "Théodore Calvi [Vautrin's sidekick], having escaped once more from the hands of justice, will in 1839 become Vautrin's secretary—when Vautrin is a Swedish lord known by the name of Halphertius" (Boussel, "Balzac et le troisième sexe," *Aesculape* 32, no. 4 (April 1951): 77.

21 Honoré de Balzac and Charles Rabou, *La Famille Beauvisage* (Paris: Potter, 1855), 2:100.

22 Ibid., 2:38.

WORKS CITED

Adam, Antoine. *Le Secret de l'aventure vénitienne: La Vérité sur Sand et Musset.* Paris: Perrin, 1938.

Adamson, Donald. *Balzac: Lost Illusions.* London: Grant and Cutler, 1981.

———. *The Genesis of "Le Cousin Pons."* Oxford: Oxford University Press, 1966.

Ahearn, Edward J. *Marx and Modern Fiction.* New Haven: Yale University Press, 1989.

Arnaud, André-Jean. *Essai d'analyse structurale du Code civil français: La Règle du jeu dans la paix bourgeoise.* Paris: R. Pichon et R. Durand-Auzias, 1973.

Aron, Jean-Paul, and Roger Kempf. *Le Pénis et la démoralisation de l'Occident.* Paris: Grasset, 1978.

Atwood, William G. *Fryderyk Chopin: Pianist from Warsaw.* New York: Columbia University Press, 1987.

Auger, Hippolyte. *Mémoires (1810–1859).* Ed. Paul Cottin. Paris: La Revue rétrospective, 1891.

Balzac, Honoré de. *The Black Sheep.* [*La Rabouilleuse,* 1847]. Trans. Donald Adamson. Harmondsworth: Penguin, 1970.

———. *La Comédie humaine.* 12 vols. Ed. Pierre-Georges Castex. Paris: Gallimard [Pléiade], 1976–1981.

———. *La Comédie humaine.* Vol. 11. Ed. Albert Prioult. Paris: Hazan, 1950.

———. *Correspondance.* Ed. Roger Pierrot. 5 vols. Paris: Garnier, 1960–1969.

———. *Cousin Bette.* [*La Cousine Bette,* 1846]. Trans. Marion Ayton Crawford. Harmondsworth: Penguin, 1965.

———. *Cousin Pons.* [*Le Cousin Pons,* 1847]. Trans. Herbert J. Hunt. Harmondsworth: Penguin, 1968.

———. *Eugénie Grandet.* [1833] Trans. Sylvia Raphael. Oxford: Oxford University Press, 1990.

———. *A Harlot High and Low.* [*Splendeurs et misères des courtisanes,* 1847]. Trans. Rayner Heppenstall. Harmondsworth: Penguin, 1970.

———. *Histoire des treize*. Ed. Pierre-Georges Castex. Paris: Garnier Frères, 1966.

———. *The Girl with the Golden Eyes*. [*La Fille aux yeux d'or*, 1834–35]. In *History of the Thirteen*. Trans. Herbert J. Hunt. Harmondsworth: Penguin, 1974. 307–91.

———. "Lettre à Hippolyte Castille." In *Oeuvres complètes*. 28 vols. Paris: Guy Le Prat, 1963. 28:487–96.

———. *Lettres à Madame Hanska*. 2 vols. Ed. Roger Pierrot. Paris: Robert Laffont, 1990.

———. *Lost Illusions*. [*Illusions perdues*, 1837–43]. Trans. Herbert J. Hunt. Harmondsworth: Penguin, 1971.

———. *Old Goriot*. [*Le Père Goriot*, 1834]. Trans. Marion Ayton Crawford. Harmondsworth: Penguin, 1985.

———. *The Rise and Fall of César Birotteau*. [*Histoire de la grandeur et de la décadence de César Birotteau, 1837*]. Trans. Ellen Marriage. New York: Carroll and Graf, 1989.

———. *Ursule Mirouët*. [1841]. Trans. Donald Adamson. Harmondsworth: Penguin, 1976.

———. *Vautrin*. In *Oeuvres complètes*. 28 vols. Paris: Guy Le Prat, 1961. 23:5–126.

Balzac, Honoré de, and Charles Rabou. *Le Comte de Sallenauve*. 5 vols. Paris: Potter, 1854.

———. *Le Député d'Arcis*. 4 vols. Paris: Potter, 1854.

———. *La Famille Beauvisage*. 4 vols. Paris: Potter, 1855.

Balzac, Honoré de, Mme. [Eveline Hanska]. *Lettres inédites à Champfleury (1851–1854)*. Ed. Lorin A. Uffenbeck and Élizabeth Fudakowska. Paris: Champion-Slatkine, 1989.

Barbéris, Pierre. *Balzac et le mal du siecle: Contribution à une physiologie du monde moderne*. 2 vols. Paris: Gallimard, 1970.

———. *Mythes balzaciens*. Paris: A. Colin, 1972.

Barry, Joseph. *Infamous Woman: The Life of George Sand*. New York: Doubleday, 1977.

Barthes, Roland. *S/Z: An Essay*. Trans. Richard Miller. New York: Hill and Wang, 1974.

Beizer, Janet L. *Family Plots: Balzac's Narrative Generations*. New Haven: Yale University Press, 1986.

Bellessort, André. *Balzac et son œuvre*. 10th ed. Paris: Perrin, 1936.

Bellos, David. *Balzac Criticism in France 1850–1900: The Making of a Reputation*. Oxford: Clarendon, 1976.

———. "Reconnaissances: Balzac et son public feminin." *Oeuvres et Critiques* 9, no. 3 (1986): 253–62.

Bérard, Suzanne Jean. *La Genèse d'un roman de Balzac: "Illusions perdues," 1837*. 2 vols. Paris: A. Colin, 1961.

Bernard, Claudie. "La Dynamique familiale dans *Ursule Mirouët* de Balzac." *French Forum* 24, no. 2 (May 1999): 179–202.

Bernheimer, Charles. *Figures of Ill Repute: Representing Prostitution in Nineteenth-Century France*. Cambridge: Harvard University Press, 1989.

Bersani, Leo. *A Future for Astyanax: Character and Desire in Literature*. New York: Columbia University Press, 1984.

Berthier, Philippe. "Balzac du côté de Sodome." *L'Année balzacienne* (1979): 144–77.

———. "Marcel et Charlus Herrera." In Van Rossum-Guyon, 94–103.

Birnberg, Jacques. "Stendhal, l'Évêque de Clogher et l'Irlande en 1822: Marginalité sexuelle et marginalité beyliste." *Australian Journal of French Studies* 26, no. 2 (1989): 148–75.

Bonnet, Marie-Jo. *Les Relations amoureuses entre les femmes du XVIe au XXe siècle*. Paris: Odile Jacob, 1995.

Borie, Jean. *Le Célibataire français*. Paris: Le Sagittaire, 1976.

Borneman, John. "Caring and Being Cared for: Displacing Marriage, Kinship, Gender, and Sexuality." *International Social Science Journal* 49, no. 4 (December 1997): 573–84.

———. "Until Death Do Us Part: Marriage/Death in Anthropological Discourse." *American Ethnologist* 23, no. 2 (1996): 215–38.

Bourdieu, Pierre. "Des familles sans nom." *Actes de la recherche en sciences sociales* 113 (June 1996): 3–5.

———. "The Field of Cultural Production, or: The Economic World Reversed." Trans. Richard Nice. In *The Field of Cultural Production*, ed. Randal Johnson. New York: Columbia University Press, 1993. 29–73.

———. "The Forms of Capital." Trans. Richard Nice. In *Handbook of Theory and Research for the Sociology of Education*, ed. John G. Richardson. New York: Greenwood, 1986. 241–58.

———. *The Logic of Practice*. Trans. Richard Nice. Stanford: Stanford University Press, 1990.

———. "On the Family as a Realized Category." *Theory, Culture, and Society* 13, no. 3 (1996): 19–26.

———. *Outline of a Theory of Practice*. Trans. Richard Nice. Cambridge: Cambridge University Press, 1977.

———. *Pascalian Meditations*. Trans. Richard Nice. Stanford: Stanford University Press, 2000.

———. *The Rules of Art: Genesis and Structure of the Literary Field*. Trans. Susan Emanuel. Stanford: Stanford University Press, 1996.

———. *"Si le monde social m'est supportable, c'est parce que je peux m'indigner": Entertien avec Antoine Spire*. Paris: L'Aube, 2002.

Boussel, Patrice. "Balzac et le troisième sexe." *Æsculape* 32, no. 4 (April 1951): 74–79.

Brooks, Peter. *Body Work: Objects of Desire in Modern Narrative*. Cambridge: Harvard University Press, 1993.

———. *The Melodramatic Imagination: Balzac, Henry James, Melodrama, and the Mode of Excess*. New York: Columbia University Press, 1985.

———. *Reading for the Plot: Design and Intention in Narrative*. New York: Vintage, 1984.
Bustarret, Claire. "Balzac et le papier." In *Balzac: Imprimeur et défenseur du livre*. Paris: Paris-Musées/Des Cendres, 1995. 81–104.
Butler, Judith. "Against Proper Objects." *differences* 6, nos. 2 and 3 (1994): 1–26.
———. *Antigone's Claim: Kinship Between Life and Death*. New York: Columbia University Press, 2000.
———. *Bodies That Matter: On the Discursive Limits of "Sex."* New York: Routledge, 1993.
———. *Gender Trouble: Feminism and the Subversion of Identity*. New York: Routledge, 1990.
Butler, Ronnie. *Balzac and the French Revolution*. London: Croom Helm, 1983.
Chasles, Philarète. *Mémoires*. 2 vols. Paris: Charpentier, 1876.
Citron, Pierre. *Dans Balzac*. Paris: Seuil, 1986.
———. "Sur deux zones obscures de la psychologie de Balzac." *L'Année balzacienne* (1967): 3–27.
Clarke, Eric O. *Virtuous Vice: Homoeroticism and the Public Sphere*. Durham: Duke University Press, 2000.
Le Code Civil: Textes antérieurs et version actuelle. Paris: Flammarion, 1997.
Cohen, Margaret. *The Sentimental Education of the Novel*. Princeton: Princeton University Press, 1999.
Courteix, René-Alexandre. *Balzac et la Révolution française*. Paris: PUF, 1997.
Creech, James. *Closet Writing/Gay Reading: The Case of Melville's "Pierre."* Chicago: University of Chicago Press, 1993.
Crompton, Louis. *Byron and Greek Love: Homophobia in Nineteenth-Century England*. Berkeley: University of California Press, 1985.
Custine, Astolphe de. "Les Amitiés littéraires in 1831." In *Paris; ou, Le Livre des cent-et-un*. 13 vols. Paris: Ladvocat, 1831–32. 5:103–128.
———. *Letters à Varnhagen d'Ense*. Ed. Roger Pierrot. Geneva: Slatkine, 1979.
———. *Mémoires et voyages, ou Lettres écrites à diverses époques, pendant des courses en Suisse, en Calabre, en Angleterre, et en Écosse*. 2 vols. Paris: Vézard, 1830.
———. *Souvenirs et portraits*. Ed. Pierre de Lacretelle. Monaco: Éditions du Rocher, 1956.
Darrow, Margaret H. *Revolution in the House: Family, Class, and Inheritance in Southern France, 1775–1825*. Princeton: Princeton University Press, 1989.
Deberdt, Raoul. "Un Grand Exciteur d'âmes: Le Maître de Balzac et de George Sand." *Revue des revues* (May 1, 1899): 265–80.
Desan, Suzanne. "Reconstituting the Social After the Terror: Family, Property, and the Law in Popular Politics." *Past and Present* 164 (August 1999): 81–121.
Dobelbower, Nicholas. "*Les Chevaliers de la guirlande:* Cellmates in Restoration France." *Journal of Homosexuality* 4, no. 3/4 (2001): 131–47.
Drevon, Marguerite, and Jeannine Guichardet. "Fameux Sexorama." *L'Année balzacienne* (1972): 257–74.

Dufay, Pierre. "Champfleury et Mme Hanska." *Mercure de France* (April 1, 1908): 565–68.

Durkheim, Émile. *The Division of Labor in Society.* [1893]. Trans. W. D. Halls. New York: Free Press, 1984.

———. *The Rules of Sociological Method.* [1895]. Ed. Steven Lukes. Trans. W. D. Halls. London: Macmillan, 1982.

Engel, David M. "How Does Law Matter in the Constitution of Legal Consciousness?" In *How Does Law Matter?,* ed. Bryant G. Garth and Austin Sarat. Evanston, Ill.: Northwestern University Press, 1998. 109–144.

Eribon, Didier. *Michel Foucault et ses contemporains.* Paris: Fayard, 1994.

———. *Papiers d'identité: Interventions sur la question gay.* Paris: Fayard, 2000.

Ezdinli, Leyla. "Rumor and Reputation: George Sand's Transvestism and the Literary Star System." Unpublished manuscript.

Faillie, Marie-Henriette. *La Femme et le Code civil dans "La Comédie humaine" d'Honoré de Balzac.* Paris: Didier, 1968.

Faderman, Lillian. *Surpassing the Love of Men: Romantic Friendship and Love between Women from the Renaissance to the Present.* New York: Quill, 1981.

Felman, Shoshana. *What Does a Woman Want? Reading and Sexual Difference.* Baltimore: Johns Hopkins University Press, 1993.

Fenet, P. A. *Recueil complet des travaux préparatoires du Code civil.* [1827–1828]. 16 vols. Osnabruck: Otto Zeller, 1968.

Finas, Lucette. *Le Toucher du rayon: Proust, Vautrin et Antinoüs.* Paris: Nizet, 1995.

Floyd, Juanita Helm. *Women in the Life of Honoré de Balzac.* New York: Holt, 1921.

Fontaney, Antoine. *Journal intime.* Ed. René Jasinski. Paris: Les Presses françaises, 1925.

Ford, Caroline. "Private Lives and Public Order in Restoration France: The Seduction of Emily Loveday." *American Historical Review* 99, no. 1 (February 1994): 21–43.

Foucault, Michel. *Dits et écrits 1954–1988.* 4 vols. Ed. Daniel Defert and François Ewald. Paris: Gallimard, 1994.

———. "Entretien avec M. Foucault." In *Dits et écrits.* 4:286–95.

———. *Ethics: Subjectivity and Truth.* Ed. Paul Rabinow. Trans. Robert Hurley et al. Volume 1 of *Essential Works of Foucault, 1954–1984.* New York: New Press, 1997.

———. "Folie, littérature, société." An interview with T. Shimizu and M. Watanabe. In *Dits et écrits.* 2:104–28.

———. "Friendship as a Way of Life." In *Ethics: Subjectivity and Truth,* 135–40.

———, ed. *Herculine Barbin. Being the Recently Discovered Memoirs of a Nineteenth-Century French Hermaphrodite.* Trans. Richard McDougall. New York: Pantheon, 1980.

———. *The History of Sexuality. Volume 1: An Introduction.* Trans. Robert Hurley. New York: Vintage, 1990.

———, ed. *I, Pierre Rivière, having slaughtered my mother, my sister and my brother . . . : A Case of Parricide in the Nineteenth Century.* [No translator indicated]. Harmondsworth: Penguin, 1978. Translation of *Moi, Pierre Rivière, ayant égorgé ma mère, ma soeur et mon frère . . . : Un Cas de parricide au XIXe siècle.* Paris: Gallimard, 1973.

———. "The Life of Infamous Men." In *Power.* Ed. James D. Faubion. Trans. Robert Hurley et al. Volume 3 of *Essential Works of Foucault, 1954–1984.* Series ed. Paul Rabinow. New York: New Press, 2000. 157–175. Translation of "La Vie des hommes infâmes." In *Dits et écrits.* 3:237–53.

———. "Sex, Power, and the Politics of Identity." In *Ethics: Subjectivity and Truth.* 163–73.

———. "The Social Triumph of the Sexual Will." In *Ethics: Subjectivity and Truth.* 157–62.

———. "Le Vrai sexe." In *Dits et écrits.* 4:115–23.

Fremy, Arnould. *Les Deux Anges.* 2 vols. Paris: Gosselin, 1833.

Freud, Sigmund. *General Psychological Theory: Papers on Metapsychology.* Ed. Philip Rieff. New York: Collier, 1963.

———. *Leonardo da Vinci and a Memory of His Childhood.* Trans. Alan Tyson. New York: Norton, 1964.

———. "Mourning and Melancholia." Trans. Joan Riviere. In *General Psychological Theory.* 164–79.

———. "On Narcissism: An Introduction." Trans. Cecil M. Baines. In *General Psychological Theory.* 56–82.

Fulchiron, Hughes. "Nature, fiction et politique: L'Adoption dans les débats révolutionnaires." In Théry and Biet, 204–20.

Fuss, Diana. *Identification Papers.* New York: Routledge, 1995.

Gager, Kristin Elizabeth. *Blood Ties and Fictive Ties: Adoption and Family Life in Early Modern France.* Princeton: Princeton University Press, 1996.

Gautier, Théophile. *Lettre à la Présidente: Voyage en Italie, 1850.* N.p.: Les Perspectives, n.d.

Gide, André. *Journal II: 1926–1950.* Ed. Martine Sagaert. Paris: Gallimard [Pléiade], 1997.

Gide, Paul. *Étude sur la condition privée de la femme.* [1867]. 2nd ed. Paris: Larose et Forcel, 1885.

Ginsburg, Michal Peled, ed. *Approaches to Teaching Balzac's "Old Goriot."* New York: Modern Language Association, 2000.

———. *Economies of Change: Form and Transformation in the Nineteenth-Century Novel.* Stanford: Stanford University Press, 1996.

Girardin, Madame de. *Lettres parisiennes du vicomte de Launay.* Ed. Anne Martin-Fugier. Paris: Mercure de France, 1986.

Goffman, Erving. *The Presentation of Self in Everyday Life.* New York: Anchor, 1959.

Guérin, Daniel. *Vautrin: Du roman à la scène et à l'écran.* Paris: Plume d'or, 1962.

Guise, René. "Un Grand homme du roman à la scène." *L'Année balzacienne* (1966): 171–216.

Guyon, Bernard. *La Pensée politique et sociale de Balzac.* Paris: Colin, 1967.

———. "Une Revue romantique inconnue: *Le Gymnase.*" *Revue de littérature comparée* 11, nos. 2 and 4 (1931): 314–21, 489–511.

Hacking, Ian. *The Taming of Chance.* Cambridge: Cambridge University Press, 1990.

Haggerty, George. *Men in Love: Masculinity and Sexuality in the Eighteenth Century.* New York: Columbia University Press, 1999.

Halperin, David M. "How to Do the History of Male Homosexuality." *GLQ: A Journal of Lesbian and Gay Studies* 6, no. 1 (2000): 87–124.

Halpérin, Jean-Louis. *L'Impossible Code civil.* Paris: PUF, 1992.

Hartog, Hendrik. "Abigail Bailey's Coverture: Law in a Married Woman's Consciousness." In *Law in Everyday Life,* ed. Austin Sarat and Thomas R. Kearns. Ann Arbor: University of Michigan Press, 1993. 63–108.

Heathcote, Owen N. "The Engendering of Violence and the Violation of Gender in Honoré de Balzac's *La Fille aux yeux d'or.*" *Romance Studies* 22 (autumn 1993): 99–112.

Hédouin, Pierre. *Mme Pauline du Chambge.* Paris: Mourgues, 1858.

Héritier, Françoise. *Masculin/Féminin: La Pensée de la différence.* Paris: Odile Jacob, 1996.

Houssaye, Arsène. *Les Confessions: Souvenirs d'un demi-siècle, 1830–1880.* 6 vols. Paris: Dentu, 1885–1891.

Hunt, Lynn. *The Family Romance of the French Revolution.* Berkeley: University of California Press, 1992.

James, Henry. *Literary Criticism: French Writers, Other European Writers. The Prefaces to the New York Edition.* Ed. Leon Edel. New York: Library of America, 1984.

Jameson, Fredric. *The Political Unconscious: Narrative as a Socially Symbolic Act.* Ithaca: Cornell University Press, 1981.

Jasinski, René. *Les Années romantiques de Théophile Gautier.* Paris: Vuibert, 1929.

Kashiwagi, Takao. *La Trilogie des "Célibataires" d'Honoré de Balzac.* Paris: Nizet, 1983.

Kelly, Dorothy. "Between Bodies and Texts: A Psychoanalytic Reading of *Le Père Goriot.*" In Ginsburg, 109–17.

———. *Fictional Genders: Role and Representation in Nineteenth-Century French Narrative.* Lincoln: University of Nebraska Press, 1989.

Kempf, Roger. *Sur le corps romanesque.* Paris: Seuil, 1968.

Knight, Diana. "Reading as an Old Maid: *La Cousine Bette* and Compulsory Heterosexuality." *Quinquereme* 12, no.1 (1989): 67–79.

Lacan, Jacques. *Les Complexes familiaux dans la formation de l'individu.* Paris: Navarin, 1984.

Lacenaire, Pierre-François. *Mémoires et autres écrits.* Ed. Jacques Simonelli. Paris: José Corti, 1991.

———. *Mémoires, poèmes et lettres.* Ed. Monique Lebailly. Paris: Albin Michel, 1968.

[Lambinet, Victor Felicien]. *Balzac mis à nu et les dessous de la Société romantique d'après les Mémoires inédits d'un contemporain.* Ed. Charles Léger. Paris: C. Gaillandre, 1928.

———. *Madame Récamier, la reine Hortense, et quelques autres: La Société mondaine et littéraire sous la Restauration et le Second Empire* . Ed. Charles Léger. Paris: Mercure de France, 1941.

Lenoir, Remi. "La Famille, une affaire d'État: Les Débats parlementaires concernant la famille (1973–1978)." *Actes de la recherche en sciences sociales* 113 (June 1996): 16–30.

Le Play, Frédéric. *Instruction sur la méthode d'observation dite des monographies des familles.* Paris: Société d'économie sociale, 1862.

Le Yaouanc, Moïse. *Nosographie de l'humanité balzacienne.* Paris: Maloine, 1959.

Lucey, Michael. *Gide's Bent: Sexuality, Politics, Writing.* New York: Oxford University Press, 1995.

———. "Practices of Posterity: Gide and the Cultural Politics of Sexuality." In *Andre Gide's Politics: Rebellion and Ambivalence,* ed. Tom Conner. New York: Palgrave, 2000. 47–71.

———. "Proust's Queer Metalepses." *MLN* 116, no. 4 (September 2001): 795–815.

Lukes, Steven. "Prolegomena to the Interpretation of Durkheim." In *Émile Durkheim: Critical Assessments,* vol. 2, ed. Peter Hamilton. London: Routledge, 1990. 318–42.

Luppé, A. de. *Astolphe de Custine.* Monaco: Éditions du Rocher, 1957.

———. "Custine, héros de Balzac: Comment l'auteur de *La Russie en 1839* entra dans *La Comédie humaine* et fut un peu Vautrin." *Le Figaro littéraire* (June 11, 1955): 5–6.

Lukács, Georg. *Studies in European Realism.* Trans. Edith Bone. London: Merlin, 1972.

———. *Writer and Critic and Other Essays.* Trans. Arthur Kahn. London: Merlin Press, 1978.

Marcus, Sharon. *Apartment Stories: City and Home in Nineteenth-Century Paris and London.* Berkeley: University of California Press, 1999.

———. "Comparative Sapphism." In *The Literary Channel: The Inter-National Invention of the Novel,* ed. Margaret Cohen and Carolyn Dever. Princeton: Princeton University Press, 2002. 251–85.

———. "Introduction." *The Physiology of Marriage,* by Honoré de Balzac. Baltimore: Johns Hopkins University Press, 1997.

———."Quelques problèmes de l'histoire lesbienne." Trans. Jean-Yves Boulard. In *Les Études gay et lesbiennes: Colloque du Centre Georges Pompidou, 23 et 27 juin 1997.* Ed. Didier Eribon. Paris: Centre Pompidou, 1998. 35–43.

Marix-Spire, Thérèse. *Les Romantiques et la musique: Le Cas de George Sand, 1804–1838.* Paris: Nouvelles éditions latines, 1954.

Martin, Xavier. "L'Individualisme libéral en France autour de 1800: Essai de

spectroscopie." *Revue d'histoire des facultés de droit et de la science juridique* 4 (1987): 87–144.
———. "L'Insensibilité des rédacteurs du Code civil à l'altruisme." *Revue historique de droit français et étranger* 60 (1982): 589–618.
———. *Nature humaine et Révolution française: Du siècle des Lumières au Code Napoléon.* Bouère: Dominique Martin Morin, 1994.
Meininger, Anne-Marie. "'Illusions perdues' et faits retrouvés." *L'Année balzacienne* (1979): 47–75.
Mérimée, Prosper. *Correspondance générale.* Vol. 3. Ed. Maurice Parturier. Paris: Le Divan, 1943.
Merlin, Maria de las Mercedes Santa Cruz y Montalvo. *Souvenirs et mémoires de madame la comtesse Merlin: Souvenirs d'une créole.* Ed. Hector Biancotti and Carmen Vásquez. Paris: Mercure de France, 1990.
Merrick, Jeffrey, and Bryant T. Ragan Jr., eds. *Homosexuality in Modern France.* New York: Oxford University Press, 1996.
Messol-Dedoin, Chantal. "La Charade et la chimère: Du récit énigmatique dans 'La Fille aux yeux d'or.'" *Poétique* 89 (February 1992): 31–45.
Michel, Arlette. *Le Mariage chez Honoré de Balzac: Amour et féminisme.* Paris: Les Belles lettres, 1978.
Miller, D. A. "Balzac's Illusions Lost and Found." *Yale French Studies* 67 (1984): 164–81.
———. "Body Bildung and Textual Liberation." In *A New History of French Literature,* ed. Denis Hollier. Cambridge: Harvard University Press, 1989. 681–87.
———. *The Novel and the Police.* Berkeley: University of California Press, 1988.
Moreau-Christophe, Louis-Mathurin. "Les Détenus." In *Les Français peints par eux-mêmes: Encyclopédie morale du dix-neuvième siècle.* 9 vols. Paris: Carmier, 1841–1850.
Moretti, Franco. *Atlas of the European Novel, 1800–1900.* London: Verso, 1998.
———. "Homo Palpitans: Balzac's Novels and the Urban Personality." Trans. Susan Fischer. In *Signs Taken for Wonders: Essays in the Sociology of Literary Forms.* Rev. ed. London: Verso, 1988. 109–29.
———. *The Way of the World: The "Bildungsroman" in European Culture.* London: Verso, 1987.
Mortimer, Armine Kotin. "Balzac's *Ursule Mirouët:* Genealogy and Inheritance." *Modern Language Review* 92, no. 4 (October 1997): 851–63.
Mozet, Nicole. "La Question de l'origine à l'origine du roman balzacien." In *Balzac: Une Poétique du roman,* ed. Stéphane Vachon. Montreal: XYZ, 1996. 285–94.
———. "*Ursule Mirouët* ou le test du bâtard." In *Balzac, Oeuvres complètes: Le Moment de "La Comédie humaine,"* ed. Claude Duchet and Isabelle Tournier. Saint-Denis: Presses universitaires de Vincennes, 1993. 217–28.
———. *La Ville de province dans l'œuvre de Balzac; L'Espace romanesque: Fantasmes et idéologie.* Paris: Société d'édition d'enseignement supérieur, 1982.

Mozet, Nicole, and Paule Petitier, eds. *Balzac dans l'Histoire*. Paris: SEDES, 2001.
Muhlstein, Anka. *Astolphe de Custine, 1790–1857: Le Dernier marquis*. Paris: Grasset, 1996.
Mulliez, Jacques. "Révolutionnaires, nouveaux pères? Forcément nouveaux pères! Le Droit révolutionnaire de la paternité." In *La Révolution et l'ordre juridique privé: Rationalité ou scandale? Actes du colloque d'Orléans, 11–13 septembre 1986*, ed. Michel Vovelle. Paris: PUF, 1988. 373–98.
Murger, Henry. *Scènes de la vie de bohème*. [1851]. Paris: Gallimard [Folio], 1988.
Nesci, Catherine. *La Femme mode d'emploi: Balzac, de la "Physiologie du mariage" à "La Comédie humaine."* Lexington, Ky.: French Forum Publishers, 1992.
Nishio, Osamu. *La Signification du Cénacle dans "La Comédie humaine" de Balzac*. Tokyo: France Tosho, 1980.
Nye, Robert A. *Masculinity and Male Codes of Honor in Modern France*. New York: Oxford University Press, 1993.
Nykrog, Per. "La Révélation de la société invisible chez Balzac." In *Balzac et les Parents pauvres*, ed. Françoise van Rossum-Guyon and Michiel van Brederode. Paris: SEDES, 1981. 11–19.
Perrod, Pierre Antoine. "Balzac et les 'majorats'." *L'Année balzacienne* (1968): 211–40.
Perrot, Michelle. "Balzac et les sciences sociales de son temps." In Mozet and Petitier, 27–36.
Petrey, Sandy. *Realism and Revolution: Balzac, Stendhal, Zola, and the Performances of History*. Ithaca: Cornell University Press, 1988.
Peytel, Adrien. *Balzac: Juriste romantique*. Paris: Ponsot, 1950.
Picq, Françoise. *Libération des femmes: Les Années-mouvement*. Paris: Seuil, 1993.
Pilbeam, Pamela. *The 1830 Revolution in France*. New York: St. Martin's Press, 1991.
Pinkney, David H. *The French Revolution of 1830*. Princeton: Princeton University Press, 1972.
Portalis, Jean-Étienne-Marie. "Discours préliminaire prononcé lors de la présentation du projet de la commission du gouvernment." In Fenet, 1:463–523.
Poumarède, Jacques. "La Législation successorale de la Révolution entre l'idéologie et la pratique." In Théry and Biet, 167–82.
Prendergast, Christopher. *Balzac: Fiction and Melodrama*. London: Edward Arnold, 1978.
———. *The Order of Mimesis: Balzac, Stendhal, Nerval, Flaubert*. Cambridge: Cambridge University Press, 1986.
Prokhoris, Sabine. *Le Sexe prescrit: La Différence sexuelle en question*. Paris: Aubier, 2000.
Proust, Marcel. *A la recherche du temps perdu*. 4 vols. Ed. Jean-Yves Tadié. Paris: Gallimard [Pléiade], 1987.
———. *Contre Sainte-Beuve*. [1954]. Ed. Bernard de Fallois. Gallimard [Idées], 1979.

———. *Correspondance.* 21 vols. Ed. Philip Kolb. Paris: Plon, 1970–1993.

———. *Remembrance of Things Past.* 3 vols. Trans. C. K. Scott Moncrieff, Terence Kilmartin, and Andreas Mayor. New York: Vintage, 1982.

Regard, Maurice. *Gustave Planche, 1808–1857: Correspondance, Bibliographie, Iconographie.* Paris: Nouvelles éditions latines, 1955.

Reid, Roddey. *Families in Jeopardy: Regulating the Social Body in France, 1750–1910.* Stanford: Stanford University Press, 1993.

Rheinstein, Max. "The Code and the Family." In *The Code Napoleon and the Common-Law World,* ed. Bernard Schwartz. New York: New York University Press, 1956. 139–61.

Robb, Graham. *Balzac: A Biography.* New York: Norton, 1994.

Rosen, Elisheva. "Droit et roman: Le Modèle balzacien." In Mozet and Petitier, 37–53.

———. "Le Personnage et la poétique du roman balzacien." In *Balzac: Une Poétique du roman,* ed. Stéphane Vachon. Montreal: XYZ, 1996. 201–12.

Rousseau, George, and Caroline Warman. "Made from the Stuff of Saints: Chateaubriand's *René* and Custine's Search for a Homosexual Identity." *GLQ: A Journal of Lesbian and Gay Studies* 7, no. 1 (2001): 1–29.

Rubin, Gayle. "Sexual Traffic." [Interview with Judith Butler]. *differences* 6, nos. 2 and 3 (1994): 62–99.

———. "The Traffic in Women: Notes on the 'Political Economy' of Sex." In *Toward an Anthropology of Women,* ed. Rayna R. Reiter. New York: Monthly Review, 1975. 157–210.

Sainte-Beuve, C.-A. *Les Consolations.* 3rd ed. Brussels: Hauman, Cattoir et comp., 1837.

———. *Correspondance générale.* 19 vols. Ed. Jean Bonnerot. Paris: Stock, 1935–83.

———. "M. Théodore Leclercq." In *Causeries du lundi.* 15 vols. 3rd ed. Paris: Garnier Frères, 1857–72. 3:526–547.

Sand, George. *Correspondance inédite George Sand—Marie Dorval.* Ed. Simone Andre-Maurois. Paris: Gallimard, 1953.

———. *Histoire de ma vie. Oeuvres autobiographiques.* 2 vols. Ed. Georges Lubin. Paris: Gallimard [Pléiade], 1971.

———. *Journal intime.* In *Oeuvres autobiographiques.* 2 vols. Ed. Georges Lubin. Paris: Gallimard [Pléiade], 1971. 2:945–71.

Sarat, Austin, and Thomas R. Kearns. "Beyond the Great Divide: Forms of Legal Scholarship and Everyday Life." In *Law in Everyday Life,* ed. Austin Sarat and Thomas R. Kearns. Ann Arbor: University of Michigan Press, 1993. 21–62.

Schehr, Lawrence C. "A Queer Theory Approach: Gender and Genre in *Old Goriot.*" In Ginsburg, 118–25.

———. *Rendering French Realism.* Stanford: Stanford University Press, 1997.

Schor, Naomi. *Breaking the Chain: Women, Theory, and French Realist Fiction.* New York: Columbia University Press, 1985.

———. *One Hundred Years of Melancholy.* Clarendon Press: Oxford, 1996.

Scott, Joan Wallach. *Only Paradoxes to Offer: French Feminists and the Rights of Man*. Cambridge: Harvard University Press, 1996.

Sedgwick, Eve Kosofsky. *Between Men: English Literature and Male Homosocial Desire*. New York: Columbia University Press, 1985.

———. *Epistemology of the Closet*. Berkeley: University of California Press, 1990.

Ségu, Frédéric. *Un Maître de Balzac méconnu: H. de Latouche*. Paris: Belles-Lettres, 1928.

Sibalis, Michael David. "The Palais-Royal and the Homosexual Subculture of Nineteenth-Century Paris." *Journal of Homosexuality* 4, no. 3/4 (2001): 117–29.

———. "The Regulation of Male Homosexuality in Revolutionary and Napoleonic France, 1789–1815." In Merrick and Ragan, 80–101.

Spoelberch de Lovenjoul, Charles de. *Histoire des oeuvres de H. de Balzac*. 2nd ed. Paris: Calmann Lévy, 1886.

Starobinski, Jean. "Sur la chlorose." *Romantisme* 31 (1981): 113–30.

Stendhal. *Correspondance générale*. 6 vols. Ed. V. Del Litto et al. Paris: Honore Champion, 1997–99.

———. *Romans et nouvelles*. 2 vols. Ed. Henri Martineau. Paris: Gallimard [Pléiade], 1952.

Stephanson, Raymond. "'Epicoene Friendship': Understanding Male Friendship in the Early Eighteenth Century, with some Speculations about Pope." *The Eighteenth Century* 38, no. 2 (1997): 151–70.

Tarn, Julien-Frédéric. *Le Marquis de Custine, ou: Les Malheurs de l'exactitude*. Paris: Fayard, 1985.

Terdiman, Richard. *Discourse/Counter-Discourse: The Theory and Practice of Symbolic Resistance in Nineteenth-Century France*. Ithaca: Cornell University Press, 1985.

Terrat, Barthélemy. "Du régime de la propriété dans le Code civil." In *Le Code civil: 1804–1904: Livre du centenaire*. 2 vols. Paris: Arthur Rousseau, 1904.

Théry, Irène, and Christian Biet, eds. *La Famille, La Loi, L'État: De la Révolution au Code civil*. Paris: Éditions du Centre Georges Pompidou, 1989.

Thompson, C. W. "Stendhal connaisseur de l''improper': De Byron à William Courtenay, lord Link et Balzac." *Stendhal Club* 29, no. 114 (January 1987): 113–39.

Thompson, Victoria. "Creating Boundaries: Homosexuality and the Changing Social Order in France, 1830–1870." In Merrick and Ragan, 102–27.

Tolley, Bruce. "Balzac et les saint-simoniens." *L'Année balzacienne* (1966): 49–66.

Tort, Michel. "Quelques conséquences de la différence 'psychanalytique' des sexes." *Les Temps modernes* 55 (June 2000): 176–215.

Troubat, Jules. *Sainte-Beuve et Champfleury: Lettres de Champfleury à sa mère, à son frère, et à divers*. Paris: Mercure de France, 1908.

Tulard, Jean. *Joseph Fiévée: Conseiller secret de Napoléon*. Paris: Fayard, 1985.

Vachon, Stéphane. "Chronologie de la rédaction et de la publication d'*Illusions perdues*." In Van Rossum-Guyon, 1–11.

Van Rossum-Guyon, Françoise, ed. *Balzac: Illusions perdues: "L'Oeuvre capitale dans l'œuvre."* Groningen: CRIN, 1988.

Vidocq, Eugène-François. *Mémoires; Les Voleurs.* [1837]. Ed. Francis Lacassin. Paris: Laffont, 1998.

Viel-Castel, Horace de. *Mémoires sur la règne de Napoléon III (1851–1864).* 2 vols. Ed. Pierre Josserand. Paris: Guy Le Prat, 1942.

Vincent-Buffault, Anne. *L'Exercice de l'amitié: Pour une histoire des pratiques amicales aux XVIIIe et XIXe siècles.* Paris: Seuil, 1995.

Waller, Margaret. "A Feminist Approach: Realism and Its Others." In Ginsburg, 98–108.

———. *The Male Malady: Fictions of Impotence in the French Romantic Novel.* New Brunswick: Rutgers University Press, 1993.

Weber, Max. *From Max Weber: Essays in Sociology.* Ed. and trans. H. H. Gerth and C. Wright Mills. New York: Oxford University Press, 1946.

Wechsler, Judith. *A Human Comedy: Physiognomy and Caricature in Nineteenth-Century Paris.* Chicago: University of Chicago Press, 1982.

Weil, Kari. "Romantic Exile and the Melancholia of Identification." *differences* 7, no. 2 (1995): 111–26.

Wilde, Oscar. "Balzac in English." In *The Artist as Critic: Critical Writings of Oscar Wilde,* ed. Richard Ellmann. New York: Random House, 1969. 29–32.

Yoshikawa, Kazuyoshi, et al. *Index général de la correspondance de Marcel Proust.* Kyoto: Presses de l'Université de Kyoto, 1998.

Zucker-Rouvillois, Élisabeth. "L'Expertise familiale ou la perte du doute scientifique." In *Au-delà du PaCS: L'Expertise familiale à l'épreuve de l'homosexualité,* ed. Daniel Borrillo, Éric Fassin, and Marcela Iacub. Paris: PUF, 1999. 111–44.

INDEX

Michael Lucey is Professor of French and Comparative Literature at the University of California at Berkeley. He is the author of *Gide's Bent: Sexuality, Politics, Writing* (1995).

Library of Congress Cataloging-in-Publication Data
Lucey, Michael.
The misfit of the family : Balzac and the social forms of sexuality / Michael Lucey.
p. cm. — (Series Q)
Includes bibliographical references and index.
ISBN 0-8223-3156-X (cloth : alk. paper)
ISBN 0-8223-3193-4 (pbk. : alk. paper)
1. Balzac, Honorâe de, 1799–1850—Political and social views. 2. Literature and society—France—History—19th century. 3. Sex in literature. I. Title. II. Series.
PQ2184.E76L83 2003 843′.7—dc21 2003001723